STUDY GUIDE

for Stiglitz's

Principles of Microeconomics

Second Edition

STUDY GUIDE

for Stiglitz's

Principles of Microeconomics

Second Edition

LAWRENCE W. MARTIN
Michigan State University

W · W · NORTON & COMPANY · NEW YORK · LONDON

Printed in the United States of America

ISBN 0-393-96932-0 (pbk.)

W. W. Norton & Company, Inc., 500 Fifth Avenue, New York, N.Y. 10110
http://www.wwnorton.com

W. W. Norton & Company, Ltd., 10 Coptic Street, London WC1A 1PU

1 2 3 4 5 6 7 8 9 0

CONTENTS

PREFACE

This Study Guide is designed to aid in your understanding, assimilation, and the use of the material in Joseph Stiglitz's *Principles of Microeconomics, Second Edition*. The chapters in this volume correspond those in the main text, and each one is divided into three parts. The first part contains a *Chapter Review*, an *Essential Concepts* section, and a *Behind the Essential Concepts* section. The *Chapter Review* begins with a brief paragraph explaining how each chapter in Stiglitz fits into the overall structure of the text. the *Essential Concepts* section is a summary of the chapter, bringing out the main points covered. *Behind the Essential Concepts* offers suggestions about how to avoid common mistakes and provides some intuitive explanations for difficult concepts. This section also brings out the similarities among related ideas and the common structure of many economic theories and concepts.

The second part of each chapter provides a "Self-Test" with true-or-false, multiple-choice, and completion questions. After reading the chapter in the text and going over the first part of the Study Guide chapter, you should take the self-test. It will help you determine those areas that need further study.

The final part of each chapter is called "Doing Economics: Tools and Practice Problems." This part is designed to teach you the basic skills of economics. The only way to do this is to sharpen up your pencil and try some exercises. If you're willing (or your teacher has assigned this material), I think you'll find the program useful. For each type of problem, there is a Tool Kit box that gives step-by-step instructions about how to use the appropriate tool, a worked problem with a step-by-step solution that follows the procedure outlined in the Tool Kit box, and several practice problems for you to do. Answers are provided at the end of each chapter.

Best of success with your course!

Part One

Introduction

Chapter 1

THE AUTOMOBILE AND ECONOMICS

Chapter Review

The story of the automobile in the United States is a rich one, introducing as it does the principal ideas of economics. The dominant idea is that economics is about the choices made by the three major groups of participants: individuals or households, firms, and the government. These choices control the allocation of resources, another central concern of economics. The automobile story also highlights the three markets on which this book focuses: product, labor, and capital. The chapter closes with a discussion of how economists use models and theories to describe the economy and why they sometimes disagree. This chapter sets the stage for the introduction of the basic economic model in Chapter 2.

ESSENTIAL CONCEPTS

1 The brief history of the automobile given here illustrates the broad and varied subject matter of economics and many of the important themes of this book. We see the importance of investors and entrepreneurs and the risks they face, and the central roles of research, technological advance, and patents. The problem of incentives appears both in the conflicting interests of Henry Ford and his investors and in the effect of high wages on his workers.

The upheavals caused by oil price increases in the 1970s and the influx of competition from foreign producers show us how the U.S. economy now functions in the world economy. Finally, a large and growing government presence has mandated environmental and safety regulations, supplied money to bail out a major producer, and provided protection against foreign competition.

2 Economics studies how **choices** are made by individuals, firms, governments, and other organizations and how those choices determine the allocation of resources. **Scarcity,** the fact that there are not enough resources to satisfy all wants, requires that choices must be made by individuals and by the economy as a whole. The fundamental questions that an economy must answer are the following:

a What is produced, and in what quantities?
b How are these goods produced?
c For whom are these goods produced?
d Who makes economic decisions, and by what process?

3 The U.S. economy is a mixed one that relies primarily on private decisions to answer the basic economic questions. **Markets,** which exist wherever and whenever exchanges occur, influence the choices of individuals and firms, but government also plays a prominent role. For

starters, the government sets the legal structure within which market forces operate. It also regulates private activity, collects taxes, produces some goods and services, and provides support for the elderly, poor, and others.

4   Trade takes place between individuals and firms in three major markets: the **product market,** the **labor market,** and the **capital market.** Figure 1.1 sketches the interactions. Notice that in general, individuals buy goods and services from firms; they also supply labor and funds for investment to firms.

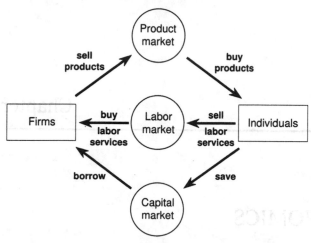

Figure 1.1

5   There are two broad branches in economics. **Microeconomics** studies the product, labor, and capital markets, focusing on the behaviour of individuals, households, firms, and other organizations that make up the economy. **Macroeconomics** looks at the performance of the economy as a whole and at such aggregate measures as unemployment, inflation, growth, and the balance of trade.

6   Economics uses models and theories, which are sets of assumptions and conclusions, to understand and predict the behaviour of the economy. Economists want to discover and interpret relationships among economic variables and especially to distinguish where there is causation and where there is only correlation.

7   Economists are frequently asked to give advice regarding public policy, and often they disagree, for two major reasons: they disagree about what is the appropriate theoretical model of the economy, and about the effects a policy will have.

BEHIND THE ESSENTIAL CONCEPTS

1   In this book you will learn many economic theories and models. Models and theories are simplified representations of the vast and complex economic world. The way that a model is made simple and workable is through assumptions. We assume that only certain factors are relevant to the problem at hand. Then we derive conclusions

from the assumptions and test the model by comparing its predictions with what we know of the world.

You need to do two different things with the models that you will come across in your study of economics. First, you must understand how the model works—specifically, what is assumed and how the conclusions follow. The second task is to evaluate how well the model explains what it is supposed to explain. As you read the many arguments and pieces of evidence, keep in mind how they fit with the model's basic assumptions and conclusions.

2   Economic **variables** are measurable, and they change. The price of potatoes is an economic variable; so is the rate of unemployment. We look for two types of relationships among these variables. First, we are interested in whether certain economic variables move together. For example, during the 1980s, the U.S. government ran up unprecedented peacetime budget deficits and also very high trade deficits. These two deficit variables were **correlated.** But we are also interested in whether a change in one variable **causes** a change in another variable. Specifically, did the high government budget deficits of the 1980s cause the large trade deficits? Before economists make conclusions, they require a sound model that shows how a change in an economic variable was caused and also some evidence that the model's assumptions are appropriate and that its predictions have actually occurred.

3   **Positive economics** focuses on questions about how the economy works. What does it do, and why does it do it? For example, how were the budget and trade deficits of the 1980s related? **Normative economics,** on the other hand, typically asks what should be done. Should we reduce the federal budget deficit? Keep in mind, however, that normative economics cannot prescribe which value to hold; it describes the appropriate policy given the value.

4   Microeconomics and macroeconomics are two ways of looking at the economy. Microeconomics looks from the bottom up; it starts with the behavior of individuals and firms and builds up to an understanding of markets and the economy as a whole. Macroeconomics, on the other hand, is a top-down look, beginning with a description of the performance of aggregate economic variables and then constructing explanations. Micro- and macroeconomics must fit together. The models that explain how individuals, firms, and markets work must be consistent with the models that we use to describe the economy as a whole. An important theme of this book is that the microeconomics in Parts One, Two, and Three provides a firm foundation for the macroeconomics to follow in Parts Four, Five, and Six.

SELF-TEST

True or False

1   Henry Ford patented the internal combustion engine.

2   Henry Ford paid his workers especially high wages because he wanted them to earn enough to buy his cars.

3   By and large, government has kept out of the automobile business.

4   Patents give exclusive rights to market an innovation for a limited period of time.

5   The U.S. government imposed a tariff on Japanese car imports in the early 1980s.

6   Economics studies how individuals, firms, governments, and other organizations make choices and how those choices determine the allocation of the economy's resources.

7   The four basic questions concerning how economies function are what is produced and in what quantities, how are the goods produced, for whom are they produced, and who makes the decisions?

8   Most resource allocation decisions are made by governments in the U.S. economy.

9   In centrally planned economies, most decisions are made by the government.

10 The three major markets are the product, labor, and insurance markets.

11 Microeconomics focuses on the behavior of the economy as a whole.

12 Macroeconomics studies the behavior of firms, households, and individuals.

13 Two economic variables are correlated if there is a systematic relationship between them.

14 When two variables are correlated, it is because changes in one cause changes in the other.

15 Normative economics deals with questions concerning how the economy actually works.

Multiple Choice

1   Henry Ford paid his workers more than the going rate chiefly because

   a   he feared that the government would set minimum wages if he paid low wages;
   b   he could thereby obtain a hard-working, productive labor force;
   c   he did not care about profits, only the well-being of his workers;
   d   his highly paid workers would buy more of his cars;
   e   his highly paid workers would pay more taxes.

2   Patents

   a   give inventors exclusive rights to produce and market their inventions for a limited time;
   b   allow inventors to charge high prices without fear of competition.
   c   provide incentives to encourage new inventions;
   d   are awarded for innovations, not ideas;
   e   all of the above.

3   In the 1980s, the U.S. government negotiated limitations on exports of Japanese automobiles to the United States. As a result,

   a   the U.S. automobile industry recaptured its lost market share;
   b   automobile prices increased;
   c   Japanese firms set up plants in the United States;
   d   the Japanese government retaliated with restrictions on exports of U.S. automobiles to Japan;
   e   b and c.

4   Because resources are scarce,

   a   questions must be answered;
   b   choices must be made;
   c   all except the rich must make choices;
   d   governments must allocate resources;
   e   some individuals must be poor.

5   Which of the following is not a fundamental question concerning how economies funtion?

   a   What is produced, and in what quantities?
   b   How are the goods produced?
   c   For whom are they produced?
   d   Who makes the decisions?
   e   All of the above are fundamental questions.

6   In market economies, the four basic questions are answered

   a   by elected representatives;
   b   in such a way as to ensure that everyone has enough to live well;
   c   by private individuals and firms, interacting in markets;
   d   according to the traditional way of doing things;
   e   by popular vote.

7   In market economies, goods are consumed by

   a   those who are most deserving;
   b   those who work the hardest;
   c   those who are politically well connected;
   d   those who are willing and able to pay the most;
   e   those who produce them.

8   Which of the following is not one of the three major markets?

   a   goods market;
   b   labor market;
   c   capital market;
   d   Common Market;
   e   all of the above.

9   The detailed study of firms, households, individuals, and the markets where they transact is called

   a   macroeconomics;
   b   microeconomics;
   c   normative economics;
   d   positive economics;
   e   aggregate economics.

10 The study of the behavior of the economy as a whole, especially such factors as unemployment and inflation, is called

   a   macroeconomics.
   b   microeconomics.
   c   normative economics.

d   positive economics.
e   market economics.

11   An economic theory or model is a

a   mathematical equation;
b   prediction about the future of the economy;
c   recommended reform in government policy that pays attention to the laws of economics;
d   set of assumptions and conclusions derived from those assumptions;
e   small-scale economic community set up to test the effectiveness of a proposed government program.

12   Which of the following is an example of causation?

a   Taxes are too high.
b   The trade deficits of the 1980s were the direct result of the decade's budget deficits.
c   During the 1980s the United States experienced high trade and budget deficits.
d   In mixed economies there is a role for government and a role for markets.
e   U.S. interest rates fell during the early 1990s.

13   Which of the following is an example of correlation?

a   The high budget deficits of the 1980s caused the trade deficits.
b   Taxes are too high.
c   During recessions, output falls and unemployment increases.
d   In mixed economies, there is a role for markets and a role for government.
e   Economics studies choices and how choices determine the allocation of resources.

14   Which of the following is an example of normative economics?

a   The high budget deficits of the 1980s caused the trade deficits.
b   During recessions, output falls and unemployment increases.
c   Lower interest rates would encourage investment.
d   Interest rates should be reduced to encourage investment.
e   Expansionary monetary policy will reduce interest rates.

15   Which of the following is an example of positive economics?

a   Taxes are too high.
b   U.S. savings rates are too low.
c   Lower interest rates would encourage investment.
d   Interest rates should be reduced to encourage investment.
e   There is too much economic inequality in the United States.

16   In the United States, the question of what is produced and in what quantities is answered

a   primarily by private decisions influenced by prices;
b   by producing what was produced the previous year;
c   primarily by government planning;
d   randomly;
e   according to majority vote.

17   In which of the following does the government determine what is produced, how, and for whom?

a   market economies;
b   mixed economies;
c   centrally planned economies;
d   tradition-bound economies;
e   all of the above

18   Choices must be made because

a   resources are scarce;
b   human beings are choice-making animals;
c   government regulations require choices to be made;
d   economic variables are correlated;
e   without choices, there would be no economics as we know it.

19   Anything that can be measured and that changes is

a   a correlation;
b   a causation;
c   a variable;
d   a value;
e   an experiment.

20   In the labor market,

a   households purchase products from firms;
b   firms purchase the labor services of individuals;
c   firms raise money to finance new investment;
d   households purchase labor services from firms;
e   borrowing and lending are coordinated.

Completion

1   Exchanges take place in _____.

2   In a _____ economy, some decisions are made chiefly by government and others by markets.

3   All the institutions involved in borrowing and lending money make up the _____ market.

4   The behavior of the economy as a whole, and especially of certain aggregate measures such as unemployment and inflation, is called _____.

5   The branch of economics that focuses on firms, households, and individuals and studies product, labor, and capital markets is called _____.

6   The statement that crime rates are higher in low-income areas is an example of _____.

7   The statement that poverty leads to crime is an example of _____.

8   Economists use _____, which are sets of assumptions, conclusions, and data, to study the economy and evaluate the consequences of various policies.

9   _____ economics rests on value judgments; _____ economics describes how the economy behaves.

10   The four basic questions that economists ask about the economy are (1) what is produced and in what quantities, (2) _____, (3) for whom are they produced, and (4) who makes the decisions?

Answers to Self-Test

True or False

1	f	6	t	11	f
2	f	7	t	12	f
3	f	8	f	13	t
4	t	9	t	14	f
5	f	10	f	15	f

Multiple Choice

1	b	6	c	11	d	16	a
2	e	7	d	12	b	17	c
3	e	8	d	13	c	18	a
4	b	9	b	14	d	19	c
5	e	10	a	15	c	20	b

Completion

1 markets
2 mixed
3 capital
4 macroeconomics
5 microeconomics
6 correlation
7 causation
8 theories or models
9 Normative, positive
10 how are these goods produced

Chapter 2

THINKING LIKE AN ECONOMIST

Chapter Review

The concept of scarcity discussed in Chapter 1 implies that choices must be made. This chapter begins to explain how economists think about choice, and how choices are influenced and coordinated by markets. A basic economic assumption is that of rational choice, which simply says that people select the alternative they prefer most from among all those that are available. The alternatives available to any particular firm or individual, of course, depend upon the choices made by other firms and individuals. All of these rational choices must somehow fit together, and markets serve the function of coordinating them. How they do so is the subject of Chapters 3 through 5.

ESSENTIAL CONCEPTS

1   The **basic economic model** includes three elements: individuals, firms, and markets. Economic decisions such as what and how much of each type of good to produce, how to produce them, what kind of career to pursue, and how to spend one's earnings are made by **rational, self-interested individuals** and **rational,**

profit-maximizing firms. Markets serve the economic role of coordinating these decisions.

2   The basic economic model assumes that markets are **perfectly competitive.** In perfectly competitive markets, there are many consumers and firms, and each is small relative to the size of the overall market. One key feature of perfect competition is that any firm charging more than the going price will lose all its customers. Without any ability to influence the market price, the firm is a **price taker.** (Later in this book, we will encounter monopolists and others known as **price makers,** who have the power to charge higher prices without losing all their customers.)

3   Private **property rights** play an important role in the basic model. They include the right to use resources in certain ways and the right to sell them in markets. These two aspects of property rights provide incentives to use resources efficiently and to transfer resources to their most valuable use. Inefficiencies can arise when property rights are ill-defined or restricted.

4   When compensation is tied to performance, people have strong incentives to work hard and be productive, but those who are more fortunate and successful also will earn higher incomes. On the other hand, distribut-

ing the output more equally undermines incentives. This **incentive-equality trade-off** is one of the basic questions facing societies: how should the tax and welfare system be constructed to balance the competing ends of providing strong incentives and promoting equality?

5   **Scarcity** implies that not everyone who desires a good or resource can have it: there is an allocation problem. In market economies, goods are allocated to the highest bidder. Another solution to the allocation problem is to **ration**. Rationing schemes include queues, first-come-first-served, lotteries, and coupons. Unless supplemented by markets, rationing schemes will likely lead to inefficiencies.

6   The basic economic model assumes that decisions are made rationally, which simply means that individuals and firms balance the benefits and costs of their decisions. Economists see rational decision making as a two-step process. First, find what alternatives are available. This step is the construction of the **opportunity set**. Next, select the best alternative from those within the opportunity set.

7   The chapter presents three types of opportunity sets. The **budget constraint** shows what combinations of goods can be consumed with a limtied amount of money. The **time constraint** indicates to what uses limited time can be put. Finally, the **production possibilities curve** depicts the combinations of goods that a firm or an entire economy can produce given its limited resources and the quality of the available technology.

8   The best alternatives in an opportunity set will lie along the outer edge. This is because people prefer more goods to less. Operating on the outer edge also implies that there will be a **trade-off**: more of one option means less of another. For example, on the budget constraint, consuming more of one good means that less money is available to spend on another good. On the time constraint, if an individual devotes more time to one activity, there is less time available for other endeavors. A society that chooses to produce more of one good must settle for less production of other goods.

9   The **opportunity cost** of a good or activity is the option forgone. The opportunity cost of consuming more of one good is consuming less of some alternative good. The opportunity cost of an activity is the other endeavor that would have been, but now cannot be, undertaken. The opportunity cost of producing one good is the necessarily lower production of another.

10   The opportunity cost, not the price, is the proper measure of the economic cost of any choice. For example, in addition to the ultimate purchase price, the opportunity cost of buying an automobile includes the time and expense devoted to investigating alternatives, searching for the best deal, and negotiating the terms.

11   Opportunity costs are measured in total and at the margin. When a firm is deciding where to locate its plant, it compares the **total costs** at each location. When a firm is considering how large a plant to build, it looks at the costs of increasing or decreasing the size. These are the **marginal costs**, the costs of a little bit more or a little bit less.

BEHIND THE ESSENTIAL CONCEPTS

1   The basic competitive model introduced in this chapter is critical to your understanding of economics. It will be expanded and applied in all the chapters that follow, but you should master the concepts given in this chapter: rational individuals choose the best combinations of goods along their budget constraints, firms maximize profits, and trading takes place in competitive markets, where each individual and firm is a price taker.

2   The opportunity set itself shows all of the alternatives that are available. Because more is generally preferred to less, however, economists focus on the outer boundary of the opportunity set. For example, Figure 2.1 shows an opportunity set for a firm that must divide its resources between the production of canned and frozen vegetables. The entire shaded area shows all of the combinations that are possible. The economist's attention is drawn to the outer edge, the production possibilities curve, because to choose a combination inside (such as point A) would be inefficient.

3   The terms "opportunity set," "budget constraint," "trade-off," and "opportunity cost" are related, but they are distinct, and you should take care to understand each one. Figure 2.2 shows the opportunity set for a student who consumes hamburgers and pizzas. The **opportunity set** shows all of the combinations of hamburgers and pizzas that are affordable. Points A and B are affordable; they lie within the opportunity set, but have the critical characteristic of lying along its outer edge, which is the budget constraint. The trade-off is that more hamburgers mean fewer pizzas. If Joe chooses B rather than A, he eats another pizza and exactly two fewer hamburgers. The trade-off be-

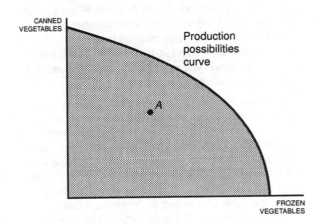

Figure 2.1

Figure 2.2

tween any two points measures the opportunity cost. In this case, the opportunity cost of this extra pizza is the two forgone burgers. When the outer edge of the opportunity set is a straight line, the trade-offs will be the same all along the line; when it is a curve, the trade-offs will change.

4 Opportunity costs are forgone alternatives—not money, not time, and not resources. For example, if you spend one hour in class tomorrow, the opportunity cost of attending that class is not the hour itself. That hour will pass whether you go to the class or not. The opportunity cost is what you would have done with that hour. It is the activity you give up. Strictly speaking, the opportunity cost of buying a book for $20 is not the money, but what would have been purchased with the $20 if it had not been spent on the book.

5 **Sunk costs**, outlays that cannot be recovered, are not opportunity costs. Because these expenditures are not affected by the choice of any alternative, they do not represent the opportunity cost of any alternative. For example, suppose that you sign a one-year lease on an apartment and are forbidden to sublet it. When you consider whether to stay in town for the summer or travel abroad, the rent owed your landlord is irrelevant. You cannot do anything about it. Regardless of which alternative you choose, you must pay the rent. The rent is a sunk cost, not an opportunity cost.

6 Be clear about the difference between total costs and marginal costs. Marginal costs are the costs of a little more or a little less of some activity. Before considering going into business, you evaluate that total opportunity costs of the enterprise—all of the costs of setting up the plant, designing and producing the product, and locating the market. When you are considering whether to produce another unit of output, however, it is the marginl opportunity cost that is important. The marginal cost of producing a little bit more is just the added cost

incurred when producing more with the plant already set up, the product designed, and the market found. These latter costs are not marginal.

7 **Diminishing returns** can be confusing at first. What the term means is that as more inputs are used in a production process, output increases at a diminishing rate. For example, suppose more migrant workers are hired to pick apples. Each additional worker results in more apples being picked in total, but the marginal contribution of the newest worker, how many extra apples are picked when he is hired, is not as great as that of the previously hired new workers. We can also say that the opportunity cost of increasing output—the marginal cost—is higher as output increases.

8 Another way to approach diminishing returns is to think about why the output of the marginal input is declining. The extra inputs are just as good at producing; however, as more are used, the production process becomes crowded. For example, when more workers are hired to pick apples, there are fewer apple trees per workers, and it is more difficult to pick apples.

SELF-TEST

True or False

1 The basic model of economics seeks to explain why people want what they want.

2 According to the basic competitive model, firms maximize profits (or stock market value).

3 Generally, inequality will be greater when society is organized to provide stronger incentives to perform efficiently.

4 A firm selling in a perfectly competitive market is a price taker because it cannot raise its price without losing all of its customers.

5 Both the right to use a resource in certain ways and the right to transfer that resource are important aspects of private property rights.

6 Commonly owned property is the reason for diminishing returns.

7 A legal entitlement—that is, the right to use a resource in certain ways but not to sell or trade it—probably prevents the resource from going to its highest valued use.

8 Lotteries are an inefficient means of allocating resources because they do not allocate goods to the highest bidder.

9 Rationing by queues wastes the time spent waiting in line.

10 The opportunity set includes only the best available alternative.

11 The production possibilities curve shows the boundary of the opportunity set.

12   The principle of diminishing returns says that as more units of any input are added to a production process, total output eventually falls.

13   If an economy is not using its resources in the most productive way, economists say that there is inefficiency.

14   Sunk expenditures do not represent opportunity costs.

15   If one pizza sells for $8 but two pizzas can be purchased for $12, the marginal cost of the second pizza is $6.

Multiple Choice

1   Which of the following is not a building block of the basic economic model?

   a   assumptions about how firms behave;
   b   assumptions about how consumers behave;
   c   assumptions about markets;
   d   assumptions about the behavior of government.
   e   All of the above are building blocks of the basic economic model.

2   Individuals and firms in the economy must make choices because of

   a   diminishing returns;
   b   rationality;
   c   scarcity;
   d   all of the above;
   e   none of the above.

3   The concept of rationality refers to

   a   the fact of scarcity;
   b   the principle of diminishing returns;
   c   the assumption that individuals have sensible goals;
   d   the assumption that individuals and firms weigh the costs and benefits of their choices;
   e   the assumption that individuals and firms are certain of the consequences of their choices.

4   A firm that cannot influence the price it sells its product for is called a

   a   price maker;
   b   price taker;
   c   rational decision maker;
   d   none of the above;
   e   all of the above.

5   In a pure market economy, incentives to work hard and produce efficiently are provided by

   a   the profit motive;
   b   government regulations;
   c   private property rights;
   d   both the profit motive and private property rights;
   e   all of the above.

6   When property is commonly owned, users

   a   do not maximize profits;
   b   violate the principle of rationality;
   c   ignore the principle of diminishing returns;
   d   have little incentive to maintain and preserve the value of the property;
   e   none of the above.

7   If owners are not allowed to sell their resources, then

   a   the resources will not go to the highest value users;
   b   the owners will not act rationally;
   c   their choices will not be limited to their opportunity sets;
   d   the market will be perfectly competitive;
   e   none of the above.

8   Allocating goods by lotteries, queues, and coupons are examples of

   a   rationing;
   b   not selling to the highest bidder;
   c   efficient ways of allocating resources;
   d   the profit motive;
   e   a and b.

9   Rationing by queues

   a   leads to an efficient allocation of resources;
   b   allocates goods to those willing to pay the most money;
   c   wastes the time spent waiting in line;
   d   is an efficient way of allocating scarce goods;
   e   a and c.

10   When goods are rationed by coupons and the coupons are not tradable,

   a   the goods do not go to the individuals who value them most;
   b   a black market may be established;
   c   individuals will not act rationally;
   d   a and b;
   e   none of the above.

11   Choices of individuals and firms are limited by

   a   time constraints;
   b   production possibilities;
   c   budget constraints;
   d   all of the above;
   e   none of the above.

12   Fred has $10 to spend on baseball cards and hamburgers. The price of baseball cards is $.50 per pack. Hamburgers sell at a price of $1.00 each. Which of the following possibilities is not in Fred's opportunity set?

   a   10 hamburgers and zero packs of baseball cards;
   b   5 hamburgers and 10 packs of baseball cards;
   c   2 hamburgers and 16 packs of baseball cards;
   d   1 hamburger and 18 packs of baseball cards.
   e   All of the above are in Fred's opportunity set.

13   The production possibilities curve

   a   shows the amounts of goods a firm or society might produce;
   b   is not a straight line because of the principle of diminishing returns;
   c   illustrates the trade-offs between goods;
   d   all of the above;
   e   none of the above.

14 Henry spends an hour shopping and buys one sweater for $30. The opportunity cost of the sweater is

 a one hour;
 b $30;
 c one hour plus $30;
 d the next-best alternative uses of the hour and the $30;
 e none of the above.

15 Renting an apartment, Jorge signs a lease promising to pay $400 each month for one year. He always keeps his word, and therefore he will pay the $400 each month whether he lives in the apartment or not. The $400 each month represents

 a an opportunity cost;
 b a sunk cost;
 c a trade-off;
 d a budget constraint;
 e diminishing returns.

16 One box of Nature's Crunch Cereal sells for $2.55. Each box comes with a coupon worth $.50 off the purchase price of another box of Nature's Crunch Cereal. The marginal cost of the second box of this product is

 a $2.55;
 b $3.05;
 c $2.05;
 d $1.55;
 e none of the above.

17 Making a rational choice involves

 a identifying the opportunity set;
 b defining the trade-off;
 c calculating the opportunity costs;
 d all of the above;
 e none of the above.

18 Fred is considering renting an apartment. A one-bedroom apartment rents for $400, and a nice two-bedroom apartment can be had for $500. The $100 difference is

 a the opportunity cost of the two-bedroom apartment;
 b the marginal cost of the second bedroom;
 c a sunk cost;
 d the marginal cost of an apartment;
 e none of the above.

19 If a firm changes from paying commissions on total sales to paying each member of its sales force a fixed salary, it will likely

 a experience lower total sales;
 b have greater equality in earnings of its sales representatives;
 c see no difference because compensation is a sunk cost;
 d a and b;
 e none of the above.

20 Reducing taxes

 a makes no difference because incentives do not matter;
 b will likely increase inequality because those who work harder can keep more of their higher earnings;
 c will likely increase inequality because those who are luckier can keep more of their higher earnings;
 d b and c;
 e none of the above.

Completion

1 Economists assume that people make choices _____, taking into consideration the costs and benefits of their alternatives.

2 A market with large numbers of buyers and sellers, each of whom cannot influence the price, is an example of _____.

3 The right of an owner of a resource to use it in certain ways and to sell it is called a _____.

4 Allocating goods and services by some means other than selling to the highest bidder is called _____.

5 The collection of all available opportunities is called the _____.

6 _____ limit choices.

7 The amount of goods that a business firm is able to produce is called its _____.

8 The idea that as more inputs are used in a production process each successive input eventually adds less to output is an example of the principle of _____.

9 The fact that more time spent studying means less time available for other activities illustrates a _____.

10 An expenditure that cannot be recovered is a _____ cost.

Answers to Self-Test

True or False

1	f	4	t	7	t	10	f	13	t
2	t	5	t	8	t	11	t	14	t
3	t	6	f	9	t	12	f	15	f

Multiple Choice

1	d	6	d	11	d	16	c
2	c	7	a	12	e	17	d
3	d	8	e	13	d	18	b
4	b	9	c	14	d	19	d
5	d	10	d	15	b	20	d

Completion

1 rationally
2 perfect competition
3 property right
4 rationing
5 opportunity set
6 Constraints
7 production possibilities
8 diminishing returns
9 trade-off
10 sunk

Doing Economics: Tools and Practice Problems

For the problem sets in this section, we reach into the economist's tool box for five important techniques, each of which will reappear throughout the remainder of the book. Three relate to the opportunity set: budget and time constraints, for which the outer edge of the opportunity set is a straight line; multiple constraints involving, for example, limits on both time and money; and production possibilities curves, which can be straight lines but more often exhibit diminishing returns and are curved. The remaining two techniques relate to costs: the distinction between sunk and opportunity costs, and the use of marginal analysis to balance costs and benefits.

STRAIGHT-LINE OPPORTUNITY SETS

The simplest type of opportunity set has an outer boundary that is a straight line. Examples include budget constraints, time constraints, and production possibilities, when there are constant returns. The budget constraint indicates what combinations of goods can be purchased with a limited amount of money. The time constraint indicates what combinations of time-consuming activities can be undertaken with a limited amount of time. The production possibilities curve (in this case it is a straight line) indicates what combinations of goods can be produced. Tool Kit 2.1 shows how to construct these opportunity sets.

Tool Kit 2.1: Plotting the Straight-Line Opportunity Set

Budget constraints, time constraints, and production possibilities are examples of straight-line opportunity sets. To draw the budget constraint you must know the size of the budget and the prices of the goods. The time constraint can be drawn given the total time available and the time requirements for each activity. To plot the production possibilities curve you need to know the resources and the technology. Follow this procedure to plot these straight-line opportunity sets.

Step one: Draw a set of coordinate axes. Label the horizontal axis as the quantity of one good or activity and the vertical axis as the quantity of the other good or activity.

Step two: Calculate the maximum quantity of the good or activity measured on the horizontal axis. Plot this quantity along the horizontal axis.

Step three: Calculate the maximum quantity of the good or activity measured on the vertical axis. Plot this quantity along the vertical axis.

Step four: Draw a line segment connecting the two points. This line segment is the relevant part of the opportunity set.

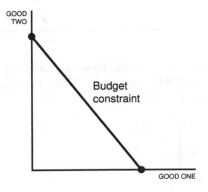

Step five: The slope is the opportunity cost of the good or activity measured on the horizontal axis. In the case of the budget constraint, it is called the relative price, the ratio of the price of the good measured on the horizontal axis divided by the price of the good measured on the vertical axis.

1   (Worked problem: budget constraint) Diana has an entertainment budget of $200 each month. She enjoys lunches with friends and going to the movies. The price of a typical lunch is $10. Movie tickets are $5 each. Construct her opportunity set.

Step-by-step solution

Step one: Draw coordinate axes and label the horizontal one "Lunches" and the vertical one "Movies." (There is no rule as to which good goes where. It would be fine if lunches were measured on the vertical axis and movies on the horizontal.)

Step two: Calculate the maximum quantity of lunches. This number is $200/$10 = 20 lunches. Plot this quantity along the horizontal axis.

Step three: Calculate the maximum quantity of movies. This number is $200/$5 = 40 movie tickets. Plot this quantity along the vertical axis.

Step four: Draw a line segment connecting these two points. This line segment is the budget constraint.

Step five: The slope of the budget constraint is 40/20 = 2. The price ratio is $10/$5 = 2. (Strictly speaking, these slopes are negative, but we follow the practice of dropping the negative sign as long as there is no confusion.)

2   (Practice problem: budget constraint) Velma Thomas must pay for both prescription medicine and nursing care for her elderly father. Each bottle of pills costs her $40, and the price of nursing care is $100 per day. She has been able to scrape together $1,000 each month for these expenses. Construct her opportunity set, going through all five steps.

3   (Practice problem: budget constraint) Construct the following opportunity sets.

a   Clothing budget per year = $900; price of suits = $300; price of shoes = $90.
b   Food budget = $200 per week; price of restaurant meals = $20; price of in-home meals = $5.
c   School expense budget = $1,200 per semester; price of books = $50; price of courses = $200.
d   Annual state transportation department budget = $100,000; cost of fixing potholes = $200; cost of replacing road signs = $500.

4   (Worked problem: time constraint) Ahmed likes to visit his invalid father across town. Each visit, including transportation and time with Dad, takes 3 hours. Another of Ahmed's favorite activities is his tango lessons. These are given downstairs in his apartment building and take only an hour each. With work and night school, Ahmed has only 15 hours each week to divide between visiting his father and tango lessons. Construct his opportunity set.

Step-by-step solution

Step one: The time constraint works very much like the budget constraint. Plot coordinate axes and label the horizontal one "Visits" and the vertical one "Lessons."

Step two: Calculate the maximum number of visits to his father. This number is 15/3 = 5 visits. Plot this quantity along the horizontal axis.

Step three: Calculate the maximum number of tango lessons. This number is 15/1 = 15 lessons. Plot this quantity along the vertical axis.

Step four: Draw a line segment connecting these two points. This line segment is the time constraint.

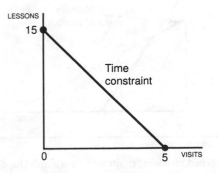

Step five: The slope of the time constraint is 15/5 = 3. The time-requirement ratio is 3/1 = 3.

5   (Practice problem: time constraint) Michael Terranova has 2 hours to make his house as clean as possible. The place needs vacuuming and dusting. He can dust one piece of furniture in 10 minutes. Each room takes 20 minutes to vacuum. Plot his time constraint.

6   (Practice problem: time constraint) Construct the following opportunity sets.

   a   Total time available = 6 hours; time required to iron each shirt = 15 minutes; time required to iron each dress = 30 minutes.
   b   Total time available = 20 days; time required to study each chapter = 1/2 day; time required to write book reports = 2 days.
   c   Total time available = 40 hours; time required to counsel each disturbed teenager = 2 hours; time required to attend each meeting = 1 hour.
   d   Total time available = 8 hours; time required to visit each client = 4 hours; time required to telephone each client = 10 minutes.

7   (Worked problem: production possibilities curve) First, assume that there is one resource, which can be used in the production of either of two goods, and that there are no diminishing returns. In this case, the production possibilities curve is a straight line, and we treat it just as we did the budget and time constraints.

   There are 25 migrant farm workers employed at San Pueblo vegetable farm. Each worker can pick 4 bushels of cucumbers an hour. Alternatively, each worker can pick 1 bushel of peppers each hour. Each worker can work 8 hours a day. Plot the daily production possibilities curve.

Step-by-step solution

Step one: Plot coordinate axes and label the horizontal one "Cucumbers" (measured in bushels) and the vertical one "Peppers."

Step two: Calculate the maximum number of cucumbers that can be picked each day. This number is 25 (workers) × 8 (hours) × 4 (bushels an hour) = 800 bushels of cucumbers. Plot this number along the horizontal axis.

Step three: Calculate the maximum number of peppers that can be picked each day. This number is 25 (workers) × 8 (hours) × 1 (bushel an hour) = 200 bushels of peppers. Plot this number along the vertical axis.

Step four: Draw a line segment connecting these two points. This line segment is the production possibilities curve.

Step five: The slope is 200/800 = 1/4, which means that the opportunity cost of 1 bushel of cucumbers is 1/4 bushel of peppers.

8   (Practice problem: production possibilities curve) Coach Hun has four assistant coaches. They make recruiting visits and also run clinics for local youth. Each can make 32 recruiting visits a week. Alternatively, each can run 8 clinics in a week. Plot the production possibilities curve.

9   (Practice problem: production possibilities curve) Construct the following opportunity sets.

   a   Total amount of land available = 10 acres of land; output of corn per acre = 2,000 bushels; output of wheat per acre = 1,000 bushels.

   b   Total amount of labor available = 40 hours; output of donuts per hour = 150; output of sweet rolls per hour = 50.

   c   Total amount of floor space available = 1,000 square feet; sales of women's sportswear per square foot = $500; sales of housewares per square foot = $200.

   d   Total amount of fuel available = 5,000 gallons; miles per gallon for tank travel = 3; miles per gallon for armored personnel carriers = 9.

MULTIPLE CONSTRAINTS

Individuals often face more than one constraint. For example, many activities cost money and take up time. This means that the opportunity set includes only those alternatives that do not exceed both the budget and time constraints. Tool Kit 2.2 shows how to combine multiple constraints into a single opportunity set. Notice how the resulting opportunity set is convex.

Tool Kit 2.2: Plotting Multiple Constraints

When activities take both time and money, opportunities will be limited by two constraints. This is one example of the problem of multiple constraints. To plot the opportunity set when more than one constraint applies, follow this three-step procedure.

Step one: Plot the first constraint. (For example, this might be the budget constraint.)

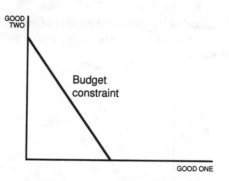

Step two: Plot the second constraint. (For example, this might be the time constraint.)

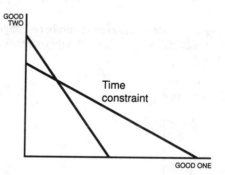

Step three: Darken the section of each constraint that lies under the other constraint. This is the outer edge of the opportunity set.

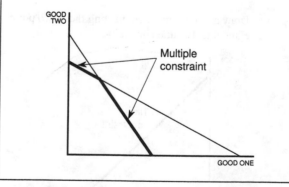

10   (Worked problem: multiple constraints) Out of work for six months, Donna feels that it is time to start looking for a job. Her father (gently) suggests that she apply in person to several of the retail stores on the west side of town. Each store application would require $5 in out-of-pocket expenses for transportation and dry

cleaning. (She realizes that only those who wear clean clothes stand any chance of receiving an offer.) Each trip would require 5 hours.

Donna's mother (not so gently) says that she should mail letters of application to a wide variety of potential employers. Each letter of application would require only $1 in mailing and copying costs and 1/2 hour of time.

Donna can devote 30 hours and $50 dollars each week to her job search campaign. Plot her opportunity set.

Step-by-step solution

Step one: Follow the procedure for plotting her budget constraint. Label the horizontal axis "Personal applications" and the vertical one "Mail applications." Your answer should look like this.

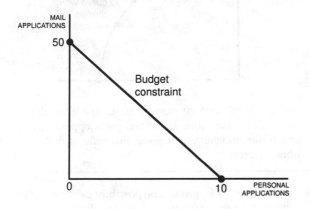

Step two: Follow the procedure for plotting her time constraint. Your answer should look like this.

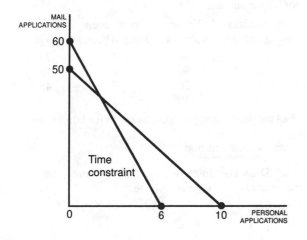

Step three: Darken the section of each constraint that lies under the other constraint. Notice that between points *A* and *B* on the diagram, it is the budget constraint that is binding, but between *B* and *C,* the time constraint is the limiting one.

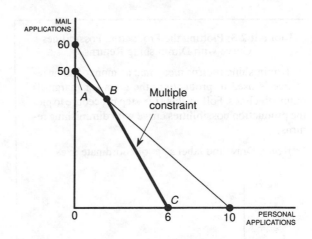

11 (Practice problem: multiple constraints) Harold's leaf-raking business is taking off. He has so many jobs to do that he is thinking of renting a leaf blower. This would cost him $20 per day. With a leaf blower, he could clean 10 lawns each day. He can only do 4 each day with his trusty rake, which costs nothing. Harold works 7 days each week, but has only $100 to spend. Plot his opportunity set for the week. (Hint: The axes should be labeled "Lawns cleaned with a leaf blower" and "Lawns raked by hand.")

12 (Practice problem: multiple constraints) The maintenance department at Alberti Van and Storage has 8 mechanic-hours to tune truck engines and replace the mufflers. It takes 1 hour to tune an engine and 1/2 hour to replace the muffler. In addition, the parts budget is only $100, the parts required to tune an engine cost $10, and each muffler costs $20. Construct the department's opportunity set.

13 (Practice problem: multiple constraints) Lamont tests swimming pools and cleans locker rooms for local country clubs. He has 20 hours available, and it takes him 1 hour to test each pool and 1/2 hour to clean each locker room. He has a budget of $50 to spend. It costs him $10 to test each pool and $1 to clean each locker room. Construct his opportunity set.

PRODUCTION POSSIBILITIES WITH DIMINISHING RETURNS

Usually, production is subject to diminishing returns. This means that as more of a resource is used in production, the extra (or marginal) output is less. In other words, although output increases, it does so at a diminishing rate. With diminishing returns the production possibilities curve acquires a convex shape. Tool Kit 2.3 shows how to plot the production possibilities curves when there are diminishing returns.

Tool Kit 2.3: Plotting the Production Possibilities Curve with Diminishing Returns

Diminishing returns mean that as more of some resource is used in production, the extra (or marginal) output declines. Follow this five-step procedure to plot the production possibilities curve with diminishing returns.

Step one: Draw and label a set of coordinate axes.

Step two: Calculate the total amount of the good measured on the horizontal axis that can be produced if all the resource is used. Plot this quantity along the horizontal axis.

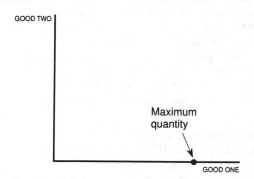

Step three: Calculate the total amount of the good measured on the vertical axis that can be produced if all the resource is used. Plot this quantity along the vertical axis.

Step four: Calculate and plot several other feasible combinations.

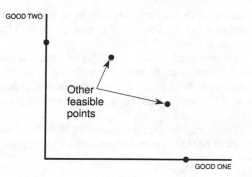

Step five: Draw a smooth curve connecting these points. This curve is the production possibilities curve.

Step six: Verify that the slope is increasing along the curve. Since the slope is the marginal opportunity cost of the horizontal axis good, this reflects diminishing returns.

14   (Worked problem: production possibilities curve with diminishing returns) Iatrogenesis, a medical laboratory, employs 4 lab technicians. Each is equally adept at analyzing throat cultures and distilling vaccines. The table below shows output per day for various numbers of lab technicians.

Technicians doing cultures	Throat cultures	Technicians doing vaccines	Vaccines
1	50	1	20
2	90	2	35
3	120	3	45
4	140	4	50

Plot the production possibilities curve for Iatrogenesis.

Step-by-step solution

Step one: Draw coordinate axes. Label the horizontal one "Throat cultures" and the vertical one "Vaccines."

Step two: Calculate the maximum number of throat cultures. If all 4 technicians do throat cultures, the number is 140. Plot this number.

Step three: Calculate the maximum number of vaccines. If all 4 technicians do vaccines, the number is 50. Plot this number.

Step four: Calculate several other feasible points. For example, if 1 technician does throat cultures, then 3 can do vaccines. Reading off the table, we see that the combination produced is 50 throat cultures and 45 vaccines. Similarly, if 2 do throat cultures and 2 do vaccines, the outputs are 90 throat cultures and 35 vaccines. Another feasible combination is 120 cultures and 20 vaccines. Plot these points.

Step five: Draw the production possibilities curve through the points that have been plotted.

Step six: Observe that, as expected, the slope gets steeper as the number of throat cultures is increased. This indicates diminishing returns.

15 (Practice problem: production possibilities curve with diminishing returns) Enormous State University has a crime problem. Members of the criminal element have stolen many bicycles and a great deal of stereo equipment. To address this crime wave, the campus police has hired 5 new officers. The following table gives the expected number of thefts for various assignments for these new officers.

New police officers assigned to bicycle duty	Reduction in bicycle thefts	New police officers assigned to dorm patrol	Reduction in thefts of stereo equipment
1	25	1	10
2	45	2	18
3	60	3	25
4	70	4	31
5	75	5	36

Plot the production possibilities curve.

16 (Practice problem: production possibilities curve with diminishing returns) Movaway Company has employed 4 maintenance inspectors for their fleet of trucks and forklifts. The following table shows how assigning inspectors leads to fewer breakdowns.

Inspectors assigned to check trucks	Reduced number of truck breakdowns	Inspectors assigned to check forklifts	Reduced number of forklift breakdowns
1	5	1	3
2	9	2	5
3	12	3	6
4	14	4	6

Plot Movaway's production possibilities curve, and verify that it shows diminishing returns.

17 (Practice problem: production possibilities curve with diminishing returns) The Dukakis vegetable farm (located on erstwhile corn-growing land in Iowa) has 800 tons of fertilizer. The following table shows how output of endive and bib lettuce is expected to respond to different amounts of fertilizer.

Fertilizer used on endive crop (tons)	Output of endive (bushels)	Fertilizer used on lettuce crop (tons)	Output of bib lettuce (bushels)
0	1,400	0	2,000
200	2,400	200	3,400
400	3,200	400	4,200
600	3,600	600	4,700
800	4,000	800	5,000

Plot the farm's production possibilities curve, and verify that it exhibits diminishing returns.

SUNK COSTS

Rational individuals make choices by carefully weighing the benefits and costs of their alternatives. Doing this requires a clear understanding of exactly what an opportunity cost is. Expenditures that cannot be recovered are not true opportunity costs. They are sunk costs and should be ignored when making decisions. Opportunity costs are foregone alternatives, and they are the only costs to consider. Tool Kit 2.4 shows how to distinguish true opportunity costs from sunk costs.

Tool Kit 2.4: Distinguishing Opportunity Costs and Sunk Costs

When an expenditure must be made regardless of what action is chosen, that expenditure is not an opportunity cost, it is a sunk cost. To find the opportunity cost of an action, it is necessary to see what is changed by undertaking that action rather than its alternative. Follow this four-step procedure.

Step one: To find the opportunity cost of an action, first specify the next-best alternative. This is what would be done if the action in question were not chosen.

Step two: Calculate the total cost for the action and its alternative.

Step three: Calculate the opportunity cost. Subtract the cost for the alternative from the cost for the action. This difference is the opportunity cost of the action.

Step four: Calculate the sunk costs. Any costs that are the same for both the chosen action and its alternative are sunk costs.

---

18   (Worked problem: opportunity costs and sunk costs) Upper Peninsula Airlines is studying the question of when to cancel flights for its Marquette to Detroit route. Flying nearly empty planes seems like bad business. The company wants to know the opportunity cost of going ahead with a scheduled round-trip flight. There are two scheduled flights each day. Here are some relevant cost data.

Salaries of crew	$ 1,000 per day
Fuel	$ 400 per round trip
Mortgage on plane	$ 100 per day
Landing fees	$ 50 in Marquette
	$ 100 in Detroit
Other in-flight costs	$ 100 per round trip

Calculate the opportunity cost of each round trip.

Step-by-step solution

Step one: The next-best alternative to going ahead with the scheduled round-trip flight is not flying.

Step two: Calculate the total cost for going ahead with the flight and canceling it. If the flight is made, the expenditures are all of those listed above. If the flight is canceled, the company saves on fuel, landing fees, and other in-flight costs. The salaries of the crew and the mortage must be paid whether the flight happens or not.

Expenditures if flight is not canceled =

$1,000 + $400 + $100 + $150 + $100 = $1,750.

Expenditures if flight is canceled = $1,000 + $100 = $1,100.

Step three: Calculate the opportunity costs: $1,750 − $1,100 = $650. This is the opportunity cost of the flight.

Step four: Calculate the sunk costs. The remaining $1,100 for salaries and mortgage are sunk costs. Whether or not the flight is canceled, these cannot be recovered.

19   (Practice problem: opportunity costs and sunk costs) Often during the summer term, courses are scheduled but canceled at Enormous State University's downtown education building. In order to see whether this is a good policy, the administration needs to know the opportunity cost of going ahead with a scheduled course offering. Here are some cost data.

Compensation for instructor	$4,000
Air conditioning and lighting	$1,000
Custodial services	$2,000
Property taxes	$2,500

Each course requires one room. Any rooms not used for summer courses can be rented to local groups for $1,200 for the summer term.

a   Find the opportunity cost of offering a course.
b   How much are sunk costs?

20   (Practice problem: opportunity cost and sunk costs) The Commerce Department is downsizing under Governor Scissorhands. It is considering offering early retirement to 8 bureaucrats in its strategic investment division. Each is 2 years from regular retirement age. (For simplicity, you may ignore discounting the second year's dollars in this problem.)

Salaries	$50,000 each (per year)
Fringe benefits	$20,000 each (per year)
Office space for all 8	$10,000 annually (lease signed for 1 more year)
Pension benefit	$20,000 each if retired (per year)

a If the 8 do receive early retirement, what is the opportunity cost?

b How much are sunk costs?

MARGINAL BENEFITS AND MARGINAL COSTS

The rational individual always considers the benefits and costs of any action. Once you decide to do something, however, there is the question of how much of it to do. Answering this question involves looking at the benefits and costs of a little more or a little less, the marginal benefits and marginal costs. Tool Kit 2.5 shows how to calculate and balance the marginal benefits and marginal costs of economic decisions.

Tool Kit 2.5: Using Marginal Benefits and Marginal Costs

The marginal benefit of an activity is the extra gain brought about by increasing that activity a little. The marginal cost is the corresponding cost. Rational individuals make efficient decisions by carefully balancing benefits and costs "at the margin." Follow this four-step procedure.

Step one: Identify the objective of the activity and the benefits and costs of various levels of the activity.

Step two: Calculate marginal benefits. These are the extra gains from a little bit more of the activity.

Step three: Calculate the marginal costs. These are the extra costs from a little bit more of the activity.

Step four: Choose the level of the activity for which the marginal benefits equal the marginal costs.

---

21 (Worked problem: marginal costs and marginal benefits) A new inoculation against Honduran flu has just been discovered. Presently, 55 people die from the disease each year. The new inoculation will save lives, but unfortunately, it is not completely safe. Some of the recipients of the shots will die from adverse reactions. The projected effects of the inoculation are given in Table 2.1.

Table 2.1

Percent of population inoculated	Deaths due to the disease	Deaths due to the inoculations
0	55	0
10	45	0
20	36	1
30	28	2
40	21	3
50	15	5
60	10	8
70	6	12
80	3	17
90	1	23
100	0	30

How much of the population should be inoculated?

Step-by-step solution

Step one: Identify the objective, benefits, and costs. The objective is to minimize total deaths from the disease and the inoculations, and the problem is to choose the percentage of the population to inoculate. The benefits are reduced deaths caused by the disease, and the costs are the deaths caused by the shots.

Step two: Calculate the marginal benefits. The first 10 percent of the population inoculated reduces deaths caused by the disease from 55 to 45. The marginal benefit of the first 10 percent is 10. From the second 10 percent (increasing the percentage from 10 to 20), the marginal benefit is 45 − 36 = 9. The schedule of the marginal benefit is given in Table 2.2.

Table 2.2

Percent of population	Marginal benefits
10	10
20	9
30	8
40	7
50	6
60	5
70	4
80	3
90	2
100	1

Step three: Calculate the marginal costs. Inoculating the first 10 percent causes no deaths. The second 10 percent (increasing the percent of the population getting the shots from 10 to 20 percent) causes 1 death. The schedule for the marginal costs is shown in Table 2.3.

Table 2.3

Percent of population	Marginal costs
0	0
10	1
20	1
30	1
40	1
50	2
60	3
70	4
80	5
90	6
100	7

Step four: Choose the level of inoculation percentage for which marginal benefits equal marginal costs. The percentage of the population to inoculate is 70. To see why this is correct, notice that inoculating 10 percent of the population saves 10 lives (marginal benefits = 10) and causes no deaths (marginal costs = 0). The net savings in lives is 10. Increasing the percentage to 20 percent saves 9 lives at a cost of 1 death. The net savings is 9 lives. Continuing as long as deaths do not rise gives 70 percent. Notice that increasing the percentage to 80 percent saves fewer people (marginal benefits = 2) than it kills (marginal costs = 4). This is a bad idea. We should stop at 70 percent.

22 (Practice problem: marginal costs and marginal benefits) The transportation department has 10 workers fixing potholes. It is considering allocating some of these workers to reprogram traffic lights. Each activity saves travel time for commuters, and this is the objective of the transportation department. Table 2.4 gives time savings of each activity as the number of workers assigned to it varies. Remember that if a worker is assigned to reprogram lights, he cannot fix potholes.

Table 2.4

Workers assigned to reprogramming	Total time saved	Workers assigned to fix potholes	Total time saved
1	100	1	125
2	190	2	225
3	270	3	305
4	340	4	365
5	400	5	415
6	450	6	455
7	490	7	485
8	520	8	510
9	540	9	530
10	550	10	540

How should the workers be assigned? (Hint: Let the number of workers assigned to reprogramming be the activity. What are the costs of assigning these workers?)

23 (Practice problem: marginal costs and marginal benefits) Bugout pesticide kills insects that eat lettuce leaves. Currently 11 leaves per head are eaten by the insects. In the right concentrations, Bugout can be effective. On the other hand, there are side effects. When the concentration is too great, leaves fall off the lettuce head. Table 2.5 shows the relationship between concentrations of Bugout, leaves eaten, and leaves fallen. What concentration should the manufacturer recommend?

Table 2.5

Concentration (parts per million)	Leaves eaten per head	Leaves fallen per head
1	7	0
2	4	1
3	2	3
4	1	6
5	0	10
6	0	15

Answers to Problems

2

3

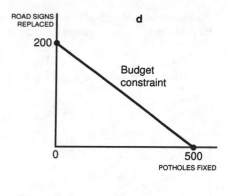

d

ROAD SIGNS REPLACED

200

Budget constraint

0   500

POTHOLES FIXED

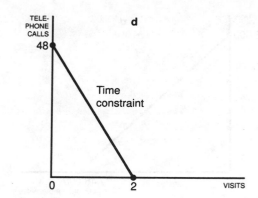

d

TELE-PHONE CALLS

48

Time constraint

0   2   VISITS

5

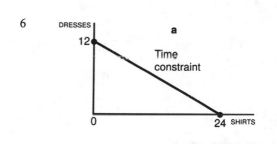

VACUUMING (ROOMS)

6

Time constraint

0   12   DUSTING (FURNITURE PIECES)

8

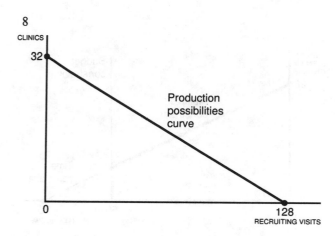

CLINICS

32

Production possibilities curve

0   128   RECRUITING VISITS

6

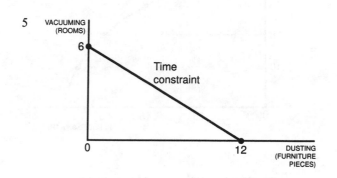

DRESSES

12

a

Time constraint

0   24   SHIRTS

BOOK REPORTS

10

b

Time constraint

0   40   STUDY

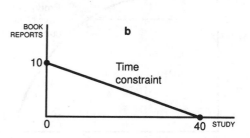

MEETINGS

40

c

Time constraint

0   20   COUNSELING SESSIONS

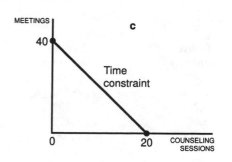

9

WHEAT (BUSHELS)

10,000

a

Production possibilities curve

0   20,000   CORN (BUSHELS)

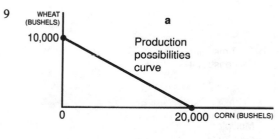

SWEET ROLLS

2,000

b

0   6,000   DONUTS

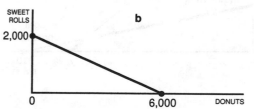

HOUSEWARES ($)

200,000

c

0   500,000   WOMEN'S SPORTSWEAR ($)

d

11

12

13

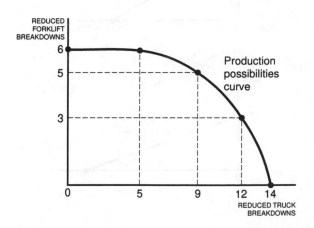

15

Reduction in bicycle thefts	Reduction in thefts of stereo equipment
0	36
25	31
45	25
60	18
70	10
75	0

16

Reduced number of truck breakdowns	Reduced number of forklift breakdowns
0	6
5	6
9	5
12	3
14	0

17

Endive (bushels)	Lettuce (bushels)
1,400	5,000
2,400	4,700
3,200	4,200
3,600	3,400
4,000	2,000

19

	Costs of holding class	Costs of canceling class
Compensation for instructor	$4,000	0
Air conditioning and lighting	$1,000	$1,000
Custodial services	$2,000	$2,000
Property taxes	$2,500	$2,500
Rent	0	− $1,200
Total	**$9,500**	**$4,300**

a   Opportunity cost = $9,500 − $4,300 = $5,200.
b   Sunk cost = $4,300.

20

	Cost of early retirements	Cost of retaining bureaucrats
Salaries	0	$50,000 × 8 × 2
Fringe benefits	0	$20,000 × 8 × 2
Office space for all 8	$ 10,000	$20,000
Pension benefit	$ 20,000 × 8 × 2	0
Total	$330,000	$1,140,000

a   Opportunity cost = $1,140,000 − $330,000 = $810,000.
b   Sunk cost = $330,000.

22   The marginal benefit of assigning a worker to reprogram the lights is the time saved; the marginal cost is the time lost because the worker was not assigned to fix potholes.

Workers assigned to reprogramming	Marginal benefits	Marginal costs
1	100	10
2	90	20
3	80	25
4	70	30
5	60	40
6	50	50
7	40	60
8	30	80
9	20	100
10	10	125

Assign 6 to reprogramming and 4 to fixing potholes.

23   The benefit of recommending higher concentrations of pesticides are the fewer leaves eaten; the costs are the leaves that fall off.

Concentration of pesticide	Marginal benefits	Marginal costs
1	4	0
2	3	1
3	2	2
4	1	3
5	1	4
6	0	5

The manufacturer should recommend a concentration of 3 ppm.

TRADE

Chapter Review

Chapter 3 takes up the key feature of markets: exchange. The fundamental aspect of market-based economies is voluntary trade. By definition, voluntary trade is mutually beneficial; it creates a surplus for both buyer and seller. If this were not true, the trade would not take place! An important insight of trade theory is the principle of comparative advantage, which shows how individuals and countries can specialize in production and thereby increase the gains they receive from trade. Economists emphasize these gains from trade and see little sense in protectionist arguments that trade between countries should be limited. The next two chapters will show how markets help realize some of the potential gains from trade.

ESSENTIAL CONCEPTS

1 Voluntary trade between rational individuals is **mutually beneficial;** it is good for both buyer and seller. Naturally, the buyer would like a lower price, and the seller prefers a higher price. Both might also benefit from better information. Nevertheless, the fact that the exchange takes place implies that given the information each has at the time of the transaction, both judge that they are better off trading than not trading.

2 Trade between individuals within a country and trade between individuals in different countries take place in markets. The three broad classes of markets are the product, labor, and capital markets. These three markets are all integrated internationally; this has led to a high degree of economic interdependence among nations.

3 Trade is many-sided, or multilateral. A typical person sells labor to an employer and uses the wages she earns both to purchase goods and services from many other firms and to save for future consumption. Similarly, a country may import more from some trading partners and export very little to those countries. With other trading partners, the country may export more than it imports. A country may also buy more goods and services than it sells abroad, and make up the difference by borrowing in capital markets or sending its workers to foreign labor markets.

4 The principle of **comparative advantage** says that individuals and countries will specialize in those goods that they are relatively more efficient in producing. To be relatively efficient means to have a lower opportunity

cost. Countries will have a comparative advantage in different goods. Each can import certain goods from abroad for a lower opportunity cost than it would incur producing them at home. Similarly, each can export to foreign countries those goods for which it has a comparative advantage.

5   Comparative advantage leads to **specialization** in trade, but specialization itself increases productivity and further lowers opportunity costs. First, individuals and countries grow more efficient at their specialties through practice. Second, producing for others allows a larger scale of operations, more **division of labor** into separate tasks, and more specialization. Finally, specialization creates conditions in which invention and innovation flourish.

6   Different countries and individuals have comparative advantages in different activities. Reasons for a comparative advantage can include natural endowments such as climate (for a country) or manual dexterity (for a tailor), human or physical capital, knowledge, and experience. These factors may be gifts of nature, or they may be the result of investment, experience, education, training, or other past actions.

7   **Protectionism** is the idea that the economy needs safeguarding against the perceived harmful effects of trade. Proponents of protectionism use many arguments; chief among them are the loss of domestic jobs, the vulnerability to foreign influences, the unfair trade practices of foreign governments, trade imbalances, and the potential damage to weak economies. To economists, none of these arguments is convincing.

BEHIND THE ESSENTIAL CONCEPTS

1   An exchange creates and divides a surplus. The surplus is the difference between the value to the seller of what is traded and its value to the buyer. If there is no surplus, the exchange does not take place; the seller simply refuses to trade if he thinks the good is worth more than the buyer is willing to pay. The division of the surplus is another matter. Both the buyer and seller will receive some of the surplus. This is what economists mean when they say that trade is mutually beneficial: each party receives some of the surplus. The buyer pays somewhat less than the maximum she is willing to pay, and the seller receives somewhat more than the minimum he is willing to accept. Of course, whatever the division of the surplus, each would prefer to receive more.

2   When individuals trade, both buyer and seller gain. Each is better off with the trade than he or she would be if the trade did not take place. Likewise, countries also gain from trade. Trade allows specialization on the basis of comparative advantage, and countries benefit from more goods and services. But although each country as a whole gains from trade, not every individual in each country is better off. Some businesses lose out to foreign competition, and some workers lose jobs. Other

businesses gain new markets, and new jobs are created. Thus, international trade creates both gains and losses, but overall, the gains outweigh the losses.

3   The problem with protectionism is that it looks only at the losers from international trade. Tariffs, quotas, and other protectionist policies can, at least temporarily, protect the losers, but only by limiting the trade. Limiting the trade means limiting the gains as well as the losses. Because the gains from trade exceed the losses, protectionism can only make matters worse for the economy as a whole.

4   To better understand comparative advantage, it helps to distinguish it from **absolute advantage.** A country has an absolute advantage in the production of a good or service if it requires fewer inputs to produce the good than another country. Comparative advantage, on the other hand, pertains to opportunity costs. As we have seen, the opportunity cost is not the inputs used in production; rather, it is the alternative use of those inputs. Thus, a country (or individual) has the comparative advantage in the production of a good or service if it has the lower opportunity cost.

For instance, assume that only labor is required to produce tomatoes or bookcases. Workers in country A can produce a carload of tomatoes in 40 hours, while workers in country B require 80 hours. Country A has an absolute advantage in producing tomatoes. To determine comparative advantage, however, we must look at how productive those workers are elsewhere in the economy. If the 40 hours of labor in country A produce 2 bookcases, but 80 hours in country B produce only 1, then country B has a comparative advantage in tomatoes. Why? Because a carload of tomatoes has an opportunity cost of 1 fewer bookcase in country B.

SELF-TEST

True or False

1   Unless the gain from trade is divided equally between buyer and seller, an exchange cannot be mutually beneficial.

2   While United States imports as a percentage of gross domestic product (GDP) have grown over the past three decades, the percentage of GDP devoted to exports has fallen.

3   Because of problems of information, problems of estimating risks, and difficulties in forming expectations about the future, many exchanges are not mutually beneficial.

4   With multilateral trade, imports from a particular country may not equal exports to that country.

5   The country that can produce a good with the least amount of labor is said to have a comparative advantage in the production of that good.

6   Trade on the basis of comparative advantage leads to complete specialization.

7   The extent of the division of labor is limited by the size of the market.

8   Comparative advantage is determined by the endowment of natural resources, human and physical capital, knowledge, and the experience that comes from specialization.

9   The marginal rate of transformation measures the trade-off between two commodities, indicating how much more of one commodity can be produced at the sacrifice of a given amount of another commodity.

10   Opposition to trade between nations is called protectionism.

11   A country that exports more than it imports will run a trade deficit.

12   Although trade benefits the country as a whole, many individuals may lose from trade in a particular product.

13   A country that runs a trade deficit must borrow from abroad.

14   The United States has comparative advantage in high-technology manufactured products, such as airplanes and computers, but must import wheat.

15   The North American Free Trade Agreement will eliminate all trade barriers between the United States, Canada, and Mexico within fifteen years.

Multiple Choice

1   Voluntary trade between two rational individuals

   a   benefits the buyer only;
   b   benefits the seller only;
   c   benefits the buyer or the seller but not both;
   d   benefits both the buyer and the seller;
   e   none of the above.

2   The gain from trade, that is, the difference between the value of a good to the buyer and its value to the seller,

   a   accrues entirely to the seller;
   b   accrues entirely to the buyer;
   c   is always divided equally;
   d   accrues to the government;
   e   none of the above.

3   When economists argue that both parties benefit from voluntary trade, they are assuming

   a   that both parties are well-informed;
   b   that both parties place the same value on the traded good;
   c   that both parties desire the same price;
   d   that the surplus is divided evenly between buyer and seller;
   e   none of the above.

4   Goods produced in the United States and sold in foreign countries are called

   a   imports;
   b   exports;
   c   either imports or exports;
   d   capital flows;
   e   none of the above.

5   For decades, Japan has imported raw materials from Australia, while Australia has purchased heavy equipment from the United States. Furthermore, Japan has exported consumer goods to the United States. This is an example of

   a   multilateral trade;
   b   bilateral trade;
   c   absolute advantage;
   d   protectionism;
   e   trade deficit.

6   If the United States has a comparative advantage in the production of a good, then

   a   fewer resources are required to produce the good in the United States;
   b   the United States also has an absolute advantage in the production of the good;
   c   the relative cost of producing the good is lower in the United States;
   d   the United States will import the good;
   e   all of the above.

7   If the United States has absolute advantage in the production of a good,

   a   production of the good in the United States is more efficient and requires fewer resources;
   b   the United States also has comparative advantage in the production of the good;
   c   the relative cost of producing the good is lower in the United States;
   d   the United States will import the good;
   e   the United States will export the good.

8   The trade-off between two commodities is called the

   a   comparative advantage;
   b   specialization;
   c   absolute advantage;
   d   marginal rate of transformation;
   e   none of the above.

9   Suppose that in the United States increasing wheat output by 1,000 tons would require a reduction in steel output of 500 tons, but in Canada increasing wheat output by 1,000 tons would require reducing steel output by 1,000 tons. Then we can infer that

   a   Canada has absolute advantage in wheat;
   b   the United States has absolute advantage in wheat;
   c   the United States will export steel;
   d   the United States has comparative advantage in steel;
   e   the United States has comparative advantage in wheat.

10   The slope of the production possibilities curve is called the

   a   marginal rate of transformation;
   b   comparative advantage;
   c   trade deficit;

d marginal benefit;

e marginal rate of production.

11 The principle of comparative advantage

    a applies only to international trade;

    b always leads to complete specialization;

    c forms the basis for the division of labor;

    d is relevant only in the absence of protection;

    e all of the above.

12 Which of the following is not a reason why specialization increases productivity?

    a Workers and countries grow more efficient by repeating the same tasks.

    b Specialization saves time needed to switch from one task to another.

    c Specialization allows larger-scale production with greater efficiency.

    d Specialization allows the assignment of tasks to those who have a comparative advantage.

    e All of the above, are reasons.

13 Important sources of comparative advantage include

    a natural endowments;

    b human and physical capital;

    c superior knowledge;

    d experience;

    e all of the above.

14 If two countries have identical relative opportunity costs,

    a there will never be any basis for trade;

    b they might specialize in the production of certain goods and acquire a comparative advantage in those goods over time;

    c each will gain from protectionist policies;

    d the country with an absolute advantage will reap all of the gains from trade;

    e none of the above.

15 When two countries trade,

    a each individual and firm in both countries benefits;

    b any individual benefits from the trades that she engages in;

    c particular groups in each country may be hurt by trade in some goods;

    d b and c;

    e none of the above.

16 Increased immigration of unskilled workers into the United States will likely

    a lower consumer goods prices;

    b make American firms more competitive in international markets;

    c lower wages of unskilled workers already in the United States;

    d all of the above;

    e a and b.

17 If a country runs a trade deficit for several years,

    a it is importing more goods and services than it exports;

    b it is exporting more goods and services than it imports;

    c it must borrow from abroad;

    d b and c;

    e a and c.

18 Which of the following is not a basis of comparative advantage?

    a natural endowments;

    b acquired endowments;

    c superior knowledge;

    d protectionism;

    e specialization.

19 With voluntary trade between countries,

    a all individuals are made better off;

    b all individuals in the larger country are made better off;

    c some individuals are made worse off, but the gainers could more than compensate the losers;

    d businesses gain but consumers lose;

    e workers lose but consumers gain.

20 The North American Free Trade Agreement will lower trade barriers between which of the following countries?

    a all countries in North America;

    b all countries in North America and the Caribbean;

    c all countries in North and South America;

    d the United States, Canada, and Mexico;

    e the United States and Canada.

Completion

1 The difference between what a person is willing to pay for an item and what she has to pay is a gain from trade, or _____.

2 If a country is relatively more efficient at producing a good than its trading partners, then that country is said to have the _____ in the production of that good.

3 _____ refers to having superior production skills or lower resource costs.

4 Because of trade possibilities, individuals and countries can produce more of what each has a comparative advantage in. This specialization or division of labor is limited by the _____ of the market.

5 _____, such as location, natural resources, and climate, are bases of comparative advantage.

6 Acquired endowments, such as physical and human _____, represent other sources of comparative advantage.

7 The doctrine that the economy of a country is injured by trade is called _____.

8   The marginal rate of transformation is the _____ of the production possibilities frontier.

9   The trade-off in producing two commodities is called the _____.

10 The _____ will reduce trade barriers among the United States, Canada, and Mexico over the next fifteen years.

Answers to Self-Test

True or False

1	f	4	t	7	t	10	t	13	t
2	f	5	f	8	t	11	f	14	f
3	f	6	f	9	t	12	t	15	t

Multiple Choice

1	d	6	c	11	c	16	d
2	e	7	a	12	e	17	e
3	e	8	d	13	e	18	d
4	b	9	e	14	b	19	c
5	a	10	a	15	d	20	d

Completion

1   surplus
2   comparative advantage
3   Absolute advantage
4   size
5   Natural endowments
6   capital

7   protectionism
8   slope
9   marginal rate of transformation
10 North American Free Trade Agreement

Doing Economics: Tools and Practice Problems

This chapter introduces comparative advantage, a very important concept. The principle of comparative advantage illustrates how individuals, firms, and countries can benefit by specializing in performing tasks or producing goods and trading with each other. This problem set will help you to identify comparative advantage and to see why comparative advantage determines the division of labor and the pattern of trade. You will also study the gains from trade when they proceed according to comparative advantage. Finally, you will use the idea of comparative advantage to construct the production possibilities curve for the case in which resources differ.

COMPARATIVE ADVANTAGE

The most important concept in exchange and production is comparative advantage. Countries have comparative advantage when their opportunity cost is lower. They will export the goods in which they have comparative advantage. Tool Kit 3.1 shows how to use production possibilities curve to

---

Tool Kit 3.1: Identifying Comparative Advantage

When a country or individual has a comparative advantage in performing some task or producing some good, that country or individual is relatively more efficient, which means that the country or individual has the lower opportunity cost. The following procedure shows how to identify comparative advantage and predict the pattern of trade. It is written for the case of two-country trade.

Step one: Plot the production possibilities curves for each country. Be sure to be consistent and measure units of the same good along the horizontal axis in each case.

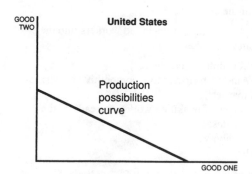

Step two: The slope of the production possibilities curve is the opportunity cost of the good on the horizontal axis, and it indicates the trade-off. The flatter slope implies comparative advantage for producing the good on the horizontal axis.

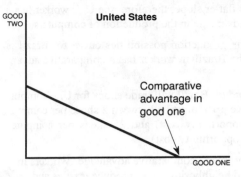

Step three: The steeper slope indicates comparative advantage for the good on the vertical axis.

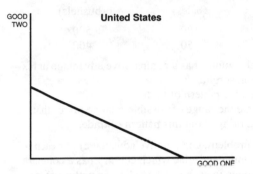

Step four: In a system of free trade, each country will produce more of the good in which it has a comparative advantage, and the relative price will lie somewhere between the opportunity costs of the two countries.

identify comparative advantage and determine the pattern or production and trade.

1   (Worked problem: comparative advantage) Workers in the United States and Brazil can produce shoes and computers. The annual productivity of a worker in each country is given in the table below.

Country	Computers	Shoes
United States	5,000	10,000
Brazil	200	5,000

a   Which country has a comparative advantage in computers? in shoes?
b   Predict the pattern of trade.
c   Indicate the range of possible relative prices that would bring about this pattern of trade.

Step-by-step solution

Step one (a): Plot the production possibilities curves. In this problem, the production possibilities curve for one worker

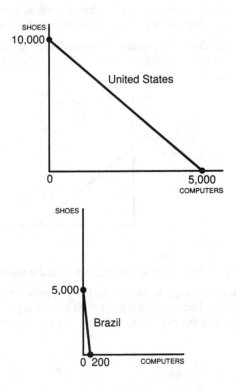

in each country will suffice. Measure computers on the horizontal axis.

Step two: The production possibilities curve for the United States has the flatter slope; therefore, the U.S. worker has a comparative advantage in the production of computers.

Step three: The production possibilities curve for Brazil is steeper, and the Brazilian worker has a comparative advantage in shoes.

Step four (b and c): Brazil will trade shoes for U.S. computers. The relative price must lie between 2 shoes per computer (the U.S. opportunity cost) and 25 shoes per computer (the Brazilian opportunity cost).

2   (Practice problem: comparative advantage) Workers in Nigeria and neighboring Niger produce textiles and sorghum. The productivities of each are given in the table below.

Country	Textiles (bales)	Sorghum (bushels)
Nigeria	100	500
Niger	50	400

   a   Which country has a comparative advantage in textiles? in sorghum?
   b   Predict the pattern of trade.
   c   Indicate the range of possible relative prices that would bring about this pattern of trade.

3   (Practice problem: comparative advantage) For each of the following, determine which country has a comparative advantage in each good, predict the pattern of trade,

and indicate the range of possible relative prices consistent with this pattern of trade.

a	Country	Fish	Wheat (bushels)
	Greece	60	80
	Poland	35	70

b	Country	Heart bypass operations	Auto parts (containers)
	United States	5,000	10,000
	Canada	3,000	9,000

c	Country	Scrap steel (tons)	Finished steel (tons)
	Thailand	20	20
	Laos	10	2

d	Country	Wine (barrels)	Wool (bales)
	Portugal	2	2
	Great Britain	4	8

GAINS FROM TRADE

When countries trade there is mutual gain, in the sense that their opportunity sets expand beyond their production possibilities curves. To exploit the potential of trade, production

---

Tool Kit 3.2: Showing the Gains from Trade

   When the pattern of trade is based upon comparative advantage, both countries can gain. Specifically, they each can consume a bundle of goods that lies beyond their own production possibilities curve. Follow these five steps.

Step one: Draw the production possibilities curve for each country, identify the country with a comparative advantage in each good, and identify the trade-offs for each country.

Step two: Choose a relative price between the trade-offs.

Step three: For the country with the comparative advantage in the horizontal-axis good, label the horizontal intercept *A* and draw a line segment from *A* with a slope equal to (–) the relative price. This line segment shows the bundles of goods that the country can consume by trading at the given relative price.

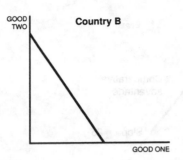

Step four: For the country with the comparative advantage in the vertical-axis good, label the vertical intercept *A* and draw a line segment from *A* with a slope equal to (−) the relative price. This line segment shows the bundles of goods that the country can consume by trading at the given relative price.

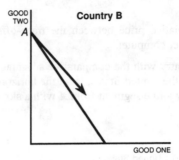

Step five: Pick a pair of consistent points, where A's exports equal B's imports, one on each line segment, and show how each country can benefit from trade.

and trade must be organized according to comparative advantage. Tool Kit 3.2 shows how both trading partners can gain from trade.

4   (Worked problem: gains from trade) This problem builds upon problem #1. Show that a worker in Brazil and a worker in the United States can benefit by trading on the basis of comparative advantage.

Step-by-step solution

Step one: Identify the country with a comparative advantage in each good and the trade-offs for each country. The U.S. worker has the comparative advantage in computers, and the trade-off is 2 shoes per computer. The Brazilian worker has the comparative advantage in shoes, and the trade-off is 25 shoes per computer.

Step two: Choose a relative price between the trade-offs. Let's choose 20 shoes per computer.

Step three: For the country with the comparative advantage in computers, which is the United States, label the horizontal intercept *A* and draw a line segment from *A* with a slope

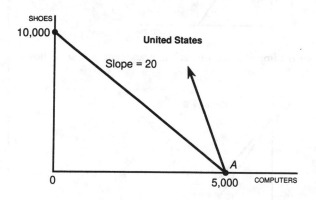

equal to –20. This line segment shows the bundles of goods that the United States can consume by trading at the given relative price.

Step four: For the country with the comparative advantage in shoes, label the vertical intercept *A* and draw a line segment

from *A* with a slope equal to –20. This line segment shows

the bundles of goods that Brazil can consume by trading at the given relative price.

Step five: Pick a pair of consistent points, one on each line segment, and show how each country can benefit from trade. Let the U.S. worker produce 4,800 computers for domestic consumption. This leaves 200 for trade. At a relative price of 20 shoes, the 200 computers trade for 4,000 shoes. Plot the point (4,000, 4,800) and label it *B*. The Brazilian worker must then produce 4,000 shoes for trade. This leaves 1,000 shoes for domestic consumption. The 4,000 shoes for trade 200 computers. Plot the point (200, 1,000) and label it *B*. At this point, the United States exports 200

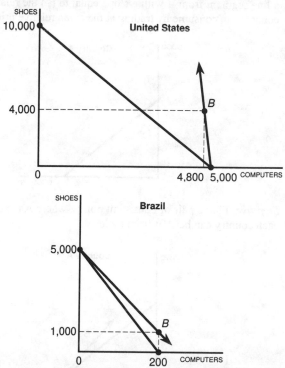

computers and imports 4,000 shoes, while Brazil imports 200 computers and exports 4,000 shoes. Trade is balanced, and each country consumes beyond its production possibilities curve.

5   (Practice problem: gains from trade) This problem builds upon problem #2. Show that workers in Nigeria and Niger can benefit by trading according to comparative advantage.

Production Possibilities with Different Resources

Free trade assigns to each country the task of producing those goods in which it has a comparative advantage. The same is true for trade between individuals. To see why this is efficient we consider the joint production possibilities curve in the case where there are two or more different types of resources that can be used in the production of two goods. To do this efficiently it is necessary to assign resources to produce the good in which they have comparative advantage.

Tool Kit 3.3: Plotting the Production Possibilities Curve When Resources Are Different

When resources differ in their productivity, plotting the production possibilities curve requires that they be assigned to produce goods according to the principle of comparative advantage. Follow these six steps.

Step one: Draw a set of coordinate axes. Label the horizontal axis as the quantity of one good and the vertical axis as the quantity of the other good.

Step two: Calculate the maximum quantities of each good that can be produced. Plot the quantity along the vertical axis and label the point *B*. Plot the quantity along the horizontal axis and label this point *A*.

Step three: Identify the resource with the comparative advantage for each good.

Step four: Choose the resource with the comparative advantage in the horizontal-axis good and assign it to produce this good, while keeping the other resource producing the vertical-axis good. Calculate the total quantities produced, and plot this point. Label it *C*.

Step five: Connect the points *BCA* with line segments. This is the production possibilities curve.

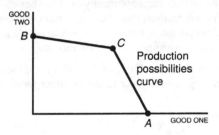

Step six: Verify that the slope is increasing. Because the slope measures the opportunity cost of the horizontal-axis good, this means that the opportunity cost is increasing, which is an implication of the principle of diminishing returns.

Tool Kit 3.3 shows how. Compare its shape with Chapter 2's opportunity sets for multiple constraints and diminishing returns.

6 (Worked problem: production possibilities curve) Harrigan and her daughter have formed a two-person firm to handle business incorporations and real estate transactions. The hours required for each type of task are given below. Each works 48 hours every week.

Lawyer	Hours required to perform each incorporation	Hours required to complete each transaction
Harrigan	4	8
Daughter	8	24

Plot their weekly production possibilities curve.

Step-by-step solution

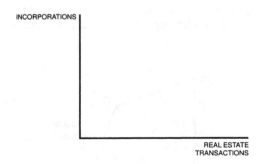

Step one: Draw and label a set of coordinate axes. Put real estate transactions on the horizontal axis and incorporations on the vertical.

Step two: Calculate the maximum number of incorporations they can do in a week. For Harrigan, this number is 48/4 = 12; for her daughter, it is 48/8 = 6. The pair can complete 18 incorporations. Plot this point along the vertical axis, and la-

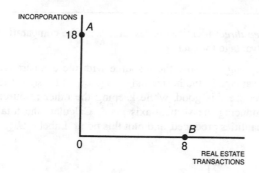

bel it *A*. Concerning real estate transactions, Harrigan can do 48/8 = 6; her daughter, 48/24 = 2. The pair can do 8. Plot this point along the horizontal axis, and label it *B*.

Step three: Identify the resource with the comparative advantage for each good. Since it takes Harrigan 8 hours to complete each real estate transaction but only 4 to do an incorporation, each real estate transaction requires enough time to do 2 incorporations. The opportunity cost of a real estate transaction for Harrigan is, then, 2 incorporations. By the same argument, the opportunity cost for her daughter is 24/8 = 3 incorporations; thus, Harrigan has the comparative advantage in real estate transactions, while her daughter has the comparative advantage in incorporations.

Step four: We assign to Harrigan the task of real estate transactions, leaving her daughter to do the incorporations. With

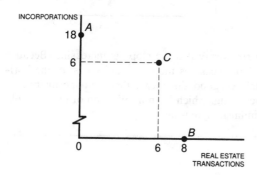

this assignment, they can do 6 incorporations and 6 real estate transactions (see step two). Plot this point, and label it *C*.

Step five: Draw line segments connecting the points. This is the production possibilities curve.

Step six: Note that between *A* and *C* the slope is 2, but be-

tween *C* and *B* the slope increases to 3. The shape of the production possibilities curve thus indicates diminishing returns.

7   (Practice problem: production possibilities curve) A farmer has 3 acres of land. Owing to various characteristics of the land, his ability to produce his two cash crops (corn and soybeans) differs on each acre. The technology of production is given in the table below.

Maximum outputs of each crop per acre (bushels)

	Acre #1	Acre #2	Acre #3
Corn	200	200	100
Soybeans	400	200	50

These figures represent the maximum output of each crop, assuming that only one crop is grown on the acre. That is, acre #1 can produce either 200 bushels of corn or 400 bushels of soybeans. Of course, the farmer can also divide the acre into one part corn and one part soybeans. For example, he can grow 100 bushels of corn and 200 bushels of soybeans on acre #1. Plot the production possibilities curve.

8   (Practice problem: production possibilities curve) Plot the following production possibilities curves.

a   Maximum harvest of each type of fish per trawler (tons)

	Trawler #1	Trawler #2	Trawler #3
Salmon	2	3	4
Tuna	2	6	6

b   Maximum amounts of pollutants removed (tons)

	Smokestack scrubbers	Coal treatment
Sulphur	100	50
Particulates	500	100

Answers to Problems

2 *a*   Nigeria has a comparative advantage in textiles. Niger has a comparative advantage in sorghum.

   b   Nigeria will trade its textiles for sorghum from Niger.

   c   The relative price will lie between 8 bushels of sorghum per bale of textiles and 5 bushels of sorghum per bale of textiles.

3 *a*   Greece has a comparative advantage in fish. Poland has a comparative advantage in wheat. Greece will trade its fish for Polish wheat. The relative price will lie between 4/3 bushels of wheat per fish and 2 bushels of wheat per fish.

   b   The United States has a comparative advantage in heart bypass operations, and Canada in auto parts. The United States will trade heart bypass operations for Canadian auto parts. The relative price will lie between 2 containers of auto parts per operation and 3 containers of auto parts per operation.

   c   Thailand has a comparative advantage in finished steel, Laos in scrap steel. Thailand will trade its finished steel for Laotian scrap steel. The relative price will lie between 5 tons of scrap steel per ton of finished steel and 1 ton of scrap steel per ton of finished steel.

d   Portugal has a comparative advantage in wine, Great Britain in wool. British wool will be traded for Portuguese wine. The relative price will lie between 1 and 2 bales per barrel of wine.

5   Choose, for example, 6 bushels of sorghum per bale of textiles as the relative price. Nigeria can produce 100 bales of textiles and trade 20 to Niger for 120 bushels of sorghum. The point (80, 120) lies outside its production possibilities curve. Niger can produce 400 bushels of sorghum and trade 120 bushels to Nigeria for 20 bales of textiles. The point (20, 280) lies outside its production possibilities curve.

7

8

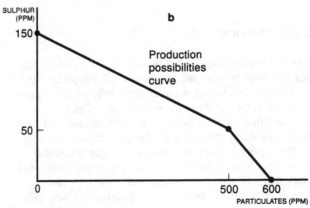

Chapter 4

DEMAND, SUPPLY, AND PRICE

Chapter Review

Trade, the markets in which it occurs, and the gains it provides for both buyers and sellers are all important ideas from Chapter 3. Chapter 4 builds the basic model of markets, which is the supply and demand model. The focus is on prices and quantities—how they are determined and how they change when other factors change. Chapter 5 then applies the supply and demand model to major areas of concern to economists: what happens to the quantity demanded or supplied when prices change, and what happens when prices do not adjust, as when the government sets price floors or ceilings.

ESSENTIAL CONCEPTS

1   Consumers **demand** goods and services. They are willing and able to pay, and given a price, they will buy a certain quantity. Several factors influence demand, but the most important is **price.** As the price falls, people buy more of the good or service; as the price rises, they purchase less. The entire relationship between the price and the quantity that a person buys is called the individual **demand curve.**

2   Adding all the individual demand curves gives the **market demand curve.** For every price, ask how much each individual will buy. Add these quantities. The result is the market demand curve, which shows the total amount of the good that will be purchased by all individuals at each price.

3   Firms **supply** goods and services. They are willing and able to produce and sell the good, and at a given price, they will sell a certain quantity. Several factors influence the supply, but the most important is price. As the price rises, producers will supply more; as the price falls, producers will supply less. The entire relationship between the price and the quantity that the producer will sell is called the individual **supply curve.**

4   Adding up all of the individual supply curves gives the **market supply curve.** For every price, ask how much each producer will sell. Add these quantities. The result is the market supply curve, which shows how much of the good will be sold by all producers at each price.

5   The price at which consumers want to buy exactly the quantity that firms want to sell is the **equilibrium price.** This quantity, which is the same for demand and

supply, is the **equilibrium quantity.** It is an equilibrium because there are no forces that would cause it to change.

6   If the price were higher than the equilibrium price, firms would want to sell more than consumers would buy. Unable to sell all of their goods, many firms would compete, by lowering prices, to attract the relatively few consumers. Because this higher price would change, it is not an equilibrium. Similarly, if the price were lower than the equilibrium price, consumers would want to buy more than firms would sell. Seeing the glut of consumers, firms would raise their prices. In sum, if the price is above equilibrium, it falls; if it is below equilibrium, it rises. When price equals the equilibrium price, it does not change.

7   Many factors affect the demand and supply. For demand, these factors include changes in income, prices of substitutes and complements, the composition of the population, and people's tastes. This is only a partial list. When one of these factors—or anything else that affects the willingness to pay for the good—changes, the entire demand curve **shifts,** and a new equilibrium must be found.

Supply is affected by changes in technology and input price—more generally, anything that causes costs to change. Again, changes in these factors **shift** the supply curve and lead to a new equilibrium.

BEHIND THE ESSENTIAL CONCEPTS

1   The demand curve is the entire range, or schedule, that indicates how many goods will be purchased at each price. At a given price, this number is called the quantity demanded. In diagrams of demand curves, the quantity demanded is measured along the horizontal axis. To find the quantity demanded, simply read it off the demand curve at the current price. Economists, students, and sometimes professors are sloppy and say "change in demand" without being clear whether they mean a shift in the demand curve or a change in the quantity demanded. The latter is brought about by a change in price, and it involves only a movement along the same demand curve. To guard against confusion in stressful situations (like tests!), say "demand curve" when you refer to the entire schedule of prices and quantities and "quantity demanded" when you want to indicate the number of goods purchased.

2   It is very important to understand why the market demand curve is drawn as it is. When the price rises, the market quantity demanded falls for two reasons. First, each individual buys less. The principle of substitution says that other available goods and services can serve as alternatives, and at higher prices, people switch to consume these substitutes. Second, some individuals find the price to be too high altogether, and they leave the market completely. When the price falls, the oppo-

site happens. People substitute away from other goods and buy more of the one with the lower price. Furthermore, the lower price attracts new consumers to the market.

3   The market supply curve slopes upward. This means that as the price rises, more is offered for sale. Again, there are two reasons. First, firms are willing to sell more at higher prices. Second, higher prices attract new products to the market.

4   Other factors that shift the demand curve include consumer income, tastes, prices of substitutes and complements, and the composition of the population. The supply curve shifts with changes in technology or input prices. While these factors are the most common causes of shifts, they do not comprise a complete list. Anything that affects the willingness and ability to pay for goods shifts the demand curve, and anything that affects costs shifts the supply curve. For example, if it rains in April, the supply of crops may increase, and the demand for umbrellas may also increase.

5   Successful supply and demand analysis proceeds in four steps:

a   Start with an equilibrium.
b   Figure out which curve shifts.
c   Shift the curve and find the new equilibrium.
d   Compare the price and quantity at the original and new equilibria.

Be careful to avoid a common pitfall. Suppose you are asked to show the effect of a change in tastes that shifts demand to the right. The failing student's analysis goes like this: "Demand shifts to the right, which increases quantity and price, but the increase in price leads producers to want to supply more, so the supply also shifts to the right." What is wrong with this answer? Stop before the "but." True, the demand shift does raise price and quantity, but that is the end of the story. The increase in price does lead producers to want to supply more. As they supply more, there is a movement along the supply curve, but not a shift. Changes in the price of a good *never shift* the demand curve for that good or the supply curve for that good; rather, changes in the price of a good cause a *movement* along the demand curve or supply curve. There is more discussion on this point and lots of practice problems in the "Doing Economics" section of this chapter.

SELF-TEST

True or False

1   Prices provide incentives to help the economy use resources efficiently.

2   As the price falls, the quantity demanded decreases.

3   The market demand curve is the sum of the quantities and prices of each individual demand.

4   The individual demand curve is an example of an equilibrium relationship.

5   One reason why the supply curve slopes upward is that at higher prices, more producers enter the market.

6   In equilibrium, there is neither excess demand nor excess supply.

7   If the price is above the equilibrium price, consumers can buy as much as they are willing.

8   If the price is below the equilibrium price, sellers cannot sell as much as they are willing.

9   The law of supply and demand says that the equilibrium price will be that price at which the quantity demanded equals the quantity supplied.

10   The individual supply curve is an example of an identity.

11   The price of diamonds is higher than the price of water because diamonds have a higher value in use.

12   A change in a consumer's income will shift her demand curve.

13   A change in the price of a good will shift its market demand curve to the right.

14   An increase in the price of a substitute will shift the demand curve for the good in question to the right.

15   A decrease in the price of a complement will shift the demand curve for the good in question to the left.

Multiple Choice

1   Market prices

   a   measure scarcity;
   b   communicate information;
   c   provide incentives;
   d   all of the above;
   e   a and b.

2   The individual demand curve for a good or service

   a   gives the quantity of the good or service the individual would purchase at each price;
   b   gives the equilibrium price in the market;
   c   shows which other goods or services will be substituted according to the principle of substitution;
   d   all of the above;
   e   a and c.

3   The idea that there are other goods or services that can serve as reasonably good alternatives to a particular good or service is called the

   a   law of demand;
   b   principle of substitution;
   c   market demand curve;
   d   principle of scarcity;
   e   none of the above.

4   If you knew the individual demand curves of each consumer, you could find the market demand curve by

   a   taking the average quantity demanded at each price;
   b   adding all of the prices;
   c   adding up, at each price, the quantities purchased by each individual;
   d   taking the average of all prices;
   e   none of the above.

5   As the price rises, the quantity demanded decreases along an individual demand curve because

   a   individuals substitute other goods and services;
   b   some individuals exit the market;
   c   some individuals enter the market;
   d   the quantity supplied increases;
   e   a and b.

6   As the price rises, the quantity demanded decreases along the market demand curve because

   a   individuals substitute other goods and services;
   b   some individuals exit the market;
   c   some individuals enter the market;
   d   the quantity supplied increases;
   e   a and b.

7   As the price rises, the quantity supplied increases along an individual supply curve because

   a   higher prices give firms incentives to sell more;
   b   the principle of substitution leads firms to substitute other goods and services;
   c   the market supply curve is the sum of all the quantities produced by individual firms at each price;
   d   b and c;
   e   none of the above.

8   As the price rises, the quantity supplied increases along the market supply curve because

   a   at higher prices, more firms are willing to enter the market to produce the good;
   b   each firm in the market is willing to produce more;
   c   the market supply curve is the sum of all the quantities produced by individual firms at each price;
   d   at higher prices, more firms substitute other goods and services;
   e   a and b.

9   If the market price is below equilibrium, then

   a   there is excess demand;
   b   there is excess supply;
   c   consumers will want to raise the price;
   d   firms will want to lower the price;
   e   all of the above.

10   If the market price is at equilibrium, then

   a   the quantity that consumers are willing to buy equals the quantity that producers are willing to sell;
   b   there is excess demand;
   c   there is excess supply;

d   there are no forces that will change the price;

e   a and d.

11   If the market price is above equilibrium, then

a   there is excess supply;

b   there is excess demand;

c   firms will not be able to sell all that they would like;

d   consumers will not be able to buy all that they would like;

e   a and c.

12   The law of supply and demand is an example of

a   an identity;

b   an equilibrium relationship;

c   a behavioral relationship;

d   none of the above;

e   all of the above.

13   The statement that market supply is equal to the sum of individual firms' supplies is an example of

a   an identity;

b   an equilibrium relationship;

c   a behavioral relationship;

d   none of the above;

e   all of the above.

14   A diamond sells for a higher price than a gallon of water because

a   luxuries always have higher prices than necessities;

b   only a few people demand diamonds, but everyone needs water;

c   the total use value of diamonds exceeds the total value of water;

d   the total cost of diamond production exceeds the total cost of water production;

e   none of the above.

15   Stationary exercise bicycles and stair-stepper machines are substitutes, according to the aerobically correct. An increase in the price of exercise bicycles will

a   shift the demand for stair-stepper machines to the right;

b   increase the price of stair-stepper machines;

c   increase the quantity of stair-stepper machine sales;

d   all of the above;

e   none of the above.

16   As people have grown more concerned about saturated fat in their diets, the demand for beef has shifted to the left. The quantity of beef sold has also fallen. This change is a

a   movement along the demand curve for beef;

b   shift in the supply curve for beef;

c   movement along the supply curve for beef;

d   a and b;

e   none of the above.

17   Which of the following is not a source of shifts in market demand?

a   an increase in consumer income;

b   a change in tastes;

c   an increase in the population;

d   a technological advance.

e   All are sources of shifts.

18   If the price of an input falls,

a   supply shifts to the left;

b   demand shifts to the right;

c   demand shifts to the left;

d   supply shifts to the right;

e   none of the above.

19   If ski-lift tickets and skiing lessons are complements, then an increase in the price of lift tickets

a   shifts demand for skiing lessons to the left;

b   shifts demand for skiing lessons to the right;

c   shifts supply of skiing lessons to the left;

d   shifts supply of skiing lessons to the right;

e   a and d.

20   A recent regulation requires tuna fishing companies to use nets that allow dolphins to escape. These nets also allow some tuna to escape. This regulation causes

a   the supply of tuna to shift to the left;

b   the demand for tunas to shift to the right;

c   the demand for tunas to shift to the left;

d   the supply of tunas to shift to the right;

e   none of the above.

Completion

1   _____ is defined as what is given in exchange for a good or service.

2   If the price of a good or service falls, the quantity demanded _____.

3   The quantity of the good or service purchased at each price is given by the _____.

4   The quantity of the good or service offered for sale at each price is given by the _____.

5   In an economic equilibrium, there are no forces for _____.

6   The law of supply and demand says that at the equilibrium price, the _____ equals the _____.

7   The statement that market supply equals market demand is an example of an _____.

8   The statement that market supply is the total of all individual supplies is an example of an _____.

9   An increase in the price of a good leads to a _____ its demand curve.

10   A change in technology leads to a _____ the supply curve.

Answers to Self-Test

True or False

1	t	4	f	7	t	10	f	13	f
2	f	5	t	8	f	11	f	14	t
3	f	6	t	9	t	12	t	15	f

Multiple Choice

1	d	6	e	11	e	16	c
2	a	7	a	12	b	17	d
3	b	8	e	13	a	18	d
4	c	9	a	14	e	19	a
5	a	10	e	15	d	20	a

Completion

1 Price
2 increases
3 demand curve
4 supply curve
5 change
6 quantity demanded, quantity supplied
7 equilibrium relationship
8 identity
9 movement along
10 shift in

Doing Economics: Tools and Practice Problems

Three techniques receive attention in this section. The first technique shows how to add individual demand and individual supply curves to get market demand and market supply curves. The next technique involves finding the equilibrium price and quantity, where the market clears. Finally, some general instructions about supply and demand analysis are given and developed in several problems. Each of these techniques is fundamental and will appear repeatedly throughout this book.

MARKET DEMAND AND MARKET SUPPLY

When the price falls, individual demanders want to buy more, and individual suppliers want to sell less. These individual demand and supply curves are behavioral relationships. The market demand and market supply curves are found by adding up all of these individual demands and supplies. Tool Kit 4.1 shows how to do this.

Tool Kit 4.1: Calculating Market Demand and Supply

The market demand is the sum of the individual demands. The market supply is the sum of the individual supplies. This tool kit shows how to add the individual demands and supplies.

Step one: Make two columns. Label the left-hand column "Price" and the right-hand column "Quantity."

Price	Quantity

Step two: Choose the highest price at which goods are demanded. Enter this in the first row of the price column.

Price	Quantity
p1	

Step three: Find how many goods each individual will purchase. Add these quantities. Enter the total in the first row of the quantity column.

Price	Quantity
p1	$Q_1 = Q_a + Q_b + Q_c + \cdots$

Step four: Choose the second highest price, and continue the process.

---

1 (Worked problem: market demand) The individual demands of Jason and Kyle for economics tutoring are given in Table 4.1. Calculate the market demand. (Jason and Kyle are the only two individuals in this market.)

Table 4.1

Jason		Kyle	
Price	Quantity	Price	Quantity
$10	6	$10	4
$ 8	8	$ 8	5
$ 6	10	$ 6	6
$ 4	12	$ 4	7

Step-by-step solution

Step one: Make and label two columns.

Price	Quantity

Step two: Choose the highest price. This is $10. Enter this in the first row under price.

Price	Quantity
$10	

Step three: Find the market quantity. Jason would buy 6; Kyle would buy 4. The total is 6 + 4 = 10. Enter 10 in the corresponding quantity column.

Price	Quantity
$10	10

Step four: Repeat the process. The next lower price is $8. Jason would buy 8; Kyle would buy 5. The total is 8 + 5 = 13. Enter $8 and 13 in the appropriate columns.

Price	Quantity
$10	10
$ 8	13

Continue. The entire market demand is given below.

Price	Quantity
$10	10
$ 8	13
$ 6	16
$ 4	19

2 (Practice problem: market demand) Gorman's tomatoes are purchased by pizza sauce makers, by submarine sandwich shops, and by vegetable canners. The demands for each are given in Table 4.2. Find the market demand.

Table 4.2

Pizza sauce		Submarine shops		Vegetable canners	
Price	Quantity (bushels)	Price	Quantity (bushels)	Price	Quantity (bushels)
$5	25	$5	5	$5	55
$4	35	$4	6	$4	75
$3	40	$3	7	$3	100
$2	50	$2	7	$2	150
$1	80	$1	7	$1	250

3 (Practice problem: market supply) The technique for finding the market supply curve is the same as for the market demand. Simply sum the quantities supplied at each price. There are three law firms that will draw up partnership contracts in the town of Pullman. Their individual supply curves are given in Table 4.3. Find the market supply curve.

Table 4.3

Jones		Jones and Jones		Jones, Jones, and Jones	
Price	Quantity	Price	Quantity	Price	Quantity
$200	0	$200	6	$200	4
$220	0	$220	8	$220	8
$240	0	$240	12	$240	10
$260	8	$260	24	$260	11

EQUILIBRIUM

In equilibrium, markets clear. The market price will settle where the quantity that demanders would like to purchase exactly equals the quantity that suppliers choose to sell. Tool Kit 4.2 shows how to find the equilibrium.

Tool Kit 4.2: Finding the Equilibrium Price and Quantity

The equilibrium price in the demand and supply model is the price at which the buyers want to buy exactly the quantity that sellers want to sell. In other words, the quantity demanded equals the quantity supplied. The equilibrium quantity in the market is just this quantity. Here is how to find the equilibrium in a market.

Step one: Choose a price. Find the quantity demanded at that price and the quantity supplied.

Step two: If the quantity demanded equals the quantity supplied, the price is the equilibrium. Stop.

Step three: If the quantity demanded exceeds the quantity supplied, there is a shortage. Choose a higher price and repeat step one. If the quantity demanded is less than the quantity supplied, there is a surplus. Choose a lower price and repeat step one.

Step four: Continue until the equilibrium price is found.

---

4 (Worked problem: equilibrium price and quantity) The supply curve and demand curve for cinder blocks are given in Table 4.4. The quantity column indicates the number of blocks sold in one year.

Table 4.4

Demand		Supply	
Price	Quantity	Price	Quantity
$2.00	50,000	$2.00	200,000
$1.50	70,000	$1.50	160,000
$1.00	100,000	$1.00	100,000
$0.75	150,000	$0.75	50,000
$0.50	250,000	$0.50	0

a Find the equilibrium price and quantity.
b If the price is $1.50, is the market in equilibrium? Will there be a surplus or a shortage? If so, what is the size of the surplus or shortage? What will happen to the price? Why?
c If the price is $0.75, is the market in equilibrium? Will there be a surplus or a shortage? If so, what is the size of the surplus or shortage? What will happen to the price? Why?

Step-by-step solution

Step one (a): Choose a price. At a price of, say, $2.00, the quantity demanded is 50,000 and the quantity supplied is 200,000.

Step two: The quantities are not equal.

Step three: There is a surplus. The equilibrium price will be lower.

Step four: Continue. Try other prices until the quantity supplied equals the quantity demanded. The equilibrium price is $1.00, where the quantity equals 100,000. We can now see the answers to parts b and c.

Step five (b): If the price is $1.50, the quantity demanded is 70,000, and it is less than the quantity supplied, which is 160,000. There is a surplus of 90,000 (160,000 − 70,000). The price will fall because producers will be unable to sell all that they want.

Step six (c): If the price is $0.75, the quantity demanded is 150,000, and it is greater than the quantity supplied, which is 50,000. There is a shortage of 100,000 (150,000 − 50,000). The price will rise because producers will see that buyers are unable to buy all that they want.

5 (Practice problem: equilibrium price and quantity) The demand curve and supply curve in the market for billboard space space along Interstate 6 are given in Table 4.5. The price is the monthly rental price. The quantity column shows numbers of billboards.

Table 4.5

Demand		Supply	
Price	Quantity	Price	Quantity
$100	5	$100	25
$ 80	8	$ 80	21
$ 60	11	$ 60	16
$ 40	14	$ 40	14
$ 20	22	$ 20	3

a   Find the equilibrium price and quantity.
b   If the price is $20, is the market in equilibrium? Will there be a surplus or a shortage? If so, what is the size of the surplus or shortage? What will happen to the price? Why?
c   If the price is $80, is the market in equilibrium? Will there be a surplus or a shortage? If so, what is the size of the surplus or shortage? What will happen to the price? Why?

6   (Practice problem: equilibrium price and quantity) Find the equilibrium price and quantity in each of the following markets.

a   The supply and demand curves for new soles (shoe repair) are given in Table 4.6.

Table 4.6

Demand		Supply	
Price	Quantity	Price	Quantity
$35	17	$35	53
$30	21	$30	37
$25	25	$25	25
$20	30	$20	15
$15	35	$15	0

b   The supply and demand curves for seat cushions are given in Table 4.7.

Table 4.7

Demand		Supply	
$8	4	$8	32
$7	8	$7	28
$6	12	$6	22
$5	16	$5	19
$4	17	$4	17

SUPPLY AND DEMAND

Supply and demand is probably the most useful technique in microeconomics. Economists use it to study how markets are affected by changes, such as tastes, technology, government programs, and many others. Supply and demand offers a wealth of insights into the workings of the economy. It is very important to master the procedure spelled out in Tool Kit 4.3.

Tool Kit 4.3: Using Supply and Demand

Supply and demand analysis provides excellent answers to questions of the following form: "What is the effect of a change in _____ on the market for _____?" You are well on your way to success as a student of economics if you stick closely to this procedure in answering such questions.

Step one: Begin with an equilibrium in the relevant market. Label the horizontal axis as the quantity of the good or service and the vertical axis as the price. Draw a demand and a supply curve and label them D and S, respectively.

Step two: Figure out whether the change shifts the supply curve, the demand curve, or neither.

Step three: Shift the appropriate curve.

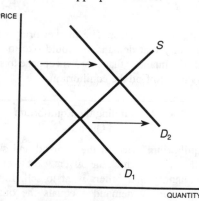

Step four: Find the new equilibrium, and compare it with the original one.

7   (Worked problem: using supply and demand) In response to concern about the fumes emitted by dry cleaning establishments, the Environmental Protection Agency has issued regulations requiring expensive filtering systems. How will this regulation affect the dry cleaning market?

Step-by-step solution

Step one: Start with an equilibrium.

Step two: Figure out which curve shifts. The mandated filtering systems increase the dry cleaning firm's costs, shifting supply to the left.

Step three: Shift the curve.

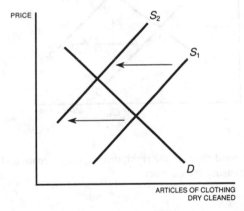

Step four: Find the new equilibrium and compare. The effect of the regulation is to raise the price and lower the quantity of clothes dry cleaned.

8   (Practice problem: using supply and demand) As the oil market comes to the realization that Kuwait's production will not return to prewar levels, the price of oil has increased by $4 per barrel. Explain the effect of this oil price increase on the market for natural gas.

9   (Practice problem: using supply and demand) For each of the following, show the effects on price and quantity. Draw the diagrams and follow the procedure.

a   an increase in income in the market for a normal good
b   a decrease in income in the market for a normal good
c   an increase in the price of a substitute
d   a decrease in the price of a substitute
e   an increase in the price of a complement
f   a decrease in the price of an complement
g   an increase in the price of an input
h   a decrease in the price of an input
i   an improvement in technology

Answers to Problems

2 | Price | Quantity (bushels) |
    | --- | --- |
    | $5 | 85 |
    | $4 | 116 |
    | $3 | 147 |
    | $2 | 207 |
    | $1 | 337 |

3 | Price | Quantity |
    | --- | --- |
    | $200 | 10 |
    | $220 | 16 |
    | $240 | 22 |
    | $260 | 43 |

5   a   Equilibrium price = $40; quantity = 14.
    b   If the price is $20, there is a shortage of 22 − 3 = 19. The price will be driven up.
    c   If the price is $80, there is a surplus of 21 − 8 = 13. The price will be driven down.

6   a   Price = $25; quantity = 25.
    b   Price = $4; quantity = 17.

8   Oil and natural gas are substitutes, and therefore the demand curve shifts to the right, the price increases, and the quantity increases.

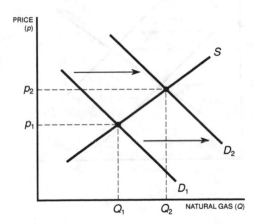

9   *a*   Demand shifts to the right, driving the price up and
        increasing the quantity.

b   Demand shifts to the left, driving the price down
      and decreasing the quantity.

c   Demand shifts to the right, driving the price up and
      increasing the quantity.

d   Demand shifts to the left, driving the price down
      and decreasing the quantity.

e   Demand shifts to the left, driving the price down
      and decreasing the quantity.

f   Demand shifts to the right, driving the price up and
      increasing the quantity.

g Supply shifts up (vertically), increasing the price
   but decreasing the quantity.

i Supply shifts down (vertically), decreasing the
   price but increasing the quantity.

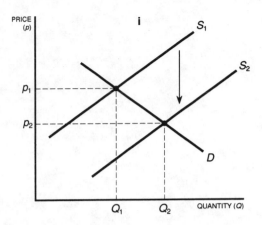

h Supply shifts down (vertically), decreasing the price
   but increasing the quantity.

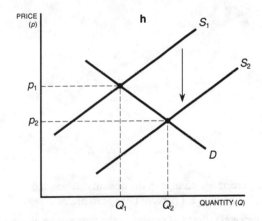

Chapter 5

USING DEMAND AND SUPPLY

Chapter Review

The model of demand and supply introduced in Chapter 4 is one of the most useful in all of the social sciences. The ideas of demand and supply form the basis of all economic study, and will be used throughout this text. This chapter develops the model in more detail and introduces the concept of elasticity. Elasticity is best thought of as "sensitivity." The price elasticity of demand, for instance, measures how sensitive the quantity demanded is to a change in price. The chapter then applies the model to the study of the effects of taxes and price controls. Chapter 6 extends the supply and demand framework to markets in which future goods and risk are exchanged.

ESSENTIAL CONCEPTS

1   When price falls, quantity demanded increases. If the demand curve is steep, the increase in quantity is smaller than it would be if the curve were flat. Although it might seem natural to measure how the quantity responds to price changes by the slope of the demand curve, economists employ the concept of **elasticity.** They do so because elasticity will produce the same measure no matter what units are used. The **price elasticity of demand**

is the percentage change in the quantity demanded brought about by a 1 percent change in price.

2   The **price elasticity of supply** is the percentage change in the quantity supplied brought about by a 1 percent change in price. It is the basic measure of how sensitive the quantity supplied is to changes in price.

3   The price elasticity of demand is greater when there are good, close substitutes available. Usually it is greater when the price is higher, because at higher prices, only those who consider the good essential remain in the market. Both the price elasticity of demand and the price elasticity of supply are greater in the long run because individuals and firms have more time to find substitutes and make adjustments.

4   When demand shifts, both the equilibrium price and quantity change. The price elasticity of supply determines which change is larger. If supply is more elastic, quantity changes by a greater percentage than price; if supply is less elastic, price changes more. Similarly, it is the price elasticity of demand that determines the relative changes in price and quantity when supply shifts. The more elastic the demand, the more quantity changes and the smaller is the change in price.

5   The economic effects of a tax are seen by focusing on the market affected by the tax. For example, a tax on the

sale of gasoline shifts the supply curve up (vertically) by the amount of the tax, raises consumer prices, and reduces the quantity of gasoline sold. Except in a case where supply or demand is perfectly inelastic or perfectly elastic, the increase in consumer price is less than the amount of the tax. This means that producers are able to pass on only part of the tax to their customers and must bear some of the burden themselves.

6   **Price ceilings,** when set below the market-clearing price, lead to shortages, which means that the quantity demanded exceeds the quantity supplied. **Price floors,** when set above the market-clearing price, result in surpluses; in this case, the quantity demanded is less than the quantity supplied. In each case, the quantity actually exchanged is less than it is at the market-clearing price.

BEHIND THE ESSENTIAL CONCEPTS

1   The concept of elasticity appears many times throughout the text, and is worth mastering. Suppose that price falls by 1 percent. We know that quantity will increase as consumers substitute toward the lower price, but by how much? The price elasticity provides the answer. It is the percent change in quantity brought on by a 1 percent change in price.

2   The relationship between elasticity and total revenue is very important. Total revenue is just price multiplied by quantity. If the price of a bicycle is $200 and there are 20 sold, then total revenue is $200 × 2 = $4,000. When price falls, total revenue is pushed down because each unit sells for less money; however, total revenue is pushed up because more units are sold. Whether on balance total revenue rises or falls depends on the elasticity. Table 5.1 helps to keep the relationship between elasticity and total revenue straight.

Table 5.1

If price rises,
  total revenue *falls* if the price elasticity of demand is greater than one (elastic).
  total revenue *rises* if the price elasticity of demand is less than one (inelastic).
  total revenue *does not change* if the price elasticity of demand equals one (unitary elasticity).

If price falls,
  total revenue *rises* if the price elasticity of demand is greater than one (elastic).
  total revenue *falls* if the price elasticity of demand is less than one (inelastic).
  total revenue *does not change* if the price elasticity of demand equals one (unitary elasticity).

3   What makes the demand for some goods (like motor boats) elastic, while the demand for others (like milk) is inelastic? The most important factor is the availability of substitutes. The **principle of substitution** says that consumers will look for substitutes when the price rises. If there are good, close substitutes available, then finding substitutes will be easy and consumers will switch. If good, close substitutes are not available, the consumers are more likely to swallow the price increase and continue purchasing the good.

4   Suppose that the government levies a tax on the supply of hotel rooms. Who pays the tax? While it is natural to think that the hotel pays the tax because it actually writes the check to the government, when you look at the issue through the lens of supply and demand, you see the value of economics. The tax increases the hotel's costs, and therefore it shifts the supply curve up and raises the price. Because they must pay higher prices for hotel rooms, consumers pay some of the tax.

5   The key to tax analysis is to find the market or markets in which the burden of the tax falls. Sometimes this is easy. A hotel room tax falls on the market for hotel rooms. In other cases, its not so clear. For example, an income tax affects the labor market, because workers must give up some of the earnings. It also affects the capital market because some of the interest earnings must be paid to the government. Once you find the relevant market, simply apply the basic method of supply and demand: start with an equilibrium, figure out which curve shifts (which side of the market is taxed), shift the curve, find the new equilibrium, and compare.

6   Price ceilings only make a difference if they are set below the market-clearing price (where the supply and demand curves intersect). A price ceiling set above the market-clearing price has no effect. Similarly, a price floor set below the market-clearing price does not do anything.

7   Price floors and ceilings also affect the quantity traded in the market. If there is a price ceiling, then the quantity demanded exceeds the quantity supplied. The supply is the short side of the market, and although consumers would like to buy more of the good, the quantity traded is what producers are willing to sell. This is shown in Figure 5.1A. With price floors, the opposite is true. The demand is the short side of the market, and the quantity traded equals the amount that consumers are willing to buy, as shown in panel B. In each case, we say that the short side of the market determines the actual quantity traded, and the actual quantity trade is less than the market-clearing quantity.

Figure 5.1

Figure 5.1

SELF-TEST

True or False

1   The price elasticity of demand is greater for goods and services that have better close substitutes.

2   The price elasticity of demand is always constant along the demand curve.

3   Total revenue increases as price falls when the demand is elastic.

4   A horizontal demand curve is perfectly elastic.

5   A vertical supply curve is perfectly inelastic.

6   If the supply curve is unitary elastic, then total revenue is constant as price changes.

7   If the supply curve is upward sloping, a rightward shift in the demand curve increases the equilibrium price and the equilibrium quantity.

8   If the demand curve is downward sloping, a rightward shift in the supply curve increases the equilibrium price and the equilibrium quantity.

9   When the demand curve is very elastic, relatively more of a tax on the production of some good or service will be borne by producers.

10   A tax on the sale of beer shifts the supply curve vertically by the amount of the tax.

11   When prices are sticky, shortages and surpluses can result in the short run.

12   A price ceiling set above the equilibrium price will have no effect on the market.

13   A price ceiling set below the equilibrium price will have no effect on the market.

14   A price floor set above the equilibrium price in the milk market will lead to a surplus of milk.

15   When demand and supply are more elastic, minimum wages set above the equilibrium wage lead to relatively more unemployment.

Multiple Choice

1   The quantity demanded is more sensitive to price changes when

   a   supply is relatively inelastic;
   b   close substitutes are available;
   c   consumers are rational;
   d   consumers are relatively more informed about quality for some goods;
   e   all of the above.

2   Suppose that price falls by 10 percent and the quantity demanded rises by 20 percent. The price elasticity of demand is

   a   2;
   b   1;
   c   0;
   d   1/2;
   e   none of the above.

3   Suppose that the price elasticity of demand is 1/3. If price rises by 30 percent, how does the quantity demanded change?

   a   Quantity demanded rises by 10 percent.
   b   Quantity demanded falls by 10 percent.
   c   Quantity demanded rises by 90 percent.
   d   Quantity demanded falls by 90 percent.
   e   Quantity demanded does not change.

4   Suppose that the price elasticity of demand is 1.5. If price falls, total revenue will

   a   remain the same;
   b   fall;
   c   rise;
   d   double;
   e   c and d.

5   Suppose that the price elasticity of demand is 0.7. The demand for this good is

   a   perfectly inelastic;
   b   inelastic;
   c   unitary elastic;
   d   elastic;
   e   perfectly elastic.

6   Which of the following are true statements concerning the price elasticity of demand?

   a   The price elasticity is constant for any demand curve.
   b   Demand is more price elastic in the short run than in the long run.
   c   If total revenue falls as price increases, the demand is relatively inelastic.
   d   a and c.
   e   None of the above.

7   If the supply curve is vertical, then the price elasticity of supply is

   a   0;
   b   inelastic.
   c   1;

d   elastic;
e   infinite.

8   The long-run elasticity of supply is greater than the short-run elasticity of supply because

a   in the long run, the stock of machines and buildings can adjust;
b   in the long run, new firms can enter and existing firms can exit the industry;
c   in the long run, customers can discover substitutes;
d   a and b;
e   all of the above.

talking about business firms, not customers

9   Suppose that supply is perfectly elastic. If the demand curve shifts to the right, then

a   price and quantity will increase;
b   quantity will increase, but price will remain constant;
c   price will increase, but quantity will remain constant;
d   neither price nor quantity will increase;
e   price will increase, but quantity will decrease.

Easy

10 Suppose that demand is perfectly inelastic, and the supply curve shifts to the left. Then

a   price and quantity will increase;
b   quantity will increase, but price will remain constant;
c   price will increase, but quantity will remain constant;
d   neither price nor quantity will increase;
e   price will increase, but quantity will decrease.

11 The price elasticity of demand for tires is 1.3, and the supply curve is upward sloping. If a $1-per-tire tax is placed on the production of tires, then the equilibrium price will

a   not change because the tax is on production and not on consumption;
b   increase by $1;
c   increase by less than $1;
d   fall by less than $1;
e   fall by $1.

less than a $1 because

12 In general, consumers bear more of a tax when the demand is

a   relatively inelastic;   - cigarettes elastic
b   unitary elastic;
c   relatively elastic;
d   such that consumers always bear the entire burden;
e   none of the above.

demand is very

13 Suppose that the supply of a good is perfectly elastic. A tax of $1 on that good will raise the price by

a   less than $1;
b $1;
c   more than $1;
d $.50;
e   none of the above.

14 A price ceiling set below the equilibrium price will

a   create a shortage;
b   increase the price;
c   create a surplus;
d   a and b;
e   have no effect.

Rent Apartments below equilibrium $ because it is too high. More buyers w/ price ceiling

15 A price ceiling set above the equilibrium price will

a   create a shortage;
b   increase the price;
c   create a surplus;
d   a and b;
e   have no effect.

pointless - ceilings are always set below

16 A price ceiling set below the equilibrium price will

a   increase the quantity demanded; - more people in market
b   increase the quantity supplied;
c   decrease the quantity supplied; - firms back out of market
d   a and c;
e   have no effect.

17 Rent control

a   creates a shortage of rental housing;
b   leads to a larger shortage in the long run;
c   lowers rents for renters who have apartments;
d   all of the above;
e   none of the above.

See Above

18 A price ceiling on insurance rates will

a   shift demand to the left;
b   shift demand to the right;
c   shift supply to the left;
d   shift supply to the right;
e   none of the above.

19 Which of the following is not a cause of surpluses or shortages?

a   price ceilings; - creates shortage
b   price floors; - creates surplus
c   taxes;
d   sticky prices; - prices don't change
e   All of the above cause surpluses or shortages.

20 Recently, the demand for housing has fallen in the northeast United States. Housing prices are sticky, and therefore

a   temporary shortages of housing have appeared;
b   temporary surpluses of housing have appeared; - demand ↓
c   the housing market has cleared; price - ↓
d   supply has also shifted to the left;
e   none of the above.

Completion

1   The percentage change in the quantity demanded as a result of a 1 percent price change is called the ___E of D___.

2   Price changes have no effect on revenue if the price elasticity of demand is ___1___.

3   If the price elasticity of demand lies between 0 and 1, then we say that demand is relatively ___inelastic___.

4   A horizontal demand curve indicates that demand is
     perfect(ly)infinite elastic [handwritten: perfectly infinitely elastic / or infinite]

5   If the supply curve is vertical, then the price elasticity
     of supply equals ___0___.

6   A $.50-per-gallon tax on the production of gasoline
     can be expected to shift the supply curve _to the_ [handwritten: vertically]
     by _.50_.

7   If demand is relatively inelastic, most of the tax is
     borne by _the consumer_

8   A price ceiling set below the equilibrium price will
     create a _shortage_

9   A price floor set above the equilibrium price will cre-
     ate a _surplus_

10   The minimum wage is an example of a _price floor_

Answers to Self-Test

True or False

1	t	4	t	7	t	10	t	13	f
2	f	5	t	8	f	11	t	14	t
3	t	6	f	9	t	12	t	15	t

Multiple Choice

1	b	6	e	11	c	16	d
2	a	7	a	12	a	17	d
3	b	8	d	13	b	18	e
4	c	9	b	14	a	19	c
5	b	10	c	15	e	20	b

Completion

1   price elasticity of demand
2   1
3   inelastic
4   perfectly elastic
5   zero
6   vertically, $.50
7   consumers
8   shortage
9   surplus
10   price floor

Doing Economics: Tools and Practice Problems

Three techniques receive attention in this section. You'll
first learn how to calculate elasticity, then how to measure
the effects of taxes, and finally how to analyze the effects of
price controls.

ELASTICITY

When price changes, how much does quantity change? Economists answer this question with the concept of elasticity. The
price elasticity of demand measures how responsive quantity
demand is to changes in the price. Similarly, the elasticity of
supply measures the responsiveness of quantity supplied to

price changes. Tool Kit 5.1 shows how to calculate elasticity.
The problems focus on elasticity of demand and illustrate the
relationship between elasticity and total revenue.

Tool Kit 5.1: Calculating Elasticity

Elasticity measures how sensitive the quantity is to
changes in price. Follow these steps to calculate elasticity.

Step one: To find the elasticity between two points on
the demand or supply curve, let p_1 and Q_1 be the price
and quantity at the first point and p_2 and Q_2 be the
price and quantity at the second point.

Step two: Substitute the prices and quantities into the
formula

$$\text{elasticity} = (Q_1 - Q_2)(p_1 + p_2)/(Q_1 + Q_2)(p_1 - p_2).$$

---

1   (Worked problem: calculating elasticity) The demand
     curve for bulletin boards is given below.

Price	Quantity
$35	800
$30	1,000
$25	1,200
$20	1,300

a   Calculate total revenue for each price.
b   Calculate the price elasticity of demand between
     $35 and $30, between $30 and $25, and between $25
     and $20. Does elasticity change along this demand?
c   Verify the relationship between elasticity and total
     revenue.

Step-by-step solution

Step one (a): Total revenue at $35 is 800 × $35 = $28,000.
Total revenue at $30 is 1,000 × $30 = $30,000. Continue,
and enter the numbers in the table.

Price	Quantity	Total revenue
$35	800	$28,000
$30	1,000	$30,000
$25	1,200	$30,000
$20	1,300	$26,000

Step two (b): Let $35 = p_1, 800 = Q_1, $30 = p_2, and 1,000 =
Q_2. Substituting into the formula gives

elasticity = (35 + 30)(1,000 − 800)/(800 + 1,000)(35 − 30)
           = 1.44, which is elastic.

Step three: Between $30 and $25,

elasticity = (30 + 25)(1,200 − 1,000)/(1,000 + 1,200)(30 − 25)
           = 1, which is unitary elastic.

Step four: Between $25 and $20,

elasticity = (25 + 20)(1,300 − 1,200)/(1,200 + 1,300)(25 − 20)
           = 0.36, which is inelastic.

Clearly, the elasticity is not constant. The demand curve is
less elastic at lower prices.

Step five (c): Between $35 and $30, where the demand is elastic, total revenue rises from $28,000 to $30,000 as price falls. Between $30 and $25, where the demand is unitary elastic, total revenue is constant at $30,000 as the price falls. Between $25 and $20, where the demand is inelastic, total revenue falls from $30,000 to $26,000 as the price falls. Check Table 5.1 to verify that these numbers are consistent with the general relationship between price elasticity of demand and total revenue.

2 (Practice problem: calculating elasticity) The demand curve for bookends is given below.

Price	Quantity
$10	70
$ 8	90
$ 6	120
$ 4	130

a Calculate total revenue for each price.
b Calculate the price elasticity of demand between each of the adjacent prices. Does elasticity change along this demand?
c Verify the relationship between elasticity and total revenue.

3 (Practice problem: calculating elasticity) For each of the following, calculate the total revenue for each price and the price elasticity for each price change, and verify the relationship between elasticity and total revenue.

a | Price | Quantity |
|-------|----------|
| $12 | 6 |
| $10 | 8 |
| $ 8 | 10 |
| $ 6 | 12 |

b | Price | Quantity |
|-------|----------|
| $100 | 80 |
| $ 80 | 85 |
| $ 60 | 90 |
| $ 40 | 95 |

c | Price | Quantity |
|-------|----------|
| $9 | 10 |
| $8 | 8 |
| $7 | 6 |
| $6 | 4 |

TAX INCIDENCE

The economic effects of taxes can be analyzed using the method of supply and demand introduced in Chapter 4. The key idea is that the burden of a tax—its incidence—does not necessarily fall on the person or firm that must deliver the money to the government. Taxes affect exchanges, and their impact must be analyzed by looking at the markets where the affected exchanges occur. The basic conclusions of this analysis are that, except when demand or supply is perfectly elastic or perfectly inelastic, consumers and producers share the burden of the tax, taxes reduce the level of economic activity, and, perhaps surprisingly, the effects of the tax are the same whether the supplier or the demander pays. Tool Kit 5.2 shows how to use supply and demand to do tax incidence.

Tool Kit 5.2: Using Supply and Demand for Tax Incidence

Supply and demand analysis shows how markets are affected by taxes and how the burden of taxes is allocated between suppliers and demanders. Follow this five-step procedure.

Step one: Start with an equilibrium in the relevant market.

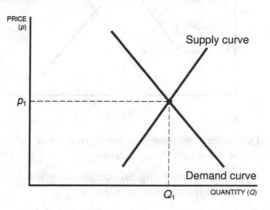

Step two: Identify whether the demander or supplier must pay the tax.

Step three: If the supplier must pay the tax, shift the supply curve up (vertically) by exactly the amount of the tax. If the demander must pay the tax, shift the demand curve down by exactly the amount of the tax.

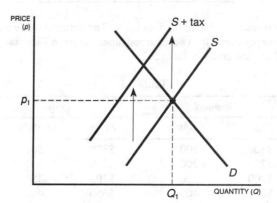

Step four: Find the new equilibrium.

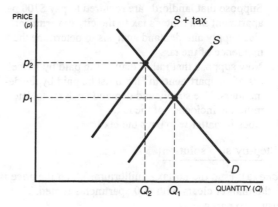

Step five: Determine the economic incidence of the tax. If the supplier must pay the tax, then use the following formulas to calculate economic incidence.

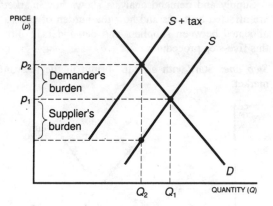

Demander's burden = new equilibrium price − original equilibrium price;

supplier's burden = original equilibrium price − new equilibrium price + tax.

If the demander must pay the tax, use the following formulas to calculate tax incidence.

Demander's burden = new equilibrium price + tax − original equilibrium price;

supplier's burden = original equilibrium price − new equilibrium price.

4   (Worked problem: tax incidence) The demand curve and supply curve for two-bedroom apartments in Takoma Park are given in Table 5.2.

Table 5.2

Demand		Supply	
Price	Quantity	Price	Quantity
$800	100	$800	500
$750	200	$750	500
$700	300	$700	450
$650	400	$650	400
$600	500	$600	300

a   Find the equilibrium price and quantity.
b   Suppose that landlords are required to pay $100 per apartment in a renter's tax to the city government. Use supply and demand analysis to determine the incidence of the tax.
c   Now suppose that rather than being paid by the sellers of an apartment, the tax must be paid by the demanders. Use supply and demand analysis to determine the incidence of the tax.
d   Does it matter who pays the tax?

Step-by-step solution

Step one (a): Find the no-tax equilibrium. When the price is $650, the market clears with 400 apartments rented. This is the answer to part a.

Step two (b): Identify whether the demander or supplier must pay the tax. For part b, the supplier pays the tax.

Step three: Because the tax is paid by sellers, the supply curve shifts up by $100, the amount of the tax. The new supply curve is found by adding $100 to the price column, as in Table 5.3.

Table 5.3

Supply	
Price	Quantity
$900	500
$850	500
$800	450
$750	400
$700	300

Step four: Find the new equilibrium. The market clears at a price of $700 and a quantity of 300.

Step five: Determine the economic incidence of the tax.

Demander's burden = new equilibrium price − original equilibrium price
$$= \$700 - \$650 = \$50.$$
supplier's burden = original equilibrium price − new equilibrium price + tax
$$= \$650 - \$700 + \$100 = \$50.$$

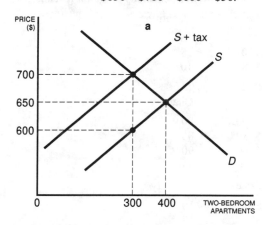

Step six (c): To answer part c, we repeat the procedure for the case where the demander must pay the tax.

Step seven (one): The original no-tax equilibrium is the same with the price equal to $650 and 400 apartments rented.

Step eight (two): In this case, the demanders pay the tax.

Step nine (three): We shift the demand curve down by $100. The new demand curve is given in Table 5.4.

Table 5.4

Demand	
Price	Quantity
$700	100
$650	200
$600	300
$550	400
$500	500

Step ten (four): The market clears at a price of $600 and a quantity of 300.

Step eleven (five): We determine the incidence as follows.

Demander's burden = new equilibrium price
+ tax − original equilibrium price.
$$= \$600 + \$100 - \$650 = \$50.$$
supplier's burden = original equilibrium price
− new equilibrium price
$$= \$650 - \$600 = \$50.$$

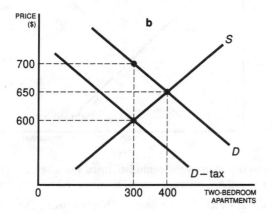

Step twelve (d): It does not matter who pays the tax! In either situation, the total amount that demanders pay is $700, the net amount that sellers receive is $600, and the equilibrium quantity is 300. The diagrams illustrate the solution.

5   (Practice problem: tax incidence) The demand curve and supply curve for unskilled labor are given in Table 5.5.

Table 5.5

Demand		Supply	
Wage	Quantity	Wage	Quantity
$6.50	1,000	$6.50	1,900
$6.00	1,200	$6.00	1,800
$5.50	1,400	$5.50	1,700
$5.00	1,600	$5.00	1,600
$4.50	1,800	$4.50	1,500
$4.00	2,000	$4.00	1,400

a   Find the equilibrium wage and quantity hired.
b   Consider the effect of the unemployment insurance tax. Suppose that it equals $1.50 per hour and is paid by the employers (they are the demanders in this market). Use supply and demand analysis to determine the incidence of this tax.
c   Now suppose that rather than being paid by the employers, the tax must be paid by the workers. Use supply and demand analysis to determine the incidence of this tax.
d   Does it matter who pays the tax?

PRICE CONTROLS

When the government interferes with the law of supply and demand and sets price controls, the effects can be analyzed with the basic method of supply and demand. To see the effects, start with an equilibrium.

The price control (if it is effective) will change the price without changing either the demand curve or the supply curve. The new equilibrium occurs at the price set by the government, but the quantity demanded is read off the demand curve, and the quantity supplied is read off the supply curve. The actual quantity transacted is always the short side of the market (the smaller of the quantity demanded and the quantity supplied).

The basic results of this analysis are that price ceilings, when set below the market-clearing price, lower the price, cause shortages, and reduce the quantity transacted. Price floors, when set above the market-clearing price, raise the price, cause surpluses, and reduce the quantity transacted. Tool Kit 5.3 shows how to use supply and demand to analyze price controls.

Tool Kit 5.3: Using Supply and Demand for Price Controls

The impact of price controls is made clear through the use of supply and demand. This four-step procedure shows how to analyze price controls.

Step one: Start with a market-clearing equilibrium.

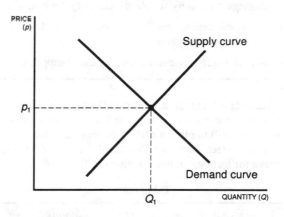

Step two: Identify the controlled price, and decide whether it is a floor or a ceiling.

Step three: Find the new equilibrium price. If it is a price floor set below the market-clearing price or a price ceiling set above the market-clearing price, then the equilibrium is the market-clearing one found in step one. If it is a price floor set above the market-clearing price or a price ceiling set below market clearing, then the controlled price is the equilibrium price.

Step four: Determine the shortage or surplus. For a price floor set above the market-clearing price, there is a surplus:

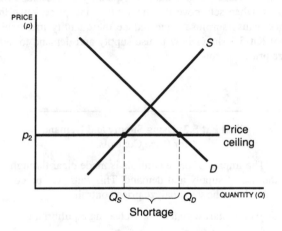

shortage = quantity supplied – quantity demanded.

For a price ceiling set below the market-clearing price, there is a shortage:

surplus = quantity demanded – quantity supplied.

6   (Worked problem: price controls) Dental bills in Yellowville rose again last year. The City Council is considering a bill to place a ceiling on fees that dentists can charge for teeth cleaning. The supply curve and demand curve for teeth cleanings are given in Table 5.6.

Table 5.6

Demand		Supply	
Price	Quantity	Price	Quantity
$65	100	$65	190
$60	120	$60	180
$55	140	$55	170
$50	160	$50	160
$45	180	$45	150
$40	200	$40	140

a   Find the equilibrium price and quantity for teeth cleanings in Yellowville.
b   The City Council passes a price ceiling ordinance, setting the maximum price at $40 per cleaning. Use

supply and demand analysis to determine the effects of the price control.

Step-by-step solution

Step one (a): Find the equilibrium price and quantity. The market clears at a price of $50 and quantity equal to 160.

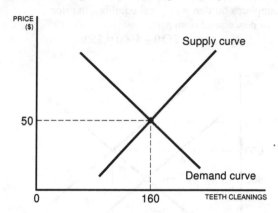

Step two (b): Identify the controlled price and whether it is a floor or a ceiling. The price control is a price ceiling set at $40.

Step three: Determine the new equilibrium price. The ceiling is below the market-clearing price; therefore, the new price is equal to the ceiling price of $40.

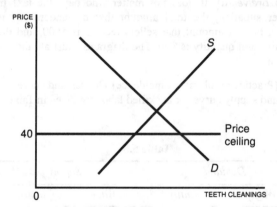

Step four: Determine the shortage or surplus. When the price is $40, the quantity demanded is 200 and the quantity supplied is 140. Although consumers would like more, there are only 140 cleanings actually performed. This results in a shortage of 200 – 140 = 60 teeth cleanings. The diagram illustrates the solution.

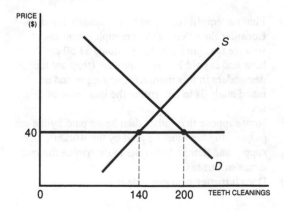

7 (Practice problem: price controls) Many states are considering price ceilings on automobile insurance premiums. In West Dakota, the supply curve and demand curve for automobile insurance policies ($250 deductible on liability, no collision) are given in Table 5.7.

Table 5.7

Demand		Supply	
Price	Quantity	Price	Quantity
$800	1,000	$800	1,800
$750	1,100	$750	1,500
$700	1,200	$700	1,200
$650	1,400	$650	900
$600	1,600	$600	600

a Find the equilibrium price and quantity.
b Suppose that a price ceiling of $650 is imposed. Use supply and demand analysis to determine the effects of the price control.

8 (Practice problem: price controls) Fearful of a restless urban population, Corporal Thug, the new supreme ruler of Costa Guano, attempts to mollify the masses with a wage increase. He mandates that employers must pay at least $8 per day. The supply and demand curves for urban labor are given in Table 5.8.

Table 5.8

Demand		Supply	
Wage	Quantity	Wage	Quantity
$8.50	400	$8.50	4,000
$8.00	600	$8.00	3,200
$7.50	700	$7.50	2,600
$7.00	800	$7.00	2,200
$6.50	900	$6.50	1,800
$6.00	1,000	$6.00	1,000

a Find the quantity demanded, the quantity supplied, and the size of the surplus or shortage, if any.
b Democracy comes to Costa Guano! Corporal Thug is overthrown and the minimum wage repealed. Use supply and demand analysis to determine the effects of the price control.

Answers to Problems

2 a

Price	Quantity	Revenue
$10	70	$700
$ 8	90	$720
$ 6	120	$720
$ 4	130	$520

b Between $10 and $8,
elasticity $= (10 + 8)(90 - 70)/(10 - 8)(90 + 70)$
$= 1.125$.

Between $8 and $6,
elasticity $= (8 + 6)(120 - 90)/(8 - 6)(120 + 90)$
$= 1$.
Between $6 and $4,
elasticity $= (6 + 4)(130 - 120)/(6 - 4)(130 + 120)$
$= 0.2$.

c When elasticity is 1.125, the demand curve is elastic, and total revenue rises from $700 to $720 as price falls. When elasticity is 1, the demand curve is unitary elastic, and total revenue remains constant at $720 as price falls. Finally, when elasticity is 0.2, the demand curve is inelastic, and total revenue falls from $720 to $520 as price falls.

3 In the following tables, the number in the elasticity column corresponding to each price refers to the elasticity over the interval between that price and the next highest price.

a

Price	Quantity	Total revenue	Elasticity
$12	6	$72	
$10	8	$80	1.57
$ 8	10	$80	1.00
$ 6	12	$72	0.64

b

Price	Quantity	Total revenue	Elasticity
$100	80	$8,000	
$ 80	85	$6,800	0.26
$ 60	90	$5,400	0.20
$ 40	95	$3,800	0.14

c

Price	Quantity	Total revenue	Elasticity
$9	10	$ 90	
$8	14	$112	2.430
$7	18	$126	1.875
$6	22	$132	1.300

5 a Wage = $5.00; quantity = 1,600.
b The new supply is given in Table 5.9.

Table 5.9

Supply	
Wage	Quantity
$8.00	1,900
$7.50	1,800
$7.00	1,700
$6.50	1,600
$6.00	1,500
$5.50	1,400

The new equilibrium wage = $5.50; quantity = 1,400. Demander's burden = $5.50 − $5.00 = $0.50; supplier's burden = $5.00 + $1.50 − $5.50 = $1.00.
c The new demand curve is given in Table 5.10.

Table 5.10

Demand	
Wage	*Quantity*
$5.00	1,000
$4.50	1,200
$4.00	1,400
$3.50	1,600
$3.00	1,800
$2.50	2,000

The new equilibrium wage = $4.00; quantity = 1,400. Demander's burden = $4.00 + $1.50 − $5.00 = $0.50; supplier's burden = $5.00 − $4.00 = $1.00.

d No. The demander's burden, supplier's burden, and equilibrium quantity are the same in each case.

7 a Price = $700; quantity = 1,200.

b Price = $650; quantity demanded = 1,400; quantity supplied = 900; shortage = 1,400 − 900 = 500.

8 a Wage = $8.00; quantity demanded = 600; quantity supplied = 3,200; surplus = 3,200 − 600 = 2,600.

b Price = $600; quantity = 1,000.

Chapter 6

TIME AND RISK

Chapter Review

When trades involve the future, as they do when individuals save, borrow money, or buy a house, people must be concerned with the time value of money and with the risk that the trade will not proceed as stipulated. Time and risk therefore affect today's demand and supply curves. This chapter explores markets for risk and insurance along with the broad class of capital markets (stock markets, foreign exchange markets, and so on) where firms raise funds to finance investment and where people transfer risks. Chapter 7 closes the introductory part of the book, with a look at the public sector and the large role government plays in the economy.

ESSENTIAL CONCEPTS

1   The value of a dollar today is greater than the value of a dollar to be received in the future. In other words, money has a time value. Any decision that involves present and future dollars must account for the time value of money. Economists calculate the present discounted value; they convert future dollars to their present equivalent. The formula for the present discounted value of $1.00 next year is $1.00/(1 + interest rate).

2   The market for loanable funds brings together all those who want to borrow and those who want to save. The price in this market is the **interest rate.** Figure 6.1 shows the demand curve for loanable funds sloping downward, which indicates that at lower interest rates, more borrowers would like to borrow more funds. The supply curve slopes upward because at higher interest rates, individuals will save more. The interest rate adjusts to clear the market, and the equilibrium quantity of savings equals the equilibrium quantity of borrowing.

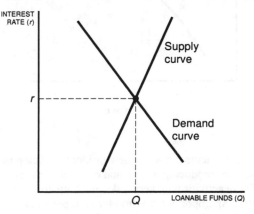

Figure 6.1

3   **Assets,** such as land, housing, stocks, and bonds, last a long time and can be bought today and sold in the future. The prices of assets are determined by supply and demand; however, supply and demand are affected by both today's conditions and what people expect future prices to be. Buyers and sellers of assets must form their **expectations** and make forecasts with care; nevertheless, they are likely to make mistakes, disagree, and revise their expectations. Changing expectations explain large changes in asset prices and make asset markets volatile and risky.

4   Most people are **risk averse** and would prefer to reduce the uncertainty about future economic conditions. The **market for risk** is a whole set of institutions and arrangements by which risk is transferred. People can manage risk by avoiding certain risk endeavors altogether, taking steps to keep options open, diversifying, and transferring risks through the **insurance market,** where individuals purchase policies that protect against the risk of specific events, such as disability or accidents.

5   There are important risks, however, for which insurance markets do not offer such protection. One reason is **adverse selection,** which means that the riskiest customers are the most likely to buy insurance. Another problem, **moral hazard,** arises because people who have bought insurance have less incentive to protect themselves against loss.

6   One of the most fundamental **trade-offs** in the economy involves **risk and incentives.** In markets for both risk and capital, when risks are reduced, so are incentives. Figure 6.2 shows the trade-off. At point *A,* there is low risk and limited incentives. Both risk and incentives increase by moving from *A* to *B.*

RISK

Risk-incentive
trade-off

B

A

INCENTIVES

Figure 6.2

7   Entrepreneurs introduce new products, develop new ways of producing goods, and create new businesses. These activities are very risky, but they are not insurable. An important function for entrepreneurs is bearing the risks of these necessary endeavors.

BEHIND THE ESSENTIAL CONCEPTS

1   The distinction between real and nominal interest rates is very important, especially in macroeconomics. When you deposit money in your bank account, the bank pays you the nominal interest rate. Say it is 5 percent. Your money grows at 5 percent each year, but your purchasing power may not, because each year prices may also be changing. Suppose that the inflation rate (the rate of increase in the general price level) is 4 percent. This means that each year goods become 4 percent more expensive, and you can buy only 5 percent – 4 percent = 1 percent more goods. The 1 percent is the real interest rate, and also the rate of increase in your purchasing power.

2   Many economic activities, from purchasing an asset to making an investment, are oriented toward the future. Households and firms must form expectations about the future. Economists distinguish three ways of forming expectations. If you think that tomorrow will be like today, then your expectations are **myopic.** You have **adaptive expectations** if you think that current trends will continue. Finally, you have **rational expectations** (and are well on your way to becoming an economist) if you use all available information, including what you learn in economics.

3   Because people are risk averse, they are willing to pay something to reduce risk. The extra payment is called the risk premium. Here is how it works. Suppose that you have a $5,000 car, and its chance of being stolen is 1 percent. Your expected payment (if uninsured) is 1 percent of $5,000, or $50. If you buy a theft insurance policy for $55, then the risk premium is $55 – $50 = $5.00. In other words, it is the amount (beyond the expected payment) received by the insurance company to bear the risk of theft.

4   **Adverse selection** and **moral hazard** are important problems, and you should be clear about the difference. Adverse selection occurs when the mix of customers is affected by the insurance contract. For example, an insurance company may find that its policyholders have more accidents than the population at large. The company reasons that high-risk people buy more insurance. **Moral hazard,** on the other hand, involves the behavior of the insured. People who have insurance may not take the same precautions as those without insurance. They may fail to buckle up or may even drive recklessly.

5   Adverse selection, moral hazard, and the risk-incentive trade-off are not limited to the insurance industry. They are pervasive in the economy. If you are a banker and charge higher interest rates, then you may find that only risky borrowers apply for loans. We say that the pool of applicants for your loans is adversely selected. It may be wise for you to move along the risk-incentive trade-off. You can do this by requiring collateral. This increases the borrower's risk—the collateral will be forfeited if she defaults—but it gives better incentives to repay the loan.

Here is another example. Suppose that you own a business and you pay your sales force a fixed salary. You may find that they do not work as hard as you would like, and sales decline. Because it is the behavior of your sales force that changes, it is called moral hazard. Again, you can move along the risk-incentive trade-off by replacing the fixed salary with a commission pay based on how much each employee sells. This policy exposes your sales force to more risk, but gives them incentives to work hard.

SELF-TEST

True or False

1 The present discounted value of a future dollar is what one would pay today for that future dollar.

2 The interest rate is the price in the market for loanable funds.

3 The nominal interest rate is the real interest rate minus the inflation rate.

4 Current prices of assets are based upon expectations about their future prices.

5 Someone who always expects that what is true today will be true tomorrow has myopic expectations.

6 Someone who expects current trends to continue has adaptive expectations.

7 People with rational expectations do not make mistakes.

8 Keeping options open only exacerbates risk.

9 The risk premium equals the expected payment.

10 Individuals demand insurance because they are risk averse.

11 The adverse selection problem arises because insurance companies are not sure about the riskiness of their customers.

12 The moral hazard problem arises because insured individuals have less incentive to protect against loss.

13 When risks are higher, so are incentives to protect against losses.

14 The individuals who are responsible for creating new businesses, new products, and new production processes are called entrepreneurs.

15 Most of the risks faced by entrepreneurs, such as the risk that the business will not succeed, cannot be insured against.

Multiple Choice

1 If you deposit $1,100 in the bank today and the interest rate on your deposit is 10 percent, how much money will be in your account at the end of one year?

a $1,200;
b $1,210;
c $121;
d $1,000;
e none of the above.

2 If you are to receive $1,100 from a client one year from today, and the interest rate is 10 percent, what is the present discounted value of that future receipt?

a $1,100;
b $1,000;
c $1,200;
d $979;
e none of the above.

3 If the interest rate increases, the present discounted value of the future returns from investment projects

a increases;
b remains unchanged;
c decreases;
d either a or b;
e none of the above.

4 If you borrow $4,000 for a used car purchase at 11 percent interest, the 11 percent is the

a real rate of interest;
b rate of inflation;
c nominal rate of interest;
d real rate of interest – nominal rate of interest;
e nominal rate of interest – rate of inflation.

5 Suppose that the interest rate offered for certificates of deposit is 8 percent. The inflation rate is expected to be 5 percent. What is the real rate of interest?

a 8 percent;
b 5 percent;
c 13 percent;
d 3 percent;
e none of the above.

6 When market prices for assets change dramatically, it is usually because of

a changes in the supply of assets;
b government price floors;
c changes in expectations about future prices;
d changes in tastes;
e changes in income.

7 People who use all available information to form expectations about the future are said to have

a myopic expectations;
b adaptive expectations;
c rational expectations;
d insider expectations;
e random walk expectations.

8 Most people are risk averse. This means they

a try to avoid or minimize serious risks;
b have myopic expectations;
c never take risks;
d focus on the nominal rate of interest;
e a and b.

9 An important market for risk is the insurance market. Which of the following is true about insurance markets?

    a Buyers are risk averse.
    b Insurance companies spread risks among its many owners.
    c Insurance companies can forecast accurately the annual amount of claims.
    d All of the above.
    e a and b.

10 For insurance companies, the selection problem refers to

    a selecting the best employees to hire;
    b selecting the right premium to charge;
    c selecting the best risks to insure;
    d selecting the best corporate logo;
    e none of the above.

11 Adverse selection

    a is a consequence of the fact that the insurance company has limited information about the riskiness of individual customers;
    b implies that those more likely to buy insurance tend to be the higher risks;
    c causes those customers with lower risk to avoid insurance at high rates;
    d makes the fraction of customers who will have an accident larger when premiums are higher;
    e all of the above.

12 Moral hazard means that

    a insurance buyers are risk averse;
    b insurance companies can predict losses accurately;
    c higher-risk individuals demand more insurance at higher prices;
    d insured individuals have less incentive to avoid accidents;
    e the premium must include an allowance for false claims.

13 An individual who sometimes drives under the influence of alcohol has a great demand for automobile insurance. This is an example of

    a adverse selection;
    b moral hazard;
    c risk aversion;
    d adaptive expectations;
    e none of the above.

14 After buying more malpractice insurance, a doctor spends less time with each patient. This is an example of

    a adverse selection;
    b moral hazard;
    c risk aversion;
    d adaptive expectations;
    e none of the above.

15 Individuals respond to risk by

    a avoiding or mitigating risks;
    b keeping options open;
    c diversifying;
    d transferring risk to others;
    e all of the above.

16 Investing in a wide variety of stocks or in mutual funds, rather than owning a single asset, is an example of

    a avoiding or mitigating risks;
    b keeping options open;
    c diversifying;
    d transferring risk to others;
    e none of the above

17 Suppose that a certain business is losing money on a certain product line. If it delays abandoning production for a while in the hopes that demand will pick up, it is

    a avoiding or mitigaing risks;
    b keeping options open;
    c diversifying;
    d transferring risk to others;
    e none of the above.

18 The risk-incentive trade-off shows that

    a insurance buyers have adaptive expectations;
    b bonds are riskier than stocks;
    c fully insured individuals have less incentive to protect against risk;
    d as risk is decreased, the moral hazard problem becomes less severe;
    e c and d.

19 For the most part, the risk of business failure is borne by

    a insurance companies;
    b corporate lawyers;
    c accounting firms;
    d entrepreneurs;
    e the loanable funds market.

20 Those who provide new businesses with capital earn higher rates of returns. This extra return is

    a a risk premium;
    b adverse selection;
    c a moral hazard;
    d diversification;
    e insurance.

Completion

1 The return received for giving up current consumption in exchange for increased future consumption is called the _____.

2 The _____ of a dollar to be received in the future shows how much that future dollar is worth today.

3 The formula used to calculate the present value of $1 next year is _____.

4 When the interest rate rises, the present discounted value of future income _____.

5 The interest rate is the price in the market for _____.

6 A savings account that pays 10 percent compounded daily will return _____ to the saver than another savings account that pays 10 percent compounded monthly.

7 The interest rate that indicates how much consumption tomorrow must be forgone for extra consumption today is the _____ interest rate.

8 The real interest rate is the nominal interest rate minus the _____.

9 Current prices of assets, such as land, depend upon _____ about their future prices.

10 The fact that insured individuals have less incentive to take precaution against accident is called _____.

Answers to Self-Test

True or False

1	t	6	t	11	t
2	t	7	f	12	t
3	f	8	f	13	t
4	t	9	f	14	t
5	t	10	t	15	t

Multiple Choice

1	b	11	e
2	b	12	d
3	c	13	a
4	c	14	b
5	d	15	e
6	c	16	c
7	c	17	b
8	a	18	c
9	d	19	d
10	c	20	a

Completion

1 interest rate
2 present value
3 $1/(1 + \text{interest rate})$
4 falls
5 loanable funds
6 more
7 real
8 inflation rate
9 expectations
10 moral hazard

Doing Economics: Tools and Practice Problems

Payments to be received in the future are not worth as much as payments received today. This statement reflects the time value of money. Decisions involving present and future costs and returns require a consistent standard for comparison. This standard is present discounted value, and it is illustrated in Tool Kit 6.1.

Tool Kit 6.1: Calculating the Present Discounted Value

To compare the worth of present and future payments, it is necessary to compute the present discounted value, which is the current dollar equivalent of an amount to be rendered in the future. Follow the steps.

Step one: Make a table with four columns, and label them as shown.

Year	Amount	Discount factor	Present discounted value

Step two: For every payment or receipt, enter the year and the amount. Let Y_1 be the amount in the first year, Y_2 the amount the second year, and so on.

Year	Amount	Discount factor	Present discounted value
1	Y_1		
2	Y_2		

Step three: Calculate the discount factor for each year. The formula is $1/(1 + r)^n$, where r is the interest rate and n is the number of years until the payment or receipt. Enter these discount factors in the table.

Year	Amount	Discount factor	Present discounted value
1	Y_1	$1/(1 + r)$	
2	Y_2	$1/(1 + r)^2$	

Step four: Multiply the number in the amount column by the corresponding discount factor. Enter the product in the present discounted value column.

Year	Amount	Discount factor	Present discounted value
1	Y_1	$1/(1 + r)$	$Y_1 \times 1/(1 + r)$
2	Y_2	$1/(1 + r)^2$	$Y_2 \times 1/(1 + r)^2$

Step five: Add the numbers in the right-hand column. The sum is the present discounted value.

Year	Amount	Discount factor	Present discounted value
1	Y_1	$1/(1 + r)$	$Y_1 \times 1/(1 + r)$
2	Y_2	$1/(1 + r)^2$	$Y_2 \times 1/(1 + r)^2$

Present discounted value $= Y_1 \times 1/(1 + r) + Y_2 \times 1/(1 + r)^2$

---

1 (Worked problem: present discounted value) Ethel has two years before retirement from a career of teaching unruly high school delinquents. Her salary is $40,000, paid at the end of each year. The school board has offered her $70,000 now to retire early. The relevant interest rate is 7 percent. In monetary terms alone, is working worth more than retiring?

Step-by-step solution

First, calculate the present discounted value of continuing to work.

Step one: Make a table with four columns, and label them as shown.

Year	Amount	Discount factor	Present discounted value

Step two: For every payment or receipt, enter the year and the amount. Ethel receives $40,000 each year for two years.

Year	Amount	Discount factor	Present discounted value
1	$40,000		
2	$40,000		

Step three: Calculate the discount factor for each year. For the first year, the discount factor is $1/(1 + .07) = 0.93$, and for the second year it is $1/(1 + .07)^2 = 0.86$. Enter these discount factors in the table.

Year	Amount	Discount factor	Present discounted value
1	$40,000	0.93	
2	$40,000	0.86	

Step four: Multiply the number in the amount column by the corresponding discount factor. Enter the product in the present discounted value column.

Year	Amount	Discount factor	Present discounted value
1	$40,000	0.93	$37,380
2	$40,000	0.86	$34,400

Step five: Add the numbers in the right-hand column. The sum is the present discounted value.

Year	Amount	Discount factor	Present discounted value
1	$40,000	0.93	$37,380
2	$40,000	0.86	$34,400

Present discounted value = $71,780.

Next, compare the lump-sum payment with the present discounted value of continuing to work. Ethel can postpone retirement and increase the present discounted value of her earnings by only $1,780. The reason that the gain is so little is that earnings come in the future and must be discounted, while the retirement bonus is paid now.

2 (Practice problem: present discounted value) The Transportation Department is considering the bids of two paving companies for repaving South Street. The Do-It-Rite firm will do the job for $200,000, and they will guarantee that their new process will make the road free of potholes for 3 years. The Let-It-Go company only charges $100,000, but estimated pothole repair costs are $40,000 each year. The interest rate is 8 percent.

  a Calculate the present discounted value of the entire cost with the Let-It-Go firm.
  b Which is the least expensive bid?

3 (Practice problem: present discounted value) Calculate the present discounted value of each of the following.

  a Interest rate equals 10 percent.

Year	Amount	Discount factor	Present discounted value
1	$10,000		
2	$15,000		

  b Interest rate equals 5 percent.

Year	Amount	Discount factor	Present discounted value
1	$ 0		
2	$20,000		

  c Interest rate equals 15 percent.

Year	Amount	Discount factor	Present discounted value
1	$5,000		
2	$5,000		
3	$5,000		

  d Interest rate equals 5 percent.

Year	Amount	Discount factor	Present discounted value
1	$ 5,000		
2	$ 0		
3	$25,000		

EXPECTED VALUE AND THE RISK PREMIUM

Markets provide incentives to take or accept risks. These incentives include the risk premium, which is the extra payment offered to one who accepts a certain risk. The ultimate consequence of the risky alternative is unknown, of course, so it is measured using the concept of expected value. Risk premiums appear in many settings, including insurance, investment, and risky employment. Tool Kit 6.2 shows how to calculate the risk premium.

Tool Kit 6.2: Calculating Expected Value and the Risk Premium

The risk premium is the extra payment that markets offer for accepting risk. It is calculated using expected value. Follow these three steps.

Step one: Identify the safe and risky alternative and also the amounts and probabilities of gain or loss.

Step two: Calculate the expected value of the risky alternative. Use the formula for expected value.

Expected value = (probability of bad event)
  (payments if bad event occurs)
  + (probability of good event)
  (payments if good event occurs).

Step three: Subtract the value of the safe alternative from the expected value of the risky alternative (calculated in step two). The difference is the risk premium.

Expected value of the risky alternative
  − value of the safe alternative =
  risk premium.

---

4   (Worked problem: risk premium) Municipal Money Managers is a small firm that provides short-term money management to municipalities and depends upon the knowledge and personal reputation of its founder. Should he die or be forced to retire for health reasons, the value of the business would fall by $200,000. The probability of this happening is 0.01. An insurance policy is available for $2,500. This policy would compensate the business in the event of the loss of the founder.

a   Point out the safe and risky alternatives.
b   What is the expected loss?
c   How much is the risk premium?

Step-by-step solution

Step one: Identify the safe and risk alternatives. Buying the insurance is the safe alternative. Bearing the risk of the loss of the founder is the risky one.

Step two: Calculate the expected value (EV) of the risky alternative.

$$EV = 0.01(-\$200,000) + 0.99(0) = -\$2,000.$$

Step three: Subtract the value of the safe from the expected value of the risky alternative. The insurance policy costs $2,500.

$$\text{Risk premium} = -\$2,000 - (\$-2,500) = \$500.$$

5   (Practice problem: risk premium) Barbara is considering leaving her safe job in state govenment to strike out on her own as a consultant. She currently earns $40,000 and estimates that the consultant business will pay $75,000 if she wins an important contract but nothing otherwise. Her best guess is that the probability of her winning the contract is 2/3.

a   Point out the safe and risky alternatives.
b   What is the expected value of the consulting business?
c   How much is the risk premium?

6   (Practice problem: risk premium) If Kim keeps her retirement savings in safe assets she expects to have $250,000 at retirement. Her brother-in-law advises that she move into derivatives. Her financial advisor points out that following the advice of the brother-in-law might result in $600,000 at retirement. Losing it all is another possibility. The probability of each is 1/2.

a   Point out the safe and risky alternatives.
b   What is the expected loss?
c   How much is the risk premium?

Answers to Problems

2   a

Firm	Cost
Do-It-Rite	$200,000
Let-It-Go	$100,000 + $\dfrac{\$40,000}{1.08}$ +

$$\frac{\$40,000}{(1.08)^2} + \frac{\$40,000}{(1.08)^3} =$$

$203,083.

b   The Do-It-Rite bid.

3   a $21,488.
    b $18,141.
    c $12,447.
    d $26,358.

5   a   Safe alternative = state government; risky alternative = consultant.
    b $75,000 × 2/3 + $0 × 1/3 = $50,000.
    c $50,000 – $40,000 = $10,000.

6   a   Safe alternative = safe assets; risky alternative = derivatives.
    b $600,000 × 1/2 + $0 × 1/2 = $300,000.
    c $300,000 – $250,000 = $50,000.

Chapter 7

THE PUBLIC SECTOR

Chapter Review

The text's focus so far has been on private markets. This is overly simple, as the history of the automobile given in Chapter 1 illustrates. While the American automobile industry consists of private firms, government has played a large role throughout the industry's history, from issuing patents and regulating safety and environmental standards to occasionally protecting domestic manufacturers from foreign competition and providing unemployment benefits to laid-off workers. This blend of the public and private sectors is called a mixed economy.

This chapter considers the economic role of the public sector and how it operates differently from the private sector. Important roles for the public sector include improving the market's allocation of resources, stabilizing the overall performance of the economy, and redistributing income. The chapter also discusses government policies and emphasizes that government action may not always succeed in correcting market failures.

ESSENTIAL CONCEPTS

1   For the most part, the economic system relies on private markets to allocate resources, but government has al-
ways played a major role. The balance between public and private sectors has changed over the years as government has taken on new responsibilities to improve perceived failures in the private economy. Government differs from private institutions in that its decisions are made by elected representatives or their appointed officers, and government has the power to force compliance with some of its orders.

2   Economists see roles for government in redistributing income and correcting market failures. These include stabilizing the economy's fluctuations, enhancing competition, and improving the performance of the economy where there are externalities, public goods, missing markets, or information problems. Government also intervenes to discourage or prohibit certain actions, overriding the principle of consumer sovereignty.

3   The **public sector** has a variety of instruments with which to accomplish its goals. It can take direct action, either producing the good or service itself or purchasing it from private firms. It can mandate private sector action, regulate private activity, or ban certain behaviors altogether. Finally, with a somewhat lighter hand, the government can provide incentives to increase or decrease certain types of actions through the use of its tax and subsidy powers.

4 While market failures imply that there is potential for improvement, government programs carry with them additional problems. Imperfect information, poor incentives for government administrators, waste, and the failure to foresee all of the consequences of government actions can cause public failures.

BEHIND THE ESSENTIAL CONCEPTS

1 **Externalities** exist whenever individuals or firms do not face the full costs and benefits of their decisions, and left alone, externalities create incentive problems. Negative externalities are costs borne by others, such as pollution, congestion, and noise. Positive externalities are benefits received by others, such as contributions for medical and other research, innovation, public parks, and endangered species preservation. Because decision makers can ignore the costs that spill over onto others, private firms overproduce negative externalities. Similarly, because they are not compensated, producers of positive externalities do not create enough. Governments can improve the allocation of resources by inducing individuals to produce fewer negative and more positive externalities.

2 **Public goods** have two important characteristics. Once they are provided, the marginal cost of another consumer's enjoying the good is zero. For example, a second, third, or fourth person can view a public statue without affecting the first person's enjoyment. The second characteristic is that it is costly to exclude individuals from enjoying the public good. Placing the statue in a private viewing area and charging admission misses the point of a monument. This feature makes it difficult for private individuals to collect enough funds to provide public goods. The fact that people can choose to enjoy public goods without paying for them is called the **free-rider** problem, and it is one reason economists often recommend that the public sector take a role in providing public goods.

3 When the private market fails to allocate resources efficiently, there is a potential role for government action. For example, when a public good such as a traffic light is needed, the government is the natural choice to provide it. When negative externalities are present, such as pollution, the government may be able to discourage them. The income distribution produced by private markets may be unacceptable, and the government may be able to redistribute it. Governments are large organizations, however, and policies do not always work as intended.

4 The existence of market failures prompts the call for more government intervention. **Government failures** justify calls for less intervention. Often what is needed is different, better government action, which harnesses market incentives to bring about a better allocation of resources.

SELF-TEST

True or False

1 The American economic system relies primarily on private markets.

2 Government's role in the economy has remained essentially unchanged since the early 1900s.

3 Services, such as police and fire protection, education, and parks, are provided mostly by state and local governments.

4 Adam Smith's "invisible hand" refers to the role of government in correcting market failures.

5 Government action is distinguished from private sector action in that government always has better information.

6 While markets often are efficient producers of wealth, they do not necessarily distribute that wealth equally.

7 Externalities are present whenever an individual or a firm can take an action without bearing all the costs and benefits.

8 The marginal cost of an additional consumer is zero for a public good.

9 The marginal cost of production is zero for a public good.

10 It is very costly to exclude those who do not pay from consuming private goods.

11 Markets for new inventions fail if those who benefit from new inventions do not pay the inventor.

12 The free-rider problem implies that private markets may not provide public goods efficiently.

13 If the private market provides too little of some good or service, then government can increase the quantity provided by subsidizing the good or service.

14 Even though markets may fail to allocate resources efficiently, government action may make matters worse.

15 Civil service rules and political pressures create incentive problems that may lead to public failures.

Multiple Choice

1 Which of the following is not one of the four basic questions an economy must answer?

a What is produced, and in what quantities?
b How are goods and services produced?
c For whom are the goods and services produced?
d Who makes the decisions?
e All of the above are basic questions.

2 Private institutions, such as business firms and not-for-profit organizations, are distinguished from government in that

a private decision makers are rational;
b government decision makers have adaptive expectations;

c   government decision makers are elected or appointed by someone who is elected;

d   government has certain powers of coercion;

e   c and d.

3   In his book *The Wealth of Nations,* Adam Smith argued that the public interest is best promoted by

a   government control of the economy;

b   the benevolence of well-meaning citizens;

c   individuals pursuing their own self-interest;

d   adherence to time-honored traditions;

e   all of the above.

4   Which of the following is not a legitimate role of government?

a   solving the problem of scarcity;   *— can never solved*

b   redistributing income;

c   stabilizing the level of economic activity;

d   correcting market failures.

e   All of the above are legitimate roles.

5   Which of the following is an example of market failure?

a   Housing is expensive.

b   The poor often cannot afford adequate health care.

c   The ostentatious displays of wealth by the rich and famous are offensive.

d   Periodic episodes of high unemployment trouble market economies.

e   All of the above.

— Market failure stabilization of Economy

6   The right to seize private property (with proper compensation) for public use is called

a   diminishing returns;

b   taxation;

c   deregulation;

d   nationalization;

e   eminent domain.

7   Which of the following is not an example of an externality?

a   environmental pollution;

b   research and development;

c   restoring buildings in decaying areas;

d   contributions to philanthropic organizations.

e   All of the above are examples of externalities.

8   When farmers irrigate their crops with water provided by the government at subsidized prices, there is

a   an externality;

b   a public good;

c   a market;

d   a patent;

e   none of the above.

9   Which of the following is (are) true of pure public goods?

a   The marginal cost of an additional individual using the good is zero.

b   It is impossible to exclude people from receiving the good.

c   They are efficiently provided through the interaction of supply and demand.

d   a and b.

e   All of the above.

10   Private markets have difficulty supplying public goods because

a   of the free-rider problem;

b   of the federal system of government;

c   the level of private activity fluctuates;

d   the income distribution is inequitable;

e   all markets are efficient.

11   One advantage that government has in the provision of public goods is that it

a   is not subject to scarcity;

b   does not face uncertainty about the demand for public goods;

c   can coerce citizens to pay for them;

d   need not always be rational;

e   none of the above.

12   The free-rider problem refers to

a   the idea that public transportation always runs large deficits;

b   the idea that when people can enjoy a public good without paying for it, they often do not contribute;

c   the idea that markets fail to allocate resources efficiently when there are externalities;

d   the idea that the marginal cost of an additional consumer enjoying a pure public good is zero;

e   none of the above.

13   Which of the following is not an example of direct government action to correct market failure?

a   A country nationalizes its banking system.

b   Tax breaks are offered for exploring for new deposits of oil.

c   A large city builds shelters for the homeless.

d   The army purchases tanks from a private firm.

e   All of the above are examples of direct action.

14   Which of the following is not an example of mandating private sector action?

a   Tuna fishers are required to use nets with larger openings so that captured dolphins may escape.

b   Electric utilities are required to install scrubbing devices in smokestacks.

c   Trucking firms are required to pay vehicle use fees.

d   a and b.

e   All of the above.

doesn't make sense

15   Consumer sovereignty means that

a   individuals are the best judges of what is in their own interest;

b   there is no role for government in product-safety regulations;

c   consumers always have good information;

d   consumers are rational decision makers;

e   a and c.

16   Which of the following is not a reason for government failure?

a imperfect information;
b government waste;
c incentives of public administrators;
d missing markets. — *Market Failures*
e All of the above are reasons for government failure.

17 Which of the following is not a reason for market failure?

a externalities;
b public goods;
c missing markets;
d lack of competition.
e All of the above are reasons for market failure.

18 Private markets may not provide information efficiently because

a information is scarce;
b information is costly to produce;
c certain types of information are public goods;
d the principle of consumer sovereignty does not apply to information;.
e private markets cannot exercise eminent domain.

19 Market failure occurs when

a there are positive externalities;
b there are negative externalities;
c there are positive or negative externalities;
d there are no externalities;.
e none of the above.

20 Government can provide incentives to produce more of some good by

a taxing it;
b subsidizing it; ← *farmers*
c banning its production;
d redistributing it;
e using the "invisible hand."

Completion

1 The failure of private markets to produce economic efficiency is called *Market Failure*

2 When an individual or firm can take an action without bearing the full costs and benefits, there is said to be an *externality*

3 Goods for which it costs nothing extra to have an additional individual enjoy are called *public goods*

4 Because it is difficult to exclude those who do not pay from benefiting from public goods, the private markets do a poor job of providing public goods. This is the *free ride* problem.

5 If the government seeks to encourage some activity, such as recycling, it can *subsidize* the activity.

6 Government's ability to seize private property for legitimate public purpose is called *eminent domain*

7 When resources are idle, the economy is operating *below* *inside* its production possibilities curve.

8 Three legitimate economic roles of government are to redistribute income, stabilize the economy, and *provides social insurance*

9 During the late 1970s and early 1980s, many regulations were reduced or eliminated in transportation, telecommunications, and banking. This process is an example of *deregulation*

10 Three instruments of government for economic purposes are taking direct action, mandating private action, and providing *incentive* to the private sector through taxes and subsidies.

Answers to Self-Test

True or False

1	t	4	f	7	t	10	f	13	t
2	f	5	f	8	t	11	t	14	t
3	t	6	t	9	f	12	t	15	t

Multiple Choice

1	e	6	e	11	c	16	d
2	e	7	e	12	b	17	e
3	c	8	a	13	b	18	c
4	a	9	d	14	c	19	c
5	d	10	a	15	a	20	b

Completion

1 market failure
2 externality
3 public goods
4 free-rider
5 subsidize
6 eminent domain
7 inside
8 reallocate resources
9 deregulation
10 incentives

Doing Economics: Tools and Practice Problems

When an activity causes positive externalities, or external benefits, the government can often improve matters through subsidies. This section explores two questions. First, how do subsidies encourage more of the subsidized activity? Our analysis will be very much like the treatment of the economic effects of taxation in Chapter 5. The other issue is why decisions are likely to be inefficient when there are externalities. This is an application of the technique of balancing marginal benefits and marginal costs introduced in Chapter 2.

SUBSIDIES

Many goods and services receive subsidies from various levels of government. Sometimes, as in the case of home ownership, the demanders benefit directly. In other cases, as with federal water projects, the subsidies are paid directly to the suppliers. Subsidies have their effects by shifting supply or demand curves, bringing about new equilibrium quantities. Tool Kit 7.1 shows how to analyze the impacts of subsidies.

Tool Kit 7.1: Using Supply and Demand to Determine the Effects of Subsidies

If subsidies are paid directly to demanders, the demand curve shifts. If paid directly to suppliers, subsidies shift the supply curve. The remainder of the analysis parallels the basic method of supply and demand. Follow these steps.

Step one: Start with a no-subsidy equilibrium in the appropriate market.

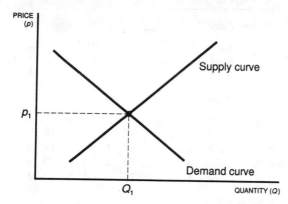

Step two: Identify the magnitude of the subsidy and whether it is paid directly to the demanders or suppliers.

Step three: If the subsidy is paid to demanders, shift the demand curve up (vertically) by exactly the amount of the subsidy. If the subsidy is paid to suppliers, shift the supply curve down by exactly the amount of the subsidy.

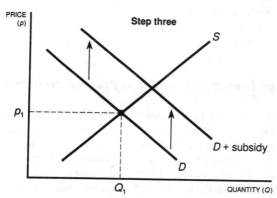

Step four: Find the new equilibrium and compare it with the original equilibrium.

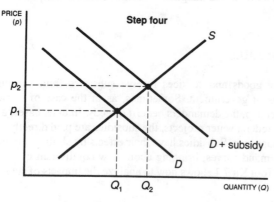

1 (Worked problem: effects of subsidies) Home ownership is treated very favorably by the U.S. tax system. The interest paid on mortgages is tax deductible, and the taxes on capital gains earned by selling at more than the purchase price can be deferred and even avoided altogether. To see how the subsidy affects the housing market, consider the market for three-bedroom bungalows in Little Spoon. The market demand and supply curves without the subsidy are given in Table 7.1.

Table 7.1

Demand		Supply	
Price	Quantity	Price	Quantity
$125,000	10	$125,000	50
$100,000	14	$100,000	42
$ 90,000	25	$ 90,000	31
$ 80,000	28	$ 80,000	28
$ 70,000	31	$ 70,000	20

a   Find the equilibrium price and quantity.
b   The tax advantages accruing to the home owner amount to $20,000 over the life of the occupancy. Calculate the demand curve with the subsidy included.
c   Find the equilibrium price and quantity with the subsidy in place. How does the subsidy change the number of bungalows sold in Little Spoon?

Step-by-step solution

Step one (a): Start with a no-subsidy equilibrium in the appropriate market. The price is $80,000; the market clears with 28 houses sold. This is the answer to part a.

Step two (b): Identify the magnitude of the subsidy and whether it is paid directly to the demanders or suppliers. The subsidy is $20,000, paid to demanders.

Step three: Because it is paid to demanders, the subsidy causes the demand curve to shift vertically by $20,000. To calculate this, add $20,000 to each entry in the price column of the demand curve. The new demand curve is given in Table 7.2, which is the answer to part b.

Table 7.2

Demand	
Price	Quantity
$145,000	10
$120,000	14
$110,000	25
$100,000	28
$ 90,000	31

Step four (c): Find the new equilibrium and compare it with the original equilibrium. The new equilibrium price is $90,000, and the market clears at 31 houses sold. The subsidy has increased the number of home owners in Little Spoon from 28 to 31. The price is $10,000 higher, so the $20,000 subsidy makes home owners only $10,000 better off. Producers share in the benefits with a $10,000 higher price. The solution is illustrated in the diagram.

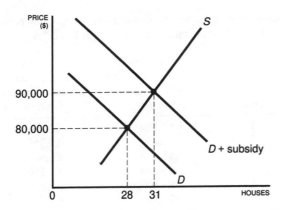

2 (Practice problem: effects of subsidies) Her eyes brightening at the thought of thousands of stressed, child-raising voters, Senator Shill has proposed child care grants of $10,000 per family. The demand and supply curves for child care services (measured in days) are given in Table 7.3.

Table 7.3

Demand		Supply	
Price (thousands)	Quantity (days)	Price (thousands)	Quantity (days)
$50	50,000	$50	100,000
$45	60,000	$45	80,000
$40	70,000	$40	70,000
$35	80,000	$35	60,000
$30	100,000	$30	50,000

a Find the equilibrium price and quantity without the subsidy.

b Calculate the demand with the subsidy.

c Find the equilibrium price and quantity with the subsidy. Compare the equilibria, and explain the effects of the subsidy.

3 (Practice problem: effects of subsidies) To promote conversion to renewable sources of energy, the government has offered various tax deductions and credits for the purchase and installation of solar water heaters. The value to a typical taxpayer of the tax provisions is $3,000. The supply and demand curves for solar water heaters are given in Table 7.4.

Table 7.4

Demand		Supply	
Price	Quantity	Price	Quantity
$8,000	1,000	$8,000	10,000
$7,000	3,000	$7,000	9,000
$6,000	5,000	$6,000	8,000
$5,000	7,000	$5,000	7,000
$4,000	9,000	$4,000	6,000
$3,000	11,000	$3,000	5,000

a Find the equilibrium price and quantity without the subsidy.

b Calculate the demand with the subsidy.

c Find the equilibrium price and quantity with the subsidy. Compare the equilibria, and explain the effects of the subsidy.

POSITIVE EXTERNALITIES

Individuals make decisions by balancing their private benefits and costs at the margin, but efficiency requires that all benefits and costs, not only the private ones, be included in the decision. Thus, when there are externalities, there are costs or benefits ignored by the individual making the decision, and this fact leads to inefficient decisions. This tool kit focuses on positive externalities and the inefficiencies that result.

Tool Kit 7.2: Showing How Positive Externalities Lead to Inefficiencies

Positive externalities occur when decision makers ignore some benefits of their actions. Follow these steps to see how this leads to inefficient decisions.

Step one: Find the private marginal benefits and costs of the relevant activity.

Step two: Find the equilibrium level of the activity, which is the level at which private marginal benefits equal marginal cost.

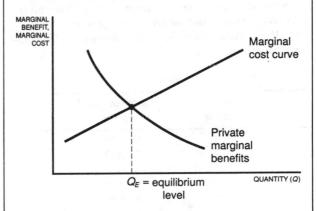

Step three: Calculate the social marginal benefits by adding the external benefit to the private marginal benefit at each level of the activity.

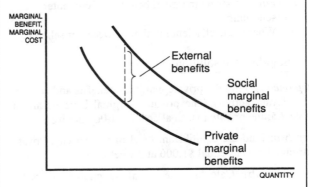

Step four: Find the efficient level of the activity, which is the level at which social marginal benefits equal marginal cost.

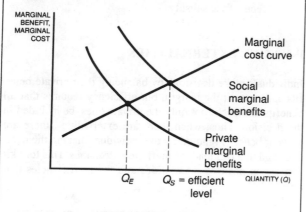

Step five: Compare the equilibrium and efficient levels of the activity.

4 (Worked problem: positive externalities) An important example of an activity that generates positive externalities is worker training. When firms train their employees, the employees not only become more productive in the job, they can also earn higher wages elsewhere. This increase in earning power is a positive externality. The QXV Corporation is considering sending some of its white-collar employees to computer school. The cost is $1,000 per week, and the private marginal benefits to QXV are given in Table 7.5. Also, the value of the external benefit is $500 per week.

Table 7.5

Weeks at school	Private marginal benefits
1	$1,500
2	$1,250
3	$1,000
4	$ 750
5	$ 500
6	$ 250

a How many weeks of computer schooling will the company provide?
b Find the social marginal benefits of computer schooling.
c What is the efficient number of weeks of schooling?

Step-by-step solution

Step one (a): Find the private marginal benefits and costs of the relevant activity. The private marginal benefits are in Table 7.5; the private marginal cost is $1,000 per week.

Step two: Find the equilibrium level of the activity. Private marginal benefits equal $1,000 at 3 weeks.

Step three (b): Calculate the social marginal benefits by

adding the external benefit to the private marginal benefit at each level of the activity. The answer is in Table 7.6.

Table 7.6

Weeks at school	Private marginal benefits	Social marginal benefits
1	$1,500	$2,000
2	$1,250	$1,750
3	$1,000	$1,500
4	$ 750	$1,250
5	$ 500	$1,000
6	$ 250	$ 750

Step four (c): Find the efficient level of the activity. Social marginal benefits equal marginal cost at 5 weeks.

Step five: Compare the equilibrium and efficient levels of the activity. The equilibrium number of weeks is 3, which is less than the efficient number, which is 5. The number of weeks provided is too low because the firm ignores the externality.

5 (Practice problem: positive externalities) ZZZX Pharmaceuticals is considering how many scientists to put to work researching a new drug for Angolan flu. Each scientist, complete with equipment and assistance, costs $200,000. The research will bring profits to ZZZX, but it will also bring about advances in viral research that other companies may build on in their own research. The private benefits are given in Table 7.7. The external marginal benefits are $150,000.

Table 7.7

Scientists	Private benefits
1	$400,000
2	$600,000
3	$700,000
4	$750,000
5	$750,000

a How many scientists will the company use? (Hint: First find the private marginal benefits.)
b Find the social marginal benefits of research scientists.
c What is the efficient number of scientists?

6 (Practice problem: positive externalities) Hillside County farmers have been advised to erect earthen dikes for erosion control. Each dike costs $2,000. The private marginal benefits are given in the second column of Table 7.8, but they do not include the external benefit that one farmer's erosion control efforts provide to her neighbors. The external benefits appear in the third column of the table.

Table 7.8

Dikes	Private marginal benefits	External marginal benefits
1	$3,000	$8,000
2	$2,000	$7,000
3	$1,500	$6,000
4	$1,000	$5,000
5	$ 500	$4,000
6	$ 0	$3,000
7	$ 0	$2,000

a How many dikes will each farmer erect?
b Find the social marginal benefits of a farmer's dikes.
c What is the efficient number of dikes?

Answers to Problems

2 a Price = $40; quantity = 70,000.
   b The new demand curve is given in Table 7.9.

Table 7.9

Demand	
Price	Quantity
$60	50,000
$55	60,000
$50	70,000
$45	80,000
$40	100,000

c The new equilibrium price is $45,000, and the quantity is 80,000. The subsidy increases the quantity from 70,000 to 80,000. Consumers are better off by $5,000 ($10,000 subsidy – $5,000 increase in price), and firms are better off by $5,000, which is the increase in price.

3 a Price = $5,000; quantity = 7,000.
   b The new demand curve is given in Table 7.10.

Table 7.10

Demand	
Price	Quantity
$11,000	1,000
$10,000	3,000
$ 9,000	5,000
$ 8,000	7,000
$ 7,000	9,000
$ 6,000	11,000

c The new equilibrium price is $7,000, and the quantity is 9,000. The subsidy increases the quantity from 7,000 to 9,000. Consumers are better off by $1,000 ($3,000 subsidy – $2,000 increase in price), and firms are better off by $2,000, which is the increase in price.

5 a 2 scientists.
   b The social marginal benefits are given in Table 7.11.

Table 7.11

Scientists	Private benefits	Private marginal benefits	Social marginal benefits
1	$400,000	$400,000	$550,000
2	$600,000	$200,000	$350,000
3	$700,000	$100,000	$250,000
4	$750,000	$ 50,000	$200,000
5	$750,000	$ 0	$150,000

c The efficient number is 4 scientists. The company chooses only 2 because it ignores the externality.

6 a 2 dikes.
   b The social marginal benefits are given in Table 7.12.

Table 7.12

Dikes	Private marginal benefits	External marginal benefits	Social marginal benefits
1	$3,000	$8,000	$11,000
2	$2,000	$7,000	$ 9,000
3	$1,500	$6,000	$ 7,500
4	$1,000	$5,000	$ 6,000
5	$ 500	$4,000	$ 4,500
6	$ 0	$3,000	$ 3,000
7	$ 0	$2,000	$ 2,000

c The efficient number of dikes is 7. Farmers only erect 2 because they ignore the external benefits.

Part Two

Perfect Markets

Chapter 8

THE CONSUMPTION DECISION

Chapter Review

The detailed study of microeconomics, the branch that focuses on the behavior of individuals and firms and builds up to an understanding of markets, begins in this chapter and continues throughout Parts Two and Three of the text. The basic competitive model of the private economy developed here is one you'll use throughout this course. Chapters 8–13 build on this model; exploring first the decisions individuals make—how much to consume, save, invest, and work—and then the decisions firms take—what and how much to produce and by what method. The entire model is put together in Chapter 13.

ESSENTIAL CONCEPTS

1   The consumer's decisions about how much of each good to purchase—that is, the demand for each—are made in a two-step procedure. First, the consumer finds how much can be consumed given the amount of money available. This step is the construction of the **opportunity set,** the outer edge of which is the **budget constraint.** Second, he chooses the best alternative along the budget constraint. Figure 8.1 depicts a budget constraint.

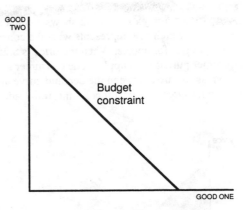

Figure 8.1

2   The budget constraint shows how much of each good can be purchased with the money available. The **slope** of the budget constraint is the **relative price** of the good measured on the horizontal axis. This relative price indicates the **trade-off:** how much of one good must be forgone to consume one more unit of the other.

3   The benefit or utility that a consumer derives from a
good is measured by how much she is willing to pay.
Consumers focus on the margin (the next unit) and continue to purchase more of the good until the *marginal
benefit equals the price.*

4   When income increases, the budget constraint shifts
out, but its slope does not change. Consumers buy more
normal goods. Goods that people buy less of as income
increases are called inferior goods, but these are the ex-
ceptions. The **income elasticity of demand** measures
how much the quantity demanded changes as income
changes. It is positive for **normal goods** and negative
for **inferior goods.**

5   When price changes, the budget constraint rotates, becoming steeper if the price of the good on the horizontal
axis rises and flatter if it falls. Introduced in Chapter 5,
the **price elasticity of demand** measures how much the
quantity demanded changes as price changes.

6   Price changes cause substitution and income effects.
Suppose the price of a good rises. Because the good is
relatively more expensive, the principle of substitution
says that consumers will shift some of their consumption to other goods. This change is the **substitution effect.** At the same time, when the price is higher, the
consumer is worse off and tends to buy less if the good
is normal but more if the good is inferior. This change is
the **income effect.**

7   **Utility** is the term economists use for the benefits that
individuals receive for consuming goods. As people
consume more of a particular good, they get smaller
increments of utility. In other words, there is **diminishing marginal utility.** When the consumer has
chosen the best bundle of goods, her utility is maximized and the marginal utility of each good equals
its price.

8   **Consumer surplus** equals the difference between what
the consumer is willing to pay for goods and the price
(what he has to pay). Figure 8.2 shows a demand curve
for apples, which also represents what the consumer is
willing to pay for apples. When the price is $.25, the
consumer purchases 8 apples. The consumer surplus,
shown as the area between the demand curve and the
price, measures the consumer's gain from trade.

Parallel

Figure 8.2

BEHIND THE ESSENTIAL CONCEPTS

1   The budget constraint shows what quantities of goods
are affordable. If you know the prices of goods and an
individual's income, you can draw her budget constraint. As you might expect, people who have the same
income and must pay the same prices have the same
budget constraint. As price changes, each individual's
budget constraint changes in the same way. The budget
constraint indicates opportunities; it says nothing about
the value that the consumer places on the goods. Individual tastes only come into the picture when the actual
choices are made.

2   The slope of the budget line depends only on prices, not
on income. Therefore, changes in income cannot change
the slope of the budget line. Changes in income bring
about a parallel shift in the budget constraint. Price
changes, on the other hand, do change the slope. The
budget constraint rotates when price changes.

3   Economists measure the responsiveness of quantity to
income or price changes by using elasticities. In this
chapter, there are two elasticities: the income elasticity
of demand and the price elasticity of demand. Elasticities are relative percentage changes. The income elasticity equals the percentage that the quantity demanded
changes when income changes by 1 percent. The price
elasticity tells the percentage change in quantity demanded as the result of a 1 percent change in price.

4   The distinction between substitution and income effects
is important, and it will reappear in the next chapter and
throughout the course. Two points are key here. First,
income effects are small in the consumption decision.
Suppose that the price of milk rises by 10 percent. If I
were spending $10 per month on milk, now I must
spend $1 more to buy the same amount of milk. This
makes me worse off by approximately $1, not a very
important change in my well-being. The income effect
captures how much extra milk can be bought with $1 of
extra income. The second point is that the relatively
more important substitution effect governs many important issues concerning the response to price changes,
such as how elastic are demand curves, whether goods
are substitutes or complements, and why taxes lead to
inefficiencies.

5   The basic economic model says that individuals balance
the benefits and costs of their decisions. It emphasizes
choice at the margin, for the next unit of a good or service. Individuals continue buying until the marginal
benefit equals the marginal cost. For the consumer, the
marginal benefit (called the marginal utility) is just how
much she is willing to pay for another unit. The marginal cost is the price. When marginal utility equals price,
the consumer has realized all the possible gains from
the purchase of the good.

6   There are two important diagrams in this chapter: the
budget constraint and the demand curve. Although each
is downward sloping, they should not be confused. The
budget constraint drawn in Figure 8.1 shows the combinations of goods that a person can afford. Quantities of

goods are measured on each axis. The demand curve drawn in Figure 8.2 shows how much of *one* good will be purchased at each price. The quantity of the good is measured on the horizontal axis, and the price is measured on the vertical.

SELF-TEST

True or False

T 1 The budget constraint indicates that the amount spent on goods cannot exceed after tax income.

T 2 The slope of the budget constraint shows the trade-off between two goods.

F 3 Income determines the slope of the budget constraint.

F 4 The amount that an individual is willing to pay for coffee is called the marginal utility of coffee.

T 5 The amount that an individual is willing to pay for an extra cup of coffee is called the marginal utility of coffee.

T 6 A rational individual will increase her consumption of a good until the marginal utility equals the price.

F 7 When income increases, the budget constraint rotates, becoming flatter.

F 8 When income increases, the consumer demands more of inferior goods.

F 9 If an individual demands more of a good when income falls, the good is a complement.

T F 10 If the income elasticity is less than zero, then the good is an inferior good.

T 11 The long-run income elasticity of demand is greater than the short-run income elasticity of demand.

T 12 If when the price of one good rises the demand for another also rises, the goods are substitutes.

F 13 If when the price of one good falls the demand for another also falls, the goods are complements. *substitutes*

T 14 When the price of a good falls, the substitution effect encourages more consumption of that good.

T 15 When the price of a normal good falls, the income effect encourages more consumption of that good.

Multiple Choice

1 Assuming that there is no saving or borrowing and a consumer's income is fixed, his budget constraint

  a defines his opportunity set;
  b indicates that total expenditures cannot be greater than total income;
  c shows that marginal utility is decreasing;
  d all of the above.
  e a and b.

2 Suppose that the price of a movie ticket is $5 and the price of a pizza is $10. The trade-off between the two goods is

  a one pizza for one movie ticket;
  b two movie tickets for one pizza;
  c two pizzas for one movie ticket;
  d $2 per movie ticket;
  e none of the above.

3 The marginal utility of a good indicates

  a that the usefulness of the good is limited;
  b the willingness to pay for an extra unit;
  c that the good is scarce;
  d that the slope of the budget constraint is the relative price;
  e none of the above.

4 Diminishing marginal utility means that

  a the usefulness of the good is limited;
  b the willingness to pay for an extra unit decreases as more of that good is consumed;
  c the good is less scarce;
  d the slope of the budget constraint is flatter as more of that good is consumed;
  e none of the above.

5 If Fred is willing to pay $100 for one espresso maker and $120 for two, then the marginal utility of the second espresso maker is

  a $20;
  b $120;
  c $100;
  d $60;
  e $50.

6 When the income of a consumer increases, her budget constraint

  a shifts outward parallel to the original budget constraint;
  b rotates and becomes steeper;
  c rotates and becomes flatter;
  d shifts inward parallel to the original budget constraint;
  e none of the above.

7 The percentage change in quantity demanded brought about by a 1 percent increase in income is

  a 1;
  b greater than zero;
  c the income elasticity of demand;
  d the price elasticity of demand;
  e none of the above.

8 If the share of income that an individual spends on a good decreases as her income increases, then the income elasticity of demand is

  a greater than 1;
  b between zero and 1;
  c zero;
  d less than 1;
  e less than zero.

9 In the long run,

  a the price elasticity of demand is greater than in the short run;

b   the income elasticity of demand is greater than in the short run;

c   the price elasticity of demand is less than in the short run;

d   the income elasticity of demand is less than in the short run;

e   a and b.

10   When the price of a good (measured along the horizontal axis) falls, the budget constraint

a   rotate, and becoming flatter;

b   rotate, and becoming steeper;

c   shifts out parallel to the original budget constraint;

d   shifts in parallel to the original budget constraint;

e   none of the above.

11   If demand for a good falls as income rises, then

a   the good is a normal good;

b   the good is an inferior good;

c   the income elasticity is less than zero;

d   the income elasticity is between zero and 1;

e   b and c.

inferior goods are less than zero

12   When the price of a good falls, the substitution effect

a   encourages the individual to consume more of the good;

b   encourages the individual to consume less of the good;

c   leads to more consumption if the good is an inferior good, but less if the good is a normal good;

d   leads to less consumption if the good is an inferior good, but more if the good is a normal good;

e   a and c.

13   When the price of a good falls, the income effect

a   encourages the individual to consume more of the good;

b   encourages the individual to consume less of the good;

c   leads to more consumption if the good is an inferior good, but less if the good is a normal good;

d   leads to less consumption if the good is an inferior good, but more if the good is a normal good;

e   a and c.

14   The rational consumer chooses her purchases for each good so that the

a   utility equals total expenditure;

b   marginal utility equals price;

c   consumer surplus equals zero;

d   marginal utility is diminishing;

e   income elasticity equals 1.

15   The difference between what the consumer is willing to pay for an item and what she has to pay is called

a   marginal utility;

b   the substitution effect;

c   consumer surplus;

d   the income effect;

e   the price elasticity of demand.

16   In general, the price elasticity of demand is greater when

a   the good is an inferior good;

b   there are good, close substitutes available;

c   there are good, close complements available;

d   the income elasticity of demand is less;

e   none of the above.

17   For normal goods, when income rises,

a   the budget constraint shifts out, parallel;

b   the demand curve shifts to the right;

c   quantity demanded increases;

d   more money is spent on the good;

e   all of the above.

18   For normal goods, as price rises,

a   the substitution effect encourages less consumption;

b   the income effect encourages less consumption;

c   the quantity demanded falls;

d   the demand for substitute goods increases;

e   all of the above.

19   For inferior goods, as price rises,

a   the substitution effect encourages less consumption;

b   the income effect encourages less consumption;

c   the income effect encourages more consumption;

d   the quantity demanded rises;

e   a and c.

20   The slope of the budget constraint depends on

a   the relative price of the goods;

b   the income of the consumer;

c   the availability of substitute goods;

d   whether the good is normal or inferior;

e   a and b.

Completion

1   The opportunity set for the consumer is defined by the _budget constraint_, which says that expenditures cannot exceed income.

2   The slope of the budget line equals the _relative price_ of the two goods.

3   The benefits of consumption are called _utility_.

4   The willingness to pay for an extra unit of some good is its _marg. utility_.

5   When income increases, the budget constraint shifts outward in a _parallel_ way.

6   The _inc. elas_ of demand measures how consumption of a good changes in response to a change in income.

7   When the price of a good changes, the budget constraint _rotates_.

8   The _price elas_ of demand measures how consumption of a good changes in response to a change in price.

9 When the price of a good falls, the ___subst.___ effect always encourages more consumption of the good.

10 The difference between what the consumer is willing to pay for an item and what she has to pay is called ___consumer surplus___.

Answers to Self-Test

True or False

1	t	4	f	7	f	10	t	13	f
2	t	5	t	8	f	11	t	14	t
3	f	6	t	9	f	12	t	15	t

Multiple Choice

1	e	6	a	11	e	16	b
2	b	7	c	12	a	17	e
3	b	8	d	13	d	18	e
4	b	9	e	14	b	19	e
5	a	10	a	15	c	20	a

Completion

1 budget constraint
2 relative price
3 utility
4 marginal utility
5 parallel
6 income elasticity
7 rotates
8 price elasticity
9 substitution
10 consumer surplus

Doing Economics: Tools and Practice Problems

The most important model in this chapter is the opportunity set for the consumer: the budget constraint. This section will first review how to construct the budget constraint and then explain how the budget constraint changes when price and income change. A somewhat more advanced topic follows, as we explore how to illustrate the substitution and income effects of price changes. Next, there are some applications: in-kind transfers and tax-subsidy schemes. Finally, we turn to marginal utility.

THE BUDGET CONSTRAINT

Because we have limited income, we must limit our purchases. The budget constraint shows what combinations of goods are affordable. Tool Kit 8.1 shows how to plot the budget constraint. After some practice problems, we study the effects of income and price changes. The basic technique is to first draw the budget constraint using the original income and price, then draw a new budget constraint using the new income and prices. Finally, we compare the old and new budget constraints.

Tool Kit 8.1: Plotting the Budget Constraint

The budget constraint shows what combinations of goods can be purchased with a limited amount of money. Constructing the budget constraint is one of the essential techniques needed in Part Two. Follow these four steps.

Step one: Draw a set of coordinate axes. Label the horizontal axis as the quantity of one good consumed and the vertical axis as the quantity of a second good consumed.

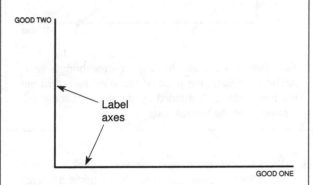

Step two: Calculate the quantity of the good measured on the horizontal axis that can be purchased if all the consumer's money is spent on it. Plot this quantity along the horizontal axis.

Step three: Calculate the quantity of the good measured on the vertical axis that can be purchased if all the consumer's money is spent on it. Plot this quantity along the vertical axis.

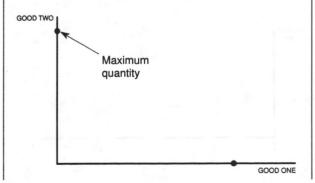

Step four: Draw a line segment connecting the two points. This line segment is the budget constraint.

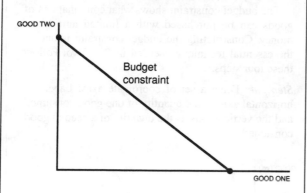

Step five: Verify that the slope of the budget constraint is (minus) the price of the good measured on the horizontal axis divided by the price of the good measured on the vertical axis.

---

1   (Worked problem: budget constraint) Dick has a budget of $500 to paint and paper the rooms in his new condominium. The price of enough paint for 1 room is $25; the price of wallpaper is $50 per room. Draw Dick's budget constraint.

Step-by-step solution

Step one: Draw a set of coordinate axes, and label the horizontal one "Rooms painted" and the vertical one "Rooms papered." (There is no rule as to which good goes on which axis. It is fine either way.)

Step two: Calculate how many rooms can be painted with the entire $500. This number is $500/$25 = 20 rooms. Plot this quantity along the horizontal axis.

Step three: Calculate how many rooms can be papered with the entire $500. This number is $500/$50 = 10 rooms. Plot this quantity along the vertical axis.

Step four: Draw a line segment connecting these two points. This line segment is the budget constraint.

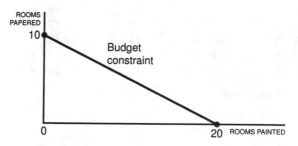

Step five: Verify the slope. The slope of the budget constraint is 10/20 = 1/2. The price ratio is $25/$50 = 1/2.

2   (Practice problem: budget constraint) Dean Lewis would like to have some of the practice pianos tuned in the charming but decaying music building. She could use some of the $1,000 in the supplies and services budget, but that money must pay for repairing broken lockers. The piano tuner charges $50 per piano, and the carpenter charges $40 per locker. Plot her budget constraint and verify that the slope is the relative price.

3   (Practice problem: budget constraint). Draw the following budget constraints.

   a   Budget for hiring groundskeepers = $100,000; price of a full-time employee = $20,000; price of a part-time employee = $8,000.
   b   Budget for food = $250; price of microwave snacks = $2.00. (Plot expenditures on all other food on the vertical axis.)
   c   Budget for landscaping = $2,000; price of lilac bushes = $50; price of cherry trees = $80.
   d   Budget for library acquisitions = $50,000; price of books = $40; price of journal subscriptions = $100.

4   (Worked problem: budget constraint with income and price changes) Bill Kutt, a somewhat diminutive and lazy student, has decided to take a course on the nineteenth-century American novel. Many books are assigned, and all are available in the abridged "Fred's Notes" versions at $8 each. The unabridged versions are $3 each. Bill has $72 to spend.

   a   Plot his budget constraint.
   b   Show how it changes when Bill finds that he has another $24 (for a total of $96).

Step-by-step solution

Step one (a): Plot Bill's budget constraint using the procedure outlined above. He can afford $72/$8 = 9 abridged and $72/$3 = 24 unabridged notes. Note that the slope is 9/24 = $3/$8, which is the ratio of the prices.

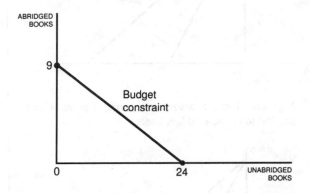

Step two (b): Plot Bill's budget constraint with $96 to spend. He can now afford $96/$8 = 12 abridged and $96/$3 = 32 unabridged notes.

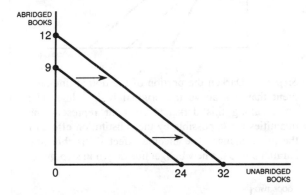

Step three: Verify that the shift in the budget constraint is parallel. The slope is 12/32 = $3/$8, which is the ratio of the prices. Because the prices have not changed, the slope has not changed. The income increase causes a parallel shift.

5   (Practice problem: budget constraint with income and price changes) Helen is nervous about graduate school. She is considering hiring a tutor for her economics course at $10 per hour. Another possibility is to attend sessions on how to improve the score of her GMAT test. These cost $30 each. She has $90.

   a   Plot her budget constraint.
   b   Oops! Unexpectedly stuck with the tab at Ernie's Ice House, Helen now has only $60 to spend. Plot her new budget constraint.

6   (Worked problem: budget constraint with income and price changes) Dissatisfied with his social life, Horatio has budgeted $400 for self-improvement. He is considering elocution lessons at $25 per hour and ballroom dancing classes at $10 each.

   a   Plot Horatio's budget constraint.
   b   Good news! A new elocution studio offers lessons at the introductory price of $20. Plot the new budget constraint.

Step-by-step solution

Step one (a): Plot the budget constraint at the $25 price. Horatio can afford $400/$25 = 16 elocution lessons or $400/$10 = 40 classes. Note that the slope is 40/16 = $25/$10, which is the ratio of the prices.

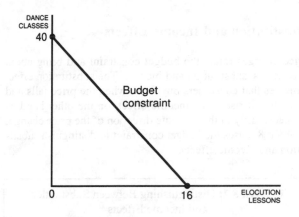

Step two (b): Plot the budget constraint at the $20 price. Horatio can now afford $400/$20 = 20 elocution lessons, which is 4 more, but he still can only buy 40 dance lessons.

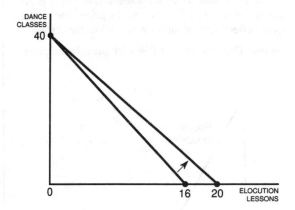

Step three: Verify that the budget constraint rotates. The slope is now 40/20 = $20/$10, which is the ratio of the new prices and is flatter. The price decrease rotated the budget constraint. The point at 0 elocution lessons and 40 dance classes does not change, because when no elocution lessons are purchased, the price change makes no difference.

7   (Practice problem: budget constraint with income and price changes) With some of her extra cash ($100 each month), Sho-Yen buys meals and blankets and donates them to the nearby shelter for the homeless. The meals cost $2 each, and she buys the blankets for $5 each.

   a   Plot her budget constraint.
   b   The supplier of meals cuts the price to $1. Plot the new budget constraint.

8   (Practice problem: budget constraint with income and price changes) For each of these problems, draw the budget constraints before and after the change. Plot "Expenditures on other goods" on the vertical axis.

   a   Income = $400; price of potatoes = $1 per sack; price of potatoes rises to $2 per sack.

   b Income = $5,000; price of therapy sessions = $100 per hour; income rises to $6,000.

   c Income = $450; price of housecleaning = $45; income falls to $225.

   d Income = $100; price of pizzas = $5; price increases to $10.

Substitution and Income Effects

Price changes rotate the budget constraint and bring about two effects, substitution and income. The substitution effect indicates that consumers buy more when the price falls and less when it rises. The income effect, on the other hand, is not necessarily in the opposite direction of the price change. Tool Kit 8.2 uses the budget constraint to distinguish substitution and income effects.

Tool Kit 8.2: Distinguishing Between Substitution and Income Effects

When the price of a good changes, there are two effects: substitution and income. These can be illustrated using the budget constraint. This technique clarifies the point that while the substitution effect is always in the opposite direction to the price change, the income effect may go either way. Follow these steps.

Step one: Draw the budget line with the original price.

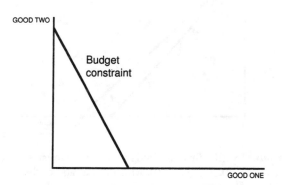

Step two: Find the chosen quantities along the budget line. Label this point *A*.

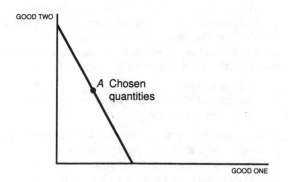

Step three: Draw the budget line with the new price.

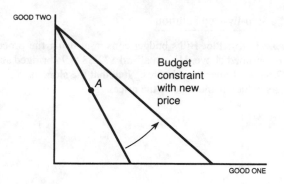

Step four: Draw a dashed line through point *A* and parallel to the *new* budget line.

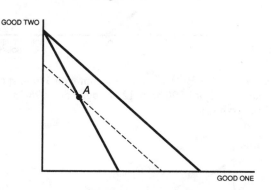

Step five: Darken the portion of the dotted-line segment that lies above the original budget line. The points along this darkened segment represent the quantities made possible by the substitution effect of the price change. The income effect shifts this line parallel out to the new budget line drawn in step three.

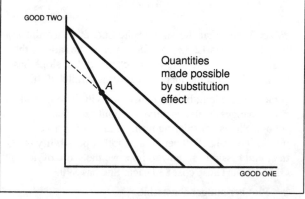

---

9   (Worked problem: substitution and income effects) Always diligent in keeping up with out-of-town friends and acquaintances, Lurleen budgets $30 per month for postage and phone calls. A long-distance call costs her $2 on average, and the price of a stamped envelope is $.30. She makes 6 calls and mails 60 letters each month.

   a Plot her budget constraint, and label the point that she has chosen.

   b Headline news! The price of a stamped envelope falls to $.20. Illustrate the substitution and income effects of the price change.

Step-by-step solution

Step one (a): Draw the original budget constraint. The maximum quantity of calls is $30/$2 = 15, and the maximum quantity of letters is $30/$.30 = 100.

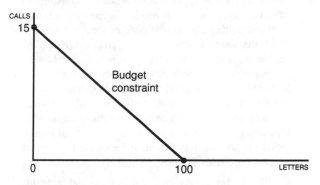

Step two: Plot and label the chosen point (6 calls, 60 letters). Note that this is on the budget constraint because (6 × $2) + (60 × $.30) = $30. Label this point *A*.

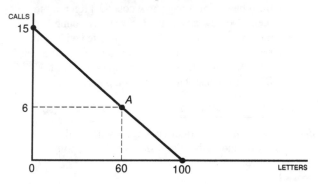

Step three (b): Draw the new budget constraint. The maximum quantities are 15 calls and 30/$.20 = 150 letters.

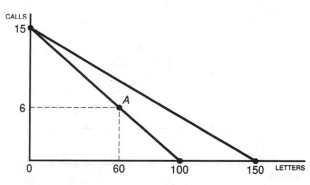

Step four: Draw a dashed line segment through *A* parallel to the new budget constraint.

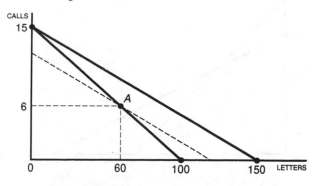

Step five: Darken the portion of the dashed line segment that lies above the original budget constraint. Notice that the substitution effect would lead Lurleen to choose a point like *B* along this segment, where the quantity of letters is greater. We say that the substitution effect of a price decrease is always to increase the quantity demanded. The income effect moves this darkened segment out to the new budget constraint. Lurleen would write more letters if letters were a normal good, but she would write fewer if letters were inferior. The income effect can go either way in principle, although most goods are normal.

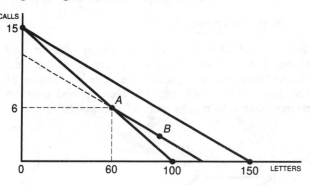

10 (Practice problem: substitution and income effects) Yves loves to wear whites for tennis. He sends his outfits to the cleaners at a price of $3.60 each. Playing tennis also requires new balls, which cost $2. Yves' tennis budget is $36 per week, which allows him his current consumption levels of 8 cans of balls and 5 clean outfits.

   a Plot his budget constraint, and show his current consumption choice.
   b The price of tennis balls has risen to $4.50. Illustrate the substitution and income effects of this price increase.

11 (Practice problem: substitution and income effects) For each of the following, illustrate the substitution and income effects of the price change. Plot "Expenditures on other goods" on the vertical axis, and pick any point on the original budget line as the quantities consumed before the price change.

   a Income = $100; price of bricks = $.10 each; price changes to $.20.
   b Income = $1,000; price of haircuts = $20; price changes to $25.
   c Income = $500; price of pies = $5; price changes to $4.
   d Income = $10; price of baseball cards = $.50; price changes to $.25

APPLICATIONS

Now that you have mastered plotting the budget constraint and analyzing how it changes when price or income changes, you are ready for some applications. The following problems look at how the budget constraint is affected by in-kind transfers, such as food stamps and tax changes. These latter problems illustrate the relationship between the substitution effect and tax distortions.

12 (Worked problem: applications) Many government programs deliver benefits in kind to people. For example, food stamps can only be used to buy food. Economists often argue that cash transfers are better. The typical food stamp recipient has $200 per week in income in addition to $80 per week in food stamps.

a   Draw the budget constraint.
b   One proposal is to substitute $80 in cash for the stamps. Draw the budget constraint that results from this proposal.
c   Which would the recipient prefer? Why?

Step-by-step solution

Step one (a): Draw the budget constraint with the food stamps. Label the axes "Food consumption in dollars" and "Expenditures on other goods." The slope is 1 because $1 less spent on other goods means $1 spent on food. Note that no more than $200 may be spent on other goods.

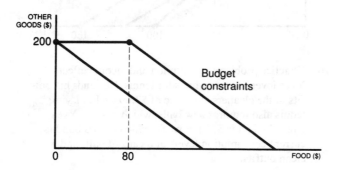

Step two (b): Draw the budget constraint with the cash grants replacing the food stamps.

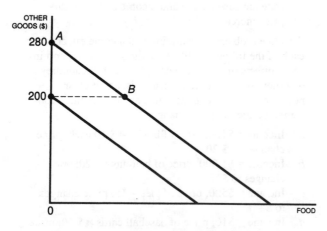

Step three (c): Compare. The difference is that the cash grant allows the recipient to choose the points between *A* and *B*. Many recipients would not choose these low levels of food consumption anyway; so there would be no difference. Some might, however, and these people would prefer the cash.

13 (Practice problem: applications) The city of Lansing, Michigan, recently planted 2 trees (worth $20 each) in every yard. The typical Lansing resident has $4,000 in disposable income this summer.

a   Plot the budget constraint with the in-kind transfer of 2 trees.

b   Plot the budget constraint with the $40 refunded through the tax system.
c   Which opportunity set is preferred? How could the tree planting be justified?

15 (Worked problem: applications) When less consumption of some good or service is needed, economists often recommend putting a tax on the good or service. One objection is that the taxes lead to higher prices, which make people worse off. If the tax revenue is refunded, however, people can be approximately as well off, yet still face higher prices for the good or service. In essence, it is possible to put the substitution effect to work and reduce consumption of the good or service without reducing the well-being of consumers very much. The city of Pleasantville is running out of room at the dump. The typical resident purchases 6 bags weekly at $.10 each.

a   Plot the budget constraint for the typical resident, and show the current consumption choice.
b   In an effort to encourage recycling and discourage disposal, the city institutes a user fee of $1.90 per trash bag. (Trash bags now cost $2.) Keeping to their "No new taxes" pledge, the city council members vote to combine the user fee with a tax refund. Each citizen receives a tax refund of $1.90 × 6 = $11.40. Plot the new budget constraint.
c   Discuss the user fee–tax refund plan.

Step-by-step solution

Step one (a): Plot the budget constraint with neither a user fee nor a tax refund. Label the resident's chosen point *A*.

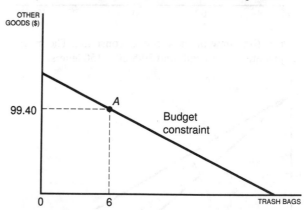

Step two (b): Plot the budget constraint with the user fee and tax refund.

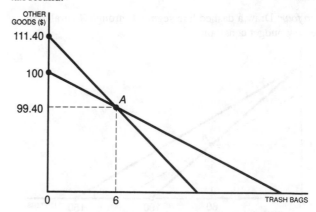

Step three (c): We see that the net effect of the entire user fee–tax refund scheme is only the substitution of the increase in the price of bags to $2. The resident is no worse off (because he can still consume as he did before the user fee), but he will be motivated to use fewer bags. (One minor flaw in the program is that as people substitute away from trash bags, they will pay less in user fees than is needed to finance the tax relief.)

16 (Practice problem: applications) Since the Gulf War, gasoline consumption has been on the mind of Senator Adam Smith. He proposes a $1-per-gallon tax on gasoline, which currently sells for $1. Assume that this tax will increase the price of gas to $2. The senator also proposes refunding the gas-tax revenues through an income tax cut large anough to allow consumers to buy the same amount of gas as before the tax.

  a Plot the budget constraint with no added gas tax.
  b Plot the budget constraint with the gas tax and the refund.
  c Columnist Kirk Jimpatrick writes, "This plan will have no effect. The government takes money away with one hand and gives it back with the other." Is he right? Why or why not?

UTILITY AND PREFERENCES

The first step in the consumption decision is to determine what is affordable—to plot the budget constraint. The second step is to choose the best bundle of goods from all those that lie along the budget constraint. Economists say that the best bundle gives the greatest utility. When the consumer has chosen the best bundle, the marginal utility (what she would be willing to pay for another unit) equals the price. Tool Kit 8.3 shows how to use marginal utility to interpret the consumption decision and also calculate consumer surplus.

Tool Kit 8.3: Using Marginal Utility to Choose the Best Bundle of Goods

The rational consumer demands the quantity of a good for which marginal equals price. The difference between what she is willing to pay and her expenditure is consumer surplus. Follow these steps to see how it works.

Step one: Identify the product price and utility (willingness to pay) for each quantity of the good.

Step two: Compute marginal utility for each quantity of the good.

　　Marginal utility = change in utility
　　　　　　　　 = utility of one fewer unit – utility.

Step three: Choose the quantity for which marginal utility equals price.

Step four: Compute her expenditure.

　　　　Expenditure = price × quantity.

Step five: Calculate consumer surplus.

　　　Consumer surplus = utility – expenditure.

---

17 (Worked problem: marginal utility) Table 8.1 gives Ching-Fan's willingness to pay (utility) for various hours of on-line access per week. On-line time is priced at $12 per hour.

  a Compute marginal utility for each hour.
  b How many hours will Ching-Fan purchase?
  c Compute his consumer surplus for this good.

Table 8.1

Number of on-line hours	Utility (willingness to pay)
0	0
1	$ 20
2	$ 38
3	$ 54
4	$ 68
5	$ 80
6	$ 90
7	$ 98
8	$104

Step-by-step solution

Step one: Identify utility for each quantity and the price. The price is $12 and utility is given in Table 8.1.

Step two: Compute marginal utility. The first unit raises utility from $0 to $20. The marginal utility is then $20 – $0 = $20. Similarly, marginal utility for the second unity equals $38 – $20 = $18. Continuing, we have the following table. Notice that marginal utility diminishes as quantity increases.

Table 8.1A

Number of on-line hours	Utility (willingness to pay)	Marginal Utility
0	0	
1	$ 20	$20
2	$ 38	$18
3	$ 54	$16
4	$ 68	$14
5	$ 80	$12
6	$ 90	$10
7	$ 98	$ 8
8	$104	$ 6

Step three: Choose the quantity for which marginal utility equals price. The price ($12) equals marginal utility when 5 hours are purchased.

Step four: Calculate expenditure. Expenditure is $12 × 5 = $60.

Step five: Calculate consumer surplus. His utility is $80 when he buys 5 hours. Consumer surplus is $80 – $60 = $20.

18 Table 8.2 gives Marneta's willingness to pay for concert tickets. The price of concerts is $20 each.

  a Compute marginal utility for ticket.
  b How many hours will Marneta purchase?
  c Compute her consumer surplus.

Table 8.2

Number of tickets	Utility (willingness to pay)
0	$ 0
1	$ 35
2	$ 65
3	$ 90
4	$110
5	$125
6	$135
7	$140

19   Table 8.3 gives Charlie's consumer surplus for tennis balls, which sell for $2 each.

a   Compute marginal utility for each can.
b   How many hours will Charlie purchase?
c   Compute his consumer surplus for this good.

Table 8.3

Number of cans of tennis balls	Utility (willingness to pay)
0	$ 0
1	$10
2	$16
3	$20
4	$22
5	$23
6	$23.50
7	$23.75

Answers to Problems

2

3

5

7

8

c

d

10

11

c   The budget constraint with the tax refund, which is shown in part b, is preferred because it allows more choices. If desired, the resident can spend as much as $4,040 on other goods, and with the in-kind transfer of trees, she can spend a maximum of $4,000 on other goods.

16

c   He is wrong. The gas tax and rebate program results in a budget constraint with more alternatives that involve less gasoline consumption. It motivates individuals to substitute other goods for gasoline.

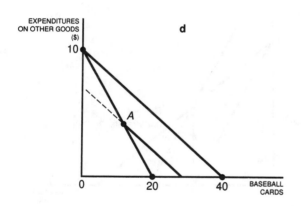

18   a

Table 8.2

Number of tickets	Utility (willingness to pay)	Marginal Utility
0	0	
1	$ 35	$35
2	$ 65	$30
3	$ 90	$25
4	$110	$20
5	$125	$15
6	$135	$10
7	$140	$ 5

13

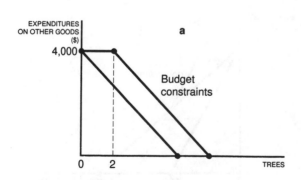

b   4.
c $110 − ($20 × 4) = $30.

19   *a*

Table 8.3

Number of cans of tennis balls	Utility (willingness to pay)	Marginal Utility
0	$ 0	
1	$10	$10
2	$16	$ 6
3	$20	$ 4
4	$22	$ 2
5	$23	$ 1
6	$23.50	$ 0.50
7	$23.75	$ 0.25

b. 4.

c. $22 − ($2 × 4) = $14.

Chapter 9

LABOR SUPPLY AND SAVINGS

Chapter Review

Chapter 8 explored the individual's decision to spend her income. This chapter continues the discussion of household decision-making. First, it examines the labor supply decision, the choice between leisure and the income needed for consumption. As with the consumption decision in Chapter 8, the individual chooses the best alternative along the budget constraint. The chapter examines how much labor time to offer, what level of education to pursue, and when to retire. Next comes the savings decision, where the trade-off pits current versus future consumption.

ESSENTIAL CONCEPTS

1   The decision to supply labor is primarily a time-allocation problem. Individuals have only so much time available, and they must divide their time between working and other activities. Any time not devoted to working and earning money, whether it is spent in recreation, sleep, chores, or errands, is called leisure. The income earned while working is available for consumption; therefore, the *trade-off* is between **leisure** and **con-**sumption, between consuming time and consuming goods.

2   The chapter focuses on the budget constraint between leisure and consumption, shown here in Figure 9.1. The slope is the wage rate, and changes in the wage rate rotate the budget constraint, causing income and substitution effects. When an individual's wage increases, leisure becomes more expensive; thus, the *substitution*

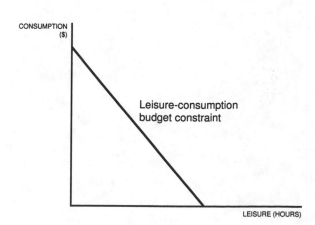

Figure 9.1

effect encourages less leisure and more work. On the other hand, the *income effect* leads the individual to want to consume more leisure, which results in less work. Because the income and substitution effects work in opposite directions, the supply curve for labor may slope upward or even bend backward.

3 There are more dimensions to labor supply than hours worked. Individuals choose whether or not to participate in the work force. They must also decide how much education and training to acquire, and when to retire. Each of these decisions can be understood as the choice of the best alternative within an appropriately specified budget constraint.

4 Government policy also affects labor supply. Taxation reduces the consumption that a given amount of labor will yield. The Social Security system affects the decision to retire through the earnings limit, by discouraging the elderly from participating in the labor force. Both the substitution and income effects of the welfare system encourage recipients to work less or not at all. Each of these policies is analyzed in terms of how it alters the leisure-consumption budget constraint.

5 According to **human capital** theory, individuals invest in education and training to acquire human capital, or skills that increase their productivity and wages. Another view is that education signals to employers which potential workers are innately more productive. This signal leads to credentials competition, the process by which people gather degrees not for any learning that takes place, but rather to show that they will be productive if hired.

6 The **savings decision** is basically a decision about *when* to consume; households choose whether to spend all of their income now, or to save it for future consumption. The **two-period budget constraint** employs the techniques we learned in Chapter 8 to show what combinations of consumption in the present and consumption in the future are affordable, given present and future incomes and the interest rate. As in Chapter 8, the slope of the budget constraint indicates the *trade-off,* and it equals the relative price. Since current consumption is measured on the horizontal axis, the slope is the **relative price of current consumption**, which is **1 plus the interest rate.**

7 When the interest rate changes, the budget constraint rotates, becoming steeper if the interest rate increases and flatter if it decreases. In exactly the same manner as Chapter 8's analysis of the consumption decision, the change in the budget constraint causes income and substitution effects. Higher interest rates make savers better off, and because current consumption is a normal good, the *income effect* makes them want to consume more today, thus reducing savings. On the other hand, higher interest rates lower the relative price of future consumption. The resulting *substitution effect* increases savings. In the decision to save, the substitution and income effects work in opposite directions.

8 There are several motives for saving. People save during their working lives to provide for retirement. This is called **life-cycle savings.** People set aside **precautionary savings** to guard against the chance of accident or illness. The **bequest motive** leads people to save for their heirs. People save to meet a particular goal, such as buying a house or starting a business. We call this motive **target savings.** Furthermore, government policies affect savings; some encourage saving, others do not. For example, Social Security benefits tend to reduce life-cycle savings because people do not feel as compelled to save for retirement. Taxes on interest lower the after-tax rate of interest and thus provide less incentive to save.

BEHIND THE ESSENTIAL CONCEPTS

1 The basic diagram for the first part of the chapter is the budget constraint for leisure and consumption. It is important to understand that this diagram is very much like the consumer's budget constraint in Chapter 8. Each shows which combinations are affordable. The slopes are the relative prices; in this case, the relative price of leisure is the wage rate. If the individual wants to consume another hour of leisure, the opportunity cost is the money that could be earned in that hour. Changes in nonwage income, such as investment returns, bring about a parallel shift in the budget constraint, but changes in the wage rate rotate it. Again, this is very similar to the Chapter 8 budget constraint.

2 Changes in the wage rate rotate the budget constraint and cause substitution and income effects. The income effect leads to more leisure (less work) when the wage rate increases. The substitution effect, on the other hand, causes less leisure (more work) when the wage rate increases. As with the savings decision, the substitution and income effects of wage changes work in opposite directions. For consumption, however, they work in the same direction. Thus, while the demand curves for goods and services are downward sloping the supply curves for savings and labor may be upward sloping or bend backward.

3 Table 9.1 may help you keep straight the substitution and income effects.

Table 9.1

If the wage rate rises,
the *substitution* effect leads to more work because leisure is more expensive.
the *income* effect leads to less work because the worker is better off and demands more leisure.
If the wage rate falls,
the *substitution* effect leads to less work because leisure is less expensive.
the *income* effect leads to more work because the worker is worse off and demands less leisure.

4 Be sure not to confuse the budget constraint with the labor supply curve. The budget constraint shows the

combinations of leisure and consumption the individual can afford given the wage rate and any nonwage income. The labor supply curve shows the quantity of labor she supplies at each wage rate. As usual, it is important to pay attention to what is measured along each axis.

5   The basic diagram in the second part of this chapter is the two-period budget constraint shown in Figure 9.2. It is important to see how similar this diagram is to the consumer's budget constraint of Chapter 8. There, the trade-off was between consuming different goods. Here, the trade-off involves consuming at different time periods. In each case, the slope is the relative price. When the relative price changes, there are substitution and income effects. Price changes rotate the budget constraint, but income changes bring about a parallel shift. This basic approach will also be used later for the labor supply decision and for other issues throughout the course.

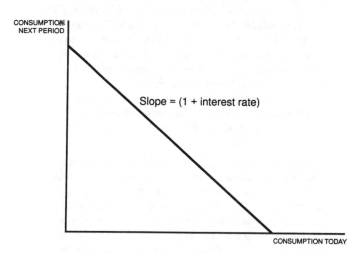

Figure 9.2

6   Think about the slope of the two-period budget constraint. If an individual desires to consume more in the future, he can save today. One dollar saved today results in (1 plus the interest rate) dollars of consumption in the future. That is, he can buy $(1 + r)$ dollars of future consumption at an opportunity cost of only 1 dollar today. Conversely, when he buys 1 more dollar of current consumption, he must give up $(1 + r)$ dollars of future consumption. The relative price of current consumption is, then, 1 plus the interest rate.

7   One plus the interest rate is also the slope of the budget constraint; therefore, only changes in the interest rate can change the slope. If the interest rate rises, the budget constraint becomes steeper. If the interest rate falls, the budget constraint becomes flatter. Income changes, either now or in the future, only shift the budget constraint in a parallel way.

8   Table 9.2 may help you keep the substitution and income effects straight.

Table 9.2

If the interest rate rises,
   the *substitution* effect leads to more savings because current consumption is relatively more expensive.
   the *income* effect leads to less savings because the saver is better off and desires to consume more today.
If the interest rate falls,
   the *substitution* effect leads to less savings because current consumption is relatively less expensive.
   the *income* effect leads to more savings because the saver is worse off and desires to consume less today

SELF-TEST

True or False

1   The percentage change in hours worked resulting from a 1 percent change in the real wage is the elasticity of supply of labor.

2   The income effect of a decrease in wages is to increase the quantity of labor supplied.

3   The substitution effect of a decrease in wages is to increase the quantity of labor supplied.

4   Investment in education is an example of human capital.

5   An increase in nonwage income rotates the budget constraint.

6   An increase in Social Security benefits will lead people, on average, to retire later.

7   The labor force participation of women has increased since World War II.

8   According to human capital theory, education increases the productivity of students, enabling them to earn more in the labor market.

9   The slope of the budget constraint equals the rate of interest.

10   As the interest rate increases, the income effect leads individuals with savings to save less.

11   As the interest rate increases, the substitution effect leads people to save less.

12   As the interest rate increases, the budget constraint shifts out in a parallel way.

13   An increase in Social Security benefits will increase national savings.

14   When the interest rate changes, the income and substitution effects work in the same direction.

15   A cut in interest taxes matters because people are concerned with the after-tax rate of interest.

Multiple Choice

1   If a person can earn $10 per hour, then the slope of the leisure-consumption budget constraint is

a   1/10;
b   10;
c   .01;
d   .10;
e   none of the above.

2   If nonwage income increases, then the budget constraint

a   rotates, becoming steeper;
b   rotates, becoming flatter;
c   shifts out parallel;
d   shifts in parallel;
e   none of the above.

3   If the wage increases, then the budget constraint

a   rotates, becoming steeper;
b   rotates, becoming flatter;
c   shifts out parallel;
d   shifts in parallel;
e   none of the above.

4   An increase in nonwage income will usually lead to

a   a decrease in the quantity of labor supplied through the substitution effect;
b   a decrease in the quantity of labor supplied through the income effect;
c   an increase in the quantity of labor supplied through the substitution effect;
d   an increase in the quantity of labor supplied through the income effect;
e   none of the above.

5   The substitution effect of a wage increase leads to

a   a decrease in the quantity of labor supply;
b   an increase in the quantity of labor supply;
c   a decrease in leisure;
d   a parallel shift in the budget constraint;
e   b and c.

6   A decrease in the marginal income tax rate will

a   cause a big increase in the quantity of labor supplied because the income effect is weaker than the substitution effect;
b   cause a big decrease in the quantity of labor supplied because the substitution effect is weaker than the income effect;
c   lead to little change in the quantity of labor supplied;
d   have no effect on the quantity of labor supplied because taxes do not affect the budget constraint;
e   none of the above.

7   Currently in the United States, the elasticity of female labor supply is

a   higher than the elasticity of male labor supply;
b   lower than the elasticity of male labor supply;
c   equal to the elasticity of male labor supply;
d   perfectly elastic;
e   irrelevant, because few women work.

8   The effective tax rate for the secondary earner in a marriage is

a   higher than for the primary earner;
b   the same as for the primary earner;
c   lower than for the primary earner;
d   irrelevant, because only one spouse works;
e   none of the above.

9   Increased lifetime wealth leads to

a   earlier retirement through the income effect;
b   later retirement through the substitution effect;
c   earlier retirement through the substitution effect;
d   later retirement through the income effect;
e   a and c.

10   Which of the following is not an example of investment in human capital?

a   formal schooling;
b   on-the-job learning;
c   technical training;
d   plant and equipment.
e   All of the above are examples.

11   The opportunity costs of attending college do not include

a   tuition expenses;
b   costs of materials and books;
c   room and board;
d   foregone earnings while attending class and studying.
e   All of the above are opportunity costs of attending college.

12   Most capital in the United States is

a   human capital;
b   credentials;
c   capital goods;
d   compensating differentials.
e   About 50 percent of the capital are goods and 50 percent human.

13   Using the budget constraint to analyze the savings decision underscores the fact that the individual is really deciding

a   when to consume;
b   what the slope of the budget constraint should be;
c   without knowing what the future will bring;
d   what the interest rate should be;
e   none of the above.

14   The slope of the intertemporal budget constraint

a   equals 1 plus the interest rate;
b   shows the trade-off between consuming now and waiting to consume;
c   indicates the relative price of current and future consumption;
d   all of the above;
e   a and b.

15   If the interest rate falls, the budget constraint

a   shifts to the left in a parallel way;
b   shifts to the right in a parallel way;
c   rotates, becoming steeper;
d   rotates, becoming flatter;
e   none of the above.

16   If the interest rate falls, the substitution effect

    a   encourages people to consume more in the future, because the relative price of future consumption is less;

    b   increases savings;

    c   decreases savings;

    d   encourages people to consume less in the future, because the relative price of current consumption is lower;

    e   c and d.

17   If the interest rate rises, the income effect for people who are saving

    a   encourages people to consume more in the future, because the relative price of future consumption is less;

    b   leads people to want to consume more both now and in the future;

    c   increases savings;

    d   decreases savings;

    e   b and d.

18   If the interest rate rises, the substitution effect increases life-cycle savings because

    a   the relative price of future consumption is higher;

    b   people are better off and want to consume more today;

    c   the budget constraint rotates, becoming flatter;

    d   people are worse off and want to consume more today;

    e   none of the above.

19   Social Security benefits are paid to retired persons

    a   from an endowment created by investing the taxes paid during their working years;

    b   out of general fund tax revenues;

    c   from Social Security taxes paid by those currently working;

    d   from revenues raised through taxing corporations;

    e   all of the above.

20   An increase in Social Security benefits will

    a   reduce national savings;

    b   increase national savings;

    c   have no effect on the national savings rate;

    d   raise savings through the income effect, but reduce savings through the substitution effect;

    e   reduce savings through the income effect, but increase savings through the substitution effect.

Completion

1   The decision concerning how much labor to supply is a choice between _____ and _____.

2   The slope of the budget line is equal to (minus) the _____.

3   When the nonwage income of an individual decreases, his labor supply _____.

4   The _____ effect of a wage decrease leads individuals to decrease their labor supply.

5   If an individual's labor supply is backward bending, then the _____ effect is stronger.

6   The labor supply of women is usually _____ elastic than the labor supply of men.

7   The relative price of consumption today and consumption tomorrow is 1 plus the _____.

8   If the interest rate increases, the budget constraint for the savings decision becomes _____.

9   The income effect of higher interest rates _____ savings.

10   The Social Security system is funded on a _____ basis, which means that benefits received by older retirees are financed through taxes paid by younger workers.

True or False

1	t	4	t	7	t	10	t	13	f
2	t	5	f	8	t	11	f	14	f
3	f	6	f	9	f	12	f	15	t

Multiple Choice

1	b	6	c	11	c	16	e		
2	c	7	a	12	a	17	e		
3	a	8	a	13	a	18	e		
4	b	9	a	14	d	19	c		
5	e	10	d	15	d	20	a		

Completion

1   leisure, consumption

2   wage

3   increases

4   substitution

5   income

6   more

7   interest rate

8   steeper

9   reduces

10   pay as you go

Doing Economics: Tools and Practice Problems

LABOR SUPPLY

The most important model in the first part of this chapter is the opportunity set for the labor supply decision: the leisure-consumption budget constraint. In this section, we first review how to construct the budget constraint. We then see how the budget constraint changes when the wage rate or nonwage income changes. As in Chapter 8, the substitution and income effects of wage changes can be illustrated using the budget constraint. Finally, there are some applications.

THE LEISURE-CONSUMPTION BUDGET CONSTRAINT

We work in order to earn money for consumption, but we give up time that could be used for leisure. Economists see the labor supply decision as involving a trade-off between leisure and consumption. The basic tool for analyzing labor supply is the budget constraint. Tool Kit 9.1 shows how to construct the leisure-consumption budget constraint.

Tool Kit 9.1: Plotting the Leisure-Consumption
Budget Constraint

The budget constraint shows what combinations of leisure and consumption can be afforded given the wage rate and the amount of nonwage income. To plot the budget constraint, follow this five-step procedure.

Step one: Draw a set of coordinate axes. Label the horizontal axis as the quantity of leisure consumed and the vertical axis as the consumption level.

Step two: If an individual chooses to do no work, leisure equals the total time available, and consumption is equal to the nonwage income. Plot this point.

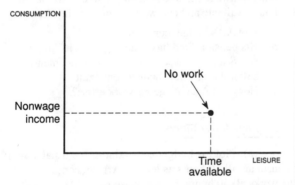

Step three: Calculate the maximum earnings if the individual consumes no leisure. Add this amount to the nonwage income, and plot this quantity along the vertical axis.

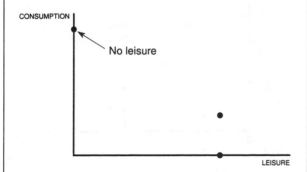

Step four: Draw a line segment connecting the two points. This line segment is the leisure-consumption budget constraint.

Step five: Verify that the slope of the budget constraint is (minus) the wage rate.

---

1   (Worked problem: leisure-consumption budget constraint) In his spare time, Mike, a student at Enormous State University, referees intramural basketball games. Each game pays $7, and if he could stand the abuse, Mike could referee as many as 60 each month. On average, each game takes 1 hour. This is not Mike's only source of income; each month his parents send him $200 for expenses.

   a   Construct Mike's budget constraint.
   b   Suppose that Mike chooses to referee 20 games. Label his chosen alternative, and indicate his total income, income from refereeing, hours worked, and leisure.

Step-by-step solution

Step one (a): Draw the two axes, and label the vertical one "Consumption" and the horizontal one "Leisure."

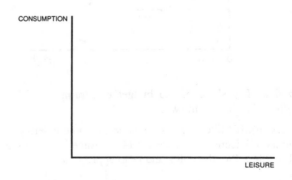

Step two: Plot the no-work consumption point. If Mike referees no games, he consumes all 60 hours as leisure. This leaves him $200 (from his parents) for consumption. Plot this point.

Step three: Calculate total income if Mike works all the time available. If he referees the maximum number of games, 60, he earns $420 from refereeing and retains the $200 from his parents. This leaves him with $620 for consumption but no time for leisure. Plot this point.

Step four: Draw a line segment between the two plotted points. This is the budget constraint.

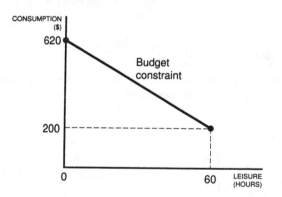

Step five: The slope of the budget constraint is (620 − 200)/60 = 7, which is the wage.

Step six (b): If Mike referees 20 games, then he is left with 40 hours of leisure, and he earns $140 in wage income for a total of $340. Plot the point, and label appropriately.

2   (Practice problem: leisure-consumption budget constraint) College professors can earn extra cash by reviewing papers for journals. Editors pay around $50 per paper for an academic opinion about whether it should be accepted for publication. Reviewing a paper takes 1 hour. Professor Cavendish has 15 hours available each month for outside work such as reviewing.

He draws $3,000 monthly from McCavendish College, and that is his only other source of income.

a   Plot Cavendish's budget constraint.
b   Suppose that the professor reviews 6 papers in March. Plot and label his chosen alternative.

3   (Practice problem: leisure-consumption budget constraint) For each of the following, draw a budget constraint. Also, choose a point along the budget constraint, and show the corresponding amount of leisure, work, nonwage income, and wage income.

	Wage	Total time	Nonwage income
a.	$25/hour	80 hours	$ 1,000
b.	$200/day	30 days	$ 0
c.	$1,000/week	50 weeks	$15,000
d.	$5/hour	100 hours	$ 0

4   (Worked problem: leisure-consumption budget constraint) When either nonwage income or the wage rate changes, the budget constraint moves. The basic technique here is to draw the budget constraint using the original nonwage income and wage rate, following the procedure shown above. Then draw a new budget constraint using the new nonwage income and wage rate. Compare the two budget constraints, and verify that the shift is parallel when nonwage income changes, but the budget constraint rotates when the wage rate changes. Art supplements his pension by repairing automatic teller machines. Each service call takes an hour, and he receives $50 per call. His pension and other nonwage income is $200 per week. Art has 30 hours available and can work as much as he likes.

a   Plot Art's budget constraint.
b   His pension fund has done well with its investments and increases Art's nonwage income to $300. Plot his new budget constraint.
c   How will Art change his work effort?

Step-by-step solution

Step one (a): Plot his budget constraint in the usual way. If he consumes all 30 hours as leisure, Art can consume $200. If he works all 30 hours, he can consume $200 + ($50 × 30) = $1,700. Note that the slope is (1,700 − 200)/30 = 50, which is the wage.

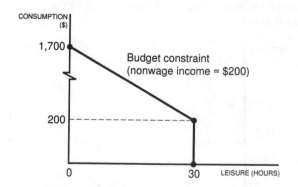

Step two (b): Plot his budget constraint with nonwage income equal to $300. His no-work consumption is now $300 + (30 × $50) = $1,800, if he works all of the available time. Note that the nonwage income increase brings about a parallel shift.

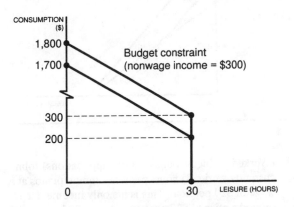

Step three (c): The change in the budget constraint is an income effect. The income effect reduces work effort when income rises. Art will work less.

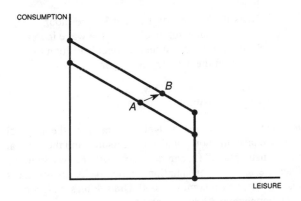

5 (Practice problem: leisure-consumption budget constraint) Liza's job as a broker requires making unsolicited, or "cold," calls to potential clients in an attempt to persuade them to put their portfolio in her hands. On average, cold calls earn Liza $10 each. She can make 4 per hour, and she can work as much as 80 hours per week. Her base salary (nonwage income) is $100 per week.

   a Plot her budget constraint.
   b Suppose that the firm offers her an increase in the base salary to $150 per week. Plot her new budget constraint.
   c Will Liza make more or fewer cold calls? Why?

6 (Practice problem: leisure-consumption budget constraint) Sara is offered a position as tour guide for a local museum. She can conduct 2 tours per hour and earn $10 each. She has no nonwage income, but she must pay 25 percent of her salary in taxes. The museum will allow her to work as much as 20 hours each week.

   a Plot her budget constraint.
   b Taxes are reduced to 20 percent. Plot her budget constraint.

7 (Practice problem: leisure-consumption budget constraint) Theodore tutors some of his fellow students in economics for $10 per hour. He also receives $2,000 in expense money per semester from his scholarship. He can work as much as 100 hours per semester.

   a Plot his budget constraint.
   b Students realize that there is a plethora of semi-intelligent grad students who will take less pay. Theodore now only receives $8 per hour. Plot his new budget constraint.

8 (Practice problem: leisure-consumption budget constraint) For each of the following, plot the budget constraint before and after the change.

   a Nonwage income = $100; wage = $20 hour; total time available = 40 hours; nonwage income changes to $0.
   b Nonwage income = $0; wage = $500/week; total time available = 52 weeks; wage changes to $300/week.
   c Nonwage income = $10,000; wage = $40/hour; total time available = 50 hours; available time increases to 60 hours.
   d Nonwage income = $500; wage = $200/week; total time available = 52 weeks; wage changes to $400/week.

SUBSTITUTION AND INCOME EFFECTS

As in the case of Chapter 8's budget constraint, price changes cause two kinds of effects: substitution and income. When the wage increases, the substitution effects motivate household to supply more labor, but the income effects indicate that they supply less labor. These concepts show how the labor supply curve can bend backward. Tool Kit 9.2 uses the budget constraint to distinguish between substitution and income effects.

Tool Kit 9.2: Distinguishing Between Substitution and Income Effects of Wage Changes

When the wage rate changes, there are two effects: substitution and income. These can be illustrated using the leisure-consumption budget constraint. This technique clarifies the fact that, as in the case of savings, the substitution and income effects work in opposite directions.

Step one: Draw the budget line with the original wage.

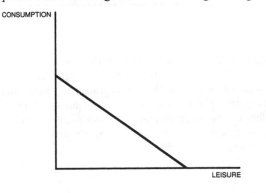

Step two: Find the chosen point along this budget line. Label this point *A*.

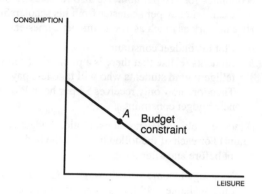

Step three: Draw the budget line with the new wage.

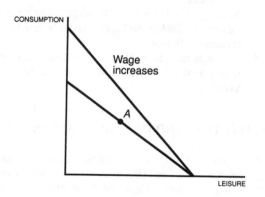

Step four: Draw a dotted line segment through point *A* and parallel to the *new* budget line.

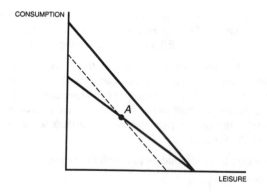

Step five: Darken the portion of the dotted line segment that lies above the original budget line. The points along this darkened segment represent the new alternatives made possible by the substitution effect of the wage change. The income effect shifts this line parallel out to the new budget line drawn in step three.

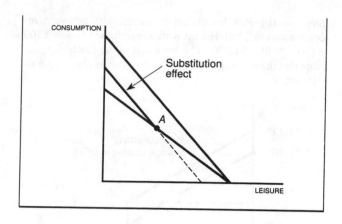

9   (Worked problem: wage changes/applications) John currently works 45 hours per week tuning pianos at a wage of $20 per hour. This is his only income. He is offered a raise to $30 per hour. He has 80 hours available for work each week.

  a   Draw the budget constraint at $20 per hour. Label his chosen alternative along this budget line.
  b   Draw the budget constraint at $30 per hour.
  c   Show the substitution effect of the wage increase. Why must the substitution effect lead John to work no less at the new, higher wage?

Step-by-step solution

Step one (a): Draw the budget constraint at the original wage. We label the horizontal axis "Leisure" and the vertical one "Consumption." If John does not work, he has 80 hours of leisure and no consumption. If he works all 80 hours (leisure = 0), he consumes $1,600. Draw John's budget constraint connecting the two points.

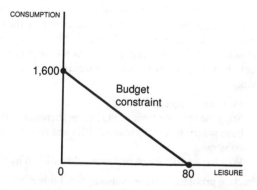

Step two: Find the chosen point along this budget line. John chooses $80 - 45 = 35$ hours of leisure, which give him $45 \times \$20 = \$900$. Label this point *A*, and note that it does lie along the budget constraint.

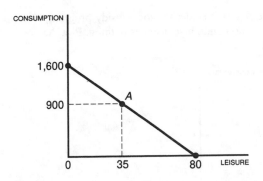

Step three (b): Draw the budget constraint when the wage is $30. The no-work alternative still offers consumption equal to $0, but now if John works the 80 hours available, he consumes $30 × 80 = $2,400. Plot and connect the two end points.

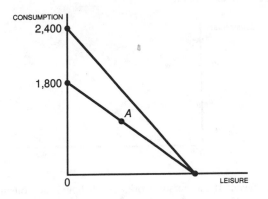

Step four (c): Draw a dotted line parallel to the $30 budget constraint through point *A*.

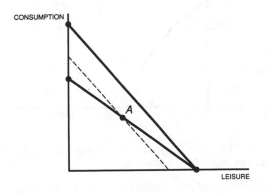

Step five: Darken the portion that lies above the budget constraint drawn in step one. These are the alternatives made possible by the substitution effect of the wage increase. All of these points involve more work than at point *A*, the alternative chosen when the wage is $20.

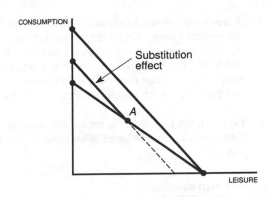

10 (Practice problem: applications) Arna loves her job as a design consultant. She can earn $60 per hour and has been able to work as much as she likes up to 50 hours per week. She has no nonwage income. She is currently working 15 hours per week.

   a Plot her budget constraint. Find her chosen alternative, and label the point *A*.

   b A new city income tax of 10 percent is passed. Arna now takes home only $54 per hour. Plot her new budget constraint.

   c Show the substitution effect of the wage decrease.

11 (Practice problem: substitution and income effects) For each of the following, draw the budget constraint with the wage in the first column and a new budget line with the wage in the second column. Pick an alternative along the first budget constraint, and show the substitution effect. There is no nonwage income.

	Old wage	New wage	Total time
a	$25/hour	$ 50/hour	80 hours
b	$200/day	$ 100/day	30 days
c	$1,000/week	$1,500/week	50 weeks
d	$5/hour	$ 4/hour	100 hours

APPLICATIONS OF THE LEISURE-CONSUMPTION BUDGET CONSTRAINT

The following applications use the leisure-consumption budget constraint. We analyze welfare programs, overtime pay, and even divorce arrangements. The basic technique is to draw the budget constraint without the policy in question, draw another budget constraint with the policy in place, and compare the two using substitution and income effects.

12 (Worked problem: application) In Smithsville, the welfare system pays $100 per week. Anyone in Smithsville can earn the minimum wage of $4.00 per hour at the local pickle plant, but welfare recipients cannot receive more than $100 per week. This means that any earnings are subtracted from welfare benefits. There are 80 hours available for work.

   a Draw the budget constraint for a Smithsville welfare recipient.

b   A new proposal would substitute a job subsidy for the welfare system. Under the job subsidy proposal, the town pays nothing to those who do not work and $.50 for every dollar earned, up to a total payment of $100. Draw the new budget constraint, and compare it with the one under the welfare system.

c   Do you think job subsidies are a better program than unconditional welfare? What other factors are involved?

Step-by-step solution

Step one (a): Draw a set of axes labeled "Leisure" and "Consumption." If the recipient does no work, she consumes $100. Plot this point, and label it *A*.

Step two: If the recipient earns $100, she loses all of her benefits and still consumes $100. At $4 per hour, $100 is earned in $100/$4 = 25 hours, which leaves 80 − 25 = 55 hours of leisure. Plot the point (100, 55). Label this point *B*.

Step three: If the recipient works all 80 hours, she consumes $4 × 80 = $320. Plot this point, and label it *C*.

Step four: Draw line segments connecting points *A* and *B* and points *B* and *C*. This is the budget constraint under the welfare system.

Step five (b): Under the job subsidy program, if the person works no hours, he consumes nothing. Plot the point (0.80). Label it *D*.

Step six: If the person earns $200, he receives the maximum subsidy, which is $100. The total consumption is then $300. To earn $200 (and consume $300) takes $200/$4 = 50 hours of work, leaving 80 − 50 = 30 hours of leisure. Plot the point (300, 30), and label it *E*.

Step seven: If the person works all 80 hours, he consumes $100 + (80 × $4) = $420. Plot the point (420, 0), and label if *F*.

Step eight: Draw line segments connecting *DEF*. This is the budget constraint for job subsidies.

13   (Practice problem: applications) The management at Acme Manufacturing is disturbed that although the typical factory worker is required to work 250 days each year, most only work 230. It proposes a $100 bonus for any employee who works more than 240 days each year. The wage of the typical factory worker is $120 per day.

a   Draw the budget constraint without the attendance bonus.

b   Draw the budget constraint with the attendance

bonus. How is attendance likely to change for the typical factory worker?

c   Suppose that the company simply gives each worker $100. How is the opportunity set different from the one with the attendance bonus?

d   Under which scheme will the typical worker work more? Why?

14 (Practice problem: applications) The Quantity Bakery Company has paid its workers $6 per hour to make donuts, cakes, and pies. There are always sweets to make, and the workers can work as many hours as they choose, up to 80 hours per week. Recently, the company union won a new contract that, although it keeps the wage at the same level, now allows for overtime pay of "time and a half" for any hours worked in excess of 40 per week.

a   Draw the budget constraint under the old contract with no provision for overtime pay.

b   Draw the budget constraint with the overtime pay.

c   What is likely to happen to the number of hours that Quantity Bakery workers work under the new contract? Explain.

15 (Practice problem: applications) Under the U.S. tax code, earnings below $20,000 or so are taxed at 15 percent. Any earnings above $20,000 incur a 28 percent tax rate. Lucinda Gamez, a private investigator, earns $800 per week, and she has 50 weeks per year available for work.

a   Draw her budget constraint if she pays no taxes.

b   Draw her budget constraint under the schedule described above. How do progressive income taxes shape the budget constraint.

16 (Practice problem: applications) Harry Gold makes $5,000 by working 20 days each month as a plumber. His wage is $250 per day, and he can work as many as 30 days each month (except February, of course). The income tax rate for Harry is 20 percent. Also, he pays $1,000 monthly in property taxes on a very nice condo down by the river. His nonwage income is $4,000 per month. (Hint: Review the solutions to problems 15 and 16 of Chapter 8.)

a   What is Harry's net wage after taxes?

b   Draw his budget constraint.

c   The new governor proposes eliminating the income tax and increasing property taxes. Harry figures that his property tax bill will rise to $2,000. Draw his budget constraint under the governor's proposed tax changes.

d   Will Harry work more or less under the new tax plan? Why?

e   Is Harry better off under the new tax plan? Why or why not?

17 (Practice problem: applications) After 10 miserable years, Al and Norma Bennet are getting a divorce. They have agreed that Norma will remain custody of their two children. Al makes $50 per hour from his job as a marriage counselor, and this is his only income. Although he could work as much as 40 hours, Al is only working 20 hours currently. The court has ruled that Al must pay $250 per week in child support regardless of his earnings. (Hint: Review the solutions to problems 15 and 16 of Chapter 8.)

a   Draw Al's (postdivorce) leisure-consumption budget constraint.

b   Many states (for example, Wisconsin and Michigan) have established fixed guidelines for child support payments. Suppose the guideline requires that noncustodial parents pay 25 percent of their income per child. Draw Al's budget line for this child care payment.

c   Under which plan will Al work more? Why?

SAVINGS

Now we turn to the saver's opportunity set: the two-period budget constraint. Given the wealth or income of the household and the interest rate, we can construct the two-period budget constraint. We see how the budget constraint is altered when income (either present or future) and interest rates change. We show the substitution and income effects by using the rotation and shift technique introduced in the last chapter. Finally, we learn some applications: different borrowing and lending interest rates, individual retirement, college and housing accounts, and how Social Security benefits affect savings.

The Two-Period Budget Constraint

When we save money, we forgo current consumption in order to increase consumption at some later date. The trade-off involves current and future consumption. Tool Kit 9.3 shows how to plot the two-period budget constraint, which is the economist's basic tool for analyzing savings.

Tool Kit 9.3: Plotting the Two-Period Budget Constraint

The two-period budget constraint shows what combinations of consumption in each period are possible, given the income and interest rate. Follow the steps.

Step one: Draw a set of coordinate axes. Label the horizontal axis consumption in period one and the vertical axis consumption in period two.

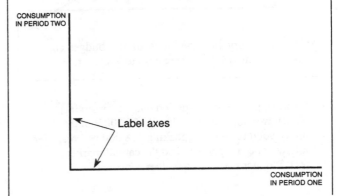

Step two: Calculate the maximum possible consumption in period one. (This quantity is the present discounted value of income.) Plot this quantity along the horizontal axis.

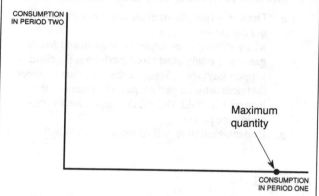

Step three: Calculate the maximum possible consumption in period two. (This quantity is the future value of income.) Plot this quantity along the vertical axis.

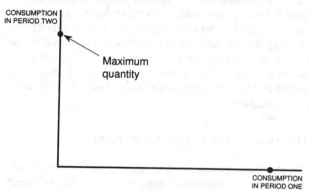

Step four: Draw a line segment connecting the two points. This line segment is the two-period budget constraint.

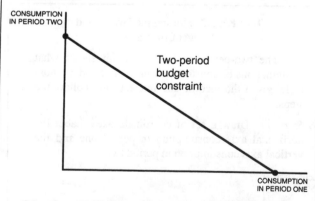

Step five: Verify that the slope of the budget constraint is (minus) $1 + r$, where r is the interest rate.

18   (Worked problem: two-period budget constraint) Nancy won the lottery! It is only $5,000, but that looks pretty good to someone making $18,000 per year. Her interest rate is 6 percent, and the capital market is perfect. Plot her two-period budget constraint.

Step-by-step solution

Step one: Draw coordinate axes, labeling the horizontal axis "Consumption now" and the vertical axis "Consumption next year."

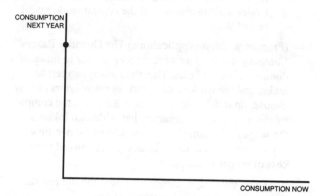

Step two: The maximum consumption today is the present discounted value of all income. Make the following table, and compute and plot the amount along the horizontal axis.

Year	Income	Discount factor	Present discounted value
Now	$23,000	1	$23,000
Next year	$18,000	1/(1.06)	$16,980

Present discounted value = $39,980.

Step three: The maximum consumption next year is

$$\$23,000 \, (1 + .06) + \$18,000 = \$42,380.$$

Plot this point.

Step four: Draw a line segment connecting the two points.

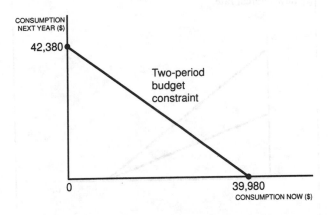

Step five: Verify that the slope equals 1 plus the interest rate. It is 42,380/39,980 = 1.06 = 1 + r.

19 (Practice problem: two-period budget constraint) Current income is $40,000. Retirement income is $15,000. The interest rate for the period between now and retirement is 150 percent. Plot the two-period budget constraint.

20 (Practice problem: two-period budget constraint) Plot the two-period budget constraints for the following.

	Interest rate	Present income	Future income
a	100%	$100,000	$ 25,000
b	50%	$ 40,000	$ 10,000
c	250%	$ 20,000	$ 0
d	80%	$ 0	$150,000

21 (Worked problem: two-period budget constraint) When the interest rate, current income, or future income changes, the two-period budget constraint moves. The basic technique here is to draw the two-period budget constraint using the original income and interest rate, and then draw a new two-period budget constraint using the new incomes and interest rate. Compare the two budget constraints and verify that the shift is parallel when either current or future income changes, but the budget constraint rotates when the interest rate changes. Michael is earning $25,000 as a secretary and expects to earn the same in the future. His interest rate is 5 percent.

a   Plot his two-period budget constraint.
b   He receives word that his aunt is sick and has one year to live. She plans to leave him $50,000. Plot his two-period budget constraint.

Step-by-step solution

Step one (a): Follow the procedure to plot the two-period budget constraint. The slope is 1 + r = 1.05, and it passes through the point $25,000 now and $25,000 next year.

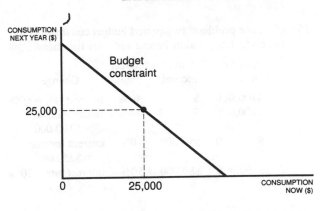

Step two (b): Plot the new budget constraint. Because the interest rate is the same, the slope does not change. The new budget constraint passes through the point $25,000 now and $75,000 next year.

22 (Practice problem: two-period budget constraint) Boris currently takes home $45,000 as a skilled lathe operator. His union contract guarantees him the same salary next year. The credit union at the plant pays 8 percent interest.

a   Plot his two-period budget constraint.
b   Boris' employer is experiencing low profits this year. He proposes that Boris accept $35,000 this year and $55,000 next year. Plot his two-period budget constraint. Does the offer shift the budget constraint? How?

23 (Practice problem: two-period budget constraint) Monica plans to retire in 20 years. She now takes home $40,000 and expects $20,000 in retirement income. The interest rate for the 20 years is 180 percent.

a   Plot her budget constraint.
b   A new broker promises her a 20-year return of 250 percent. She believes him. Plot her new budget constraint.

24 (Practice problem: two-period budget constraint) The Coddingtons now take home $375,000 per year, but they have no retirement income planned. Their portfolio will earn them 100 percent over the 12 years left until retirement.

a   Plot their budget constraint.
b   Tax increases reduce their after-tax return to 60 percent. Plot their new budget constraint.

25 (Practice problem: two-period budget constraint) Plot the budget constraints before and after the change.

	Current income	Future income	Interest rate	Change
a	$100,000	$ 0	40%	interest rate = 60%
b	$100,000	$ 0	40%	future income = $100,000
c	$ 0	$50,000	10%	current income = $25,000
d	$ 60,000	$80,000	50%	interest rate = 20%

SUBSTITUTION AND INCOME EFFECTS

As in the case of the other budget constraints that you have studied, price changes cause two kinds of effects: substitution and income. When the interest rate increases, the substitution effects motivate household to save more, but the income effects indicate that they save less. These concepts show why the supply curve of savings may bend backward. Tool Kit 9.4 uses the budget constraint to distinguish between substitution and income effects of changes in interest rates.

Tool Kit 9.4: Distinguishing Between Substitution and Income Effects of Changes in Interest Rates

When the interest rate changes, there are two effects: substitution and income. These effects can be illustrated by using the two-period budget constraint. Follow this procedure.

Step one: Draw the two-period budget line with the original interest rate.

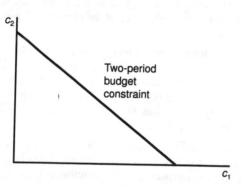

Step two: Find the chosen current and future consumption level along this budget line. Label this point A.

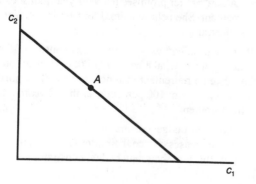

Step three: Draw the two-period budget line with the new interest rate.

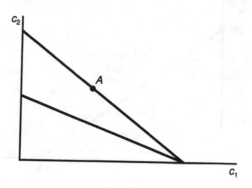

Step four: Draw a dotted line segment through point A and parallel to the *new* budget line.

Step five: Darken the portion of the dotted line segment that lies above the original budget line. The points along this darkened segment represent the quantities made possible by the substitution effect of the interest rate change. The income effect shifts this line out in a parallel way to the new budget line drawn in step three.

---

26 (Worked problem: substitution and income effects) Show the substitution and income effects of the change n the rate of return for Monica's portfolio in problem 23. She is currently saving $5,000 per year.

Step-by-step solution

Step one: Draw the two-period budget constraint with the interest rate equal to 180 percent. It must pass through the point ($40,000, $20,000).

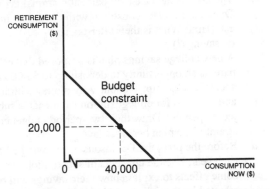

Step two: Label Monica's current consumption ($40,000 − $5,000 = $35,000) point *A*.

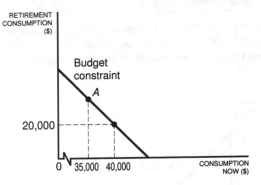

Step three: Draw the two-period budget constraint with the interest rate equal to 250 percent. It also must pass through the point ($40,000, $20,000).

Step four: Draw a dotted line with a slope of 1 + 2.50 = 3.50 through *A*.

Step five: Darken the portion of the dotted line that lies above the original budget constraint drawn in step one. These are the alternatives made possible by the substitution effect of the interest rate change. All of these involve more savings; thus, the substitution effect of an increase in the interest rate is an increase in savings. The income effect shifts this darkened line segment out parallel to the budget constraint drawn in step two and reduces savings.

27 (Practice problem: substitution and income effects) Show the substitution and income effects for the change in the Coddingtons' after-tax interest rate in problem 24. Currently they have no savings.

28 (Practice problem: substitution and income effects) Show the substitution and income effects for parts a through d in problem 25. In each case, savings equal $10,000 before the interest rate changes.

APPLICATION OF THE TWO-PERIOD BUDGET CONSTRAINT

The following applications show how the two-period budget constraint can be used to analyze imperfect capital markets, Social Security, and government programs that affect savings incentives. Again, the procedure is to draw budget constraints with and without the feature of interest and compare using substitution and income effects.

29 (Worked problem: applications) If the capital market were perfect, then the interest rates for borrowing and lending would be the same. The rates for borrowing, however, are higher. Haywood and Myrna take home $40,000 each year. They can earn 4 percent on any savings, but they must borrow at 14 percent. Plot their two-period budget constraint.

Step-by-step solution

This is an application of the opportunity set with multiple constraints introduced in Chapter 2.

Step one: Plot the budget constraint with the 4 percent interest rate. The slope is 1.04, and it passes through the point $40,000 now and $40,000 next year.

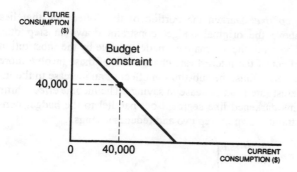

Step two: Plot the budget constraint with the 14 percent interest rate. The slope is 1.04, and it passes through the point $40,000 now and $40,000 next year.

Step three: Darken the portion of each budget constraint that lies under the other constraint.

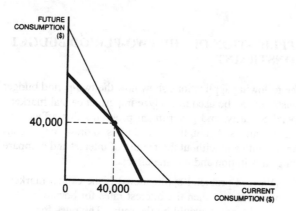

30   (Practice problem: applications) Bob takes home $20,000 this year, but he anticipates taking home $30,000 next year. He can earn 8 percent on savings, but he has a poor credit rating and must pay 19 percent to borrow. Plot his two-period budget constraint.

31   (Worked problem: applications) Concern about low U.S. savings rates, among other motivations, has prompted a number of proposals for tax-exempt savings accounts. They range from the Bush administration's family savings accounts to special tax-exempt accounts for college expenses or down payments on a first home. The Davidsons take home $100,000 per year after taxes. If he gets his grades up, David, their

son, will enter college in 3 years. The Davidsons can earn a 25 percent real rate of return before taxes over the three-year period.

a   Draw their two-period budget constraint.
b   The Davidsons face a 40 percent marginal tax rate. Draw their budget constraint with the tax on interest. (Hint: What is their after-tax real rate of return on savings?)
c   A new college savings plan is proposed that offers parents an opportunity to deposit up to $3,000 in a special tax-exempt account. Any money withdrawn and not used for college tuition payments is subject to penalty. Draw their two-period budget constraint if the plan becomes law.
d   Before the plan, the Davidsons were saving $3,500 each year. Use the concepts of substitution and income effects to explain how their savings will be affected by the college savings plan.

Step-by-step solution

Step one (a): Plot the two-period budget constraint. The slope is $1 + 0.25 = 1.25$, and the budget constraint must pass through the point where current and future income are each $100,000.

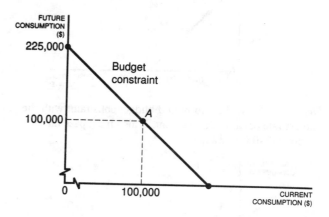

Step two (b): Plot the two-period budget constraint with the tax on interest. Taxes take 40 percent of the interest, so their after-tax interest rate for the three years is 15 percent. The slope is now 1.15. Interest taxes make the budget constraint flatter.

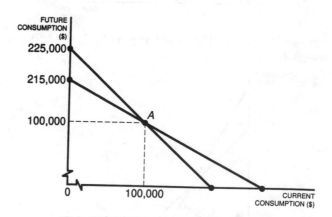

Step three (c): The college savings plan allows the Davidsons to save along the tax-free budget constraint, where the slope is 1.25 until their savings reach $3,000. At that point (*B*), there is a kink, and the slope of the budget constraint returns to the flatter after-tax slope of 1.15.

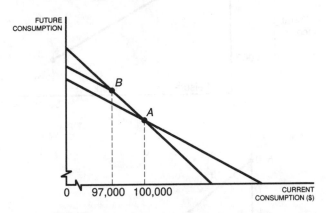

Step four (d): Since the Davidsons save more than $3,000, the program will have only an income effect. The program will not change their after-tax marginal rate of return, because only the first $3,000 of savings is tax exempt.

32 (Practice problem: applications) The Shades do not know where they will find the money to send their four bright but impecunious children to college in 5 years. They make $26,000 per year and have been unable to save a nickel. Their marginal tax rate is 20 percent, and they could earn 40 percent interest on savings over the 5-year period.

   a Plot the Shades' two-period budget constraint ignoring the tax on interest.

   b Plot their two-period budget constraint including the tax on interest.

   c Plot their two-period budget constraint under the college savings plan spelled out in problem 31.

   d Use the concepts of substitution and income effects to explain how their savings will be affected by the college savings plan.

33 (Worked problem: applications) Social Security reduces the incentives that individuals have to save for retirement, and because it is financed on a pay-as-you-go basis, it reduces national savings. Melissa is already fantasizing about retirement, even though it is 40 years away. She estimates that a dollar deposited today will return $3.50 in interest when she retires. She currently takes home $25,000 after paying taxes, including $3,250 annually in Social Security taxes, and expects to draw $14,625 in Social Security benefits. Although she is thinking about retirement, Melissa has no savings.

   a Calculate the present discounted value of Melissa's Social Security benefits.

   b Draw her two-period budget constraint, and label her levels of consumption now and in the future.

   c Suppose that the entire Social Security system (taxes and benefits) is eliminated. Draw her two-period budget constraint.

   d How much does Melissa save?

Step-by-step solution

Step one (a): The present discounted value of her benefit payment is $14,625/(1 + r) = $3,250, which is exactly her taxes.

Step two (b): Draw Melissa's two-period budget constraint. Label the axes "Current consumption" and "Consumption 40 years in the future." The slope is $1 + r$, and the interest rate for the 40-year period is 350 percent. Also, the budget constraint must pass through her current choice: $25,000 now and $14,625 in 40 years.

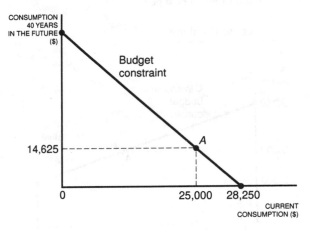

Step three (c): Eliminating Social Security reduces her future income to $0, but because she no longer pays Social Security taxes, her current after-tax income rises to $28,250. Because the present discounted value of her two-period income does not change, the budget constraint does not change. (In general, the Social Security system shifts out the budget constraint for low-income people and shifts it in for high-income people.)

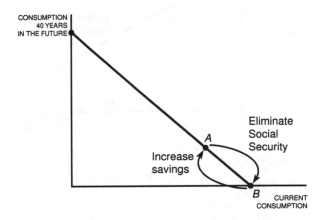

Step four (d): Because Melissa has the same budget constraint, she chooses the same point. This means that she must save $3,250 (which returns $14,625 in 40 years), which is exactly the amount she now pays in taxes. Eliminating Social Security would (for Melissa) lead to the same consumption, but greater national savings.

34 (Practice problem: applications) Melissa's uncle is only 10 years from retirement. He can expect to re-

ceive $1 in interest for every $1 saved for retirement. He takes home $50,000 annually, saves $10,000, and expects Social Security benefits of $20,000 when he retires.

a Plot his two-period budget constraint.
b Suppose that the American Association of Retired Persons has a banner year lobbying Congress and wins a 50 percent increase in benefits. Taxes also rise, so that the budget constraint of Melissa's uncle does not change. How will his earnings change? How will his consumption now and during retirement change?

Answers to Problems

2

3

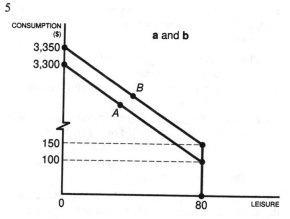

c Liza will make fewer cold calls, she will consume more leisure when her income increases, as shown by the movement from point *A* to point *B*.

6

7

8

d

10

11

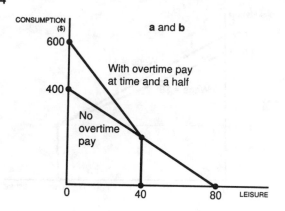

c   All the new alternatives made possible by the overtime provision involve working more than 40
hours. Work time probably will increase.

d   An unconditional bonus of $100 simply shifts the
budget constraint up in a parallel way, causing an
income effect. The typical worker consumes more
leisure at point C. The attendance bonus does not
offer the points along the dashed budget constraint. Point B or another point involving even
more work will be chosen. Clearly, there is a
greater incentive to work with the attendance
bonus.

a $200/day.
d   He will work more because the tax change offers
him new alternative with more work. In effect it
leaves him with the substitution effect of a wage
increase, with the income effect being canceled
by the property tax increase.
e   He is better off because he can continue to
choose point A, but he also has some new alternatives.

17

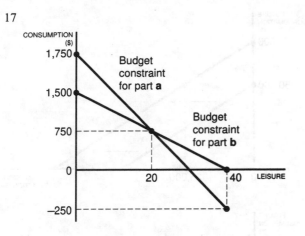

c   Al will likely work more under the lump-sum child
    care requirement. The other system leaves him
    with the substitution effect of a wage decrease.

19

20

22

32

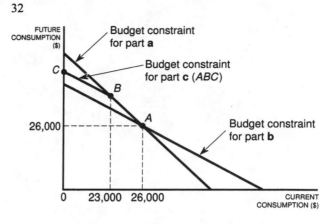

d If the Shades save less than $3,000, the program has both substitution and income effects. If they save more than $3,000, there is only an income effect.

34

30

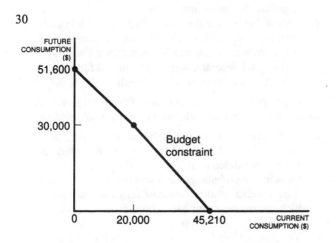

A STUDENT'S GUIDE TO INVESTING

Chapter Review

Chapter 10 moves on from the budget constraint to explore what the household does with its savings. This is the investment decision. Financial markets offer a wide array of investment opportunities, from savings accounts to Treasury bills to corporate stock, all with different characteristics. Why investors value certain characteristics of assets and how returns to assets reflect these characteristics form the central focus of this chapter. Chapter 10 completes the discussion of the household's role in capital markets.

ESSENTIAL CONCEPTS

1 **Financial investments** are purchases of financial assets in the expectation of receiving a return. Among the most important are bank deposits, housing, bonds, shares of stock, and mutual funds.

   a Bank deposits include savings accounts and certificates of deposit. Insured by the Federal Deposit Insurance Corporation, they are safe and liquid.

   b Housing is a tax favored investment in that property taxes and interest are deductible, and capital gains taxation usually can be avoided. Housing investment is risky and illiquid, however.

   c Bonds, which are promises to pay a fixed amount in a specified number of years, are a way for businesses and government to borrow. Bondholders bear the risk of default and/or inflation.

   d Shares of stock represent ownership rights in corporations. Investors hold stock in the hopes of receiving dividends and capital gains.

   e Mutual funds combine money from many different investors and purchase a wide variety of assets. This is called diversification. Although they are not insured by the federal government, mutual funds are safer than individual stocks or bonds.

2 There are four important properties of financial investments: expected return, risk, tax treatment, and liquidity.

   a Since returns are uncertain, the investor must balance the high returns with the low. The **expected return** is calculated by multiplying the possible returns by the probability each will occur.

   b Assets with a greater chance of very low and very high returns are **risky**. Most individuals are **risk averse**; they prefer safer assets.

   c The returns from some assets, such as housing and municipal bonds, are taxed less than the returns from other assets. The **tax advantages** make these assets more appealing to investors.

    d The ease with which an investment can be converted to cash is called **liquidity.** Bank accounts are very liquid; housing is illiquid. Most investors prefer liquidity.

3 The **efficient market theory** says that market prices reflect the characteristics of assets, incorporate all currently available information, and change unpredictably. An important implication of this theory is that without inside information, investors cannot continue to earn more than average returns.

4 The chapter closes with some investment advice. Although unlikely to appear on a test, this advice is immensely valuable.

    a Carefully evaluate the characteristics of each asset you own as it relates to your personal situation.
    b Diversify. Give your portfolio a broad base.
    c Consider all your risks, not just those in your financial investment portfolio.
    d Think again before you imagine that you can beat the market.

BEHIND THE ESSENTIAL CONCEPTS

1 What do investors want from their financial assets? In addition to high expected returns, individuals value the characteristics of investments with low risk, favorable tax treatment, and liquidity. The demand for investments with these characteristics is higher; therefore, their price is higher. The fact that market prices are higher for assets with desirable characteristics—in other words, that asset prices reflect these characteristics—is one of the central ideas of efficient market theory.

2 Assets that pay higher returns in bad times are especially valuable. When the economy is in recession, the typical individual loses money on investments. People do not like to see their wealth fluctuate and are willing to pay something to smooth out these ups and downs. Assets that pay higher returns when the economy is weak help to stabilize the overall portfolio. Again, efficient market theory predicts that the prices of these assets will be higher.

3 Efficient market theory says that prices also reflect all available information. For example, when Iraq invaded Kuwait in August 1990, the prices of oil and oil stocks shot up immediately. The new information that oil would be in short supply in the future made firms that owned large oil reserves worth more, and their stock prices immediately reflected this additional worth.

4 Many people are mystified by the notion that in an efficient market, asset prices change randomly. Once you understand the logic, however, you can see why this must be true. Since market prices reflect available information, you can only beat the market if you have information others do not. Anyone who had known in April 1990 that Iraq would invade Kuwait could have bought oil stocks before their prices rose. Once the invasion

happened, however, it was too late. Prices had already risen. Since the invasion was a surprise, the sudden changes in the prices of oil stocks were also surprises. This is what is meant by random movements in prices: the changes are unpredictable, though they are not without rational cause.

SELF-TEST

True or False

1 The ease with which an asset can be converted to cash is called its liquidity.

2 To find the expected return, simply take the average of the possible returns.

3 Housing is a tax-favored investment because interest is tax deductible and capital gains taxes may be postponed.

4 If the interest rate rises, bond prices fall.

5 Bondholders bear no risk from inflation.

6 If a company goes bankrupt, bondholders are paid before stockholders.

7 The portion of a company income not paid to stockholders in dividends is called retained earnings.

8 Risky assets pay higher rates of return on average.

9 Illiquid assets pay lower rates of return on average.

10 An increase in the price of a share of stock is called a capital gain.

11 If stock prices vary randomly, then the market cannot be efficient.

12 Owing to the quality of their research staffs, most mutual funds continue to earn more than the market rate of return year after year.

13 Because most people prefer safe, tax-favored, liquid assets, those assets yield higher returns.

14 A fund that gathers money from many investors and purchases a range of assets is called a mutual fund.

15 If stock prices reflect all available information, then changes in price must result from unanticipated events and must be random.

Multiple Choice

1 Which of the following are financial investments?

    a stocks;
    b bonds;
    c money market accounts;
    d certificates of deposit;
    e all of the above.

2   Which of the following are real investments?

   a   preferred stock;

   b   mutual funds;

   c   purchases of new factories;

   d   bank accounts;

   e   none of the above.

3   Liquidity refers to

   a   the correlation of the return on an asset and the market return;

   b   the term to maturity of a bond;

   c   the ease with which an asset can be converted into cash;

   d   the likelihood that an investor will be repaid if a corporation goes bankrupt;

   e   a and d.

4   Which of the following is not a risk borne by bondholders?

   a   The market interest rate may rise, causing the price of the bond to fall.

   b   Inflation may lower the real value of the fixed return.

   c   A corporation may go bankrupt and default on the bond.

   d   At the end of the term, even if it does not default, a company may not pay a bondholder what she expected to receive.

   e   All of the above are risks of holding bonds.

5   Junk bonds are

   a   highly risky bonds usually issued by firms with high debt levels;

   b   bonds that must be held by the original purchaser and cannot be sold;

   c   bonds that have procyclical returns;

   d   bonds that are not convertible into stock;

   e   bonds issued by firms in the used vehicle industry.

6   The amount of a firm's earnings not paid out to stockholders as dividends is called

   a   economic profits;

   b   the average return;

   c   retained earnings;

   d   liquidity;

   e   accounting profits.

7   If an investor sells a share of stock for more than he paid for it, he earns a

   a   liquidity premium;

   b   capital gain;

   c   retained earning;

   d   risk premium;

   e   procyclical return.

8   Who must be repaid before owners of common stock when the firm goes bankrupt?

   a   bondholders;

   b   owners of preferred stocks;

   c   creditors;

   d   the Internal Revenue Service;

   e   all of the above

9   Suppose that an antique automobile purchased for $25,000 is to be sold next year. The investor thinks that the sales price may be $20,000 or $40,000, and the probability of each price is one-half. What is its expected return?

   a $5,000;

   b $30,000;

   c $35,000;

   d   –$5,000;

   e   none of the above

10   If there were no differences between assets other than the ways in which they produced returns, then

   a   the expected returns to all assets would be the same;

   b   the returns to stock ownership would exceed the returns to bond holding;

   c   assets that paid returns through capital gains would pay more than assets that paid returns through interest or dividends;

   d   no investor would hold bonds;

   e   none of the above.

11   Why are stocks risky financial investments?

   a   The price of the stock may go up or down.

   b   The amount of the dividend payment may go up or down.

   c   The firm may go bankrupt.

   d   All of the above.

   e   a and c.

12   Most investors are risk averse. This means that they will

   a   never purchase risky assets;

   b   look only at the risk of an investment, not the expected return;

   c   always prefer bonds to stocks;

   d   always prefer bank accounts to bonds because bank accounts are insured by the Federal Deposit Insurance Corporation;

   e   prefer safe to risky assets of equal expected return.

13   Suppose that an asset has a one-half probability of earning 30% and a one-half probability of earning nothing. Its expected return equals

   a   0;

   b   15 percent;

   c   25 percent;

   d   30 percent;

   e   100 percent.

14   When investors, seeking the highest rate of return, bid up the prices of profitable assets, they are engaging in

   a   diversification;

   b   liquidity;

   c   insurance;

   d   capital gains;

   e   arbitrage.

15   State and municipal bonds yield

   a   lower returns than corporate bonds chiefly because they are less risky;

b   higher returns than corporate bonds chiefly because they are more liquid;

c   lower returns than corporate bonds of equivalent risks and liquidity because interest on them is tax-exempt;

d   higher returns than corporate bonds of equivalent risk and liquidity because interest on them is tax-exempt;

e   returns equal to those paid by corporate bonds of equivalent risk and liquidity because interest on them is tax-exempt.

16   Housing is a tax-favored investment in that

a   mortgage interest is tax deductible;
b   housing is liquid;
c   it is possible to avoid capital gains taxes on housing;
d   housing is financed by municipal bonds;
e   a and c.

17   Which of the following assets is most liquid?

a   stocks;
b   bonds;
c   bank accounts;
d   housing;
e   mutual funds.

18   The demand for an asset depends on its

a   liquidity;
b   average returns;
c   risk;
d   tax treatment;
e   all of the above.

19   Efficient market theory says that

a   all assets are perfectly liquid;
b   all assets are treated the same by the tax system;
c   asset characteristics are perfectly reflected in their prices;
d   average returns are equal for all assets;
e   a, b, and d.

20   The advice to diversify your portfolio means

a   own a wide variety of assets with different risks;
b   stay away from risky assets;
c   choose only assets with procyclical returns;
d   follow a random walk strategy;
e   none of the above.

Completion

1   Purchases of new factories and machinery are examples of _____ investment.

2   Purchases of stocks and bonds and deposits in money market accounts are examples of _____ investment.

3   _____ refers to the ease with which an investment can be turned into cash.

4   An unexpected decline in the rate of interest causes the prices of bonds to _____.

5   Because most individuals are _____, risky assets must offer a higher average return than safe assets.

6   In general, stocks that go up in value when the economy is weak are worth _____ than stocks that go up in value during good economic times.

7   Because municipal bonds are exempt from taxes, their prices are _____ than prices for comparable taxable bonds.

8   The demand for an asset depends upon its average return, _____, tax treatment, and liquidity.

9   To find the expected return on an asset, multiply the possible returns by the corresponding _____.

10   The theory that market prices perfectly reflect the characteristics of assets is called the _____ theory.

Answers to Self-Test

True or False

1	t	6	t	11	f
2	f	7	t	12	f
3	t	8	t	13	f
4	t	9	f	14	t
5	f	10	t	15	t

Multiple Choice

1	e	2	c	3	c	4	d
5	a	6	c	7	b	8	e
9	a	10	a	11	d	12	e
13	b	14	e	15	c	16	e
17	c	18	e	19	c	20	a

Completion

1   real
2   financial
3   Liquidity
4   rise
5   risk averse
6   more
7   higher
8   risk
9   probabilities
10   efficient market

Doing Economics: Tools and Practice Problems

The concept of expected returns appears for the first time in this chapter. We study how to calculate the expected return on an investment and what it means. We go on to consider the opportunity set for the investor and learn how he perceives trade-offs of risk and expected return, and also liquidity and returns. The last issue we take up is the relationship between bond prices and interest rates. A few problems use the concept of present value (introduced in Chapter 6) to show why an increase in interest rates leads to a decrease in bond prices.

EXPECTED RETURNS

When we purchase an asset, we do not know exactly what it will earn in the future. Investors calculate the expected return, which is the average of all the possible returns. The expected return is one of the important desirable properties of financial investments. Tool Kit 10.1 shows how to calculate expected returns.

Tool Kit 10.1: Calculating Expected Returns

Because the returns on financial investments come in the future, at the time the decision is made an investor is uncertain about what the returns will actually be. Good investors think carefully about all the possibilities and calculate the expected returns.

Step one: Make a three-column table showing all the possible returns in the left-hand column and the corresponding probabilities in the middle column.

Returns	Probability	Product
r_1	P_1	
r_2	P_2	

Step two: Multiply each possible return by its probability, and enter the product in the right-hand column.

Returns	Probability	Product
r_1	P_1	$r_1 \times P_1$
r_2	P_2	$r_2 \times P_2$

Step three: Add the numbers in the right-hand column. The sum is the expected return.

Returns	Probability	Product
r_1	P_1	$r_1 \times P_1$
r_2	P_2	$r_2 \times P_2$

Average returns $= (r_1 \times P_1) + (r_2 \times P_2)$.

---

1 (Worked problem: expected returns) Envious of his brother's life-style, Dr. Mendez is considering investing in one of his brother's real estate ventures. His brother promises a return of 100 percent in one year, but Dr. Mendez thinks the probability that this will happen is only 1/4. More likely (probability = 1/2) is a return of 8 percent. Finally, there is another 1/4 probability that the project will go under and the doctor will lose all his money (return = −100 percent). Calculate the expected return.

Step-by-step solution

Step one: Make a table, and enter the possible returns and the corresponding probabilities.

Returns	Probability	Product
100%	1/4	
8%	1/2	
−100%	1/4	

Step two: Multiply each return by its probability, and enter the result.

Returns	Probability	Product
100%	1/4	25%
8%	1/2	4%
−100%	1/4	−25%

Step three: Add the numbers in the right-hand column.

Returns	Probability	Product
100%	1/4	25%
8%	1/2	4%
−100%	1/4	−25%

Expected returns = 4%.

Thus, in spite of the considerable risk, the investment pays an average of only 4 percent. The good doctor should stick to medicine and put his money in a safe investment.

2 (Practice problem: expected returns) Black Dust, Montana, flush with a consultant's prediction of its future as a high-technology center, is issuing bonds for a new city government building. The bonds pay 20 percent. Most financial analysts think the probability of default is 1/10. In case of default, the bondholders lose their investments (returns = −100 percent). Calculate the expected return on the Black Dust bond.

3 (Practice problem: expected returns) Calculate the expected return on each of the following.

a
Returns	Probability	Product
50%	1/4	
12%	5/8	
−100%	1/8	

b
Returns	Probability	Product
10%	1/4	
20%	3/4	

c
Returns	Probability	Product
200%	1/3	
40%	1/3	
−100%	1/3	

d
Returns	Probability	Product
50%	1/3	
12%	2/3	

RISK AND RETURNS

There are four desirable characteristics of financial investments: expected returns, risk, tax treatment, and liquidity. Seeking the best combination of these characteristics, an investor faces trade-offs. Some problems show how this trade-off looks to a potential investor.

4 (Worked problem: risk and returns) The table below gives the returns on six bond issues if there is no default, and also the probabilities of default for each. If there is a default, the investor loses all of her money (returns = −100 percent). Also, note that if the probability

of default is 0.1, then the probability of not experiencing a default must be 0.9.

a   Compute the expected return for each bond.
b   Measure risk as the probability of default. Construct the opportunity set, and interpret its outer edge as the risk-return trade-off.
c   Are there any bonds a rational investor would never buy? Why or why not?

Company	Returns (if no default)	Probability of default
Do Music Co.	5%	0
Re Music Co.	19%	0.1
Mi Music Co.	30%	0.2
Fa Music Co.	12%	0.05
Sol Music Co.	8%	0.02
Fred's Music Co.	15%	0.07

Step-by-step solution

Step one (a): Calculate the expected returns for each bond. Follow the procedure for calculating expected returns.

Do Music Co.	$(5\% \times 1) - (100\% \times 0) = 5\%$
Re Music Co.	$(19\% \times .9) - (100\% \times .1) = 7.1\%$
Mi Music Co.	$(30\% \times .8) - (100\% \times .2) = 4\%$
Fa Music Co.	$(12\% \times .95) - (100 \times .05) = 6.4\%$
Sol Music Co.	$(8\% \times .98) - (100\% \times .02) = 5.84\%$
Fred's Music Co.	$(15\% \times .93) - (100\% \times .07) = 6.95\%$

Step two (b): Plot the expected returns on the vertical axis and risk (measured as the probability of default) on the horizontal. This is the risk-return trade-off.

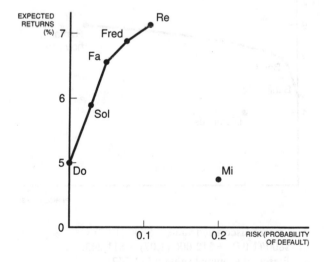

Step three (c): Since Mi Music Co.'s bonds do not lie on the outer edge, no one will buy them. All of the other issues offer higher average returns and lower risk, as shown in the figure.

5   (Practice problem: risk and returns) The four hospitals in Greenville are racing to install the latest medical technologies. Each is trying to raise money in the bond market, and their returns and default risks are given below. If there is a default, the return is −100 percent.

a   Calculate the expected returns for each.

b   Plot the risk-return trade-off.

Hospital	Returns (if no default)	Probability of default
Northside	6%	0
Southside	18%	0.09
Eastside	22%	0.1
Westside	12%	0.05

6   (Practice problem: risk and returns) The Kannapans have set aside some money in case of emergency. They are considering where to invest it, but they are concerned about how quickly they will have access to the money when it is needed. The four possible assets, their returns, and the times needed to withdraw the principal (or sell the asset) are given below. Construct the liquidity-return trade-off.

Asset	Returns	Waiting period
Bank account	5%	none
Bond	7%	2 days
Diamonds	4%	1 week
Rental housing	9%	1 month

BOND PRINCES AND INTEREST RATES

When interest rates rise, bond prices fall. This fact of financial markets follows from the concept of present discounted value, introduced in Chapter 6. The market price for a bond is the present discounted value of the promised repayments.

7   (Worked problem: present value) Bonds issued by Hitek, Inc., promise to pay $100 at the end of the year for 2 years. In addition, the face value equal to $1,000 is repaid at the end of 3 years. The market interest rate is 8 percent.

a   Calculate the present discounted value of the bond.
b   The interest rate rises to 10 percent. Recalculate the bond value.

Step-by-step solution

Step one (a): Make a table, and enter the years and the payments.

Year	Amount	Discount factor	Present discounted value
1	$ 100		
2	$ 100		
3	$1,000		

Step two: Calculate and enter the discount factors for each year. For the first year, the discount factor is $1/(1 + .08) = 0.92$. For the second year, it is $1/(1 + .08)^2 = 0.85$, and for the third, it is $1/(1 + .08)^3 = 0.78$.

Step three: Multiply the amounts by the corresponding discount factor. Enter the product in the right-hand column.

Step four: Add the numbers in the right-hand column.

Year	Amount	Discount factor	Present discounted value
1	$ 100	0.92	$ 92
2	$ 100	0.85	$ 85
3	$1,000	0.78	$780

Present discounted value = $957.

Step five (b): Repeat the procedure for a 10 percent interest rate. The table looks like this.

Year	Amount	Discount factor	Present discounted value
1	$ 100	0.90	$ 90
2	$ 100	0.81	$ 81
3	$1,000	0.73	$730

Present discounted value = $901.

The rise in the interest rate from 8 percent to 10 percent causes the bond price to fall by $56 ($957 − $901). It should be clear why ripples in interest rates cause waves in the bond market.

8   (Practice problem: present value) Deuce Hardwear, a franchiser of motorcycle clothing, has issued a bond that promises to pay $800 at the end of each of the next two years and $12,000 at the end of the third year. The interest rate is 7 percent.

a   Calculate the present discounted value of the bond.
b   The interest rate falls to 6 percent. How much does the price of the bond change?

9   (Practice problem: present value) For each of the following, calculate the change in the price of the bond.

a   The interest rate falls from 10 percent to 8 percent.

Year	Amount	Discount factor	Present discounted value
1	$ 88		
2	$ 88		
3	$1,000		

Present discounted value = $

b   The interest rate rises from 10 percent to 13 percent.

Year	Amount	Discount factor	Present discounted value
1	$ 800		
2	$ 700		
3	$13,000		

Present discounted value = $

Answers to Problems

2   Expected return = (9 × 20) − (.1 × 100) = 8%.

3   a   7.5%.
    b   17.5%.
    c   46.7%.
    d   24.7%.

5   a   The expected returns for each bond are given in the table.

Hospital	Returns (if no default)	Probability of default	Expected returns
Northside	6%	0	6%
Southside	18%	0.09	7.38%
Eastside	22%	0.1	9.8%
Westside	12%	0.05	6.4%

6

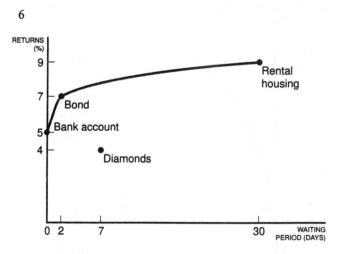

8   a   Present discounted value = $800/(1.07) + $800/(1.07)² + $12,000/(1.07)³ = $11,243.
    b   Present discounted value = $11,542.

9   a   Price of the bond rises from $904 to $950.
    b   Price of the bond falls from $11,073 to $10,263.

Chapter 11

THE FIRM'S COSTS

Chapter Review

One side of the competitive model, the household's, is complete. Business enterprises—firms—occupy the other side. This chapter begins the discussion of the role of firms in a market-based economy. We learn about the production function, which summarizes the relationship between the inputs that the firm demands (especially in the labor market) and the outputs that it supplies in the product market. Payments to purchase inputs make up most of the firm's costs, and this chapter treats these costs in depth. How the costs are balanced against revenues is the subject of Chapter 12.

ESSENTIAL CONCEPTS

1   In the basic competitive model, the firm's objective is to maximize its market value. Because the value of the firm depends on its profit-making potential, another way to put this is to say the firm's objective is to maximize its (long-term) profits. **Profits** equal revenues minus costs, and revenues are simply price times quantity.

2   The **production function** shows the relationship between inputs and outputs. The increase in output resulting from a small increase in the use of an input is called the **marginal product.** The **principle of diminishing returns** states that as more of one input is used, holding other inputs fixed, the marginal product declines. While diminishing returns represent the usual case, some production functions exhibit **increasing returns,** where the marginal product increases as more of an input is used. If doubling the input doubles the output, then there are **constant returns.** Inputs that do not change as output changes are called **fixed inputs**; inputs that do change with output are called **variable inputs.**

3   There are costs associated with each type of input: either **fixed costs,** which do not change when output changes, or **variable costs,** which do. The important concept to grasp is how the various measures of costs change as output changes. The **average cost** curve is typically U-shaped; the **marginal cost** curve lies below it when average cost falls, equals average cost at the minimum, and lies above it when average cost increases.

4   The **principle of substitution** says that as the price of an input increases, firms substitute other inputs. The firm always chooses the least-cost production technique. In the long run, all inputs are variable; the firm has more choices. The **long-run average cost curve** is the lower boundary of all possible short-run average cost curves.

5   In the long run, firms can increase in the same proportion, there are **constant returns to scale** if output increases in the same proportion. If output increases by less, there are **diminishing returns to scale**. **Increasing returns to scale** imply that output increases by a greater proportion than do inputs. **Economies of scope** refer to the cost savings from producing several goods together rather than separately.

BEHIND THE ESSENTIAL CONCEPTS

1   Of the many diagrams in this chapter, there are four that you should master. Each is explained below. Notice how the economic idea (such as diminishing returns or increasing returns to scale) determines the shape of the curves.

   a   The first diagram to master is the production function (Figure 11.1, which is similar to Figure 11.4 in the text). The production function indicates how output (measured on the vertical axis) changes as the quantity of the variable input (measured on the horizontal axis) changes. There are two important facts to know. The first is that the shape indicates whether the production function has diminishing, constant, or increasing returns. Figure 11.1 shows diminishing returns. Also, the slope of the line from the origin to the curve is equal to the average product.

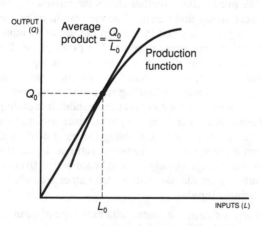

Figure 11.1

   b   The second diagram is the total cost curves, shown in Figure 11.2 (which summarizes Figure 11.5 A, B, and C of the text). Output is measured along the horizontal axis, and cost along the vertical one. Again, there are two important features to observe. First, total cost is the sum of fixed and variable costs. Because by definition fixed costs don't change, the

difference between the parallel variable and total cost curves equals fixed cost. The second feature is that the total cost curve inherits its shape from the production function. This will be explored in the analysis part of this chapter.

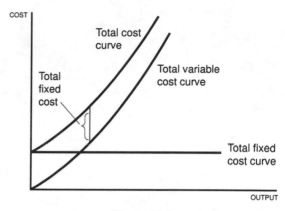

Figure 11.2

   c   Third, there is the average cost–marginal cost diagram, shown in Figure 11.3 (which duplicates Figure 11.6 in the text). The important concept here is the relationship between the marginal and average cost curves. The average cost curve is typically U-shaped. When marginal cost is below average cost, average cost is downward sloping. Marginal cost equals average cost at the minimum of average cost, and marginal cost is above average cost when average cost is upward sloping. Average cost falls as fixed costs are spread over more units. Average cost rises because diminishing returns drive the marginal cost curve above the average cost curve.

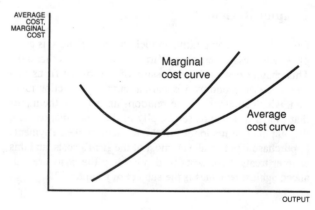

Figure 11.3

   d   Finally, there is the long-run average cost curve. For every production process, there are fixed inputs and an associated average cost curve. The long-run average cost curve is the lower boundary, as shown in Figure 11.4 (which duplicates Figure 11.14 in the text). The curve is drawn flat, which represents constant returns of scale.

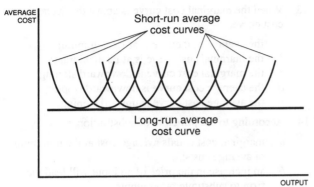

AVERAGE COST

Short-run average cost curves

Long-run average cost curve

OUTPUT

Figure 11.4

2 In reviewing these four diagrams, keep in mind three pointers.

a Remember to note what is measured along each axis. It's easy to make the mistake of memorizing the shapes of the curves while forgetting how to label the axes.

b Note the relationships among the curves, especially the marginal cost and average cost relationship.

c The shape of the curves illustrate the economic properties. It's important to be able to recognize economic properties like diminishing returns and economies of scale in the diagrams of production functions and cost curves.

3 Diminishing returns refer to production processes in which some, but not all, inputs are variable. Diminishing returns imply that the marginal product decreases as more inputs are used. Economists add the words "to scale" when describing a production process in which all inputs are variable. Thus, decreasing returns to scale mean that as all inputs are increased in a certain proportion, output increases by less.

SELF-TEST

True or False

1 According to the basic competitive model, firms maximize profits.

2 Firms in competitive markets are price takers.

3 The marginal product is the last unit of output.

4 The principle of diminishing returns says that as more of one input is added, while other inputs remain unchanged, the marginal product of the added input diminishes.

5 With constant returns, if all inputs are increased by one-third, then output increases by one-third.

6 Costs associated with inputs that change as output changes are called variable costs.

7 Total costs are the sum of average and marginal costs.

8 If labor is the only variable input, then marginal cost equals the wage divided by the marginal product.

9 The average variable cost curve lies below the average total cost curve.

10 The marginal cost curve intersects the average cost curve at the minimum of the marginal cost curve.

11 If the price of an input rises, the firm will substitute other inputs to some extent, but its cost curves will still shift up.

12 Short-run average cost curves are typically U-shaped.

13 If there are economies of scale, the long-run average cost curve slopes downwards.

14 The long-run average cost curve is the lower boundary of all short-run average cost curves.

15 Economies of scope imply that producing a set of goods is cheaper than producing each of them singly.

Multiple Choice

1 In the basic competitive model, a firm that charges more than the going price

a will lose some of its customers slowly over time;
b will lose all its customers;
c may keep its customers if its goods are of higher quality than those of its competitors;
d will lose no customers if its price equals its marginal cost;
e none of the above.

2 The statement that firm in competitive markets are price takers means that

a firms accept the price set by the market;
b firms maximize profits;
c production has constant returns;
d marginal cost is upward sloping;
e average cost equals marginal cost at the minimum of average cost.

3 Profits equal

a fixed costs minus average costs;
b revenues minus fixed costs;
c revenues minus variable costs;
d price minus average cost;
e revenues minus total cost.

4 The marginal product of an input is

a the cost of producing one more unit of output;
b the extra output that results from hiring one more unit of the input;
c the cost required to hire one more unit of the input;
d output divided by the number of inputs used in the production process;
e a and c.

5 According to the principle of diminishing returns,

a as more of one input is added, the marginal product of the added input diminishes;
b as more of one input is added, holding other inputs unchanged, the marginal product of the added input diminishes;

c   as more of the output is produced, the cost of production diminishes;

d   as more of the output is produced, the marginal cost of production diminishes;

e   none of the above.

6   If the production function exhibits increasing returns,

a   the marginal product of input increases with the amount produced;

b   the marginal cost increases with output;

c   productivity is higher;

d   the production function is downward sloping;

e   a and d.

7   If, when the total quantity of all inputs is doubled, output exactly doubles, the production function exhibits

a   constant returns;

b   diminishing returns;

c   increasing returns;

d   economies of scale;

e   none of the above.

8   Fixed inputs are

a   inputs that cannot be moved;

b   inputs that can be purchased in only one fixed configuration;

c   inputs that can be purchased at a fixed price;

d   inputs that do not depend on the level of output;

e   none of the above.

9   Fixed costs

a   are the costs associated with fixed inputs.

b   do not change with the level of output;

c   include payment to some variable factors;

d   all of the above;

e   a and b.

10   The relationship between the marginal product of labor and the marginal cost of output is the following.

a   Marginal cost is the inverse of marginal product.

b   Marginal cost equals the wage divided by the marginal product.

c   Marginal cost is downward sloping when marginal product is downward sloping.

d   Marginal cost is constant, but marginal product is subject to diminishing returns.

e   b and d.

11   The principle of diminishing returns implies that

a   marginal product diminishes as more of the input is hired;

b   marginal cost increases with the level of output;

c   productivity is higher in large firms;

d   all of the above;

e   a and b.

12   Total cost equals

a   the sum of fixed and variable costs;

b   the product of fixed and variable costs;

c   the ratio of fixed and variable costs;

d   the sum of average costs and average variable costs;

e   none of the above.

13   When the marginal cost curve is above the average cost curve,

a   the average cost curve is at its minimum;

b   the marginal cost curve is at its maximum;

c   the marginal cost curve is downward sloping;

d   the average cost curve is downward sloping;

e   the average cost curve is upward sloping.

14   According to the principle of substitution,

a   marginal cost equals average cost at the minimum of average costs;

b   an increase in the price of an input will lead the firm to substitute other inputs;

c   a decrease in the price of an input will lead the firm to substitute other inputs;

d   if the firm does not know its marginal cost curve, it can substitute its average cost curve;

e   none of the above.

15   The difference between the long run and the short run is

a   that in the short run, there are constant returns, but not in the long run;

b   that in the long run, all inputs can be varied;

c   three months;

d   that in the short run, the average cost is decreasing, but it is increasing in the long run;

e   a and b.

16   In the short run, the typical average cost curve is

a   upward sloping;

b   downward sloping;

c   U-shaped;

d   horizontal;

e   none of the above.

17   The long-run average cost curve is

a   the sum of the short-run average cost curves;

b   the lower boundary of the short-run average cost curves;

c   the upper boundary of the short-run average cost curves;

d   horizontal;

e   none of the above.

18   The long-run average cost curve

a   may slope down because of overhead costs;

b   may eventually slope up because of managerial problems;

c   always exhibits increasing returns to scale;

d   a and c;

e   a and b.

19   The concept of increasing returns to scale means that

a   it is more expensive to produce a variety of goods together than to produce them separately;

b   it is more expensive to produce a large quantity than a small quantity;

c   the average cost of production is lower when a larger quantity is produced;

d   the marginal cost curve is downward sloping;

e   a and b.

20   The concept of economies of scope means that

   a   it is less expensive to produce a variety of goods
       together than to produce them separately;
   b   it is more expensive to produce a large quantity
       than a small quantity;
   c   the average cost of production is lower when a
       larger quantity is produced;
   d   the marginal cost curve is downward sloping;
   e   a and b.

Completion

1   The relationship between the inputs used in production
    and the level of output is called the _____.

2   The increase in output that results from using one
    more unit of an input is the _____.

3   The principle of _____ says that as more and
    more of one input is added, while other inputs remain
    unchanged, the marginal product of the added input di-
    minishes.

4   Costs that do not depend upon output are called
    _____ or overhead costs.

5   The _____ is the extra cost of producing one
    more unit of output.

6   The marginal cost curve intersects the average cost
    curve at the _____ of the _____ cost
    curve.

7   If marginal costs are above average costs, then pro-
    ducing an additional unit will _____ the aver-
    age.

8   An increase in the price of one input will lead a firm
    to substitute other inputs. This is a statement of the
    _____ _____.

9   If the average cost is lower when the firm produces a
    larger quantity, then there are economies of
    _____.

10 If it is less expensive to produce a variety of goods to-
    gether than to produce each good separately, then there
    are economies of _____.

Answers to Self-Test

True or False

1	t	6	t	11	t
2	t	7	f	12	t
3	f	8	t	13	t
4	t	9	t	14	t
5	t	10	f	15	t

Multiple Choice

1	b	6	a	11	e	16	c
2	e	7	a	12	a	17	b
3	e	8	d	13	e	18	e
4	b	9	e	14	b	19	c
5	b	10	b	15	b	20	a

Completion

1   production function
2   marginal product
3   diminishing returns
4   fixed
5   marginal cost
6   minimum, average
7   raise
8   principle of substitution
9   scale
10 scope

Doing Economics: Tools and Practice Problems

There is quite a bit of technical detail in this chapter, including production functions and a host of cost curves. First, we
will explore the production function, calculating the marginal and average product and plotting the curves. It is important to understand how the shape of the production function
exhibits diminishing, constant, or increasing returns. Next,
we turn our attention to the cost curves; we calculate the
various cost concepts and plot the curves. Again, it is important to understand the relationships between the curves and
the economic meaning of the shapes of the curves.

THE PRODUCTION FUNCTION

The relationship between inputs and outputs is given by the
production function. It shows how much output will result
from the efficient use of each possible quantity of the inputs. Economists are interested also in the marginal product,
the extra returns brought about by using one more input, and
the average product, output per input. In order to understand
the decisions of firms, you must understand the production
function and its relationship to marginal and average product. Table 11.1 lists the key facts and Tool Kit 11.1 shows
how to calculate and graph the key concepts.

Table 11.1
Production Function

The marginal product is the slope of the production
    function:
    marginal product = change in output/change in number
    of inputs.
The average product is the slope of a line from the origin
    to the production function:
    average product = output/input.
If returns are diminishing,
    the marginal product is decreasing.
    the slope of the production function is becoming flatter.
If returns are constant,
    the marginal product is constant.
    the slope of the production function is constant.
If returns are increasing,
    the marginal product is increasing.
    the slope of the production function is becoming steeper.

Tool Kit 11.1: Calculating and Graphing Marginal and Average Products

The production function summarizes the relationship between inputs and outputs. It is important to understand its relationship with the marginal and average product, which can be calculated from the information in the production function and also can be derived from the graph of the production function. Here is how it is done.

Step one: Identify and graph the production function.

Step two: Calculate the average product, which is output per unit of the input:

average product = output/number of inputs.

The average product is the slope of a line from the origin to the production function.

Step three: Calculate the marginal product, which is the extra output resulting from the use of one more unit of the input:

marginal product = change in output/change in input.

The marginal product equals the slope of the production function.

1 (Worked problem: marginal and average products) Table 11.2 gives the production function for keyboards at Tek-Tek computer products.

Table 11.2

Number of workers	Output	Average product	Marginal product
1	80		
2	150		
3	210		
4	260		
5	300		

a   Compute the average and marginal product, and fill in the table.
b   Plot the production function. For each point, verify that the slope of the line from the origin to the production function equals the average product.
c   Between each two adjacent points on the production function, verify that the slope equals the marginal product.

d   Does the production function exhibit diminishing, constant, or increasing returns?

Step-by-step solution

Step one (a): Identify and graph the production function. This is given in Table 11.2.

Step two: Calculate and graph the average product. The average product is output divided by the number of workers. If output is 80, the average product is 80/1 = 80. Enter this number. If output is 150, the average product is 150/2 = 75. Complete the average product column. The result is given in Table 11.3.

Table 11.3

Number of workers	Output	Average product	Marginal product
1	80	80	80
2	150	75	70
3	210	70	60
4	260	65	50
5	300	60	40

Step three: Calculate the marginal product. The marginal product is the extra output resulting from using one more input. The marginal product of the first worker is 80. Enter this number. When the second worker is used, output rises to 150. The marginal product of this worker is 150 − 80 = 70. Enter this number. Complete the marginal product column. Table 11.3 gives the result.

Step four (b): Plot the production function.

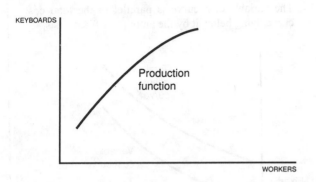

Step five: Choose a point on the production function, and verify that the slope of a line from the origin to that point is equal to the average product. Choose the point labelled *A*, where output is 210 and the number of workers is 3. Draw a line from the origin to point *A*. The slope is rise/run = 210/3 = 70, which is the average product.

Step six (c): Verify that the slope of the production function is the marginal product. The slope of the production function between *A* and *B*, where output is 300 and the number of workers is 5, is (300 − 260)/(5 − 4) = 40, which is the marginal product of the fourth worker.

Step seven (d): The marginal product is decreasing; this indicates diminishing returns.

2 (Practice problem: marginal and average products) Table 11.4 gives the production function for the insect spray Nobeetle at Bugout Pesticide Company.

Table 11.4

Number of workers	Output	Average product	Marginal product
1	1,200		
2	2,200		
3	3,000		
4	3,600		
5	4,000		

a Compute the average and marginal products, and fill in the table.
b Plot the production function. For each point, verify that the slope of the line from the origin to the production function equals the average product.
c Between each two adjacent points on the production function, verify that the slope equals the marginal product.
d Does the production function exhibit diminishing, constant, or increasing returns?

3 (Practice problem: marginal and average products) For the following production functions, answer parts a through d in problem 2.

a Bedford Waterbeds

Number of workers	Output	Average product	Marginal product
1	24		
2	42		
3	57		
4	68		
5	75		

b Worry-Free Insurance

Number of sellers	Policies	Average product	Marginal product
10	200		
20	500		
30	700		
40	800		
50	850		

COST

A firm's costs are its payments to inputs. Some of these inputs are fixed and some are variable. We are interested in the total cost curves and also in average and marginal costs. Thus we have many cost curves. Table 11.5 summarizes the important information about cost curves and Tool Kit 11.2 shows how to calculate and graph the key concepts.

Tool Kit 11.2: Calculating and Graphing Cost Measures

There are two sets of cost curves: the total curves (total cost, fixed cost, and variable cost) and the average-marginal curves (average cost, marginal cost). It is important to be able to calculate each of the cost concepts and also to recognize their relationships on the graphs. Follow along.

Step one: Identify and graph the total cost curve.

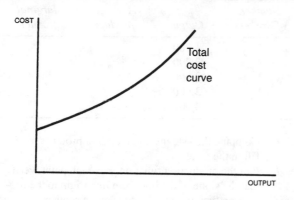

Step two: Calculate and graph the variable cost curve:

variable cost = total cost − fixed cost.

The variable cost curve is parallel to the total cost curve, lying below it by the amount of fixed costs.

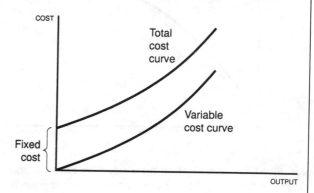

Step three: Calculate and graph the average cost curve: average cost = total cost/output.

Average cost equals the slope of a line from the origin to the total cost curve.

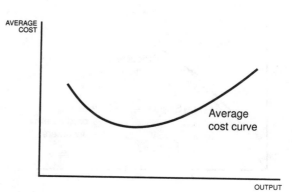

Step four: Calculate and graph the marginal cost curve: marginal cost = change in cost/change in output.

Marginal cost is the slope of the total cost curve.

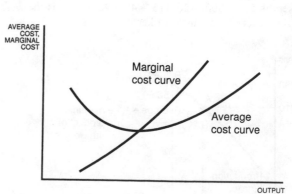

Table 11.5 summarizes the key information about cost curves.

Table 11.5
Cost Curves

Variable cost is parallel to the total cost curve, and below it by the amount of fixed cost:
variable cost = total cost – fixed cost.

Marginal cost is the slope of the total cost curve:
marginal cost = change in total cost/change in output.

Average cost is the slope of the line from the origin to the total cost curve:
average cost = total cost/output.

If returns are diminishing,
the marginal cost is increasing.
the slope of the total cost curve is becoming steeper.

If returns are constant,
the marginal cost is constant.
the slope of the total cost curve is constant.

If returns are increasing,
the marginal cost is decreasing.
the slope of the total cost curve is becoming flatter.

If marginal cost is below average cost,
the average cost curve is decreasing.

If marginal cost equals average cost,
the average cost curve is at its minimum.

If marginal cost is above average cost,
the average cost curve is increasing.

---

4   (Worked problem: cost curves) The total fixed costs at Stay-Brite Cleaning Company are $100,000. Table 11.6 gives their total costs for different levels of output measured in truckloads of Stay-Brite Cleaning Solution.

Table 11.6

Output	Total cost	Variable cost	Average cost	Marginal cost
1,000	$180,000			
2,000	$280,000			
3,000	$420,000			
4,000	$600,000			
5,000	$800,000			

a   Compute variable, average, and marginal cost, and enter in the table.
b   Plot the total cost and variable cost curves on one diagram, and verify the relationships given in Table 11.5.
c   Plot the average cost and marginal cost curves, and verify the marginal-average relationship.
d   Do the cost curves exhibit increasing, constant, or diminishing returns?

Step-by-step solution

Step one(a): Identify and graph the total cost curve.

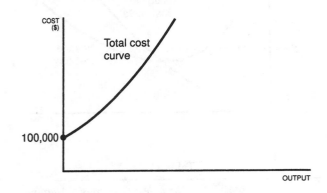

Step two: Calculate and graph the variable cost curve. Variable cost is just the difference between total cost and total fixed cost. The variable cost of 1,000 units is $180,000 – $100,000 = $80,000. Enter this number. Complete the variable cost column.

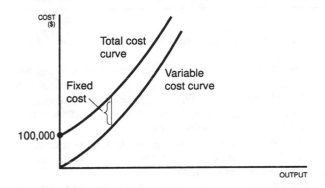

Step three: Calculate and graph the average cost curve. Average cost is total cost divided by output. The average cost of 1,000 units is $180,000/1,000 = $180. Enter this number. Complete the average cost column.

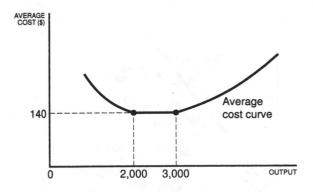

Step four: Calculate and graph the marginal cost curve. Marginal cost is the extra cost of producing one more unit. The marginal cost per unit for the first 1,000 units is $80,000/1,000 = $80. Enter this number, and continue to fill in the column. The complete information appears in Table 11.7.

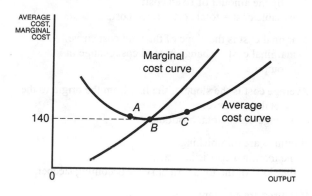

is rising; they are equal at *B*, which is the minimum of average cost; and marginal cost is above average cost at *C*, where average cost is rising.

Table 11.7

Output	Total cost	Variable cost	Average cost	Marginal cost
1,000	$180,000	$ 80,000	$180	$ 80
2,000	$280,000	$180,000	$140	$100
3,000	$420,000	$320,000	$140	$140
4,000	$600,000	$500,000	$150	$180
5,000	$800,000	$700,000	$160	$200

Step five (b): Choose a point on the total cost curve, and verify the relationships.

Variable cost is parallel to total cost. For example, between *A* and *B*, the slope of the total cost curve is ($600,000 − $420,000)/(4,000 − 3,000) = 180. The slope of the variable cost curve for the same levels of output is ($500,000 − $320,000)/(4,000 − 3,000) = 180.

The variable cost curve lies below the total cost curve by the amount of fixed cost. The difference all along the curves is $100,000, which is fixed cost.

The slope of the total cost curve equals marginal cost. Between *A* and *B*, the slope is 180, which is the marginal cost at 4,000 workers.

The slope of a line from the origin to the total cost curve equals average cost. Between the origin and point *A*, the slope of the line is $420,000/3,000 = 140, which is average cost.

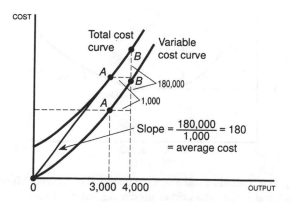

Step six (c): Plot the average and marginal cost curves, and verify the average-marginal relationship. As you can see, marginal cost is above average cost at *A*, where average cost

Step seven: The cost curves exhibit diminishing returns. Marginal cost is increasing, and total cost is becoming steeper.

5   (Practice problem: cost curves). The fixed costs at Pestle Mortar Company are $50,000. Table 11.8 gives their costs for different levels of output measured in mortars.

Table 11.8

Output	Total cost	Variable cost	Average cost	Marginal cost
1,000	$ 250,000			
2,000	$ 500,000			
3,000	$ 800,000			
4,000	$1,200,000			
5,000	$1,800,000			

a   Compute variable, average, and marginal costs, and enter in the table.
b   Plot the total cost and variable cost curves on one diagram, and verify the relationships given in Table 11.5.
c   Plot the average cost and marginal cost curves, and verify the marginal-average relationship.
d   Do the cost curves exhibit increasing, constant, or diminishing returns?

6   (Practice problem: cost curves) For the following cost data, answer parts a through d in question 5.

a   Fixed costs are $1,000.

Output	Total cost	Variable cost	Average cost	Marginal cost
10	$1,500			
20	$2,200			
30	$3,000			
40	$4,000			
50	$6,000			

b   Fixed costs are $0.

Output	Total cost	Variable cost	Average cost	Marginal cost
100	$1,000			
200	$1,800			
300	$2,400			
400	$2,800			
500	$3,200			
600	$3,600			

c   Fixed costs are $80,000.

Output	Total cost	Variable cost	Average cost	Marginal cost
1	$140,000			
2	$180,000			
3	$220,000			
4	$260,000			
5	$300,000			
6	$340,000			

Answers to Problems

2   a   The marginal and average products are given in Table 11.9.

Table 11.9

Number of workers	Output	Average product	Marginal product
1	1,200	1,200	1,200
2	2,200	1,100	1,000
3	3,000	1,000	800
4	3,600	900	600
5	4,000	800	400

b   The production function is drawn in the figure. The average product for 3 workers, which is 1,000, is shown as the slope of the line from the origin to point B.

c   The marginal product of the 4th worker, which is 600, is shown as the slope between points B and C.

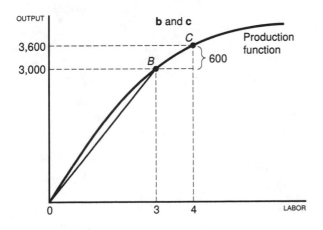

d   The production function exhibits diminishing returns.

3   a   Bedford Waterbeds—diminishing returns

Number of workers	Output	Average product	Marginal product
1	24	24	24
2	42	21	18
3	57	19	15
4	68	17	11
5	75	15	7

b   Worry-Free Insurance—diminishing returns

Number of sellers	Policies	Average product	Marginal product
10	200	20.0	20
20	500	25.0	30
30	700	23.3	20
40	800	20.0	10
50	850	17.0	5

5   a   The completed table is given in Table 11.10.

Table 11.10

Output	Total cost	Variable cost	Average cost	Marginal cost
1,000	$ 250,000	$ 200,000	$250	$200
2,000	$ 500,000	$ 450,000	$250	$250
3,000	$ 800,000	$ 750,000	$267	$300
4,000	$1,200,000	$1,150,000	$300	$400
5,000	$1,800,000	$1,750,000	$360	$600

b   The diagram shows the total cost and variable cost curves. The variable cost curve is parallel and lies below the total cost curve by $50,000, which is the amount of fixed cost.

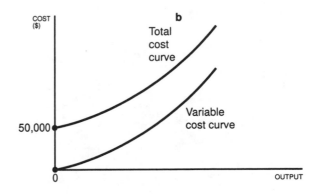

c   The diagram shows the average and marginal cost curves. Average and marginal costs are equal at $250, which is the minimum of the average cost curve. Average cost rises after this point, while marginal cost hovers above.

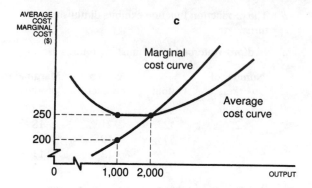

d   The cost curves exhibit diminishing returns.

6   The completed cost tables appear below.

a   These cost curves show diminishing returns.

Output	Total cost	Variable cost	Average cost	Marginal cost
10	$1,500	$ 500	$150	$ 50
20	$2,200	$1,200	$110	$ 70
30	$3,000	$2,000	$100	$ 80
40	$4,000	$3,000	$100	$100
50	$6,000	$5,000	$120	$200

b   These cost curves show increasing returns.

Output	Total cost	Variable cost	Average cost	Marginal cost
100	$1,000	$1,000	$10.00	$10
200	$1,800	$1,800	$ 9.00	$ 8
300	$2,400	$2,400	$ 8.00	$ 6
400	$2,800	$2,800	$ 7.00	$ 4
500	$3,200	$3,200	$ 6.50	$ 4
600	$3,600	$3,600	$ 6.00	$ 4

c   These cost curves show increasing returns until output equals 2, and constant returns thereafter.

Output	Total cost	Variable cost	Average cost	Marginal cost
1	$140,000	$ 60,000	$140,000	$60,000
2	$180,000	$100,000	$ 90,000	$40,000
3	$220,000	$140,000	$ 73,333	$40,000
4	$260,000	$180,000	$ 65,000	$40,000
5	$300,000	$220,000	$ 60,000	$40,000
6	$340,000	$260,000	$ 56,667	$40,000

Chapter 12

PRODUCTION

Chapter Review

This chapter moves the discussion from the firm's costs to decisions firms must make regarding production. In the process, it shows the role of the firm in the competitive model. The firm is a supplier in product markets and a demander in input markets, especially in labor markets. The chapter also explains why and when new firms will enter an industry and why and when existing firms will shut down. Each of these issues requires carefully distinguishing opportunity costs from sunk costs, and profits from rents. This close examination of the firm's production decision completes the discussion of all the individual parts of the basic competitive model that began in Chapter 8. What remains is to put them together and evaluate how the model works. This is done in Chapter 13.

ESSENTIAL CONCEPTS

1 Firms choose output to **maximize profits.** Profit is the difference between total revenue and total costs. The output decision can be illustrated in two ways. One way, shown in Figure 12.1A, is to draw the total revenue and total cost curves and find the quantity where the total revenue curve is above the total cost curve by the greatest amount. At this point, the curves are parallel and their slopes are equal. The second way, shown in panel B, uses the marginal revenue curve. The slope of the total revenue curve is marginal revenue, which for the competitive firm equals the price of its product. The slope of the total cost curve is marginal cost. Therefore, at this point, marginal revenue (price) equals marginal cost, and profit maximization can be shown by the intersection of these two curves.

2 If the market price for a good or service exceeds the minimum average cost, then it pays new firms to enter the market. In deciding whether to *exit* the market, however, a firm must pay attention to those costs it cannot recover. Costs that the firm must pay whether or not it leaves the market are called **sunk costs.** The firm should stay in the market whenever it can earn revenues greater than all the costs not sunk. If all the fixed costs are nonrecoverable sunk costs, then the firm will exit when price falls below the minimum of the average variable cost curve.

3 The *supply curve of the firm* is the marginal cost curve above the minimum price needed to keep the firm from exiting. The *market supply curve* is the sum of the quantities supplied of all firms in the market, and it takes

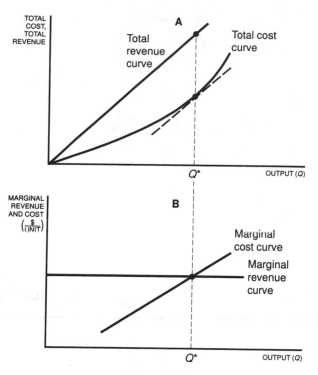

Figure 12.1

into account both the adjustments made by existing firms and the new entrants attracted to the market as the price rises. This curve is more elastic in the long run than in the short run, because existing firms have time to adjust to the lowest-cost production techniques and new firms have time to enter the market and produce.

4   When the going price in a competitive industry exceeds the minimum of the average cost, new firms will enter. The reason is that they will be able to earn higher profits in this industry than elsewhere in the economy. (Recall that the normal rate of return to captial is included in average cost.) Competition thus forces all firms to produce at minimum cost and drives any inefficient firms out of the market. In a similar vein, the theory of **contestable markets** argues that the threat of entry alone will compel a firm to earn zero profits even if it is the only one in the industry.

5   Firms exit an industry when they can no longer earn enough revenues to cover their costs, but the focus is on recoverable costs. Sunk costs are ignored in making the exit decision. The existence of significant sunk costs breaks down the theory of contestible market. The threat of entry is not so strong if the entrant risks losing its investment.

6   The firm's demand for inputs follows from its decision about how much to produce. More formally, the demand for an input is the **value of its marginal product,** which equals its marginal product (how much extra output the marginal input produces) times the product price (how much revenue the firm receives in selling the output). Again, the market demand is just the sum of the quantities demanded by all firms in the market. Because labor is by far the most important input in production, it is

used as the main example of an input in the text. Nevertheless, the demand for any input is the value of its marginal product.

BEHIND THE ESSENTIAL CONCEPTS

1   It is important that cost include all opportunity costs of production borne by the firm. Not only are such explicit costs as wages, energy, raw materials, and interest included, but also more subtle *opportunity costs* are taken into account, such as the value of the entrepreneur's time or the alternative earnings on the equity invested by the owners of the firm. These are considered opportunity costs because if the firm did not produce, the entrepreneur would devote time to some other activity, and the owners would take their investment capital elsewhere.

When a firm is making zero *economic* profits, its revenues are sufficient to cover all costs, including normal returns on the invested financial capital. An economist would say that the firm is only making enough to compensate the owners for the opportunity cost of putting their money into the firm. An accountant would view the situation differently, saying that a firm earning normal returns was actually making positive accounting profits.

2   Another difference between the way economists and accountants view profits concerns rent. **Rent** is the return to anything that is supplied inelastically. For example, suppose a firm's superior location enables it to earn 50 percent more than its competitors. An accountant would say that this firm's profits are 50 percent higher. An economist would call this extra return a rent, because the firm's earnings are higher than the minimum necessary to induce it to stay in its location. Although land is a good example, the concept of rent applies to any payment to a factor of production above the minimum necessary to bring the factor on to the market.

3   Sunk costs and fixed costs are distinct ideas. *Sunk costs* cannot be recovered no matter what the firm does. The firm can shut down production, sell off all its assets, and even go out of business, but it cannot recover its sunk costs. *Fixed costs* do not change as output changes, but they may be recoverable if the firm exits the industry. For example, the firm may own a plant, and the alternative earnings (the opportunity cost) of its plant do not depend on whether the firm produces a little or a great deal of output. If the firm can sell the factory when it exits the industry, then the costs of the plant are fixed but not sunk.

4   There is only one way to maximize profits. If the firm produces goods for the least cost and sets price equal to marginal cost, then it must set the input price equal to the value of the marginal product of that input. Thus, the profit-maximizing demand for labor is just the other side of the coin of the profit-maximizing supply of output. This fact is illustrated in Figure 12.2, where in panel A the firm sets the product price equal to marginal cost and produces Q^* units of output. (Note that this is

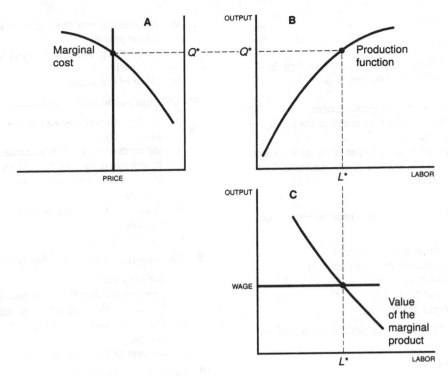

Figure 12.2

the usual diagram turned on its side.) The production function, drawn in panel B, shows that this level of output requires L^* hours of labor. Finally, panel C shows that when the firm sets the wage equal to the value of the marginal product of labor, it chooses exactly L^* hours of labor.

5   The competitive firm has four basic decisions to make: when to enter, when to exit, how much to produce, and how many inputs to hire. Table 12.1 summarizes the decision rules.

Table 12.1

Entry	Enter when price > minimum average cost.
Exit	Exit when revenues < nonrecoverable costs.
Supply	Produce the quantity of output for which price equals marginal cost.
Demand	Hire the quantity of inputs for which the input price equals the value of the marginal product.

SELF-TEST

True or False

1   The firm is choosing the profit-maximizing level of output when price equals marginal cost.

2   The firm is choosing the profit-maximizing level of any input when the input price equals the value of the marginal product.

3   The value of the marginal product equals the marginal product divided by the wage.

4   In the competitive model, marginal revenue is less than price because increasing output leads to a fall in price.

5   All fixed costs are sunk, but not all sunk costs are fixed.

6   Accounting profits are always less than economic profits.

7   In the long run in a competitive industry, economic profits are zero for any potential entrant.

8   Firms exit the industry when price falls below the minimum of the average cost.

9   A firm will enter an industry if the price is above the minimum of the average variable cost curve.

10   Economic rent is any payment to an input in excess of that needed to keep the input in its current use.

11   Land is the only input that can earn economic rent.

12   The long-run supply is more elastic than the short-run supply for the industry but not for the individual firm.

13   The long-run supply curve is the sum of the supply curves of individual firms, including those that enter at high prices.

14   Even if a firm's supply curve is upward sloping in the short run, it may be perfectly elastic in the long run.

15   Correctly measured, total cost should include all opportunity costs of operating.

Multiple Choice

1   Marginal revenue

    a   is less than price for the competitive firm because as it sells more output, it must lower the price;

    b   equals price for the competitive firm;

    c   is the revenue that the firm receives for selling another unit of output;

    d   is the extra profit that the firm receives from selling another unit of output, after accounting for all opportunity costs;

    e   b and c.

2   The firm supplies the profit-maximizing level of output when

    a   marginal revenue equals price;

    b   marginal revenue equals marginal cost;

    c   economic profits are zero;

    d   accounting profits are zero;

    e   sunk costs equal fixed costs.

3   The extra cost of producing an additional unit of output is called

    a   marginal cost;

    b   fixed cost;

    c   overhead cost;

    d   sunk cost;

    e   marginal revenue.

4   It pays a firm to enter a market whenever

    a   the market price is greater than the minimum average cost at which the firm can produce;

    b   the firm can earn revenues greater than any nonrecoverable costs;

    c   price is greater than the minimum of the average variable cost curve;

    d   price equals marginal cost;

    e   marginal revenue equals marginal cost.

5   The firm should exit the market whenever

    a   it cannot earn revenues equal to at least its nonrecoverable costs;

    b   price is less than marginal cost;

    c   price is less than the minimum of the average cost curve;

    d   price is less than the minimum of the average variable cost curve;

    e   all of the above.

6   Sunk costs are

    a   costs that do not change when output changes;

    b   the costs of starting the business;

    c   nonrecoverable costs;

    d   variable costs;

    e   opportunity costs.

7   Which of the following is true?

    a   Accounting costs are always greater than economic costs.

    b   Economic costs are always greater than accounting costs.

    c   Accounting profits are always greater than economic profits.

    d   Economic profits are always greater than accounting profits.

    e   None of the above.

8   The firm's economic costs include

    a   the opportunity cost of the time of the entrepreneur;

    b   the revenue that could be earned in alternative uses by the assets that the firm owns;

    c   the return on the equity invested in the firm by the owners;

    d   depreciation on company-owned buildings and machinery;

    e   all of the above

9   The long-run supply curve for the industry is

    a   perfectly elastic;

    b   more elastic than the short-run supply curve;

    c   less elastic than the short-run supply curve;

    d   the lower boundary of the short-run supply curves;

    e   the sum of the short-run supply curves.

10   Economic rent refers to

    a   economic profit minus sunk cost;

    b   any payment to an input above the minimum needed to keep the input in its present use;

    c   payments from tenants to landlords;

    d   the wages of especially skilled labor;

    e   revenues received by efficient firms.

11   In the basic competitive model, profits are driven to zero. This means that

    a   revenues are just enough to cover all nonrecoverable costs;

    b   revenues are just enough to cover all costs, including the opportunity cost of invested financial capital;

    c   price equals the minimum of the average variable cost curve;

    d   accounting profits are equal to zero;

    e   b and d.

12   When price is greater than the minimum of the average variable cost curve, the firm

    a   enters the market;

    b   exits the market;

    c   may continue or exit depending upon the magnitude of sunk costs;

    d   shuts down production but does not exit;

    e   enters the market only if overhead costs are zero.

13   The market supply curve

    a   is the sum of the quantities of the supply curves of all of the firms;

    b   is less elastic than the supply curves of all of the firms;

    c   is the marginal cost curve of the last firm to enter the market;

d is always horizontal;

e none of the above.

14 The value to the firm of hiring one more worker is

a equal to marginal cost;

b equal to marginal revenue;

c equal to the marginal product of labor;

d equal to the marginal product of labor multiplied by the product price;

e equal to the marginal product of labor multiplied by the wage.

15 The value of the marginal product is

a the revenue that the firm receives for the last unit of output;

b the revenue that the firm receives for entering the market;

c the marginal product multiplied by the wage;

d the marginal product multiplied by the product price;

e none of the above.

16 The market demand for labor equals

a the market supply of output;

b the sum of the demands for labor of all the firms;

c the wage;

d the marginal product of labor;

e none of the above.

17 If all of a firm's fixed costs are sunk, then it shuts down when

a price is less than marginal cost;

b price is less than the minimum of the average cost curve;

c price is less than the minimum of the average variable cost curve;

d accounting profits fall below zero;

e economic profits fall below zero.

18 If none of a firm's fixed costs are sunk, then it shuts down when

a price is less than marginal cost;

b price is less than the minimum of the average cost curve;

c price is less than the minimum of the average variable cost curve;

d economic profits fall below zero;

e b and d.

19 If a firm with a U-shaped short-run average cost curve doubles its output by doubling the number of plants and keeps its average cost the same, then the long-run supply is

a perfectly elastic;

b perfectly inelastic;

c upward sloping;

d downward sloping;

e none of the above.

20 The real product wage is equal to

a the value of the marginal product of labor;

b the marginal cost;

c the product price;

d the wage divided by the marginal product;

e the wage divided by the product price.

Completion

1 The extra revenue that a firm receives for selling another unit of output is the _____.

2 In the basic competitive model, the marginal revenue equals the _____.

3 The extra cost that the firm bears for producing another unit of output is the _____.

4 The level of output that maximizes profits is found by setting _____ equal to _____.

5 The supply curve of the competitive firm is the same as the _____ curve when price is high enough to keep the firm in the market.

6 Costs that are not recoverable are called _____ costs.

7 Economic profits equal revenues received in excess of all _____ costs of operating the firm.

8 The demand for inputs is the _____ of the _____.

9 New firms enter the industry whenever price is greater than the minimum of the _____ curve.

10 The value of the marginal product is found by multiplying the _____ by the _____.

Answers to Self-Test

True or False

1	t	4	f	7	t	10	t	13	t
2	t	5	f	8	f	11	f	14	t
3	f	6	f	9	f	12	f	15	t

Multiple Choice

1	e	6	c	11	b	16	b
2	b	7	e	12	c	17	c
3	a	8	e	13	a	18	e
4	a	9	b	14	d	19	a
5	a	10	b	15	d	20	e

Completion

1 marginal revenue

2 price

3 marginal cost

4 price, marginal cost

5 marginal cost

6 sunk

7 opportunity

8 value, marginal product

9 average cost

10 marginal product, product price

Doing Economics: Tools and Practice Problems

The firm's decision of how much output to supply requires marginal benefit and marginal cost reasoning. So does the firm's demand for labor or any other input. In this section, we will do problems involving the profit-maximizing quantity of output and corresponding quantities of inputs. Next, we will investigate the entry and exit decisions, reviewing opportunity and sunk costs. A good understanding of costs allows us to derive the entire supply curve of output. Finally, we will tackle a capstone problem that integrates the production function, cost curves, entry decision, exit decision, supply curve, and demand curve for the competitive firm.

SUPPLY OF OUTPUT

Firms must decide how much output to offer for sale. This supply decision involves balancing marginal revenue and marginal cost. Competitive firms are price takers, so marginal revenue equals price. All this implies that price must equal marginal cost, and this is the rule for profit maximization in the supply of output. Tool Kit 12.1 shows how to solve the problem of how much output to supply.

Tool Kit 12.1: Finding the Quantity of Output to Supply

The quantity of output that maximizes the firm's profits is found by setting marginal revenue equal to marginal cost. When the firm is a price taker, the marginal revenue equals the product price. The rule is then to find the quantity for which price equals marginal cost.

Step one: Calculate the marginal cost for each unit of output.

Step two: Identify the market price.

Step three: Find the greatest level of output for which price equals marginal cost. This is the quantity supplied.

---

1   (Worked problem: quantity supplied) Barbara's Carpet Cleaners has fixed costs of $100 per month and a total cost curve as given in Table 12.2. Output is the number of carpets cleaned.

Table 12.2

Output	Total cost
10	$ 200
20	$ 320
30	$ 460
40	$ 620
50	$ 800
60	$1,000

a   The current price for cleaning a carpet is $18. How many carpets must be cleaned to maximize profits? What will the profit be?

b   Suppose that the price falls to $14. Calculate the profit-maximizing output and the total profits.

Step one (a): Marginal cost is the extra cost of cleaning another carpet. When output is increased from 0 to 10, total costs increase by $200 − $100 = $100; therefore, the marginal cost is $100/10 = $10. Derive the marginal cost curve shown in Table 12.3.

Table 12.3

Output	Total cost	Marginal cost
10	$ 200	10
20	$ 320	12
30	$ 460	14
40	$ 620	16
50	$ 800	18
60	$1,000	20

Step two: Identify the market price. It is $18.

Step three: Find the greatest level of output for which price equals marginal cost. The $18 price equals marginal cost when output is 50.

Step four: Calculate profits. Profits equal revenues minus costs. Revenues equal $900 (50 × $18); profits equal $900 − $800 = $100. So the firm makes profits equal to $100.

Step five (b): If the price falls to $14, then price equals marginal cost at 30 units. Profits = (30 × $14) − $460 = −$40, and the firm loses $40.

2   (Practice problem: quantity supplied) The fixed cost for Martin Block, Inc., is $10,000. The company's cost curve is given in Table 12.4.

Table 12.4

Output	Total cost	Marginal cost
10,000	$21,000	
20,000	$32,100	
30,000	$43,300	
40,000	$54,600	
50,000	$66,000	
60,000	$77,500	

a   The current price for blocks is $1.12. Find the profit-maximizing quantity of blocks to produce. What will the profit be?

b   Suppose that the price rises to $1.15. Calculate the profit-maximizing output and the total profits.

3   (Practice problem: quantity supplied) For each of the following, find the profit-maximizing output level, and calculate total profits.

a   Fixed costs = $40,000; price = $600.

Output	Total cost	Marginal cost
100	$ 80,000	
200	$120,000	
300	$170,000	
400	$230,000	
500	$300,000	
600	$380,000	
700	$470,000	

b   Fixed costs = $900; price = $3.00.

Output	Total cost	Marginal cost
1,000	$ 1,900	
2,000	$ 2,900	
3,000	$ 4,600	
4,000	$ 6,600	
5,000	$ 9,400	
6,000	$12,400	
7,000	$16,000	
8,000	$20,000	

c   Fixed costs = $0; price = $80.

Output	Total cost	Marginal cost
1	$ 40	
2	$ 90	
3	$150	
4	$210	
5	$280	
6	$360	
7	$450	
8	$550	

DEMAND FOR INPUTS

Profits are always maximized by setting marginal revenue equal to marginal cost. When the firm is a price taker in both product and input markets, the marginal revenue from hiring another input is the value of the marginal product, which is the marginal product of that input multiplied by the product price. The marginal cost of hiring another input is the input price. In the case of labor, the input price is the wage. Tool Kit 12.2 shows how to solve for the input demand.

Tool Kit 12.2: Finding the Quantity of an Input to Demand

The demand for an input is its value of the marginal product. This is found by multiplying the marginal product by the product price. Follow this five step procedure to determine the profit maximizing quantity of an input.

Step one: Calculate the marginal product for each level of the input.

Step two: Identify the product price.

Step three: Compute the value of the marginal product by multiplying the marginal product by the product price for each level of the input:

value of the marginal product =
marginal product × product price.

Step four: Identify the input price. (In the case of labor, this is the wage.)

Step five: Find the level of the input for which the value of the marginal product equals the input price. This is the quantity demanded.

---

4   (Worked problem: quantity demanded) The new company The Hair Cuttery is ready to start hiring. The price of haircuts is $8, and the production function is given in Table 12.5.

Table 12.5

Stylists	Haircuts per day	Marginal product	Value of the marginal product
1	8		
2	16		
3	23		
4	29		
5	34		
6	38		

a   The wage paid to hair stylists is $40 per day. Find the profit-maximizing number of hair stylists to hire.

b   Suppose that the wage rises to $64 per day. Find the number of hair stylists that maximizes profits.

Step-by-step solution

Step one (a): The marginal product is the extra output that results from hiring one more input. When the first hair stylist is hired, output rises from 0 to 8. The marginal product is 8. Enter this number. When the second hair stylist is hired, output rises from 8 to 16. The marginal product is 16 − 8 = 8; enter this number and continue. The marginal product column is given in Table 12.6.

Table 12.6

Stylists	Haircuts per day	Marginal product	Value of the marginal product
1	8	8	
2	16	8	
3	23	7	
4	29	6	
5	34	5	
6	38	4	

Step two: The product price is $8.

Step three: The value of the marginal product equals the product price multiplied by the marginal product. The value of the marginal product of the first worker is 8 × $8 = $64. Continue to enter the results in the appropriate column. The completed information is given in Table 12.7.

Table 12.7

Stylists	Haircuts per day	Marginal product	Value of the marginal product
1	8	8	$64
2	16	8	$64
3	23	7	$56
4	29	6	$48
5	34	5	$40
6	38	4	$32

Step four: The wage is $40 per day.

Step five: Profits are maximized when the wage is set equal to the value of the marginal product. The wage is $40, which equals the value of the marginal product when 5 hair stylists are hired.

Step six (b): When the wage is $64, it equals the value of the marginal product if 2 stylists are hired.

5   (Practice problem: quantity demanded) Moe's Lawn Service mows lawns for $20 each. Moe's production function is given in Table 12.8. Output is measured as the number of lawns mowed.

Table 12.8

Workers	Output per day	Marginal product	Value of the marginal product
1	5.0		
2	9.0		
3	13.0		
4	16.5		
5	19.5		
6	22.0		
7	24.0		

Moe pays his lawn mowers $40 per day.

a   Find the profit-maximizing number of mowers to hire.

b   Suppose that the wage rises to $70 per day. Find the profit-maximizing number of mowers to hire.

6   (Practice problem: quantity demanded) For each of the following, complete the table and find the profit-maximizing number of inputs.

a   Product price = $10; wage = $100 per day.

Workers	Output per day	Marginal product	Value of the marginal product
10	200		
20	360		
30	500		
40	620		
50	720		
60	800		

b   Product price = $10,000; wage = $10,000 per month.

Workers	Output per day	Marginal product	Value of the marginal product
10	20		
20	40		
30	55		
40	65		
50	70		
60	70		

c   Product price = $5; input price = $40.

Workers	Output per day	Marginal product	Value of the marginal product
1,000	10,000		
2,000	18,000		
3,000	25,500		
4,000	31,500		
5,000	36,000		
6,000	40,000		

ENTRY AND EXIT

A firm should seize the opportunity and enter an industry whenever it can make positive (or at least zero) economic profits. This occurs when price is greater than the minimum of the average cost curve. A firm should give up and exit an industry whenever it can no longer earn revenues in excess of its nonrecoverable costs. If all fixed costs are recoverable, then the firm exits whenever price falls below the minimum of the average cost curve. If none of the fixed costs are recoverable, then the firm exits when price falls below the minimum of the average *variable* cost curve. If some costs are recoverable, the exit price lies somewhere in between. Tool Kit 12.3 explores this idea.

Tool Kit 12.3: Determining Entry and Exit Prices

Firms enter the market when the price rises above the minimum average cost. They exit when the price falls below the minimum average recoverable cost. Follow this procedure to find these prices.

Step one: Calculate the average cost for each level of output.

Step two: Find the minimum average cost; this is the entry price. When the price is greater than or equal to the minimum average cost, then the firm should enter the market.

Step three: Identify all costs that are not sunk (nonrecoverable).

Step four: Calculate the average of the costs that are not sunk.

Step five: Find the minimum average nonsunk cost; this is the exit price. When the price falls below this level, the firm should exit the market.

---

7   (Worked problem: entry and exit prices) Let's return to Barbara's Carpet Cleaners in problem 1. The total cost curve is given in Table 12.9.

Table 12.9

Output	Total cost
10	$ 200
20	$ 320
30	$ 460
40	$ 620
50	$ 800
60	$1,000

a   Find the entry price, which is the minimum price that will induce the firm to enter the market.

b   Assume that all the fixed costs are sunk. Find the exit price, which is the maximum price that will induce the firm to exit the market.

c   Now assume that $50 of the fixed cost is recoverable. Find the exit price.

Step-by-step solution

Step one (a): Calculate the average cost for each level of output, and enter in the table. The average cost at 10 carpets is $200/10 = $20. Continue to fill in the column as in Table 12.10.

Table 12.10

Output	Total cost	Average cost
10	$ 200	$20.00
20	$ 320	$16.00
30	$ 460	$15.33
40	$ 620	$15.50
50	$ 800	$16.00
60	$1,000	$16.66

Step two: The minimum of the average cost curve is $15.33, and this is the entry price. This is the answer to part a.

Step three (b): Identify the costs that are not sunk. If all fixed costs are sunk, then only the variable costs can be recovered. In this case, the exit price is the minimum of the average variable cost curve. First, compute variable cost by subtracting fixed costs from total cost. The variable cost for 10 units of output is $200 – $100 = $100. Continue to fill in this column as in Table 12.11.

Table 12.11

Output	Total cost	Variable cost
10	$ 200	$100
20	$ 320	$220
30	$ 460	$360
40	$ 620	$520
50	$ 800	$700
60	$1,000	$900

Step four: Compute average variable cost. For 10 carpets, the average variable cost is $100/10 = $10. Enter the results as given in Table 12.12.

Table 12.12

Output	Total cost	Variable cost	Average variable cost
10	$ 200	$100	$10
20	$ 320	$220	$11
30	$ 460	$360	$12
40	$ 620	$520	$13
50	$ 800	$700	$14
60	$1,000	$900	$15

Step five: The minimum of the average variable cost curve is $10; therefore, the firm should exit when the price falls below $10. This is the answer to part b.

Step six (c): Only $50 is sunk; thus, the firm exits when revenues fall below variable costs plus $50. To find the recoverable costs, simply add $50 to the variable cost. Next, find the average of these numbers, and the minimum of these averages is the exit price. The results appear in Table 12.13.

Table 12.13

Output	Variable cost	Recoverable cost	Average recoverable cost
10	$100	$150	$15.00
20	$220	$270	$13.50
30	$360	$410	$13.66
40	$520	$570	$14.25
50	$700	$750	$15.00
60	$900	$950	$15.83

The minimum of the average recoverable cost column is $13.50, which is the exit price. When the price is $13.50, the firm loses $50, which means that revenues cover all but the nonrecoverable costs.

8   (Practice problem: entry and exit prices) Now let's return to Martin Block in problem 2. The total cost curve is reprinted in Table 12.14. Fixed costs equal $10,000.

Table 12.14

Output	Total cost
10,000	$21,000
20,000	$32,100
30,000	$43,300
40,000	$54,600
50,000	$66,000
60,000	$77,500

a   Find the entry price, which is the minimum price that will induce the firm to enter the market.

b   Assume that all of the fixed costs are sunk. Find the exit price, which is the maximum price that will induce the firm to exit the market.

9   (Practice problem: entry and exit prices) Find the entry price and the exit price for the firms in problem 3. Assume that all the fixed costs are sunk.

10 (Worked problem: applications) The competitive firm is a price taker in product and input markets. It has a production function and a level of fixed costs. Given this information, we can derive all the firm's cost curves, its supply curve, its demand curve, and the price at which it will enter or exit the industry. Remo's Repos recovers the automobiles of delinquent borrowers. Local banks pay him $50 per car recovered. Remo hires agents at $100 per night to repossess the cars. He

runs a low-budget operation with fixed costs of only $500. The production function is given in Table 12.15, where output is measured as the number of cars repossessed.

a   Complete the table below, and calculate the profit-maximizing number of agents to hire.

Table 12.15

Agents	Output	Marginal product	Value of the marginal product
1	8		
2	15		
3	21		
4	26		
5	30		
6	33		
7	35		
8	36		
9	37		

b   Complete the cost table below, and calculate the profit-maximizing number of automobiles to repossess.

Output	Total cost	Variable cost	Average cost	Average variable cost	Marginal cost

c   Verify that the number of agents hired repossesses the quantity of output produced.
d   Find the entry price.
e   Assume that the fixed costs are sunk, and find the exit price.

Step-by-step solution

Step one (a): Follow along with the solution to problem 4, and complete the table given above. The results are given in Table 12.16.

Table 12.16

Agents	Output	Marginal product	Value of the marginal product
1	8	8	$400
2	15	7	$350
3	21	6	$300
4	26	5	$250
5	30	4	$200
6	33	3	$150
7	35	2	$100
8	36	1	$ 50
9	37	1	$ 50

Step two: Set the input price ($100) equal to the value of the marginal product, which is $100 when 7 agents are hired.

Step three (b): Compute the cost for each output level in the production function. For 8 cars repossessed, 1 agent is hired

at $100 and fixed costs are $500; therefore, total costs equal $100 + $500 = $600. Enter this number. For 15 cars, 2 agents at $100 each added to the $500 gives a total cost of $700. Continue and complete the total cost column. The result is given in Table 12.17.

Table 12.17

Output	Total cost
8	$ 600
15	$ 700
21	$ 800
26	$ 900
30	$1,000
33	$1,100
35	$1,200
36	$1,300
37	$1,400

Step four: Follow the solution to problems 1 and 7, and complete the table. Be careful with marginal cost. For example, the marginal cost at 8 cars is ($600 − $500)/8 = $12.50. The marginal cost at 15 cars is ($700 − $600)/(15 − 8) = $14.29. The complete information is given in Table 12.18.

Table 12.18

Output	Total cost	Variable cost	Average cost	Average variable cost	Marginal cost
8	$ 600	$100	$75.00	$12.50	$ 12.50
15	$ 700	$200	$46.66	$13.33	$ 14.29
21	$ 800	$300	$38.09	$14.28	$ 16.66
26	$ 900	$400	$34.61	$15.38	$ 20.00
30	$1,000	$500	$33.33	$16.66	$ 25.00
33	$1,100	$600	$33.33	$18.18	$ 33.33
35	$1,200	$700	$34.28	$20.00	$ 50.00
36	$1,300	$800	$36.11	$22.22	$100.00
37	$1,400	$900	$37.83	$24.32	$100.00

Step five: Set price equal to marginal cost. The price is $50, which equals marginal cost when 35 cars are repossessed.

Step six (c): Check the production function to make sure that when 7 agents are hired, 35 cars are repossessed.

Step seven (d): The entry price is the minimum of the average cost curve, which is $33.33. Note that marginal cost equals average cost at the minimum of the average cost curve.

Step eight (e): The exit price for the case in which all fixed costs are sunk is the minimum of the average variable cost, which is $12.50. Again, note that at the minimum of average variable cost, it is equal to marginal cost.

11   (Practice problem: applications) Perry's Perfect Pet Place hires people to bathe dogs. Perry pays the bather $20 per day and charges the dogs $10 per bath. His fixed costs are $50. The production function is given in Table 12.19.

a   Complete the table below, and calculate the profit-maximizing number of bathers to hire.

Table 12.19

Bathers	Baths	Marginal product	Value of the marginal product
1	6		
2	11		
3	15		
4	18		
5	20		
6	21		

b   Complete the cost table below, and calculate the profit-maximizing number of dogs to bathe.

Output	Total cost	Variable cost	Average cost	Average variable cost	Marginal cost

c   Verify that the number of bathers hired does give the profit-maximizing number of baths.
d   Find the entry price.
e   Assume that the fixed costs are sunk, and find the exit price.

Answers to Problems

2 a   The marginal cost is given in Table 12.20.

Table 12.20

Output	Total cost	Marginal cost
10,000	$21,000	—
20,000	$32,100	$1.11
30,000	$43,300	$1.12
40,000	$54,600	$1.13
50,000	$66,000	$1.14
60,000	$77,500	$1.15

When the price is $1.12, output is 30,000, and profits equal ($1.12 × 30,000) – $43,300 = –$9,400.
b   When the price is $1.15, output is 60,000, and profits equal ($1.15 × 60,000) – $77,500 = –$8,500.

3 a   The marginal cost is given in Table 12.21.

Table 12.21

Output	Total cost	Marginal cost
100	$ 80,000	$400
200	$120,000	$400
300	$170,000	$500
400	$230,000	$600
500	$300,000	$700
600	$380,000	$800
700	$470,000	$900

Output = 400; profits = ($600 × 400) – $230,000 = $10,000.
b   The marginal cost is given in Table 12.22.

Table 12.22

Output	Total cost	Marginal cost
1,000	$ 1,900	$1.00
2,000	$ 2,900	$1.00
3,000	$ 4,600	$1.70
4,000	$ 6,600	$2.00
5,000	$ 9,400	$2.80
6,000	$12,400	$3.00
7,000	$16,000	$3.60
8,000	$20,000	$4.00

Output = 6,000; profits = ($3.00 × 6,000) – $12,400 = $5,600.
c   The marginal cost is given in Table 12.23.

Table 12.23

Output	Total cost	Marginal cost
1	$ 40	$ 40
2	$ 90	$ 50
3	$150	$ 60
4	$210	$ 60
5	$280	$ 70
6	$360	$ 80
7	$450	$ 90
8	$550	$100

Output = 6; profits = (6 × $80) – $360 = $120.

5   The value of the marginal product is given in Table 12.24.

Table 12.24

Workers	Output per day	Marginal product	Value of the marginal product
1	5.0	5.0	$100
2	9.0	4.0	$ 80
3	13.0	4.0	$ 80
4	16.5	3.5	$ 70
5	19.5	3.0	$ 60
6	22.0	2.5	$ 50
7	24.0	2.0	$ 40

a   When the wage is $40, it equals the vmp if 7 are hired.
b   When the wage is $70, it equals the vmp if 4 are hired.

6 a   The value of the marginal product is given in Table 12.25. The quantity demanded is 50 workers.

Table 12.25

Workers	Output per day	Marginal product	Value of the marginal product
10	200	20	$200
20	360	16	$160
30	500	14	$140
40	620	12	$120
50	720	10	$100
60	800	8	$ 80

  b   The value of the marginal product is given in Table 12.26. The quantity demanded is 40 workers.

Table 12.26

Workers	Output per day	Marginal product	Value of the marginal product
10	20	2.0	$20,000
20	40	2.0	$20,000
30	55	1.5	$15,000
40	65	1.0	$10,000
50	70	0.5	$ 5,000
60	70	0	$ 0

  c   The value of the marginal product is given in Table 12.27. The quantity demanded is 2,000 workers.

Table 12.27

Workers	Output per day	Marginal product	Value of the marginal product
1,000	10,000	10.0	$50.00
2,000	18,000	8.0	$40.00
3,000	25,500	7.5	$37.50
4,000	31,500	6.0	$30.00
5,000	36,000	4.5	$22.50
6,000	40,000	4.0	$20.00

8   The cost measures are given in Table 12.28.

Table 12.28

Output	Total cost	Average cost	Variable cost	Average variable cost
10,000	$21,000	$2.10	$11,000	$1.10
20,000	$32,100	$1.61	$22,100	$1.11
30,000	$43,300	$1.43	$33.300	$1.11
40,000	$54,600	$1.37	$44,600	$1.12
50,000	$66,000	$1.32	$56,000	$1.12
60,000	$77,500	$1.29	$67,500	$1.13

  a   Entry price = $1.29.
  b   Exit price = $1.10.

9   *a*   The cost measures appear in Table 12.29.

Table 12.29

Output	Total cost	Average cost	Variable cost	Average variable cost
100	$ 80,000	$800	$ 40,000	$400
200	$120,000	$600	$ 80,000	$400
300	$170,000	$567	$130,000	$433
400	$230,000	$575	$190,000	$475
500	$300,000	$600	$260,000	$520
600	$380,000	$633	$340,000	$567
700	$470,000	$671	$430,000	$614

  Entry price = $567; exit price = $400.
  b   The cost measures appear in Table 12.30.

Table 12.30

Output	Total cost	Average cost	Variable cost	Average variable cost
1,000	$ 1,900	$1.90	$ 1,000	$1.00
2,000	$ 2,900	$1.45	$ 2,000	$1.00
3,000	$ 4,600	$1.53	$ 3,700	$1.23
4,000	$ 6,600	$1.65	$ 5,700	$1.43
5,000	$ 9,400	$1.88	$ 8,500	$1.70
6,000	$12,400	$2.07	$11,500	$1.92
7,000	$16,000	$2.29	$15,100	$2.16
8,000	$20,000	$2.50	$19,100	$2.39

  Entry price = $1.45; exit price = $1.00.
  c   The cost measures appear in Table 12.31.

Table 12.31

Output	Total cost	Average cost	Variable cost	Average variable cost
1	$ 40	$40.00	$ 40	$40.00
2	$ 90	$45.00	$ 90	$45.00
3	$150	$50.00	$150	$50.00
4	$210	$52.50	$210	$52.50
5	$280	$56.00	$280	$56.00
6	$360	$60.00	$360	$60.00
7	$450	$64.29	$450	$64.29
8	$550	$68.75	$550	$68.75

  Entry price = $40; exit price = $40.

11   *a*   The complete information is given in Table 12.32.

Table 12.32

Bathers	Baths	Marginal product	Value of the marginal product
1	6	6	$60
2	11	5	$50
3	15	4	$40
4	18	3	$30
5	20	2	$20
6	21	1	$10

Perry should hire 5 bathers.

b The completed cost information appears in Table 12.33.

Table 12.33

Output	Total cost	Variable cost	Average cost	Average variable cost	Marginal cost
6	$ 70	$ 20	$11.67	$3.33	$ 3.33
11	$ 90	$ 40	$ 8.18	$3.64	$ 4.00
15	$110	$ 60	$ 7.33	$4.00	$ 5.00
18	$130	$ 80	$ 7.22	$4.44	$ 6.33
20	$150	$100	$ 7.50	$5.00	$10.00
21	$170	$120	$ 8.10	$5.71	$20.00

Perry should sell 20 baths.

c 5 bathers complete 20 baths.

d Entry price = $7.22.

e Exit price = $3.33.

Chapter 13

COMPETITIVE EQUILIBRIUM

Chapter Review

The elements of the basic competitive model have been presented over the last six chapters of the text. In Chapter 13, these elements—from individuals and their decisions regarding consumption, savings, investment, and work, to firms and their choices regarding production and costs—are brought together in the general equilibrium model. The focus of the model is on the interdependencies of the product, labor, and capital markets. Another major topic is a normative one: how well does the competitive economy perform? The notion of Pareto efficiency provides a tool with which economists can evaluate how well the market economy answers the basic economic questions. This chapter completes the presentation of the competitive model and closes Part Two. In Part Three, attention shifts to imperfect markets.

ESSENTIAL CONCEPTS

1   Partial equilibrium analysis looks at one market in isolation. This kind of analysis can be inappropriate if changes in the market under consideration cause disturbances in the rest of the economy, which then feed back in an important way to the original market. General equilibrium analysis takes into account the relationships among different markets and keeps track of the interactions.

2   The basic competitive three-market model is a relatively simple general equilibrium model, and is very good for analyzing the interactions among markets. The three markets are the labor, capital, and product markets. They are interdependent in that as the price changes in one market, demand and supply curves shift in the others. In general equilibrium, the three prices (wage, interest rate, and product price) are set so that each market clears.

   a   Demand equals supply in the labor market.
   b   Demand equals supply in the capital market.
   c   Demand equals supply in the goods market.

3   Another view of the general equilibrium of the economy is given by the circular flow model. The simple version given in Figure 13.1 shows that households supply labor and financial capital to firms and demand products. Firms demand labor and capital and supply products. The flows of funds balance. For example, the revenues that firms receive for the sale of their goods equal the payments to labor as wages and to capital as dividends and interest. The circular flow model can be expanded

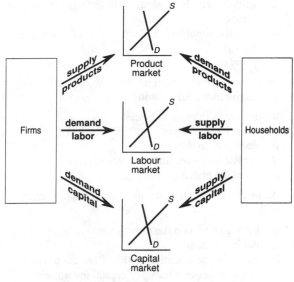

Figure 13.1

to keep track of flows between one country and the rest of the world and between the private sector and the government.

4   The concept of efficiency used by economists is called **Pareto efficiency**. An allocation of resources is Pareto efficient if there is no way to reallocate resources to make anyone better off without hurting someone else. The equilibrium of the competitive economy is Pareto efficient. There is **exchange efficiency** because the goods and services produced by the economy are distributed efficiently among individuals, **production efficiency** because the economy is on its production possibilities curve, and **product-mix efficiency** because the mix of goods matches consumers' tastes.

5   Free-market economists take the view that the basic competivive model provides a good description of the world and they see a quite limited role for government. Imperfect-market economists, on the other hand, take the competitive model as an important base but move beyond its boundaries to investigate circumstances where the economy is inefficient. Although they see the role for government in market failures, all economists caution that this does not necessarily imply that any particular government intervention will improve matters. Effective government intervention requires careful consideration of the reasons for market inefficiencies and the design of the remedy.

BEHIND THE ESSENTIAL CONCEPTS

1   The interdependencies of markets demonstrate another facet of the principle of substitution. When the price of one good rises, the demand for its substitutes rises, while the demand for its complement falls. When the price of one input rises, firms substitute other inputs. A change in the capital market affects the wealth of con-

sumers and the costs of firms. The economy is a spider's web, and a movement in any one part reverberates throughout the whole.

2   Even though there are connections among all markets, in many cases the effects beyond a single market may be small. When this is true, it is sufficient to concentrate on the one market, that is, to employ partial equilibrium analysis, and ignore any general equilibrium repercussions. The art of economic analysis is to bring to light the important general equilibrium considerations and leave aside the portion of the economy that remains relatively unaffected.

3   If a firm produces several goods and there exists a way to rearrange its production and increase the output of one good without reducing the output of any other, an economist would say that this firm is inefficient. The firm is wasting inputs, because it is not getting the maximum output from the inputs. The output of the economy is the satisfaction (the utility) of its members. Therefore, if the economy is doing things one way, and there exists another way to do things that increases the utility of one individual (makes her better off) without reducing the utility of anyone else, then, just like the firm above, the economy is inefficient. Pareto efficiency is a natural definition of efficiency for the economy, the important output of which is ultimately not goods and services but human satisfaction.

SELF-TEST

True or False

1   A general equilibrium analysis takes into account all the important interactions among markets.

2   A partial equilibrium analysis focuses on one market only.

3   General equilibrium and partial equilibrium analyses always differ quite dramatically.

4   For the most part, in the capital market, firms are demanders and households are suppliers.

5   In the product market, firms are demanders and households are suppliers.

6   In the labor market, firms are demanders and households are suppliers.

7   The economy is in equilibrium when most of its markets clear.

8   In the circular flow model, the flows to households must equal the flows from households.

9   In the circular flow model, exports plus funds lent abroad must equal imports plus money borrowed from abroad.

10   The allocation of resources is Pareto efficient in competitive equilibrium.

11   The allocation of resources is equal in competitive equilibrium.

12   Pareto efficiency means that everyone can be made better off by some reallocation of resources.

13   Imperfect-market economists despair of the market's ability to produce efficient outcomes and advocate government control over the economy.

14   All points along the production possibilities curve are Pareto efficient.

15   Pareto efficiency requires exchange efficiency, production efficiency, and product-mix efficiency.

Multiple Choice

1   When an analysis focuses on the interactions between markets, it is called

   a   partial equilibrium;
   b   interactive equilibrium;
   c   disequilibrium;
   d   general equilibrium;
   e   none of the above;

2   When an analysis looks only at the changes in one market, it is called

   a   partial equilibrium;
   b   interactive equilibrium;
   c   disequilibrium;
   d   general equilibrium;
   e   none of the above;

3   In a general equilibrium model, the supply of labor depends upon

   a   product prices;
   b   the wage;
   c   interest rates;
   d   a and b;
   e   all of the above.

4   In a general equilibrium model, the supply of products depends upon the wage and interest rates because

   a   these input prices affect costs;
   b   household income is affected by changes in the wage and interest rates;
   c   households can substitute leisure or future consumption for current products;
   d   the demand for capital depends upon the wage rate;
   e   all of the above.

5   Which of the following is not necessarily true when the economy is in full, general equilibrium?

   a   The supply of labor equals the demand.
   b   The supply of products equals the demand.
   c   The supply of capital equals the demand.
   d   The distribution of income is fair.
   e   All of the above are true when the economy is in equilibrium.

6   A increase in immigration will

   a   shift the supply of labor to the left, decreasing wages;
   b   shift the supply of labor to the right, decreasing wages;

   c   shift the supply of products to the right, decreasing prices;
   d   shift the supply of products to the left, increasing prices;
   e   b and c.

7   In general equilibrium, a tax on business profits will be paid by individuals through

   a   increases in product prices;
   b   decreases in wages;
   c   decreases in dividends;
   d   capital losses on stock ownership;
   e   all of the above.

8   An increase in the tax rate on commercial property will

   a   have no effect on the returns to other forms of capital investment;
   b   cause financial capital to flow from commercial property to other forms of capital investment, reducing the average return to capital;
   c   have no effect on the allocation of financial capital;
   d   have no effect on the returns to capital because all investments must be equally profitable in equilibrium;
   e   a and c.

9   If the allocation of resources is Pareto efficient,

   a   the distribution of income is fair;
   b   there is a way to reallocate resources and make everyone better off;
   c   there is a way to reallocate resources and make some people better off without hurting others;
   d   there is no way to reallocate resources and make anyone better off without hurting some other person;
   e   none of the above.

10   In the basic circular flow model,

   a   households demand goods and services;
   b   firms supply goods and services;
   c   households supply labor and financial capital;
   d   firms demand labor and financial capital;
   e   all of the above.

11   The circular flow model shows that

   a   some taxes are paid by businesses and some by households;
   b   all taxes are paid by businesses through either lower product prices, higher wages, or higher costs of capital;
   c   all taxes are paid by households through either higher product prices, lower wages, or lower returns to capital;
   d   the government pays all taxes;
   e   none of the above.

12   Which of the following probably does not require a general equilibrium analysis?

   a   a corporate income tax;
   b   a ban on foreign investment;

c a national sales tax;

d elimination of trade restrictions.

e All of the above require general equilibrium analysis.

13 Which of the following probably requires only a partial equilibrium analysis?

a an increase in the supply of green beans;

b stricter antipollution regulations;

c a reduction in the size of the military by one-half;

d an end to agricultural price supports;

e all of the above.

14 According to the circular flow model, if the personal income tax is cut, then

a government borrowing must increase;

b some other tax must be increased;

c government spending must decrease;

d either b or c;

e either a, b, or c.

15 Free-market economists believe that

a market outcomes are usually efficient;

b the market's determination of the distribution of income is just;

c markets cannot be relied upon to produce efficient outcome;

d the market brings about production efficiency but not exchange efficiency;

e the market brings about exchange efficiency but not production efficiency.

16 Imperfect-market economists believe that

a market outcomes are usually efficient;

b the market's determination of the distribution of income is just;

c markets cannot be relied upon to produce efficient outcomes;

d the market brings about production efficiency but not exchange efficiency;

e the market brings about exchange efficiency but not production efficiency.

17 Exchange efficiency means that

a the distribution of the goods and services that the economy produces is efficient;

b the distribution of the goods and services that the economy produces is equitable;

c the economy is operating along its production possibilities curve;

d a and b;

e all of the above.

18 Production efficiency means that

a the mix of goods and services that the economy produces reflects the preferences of consumers;

b the economy is operating along its production possibilities curve;

c the distribution of what the economy produces is efficient;

d the distribution of what the economy produces is equitable;

e all of the above.

19 Which of the following is not implied by Pareto efficiency?

a exchange efficiency;

b production efficiency;

c efficiency of the product mix.

d All individuals share equally in the decisions that the economy makes.

e All of the above are implied by Pareto efficiency.

20 If the competitive model is an accurate depiction of the economy, then

a the allocation of resources is Pareto efficient;

b the distribution of income may be quite unequal;

c the economy is operating on the production possibilities curve;

d the economy is operating on the utility possibilities curve;

e all of the above.

Completion

1 Focusing on a single market while ignoring any spillover effects on other markets is called _____ analysis.

2 _____ analysis takes into account all the interactions and interdependencies between various parts of the economy.

3 In the simple circular flow model of the economy, households _____ labor and savings (financial capital) to firms and _____ goods and services.

4 In the simple circular flow model of the economy, firms _____ labor and financial capital from households and _____ goods and services.

5 When there is no way to make anyone better off without hurting someone else, the allocation of resources is _____.

6 _____ requires that the economy's output of goods and services be distributed efficiently among its consumers.

7 When the economy is productively efficient, it is operating on its _____ curve.

8 The view that the basic competitive model gives a good description of the world is held by _____.

9 _____ believe that there are many examples of market failure and that well-designed government intervention can improve matters.

10 Environmental degradation and unemployment are examples of _____.

Answers to Self-Test

True or False

1	t	4	t	7	f	10	t	13	f
2	t	5	f	8	t	11	f	14	f
3	f	6	t	9	f	12	f	15	t

Multiple Choice

1	d	6	e	11	c	16	c
2	a	7	e	12	e	17	a
3	e	8	b	13	a	18	b
4	a	9	d	14	e	19	d
5	d	10	e	15	a	20	e

Completion

1 partial equilibrium
2 General equilibrium
3 supply, demand
4 demand, supply
5 Pareto efficient
6 Exchange efficiency
7 production possibilities

8 free-market economists
9 Imperfect-market economists
10 market failure

Doing Economics: Tools and Practice Problems

The skill in general equilibrium analysis lies in choosing which interdependencies are important and which can be left aside. In this problem set, we first use the three-market model to analyze the effects of major changes in the economy: the introduction of a national sales tax, an important technological advance, and an increase in savings. Finally, there are a few problems that focus on the connections between two markets. We consider corporate taxation, compensating differentials, and natural resource prices.

Tool Kit 13.1: Using General Equilibrium Analysis

When doing general equilibrium analysis, keep the following procedure in mind.

Step one: Identify the relevant markets.

Step two: Start with an equilibrium in each market, as in the figure.

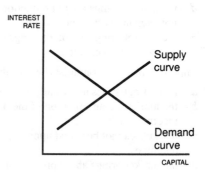

Step three: Identify a change, and determine which curves shift as a direct result of the change. In the second row of the figure, the demand for labor shifts outwards.

Step four: Shift the curves, and find the new equilibrium. In the general equilibrium model, this is only a temporary equilibrium because there are second-round effects to be accounted for. Observe which prices have changed. In the diagram, wages increase.

Step five: Determine which curves shift as a result of the price changes observed in step four.

Step six: Shift the curves, as shown here by lower supply in the product market and higher demand in the capital market, and find the new equilibrium.

Step seven: Stop. Usually a second round is enough. Compare the new equilibrium with that in step two.

1 (Worked problem: general equilibrium analysis) There are three major markets: labor, capital, and product. They are interrelated in that the prices in other markets cause the demand curves and supply curves to shift. Because of this interdependence, there will be important second-round effects in the three-market model. Most European countries have value-added taxes, a type of national sales tax.

a Use the three-market model to evaluate the effects of a value-added tax.

b Who pays the value-added tax?

Step-by-step solution

Step one (a): Identify the relevant markets. We will use the labor, capital, and product markets.

Step two: Start with an equilibrium in each market.

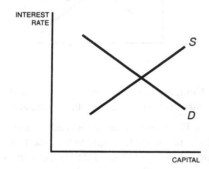

Step three: The value-added tax shifts the product market supply curve up by the amount of the tax. (This step is exactly like the analysis of the effects of taxes in Chapter 5.)

Step four: Find the new (temporary) equilibrium. Note that some of the tax is paid by consumers in the form of higher product prices. On the other hand, firms also receive less after the tax. This completes the first round.

Step five: Determine which curves shift as a result of the price changes observed in step four. The lower net of tax product prices observed in step four implies that the value of the marginal product of inputs is lower. This means that the demand curve for labor and the demand curve for capital must shift to the left.

Step six: Shift the curves, and find the new equilibrium.

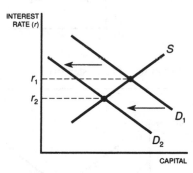

Step seven: Compare the new equilibrium with that in step two. We see that the wage and the interest rate are lower.

Step eight (b): The value-added tax is paid for in three ways. First, it is shifted forward to consumers in the form of higher product prices. Second, it is shifted backward to workers through lower wages. Third, it is shifted backward to savers in terms of lower interest rates. A vital lesson of the general equilibrium approach is that all taxes are ultimately paid by individuals. A partial equilibrium treatment in the product market alone would imply that firms pay some of the tax. The full general equilibrium analysis reveals that the producers' share of the tax is passed backward to workers and savers.

2   (Practice problem: general equilibrium analysis) A substantial share in the growth of developed countries is accounted for by technological advance, by improvements in how goods and services are produced, and by the introduction of new and better products. The hope for continued economic progress rests on technological advance in production. Use the three-market model to analyze the effects of a major technological advance.

a   Start with an equilibrium in the three markets.
b   Better technology increases the marginal products of labor and capital. Which curves are shifted? (Hint: Remember the formula for the value of the marginal product and the relationship between marginal product and marginal cost.)
c   In the second round, how does the equilibrium change?

3   (Practice problem: general equilibrium analysis) Many people are concerned about relatively low savings rate. One cause for optimism is that the aging of the relatively large baby boom generation will lead to more savings. Suppose that households decrease their consumption and increase their savings. Trace through the effects using the three-market model.

4   (Worked problem: general equilibrium analysis) Often when a change occurs in one market, there is another market closely linked to the first. In these cases, both markets must be included in the analysis. Investors seeking the highest possible returns can choose to buy stock in corporations or to invest their money in other noncorporate businesses. If the returns were higher in the corporate sector of the economy, then no one would invest in the noncorporate sector. If the returns were higher in the noncorporate sector, all money would flow out of the corporate sector. In equilibrium, then, the rate of return must be equal in the two sectors.

a   Illustrate an equilibrium in the markets for corporate and noncorporate investment.
b   In the United States, corporations must pay taxes on their income. The corporate income tax is in addition to the taxes paid by investors on their dividend income. Show how a tax on corporate income affects the market for corporate investment.
c   Show how the noncorporate investment market will adjust to restore both markets to equilibrium.
d   Who pays the corporate income tax?

Step-by-step solution

Step one (a): Start with an equilibrium. In this case, not only must supply and demand be equal in each market, but also each market must pay the same returns.

Step two (b): Determine which curve shifts. The corporate tax is paid by the demanders (corporations); therefore, the demand curve in the market for corporate investment shifts down.

Step three: The (temporary) equilibrium in the market for corporate investment has a lower rate of return than in the market for noncorporate investment.

Step four (c): Determine the effects in the noncorporate investment market. Because they can earn higher after-tax returns in the noncorporate sector, corporate investors will move their money. The supply of corporate investment will shift left, and the supply of noncorporate investment will shift right, until the returns are equal.

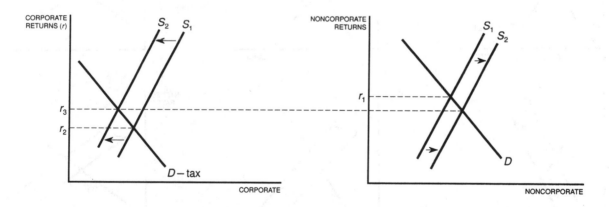

Step five (d): Find the new equilibrium and compare. In the new equilibrium, the returns are equal in each sector, but overall the returns are lower. We conclude that the corporate tax is paid by both noncorporate and corporate investors.

5   (Practice problem: general equilibrium analysis) Differences in wages that reflect differences in the characteristics of jobs are called compensating differentials. Truck drivers who haul freight over long distances are paid more than those who drive local routes. Suppose that the difference is $50 per week in equilibrium.

   a   Start with an equilibrium in the markets for local truck drivers and long-haul drivers. Be sure that the difference in wages is $50 per week.

   b   A new policy, agreed upon by both union and management, specifies that each driver must earn the same amount. Explain how the markets will adjust.

6   (Practice problem: general equilibrium analysis) Many people are concerned about the possible exhaustion of the limited supplies of natural resources, such as oil. To understand the economics of this issue, consider a two-period problem. Known reserves of oil equal 100,000 barrels. The oil can be sold now or be saved and sold in the future period. The discount rate is 50 percent over the time between the periods. The demand is the same now and in the future, and it is given in Table 13.1.

Table 13.1

Price	Quantity	Present discounted value of the future price
$50	20,000	
$45	30,000	
$40	40,000	
$35	55,000	
$30	70,000	
$25	80,000	
$20	90,000	
$10	100,000	

a Calculate the present discounted value of each of the prices for the future demand. This is the current value of waiting to sell at the future price.

b If the current price is greater than the present discounted value of the future price, all the oil will be sold today. If the reverse is true, the oil will be sold in the future. In equilibrium, current price must equal the present discounted value of the future price, and the total quantity sold in both periods

must equal 100,000 barrels. Find the equilibrium price today, the price in the future, and the quantity sold in each period.

Answers to Problems

2 a The initial equilibrium price is p_1, the wage is w_1, and the interest rate is r_1.

b The technical advance shifts the demands for labor and capital to the right because both factors are made more productive, and it shifts the supply of products to the right because costs are lower. The product price falls to p_2, the wage rises to w_2, and the interest rate rises to r_2.

c In the second round, the supply curve for products shifts left (mitigating the effects of the original shift) because wages and interest rates are higher. The demand curves for labor and capital shift back to the left (offsetting somewhat the effects of the original shift) because product prices are lower. (Recall that the demand for a factor of production is the value of the marginal product, which is price multiplied by marginal product.) The ultimate price is p_3, which is higher than p_1 but lower than p_2, because of the general equilibrium repercussions. Similarly, w_3 is greater than w_1 and r_3 is greater than r_1, but the changes are less great than a partial equilibrium analysis would imply.

3   a   The initial equilibrium price is p_1, the wage is w_1, and the interest rate is r_1.
     b   As people consume less, the demand for output falls. As they save more, the supply shifts to the right in the capital market. Product prices and interest rates fall as a result.
     c   In the second round, the fall in interest rates shifts the supply of output to the right and further reduces product prices. The fall in product prices, observed in part b, reduces the demand for capital and leads to a further decrease in the interest rate. In the labor market, demand shifts up because of lower interest rates, but shifts down because of lower product prices. The ultimate impact on the wage is not certain.

a

b

c

5 *a*   In the initial equilibrium, both markets clear, and the weekly wage is $50 higher in the long-haul market.

b   When the same wage is paid in the two markets, there is a shortage of long-haul drivers, and a surplus of drivers in the local market.

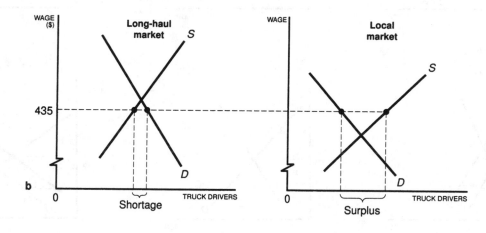

6 *a*   The present discounted value of the future price is given in Table 13.2.

Table 13.2

Price	Quantity	Present discounted value of the future price
$50	20,000	$50/(1 + $.50) = $33.33
$45	30,000	$30.00
$40	40,000	$26.67
$35	55,000	$23.33
$30	70,000	$20.00
$25	80,000	$16.67
$20	90,000	$13.33
$10	100,000	$ 6.67

b   The current price is $30, and 70,000 barrels are sold. The future price is $45, and 30,000 barrels are sold. The total is 70,000 + 30,000 = 100,000. The present discounted value of the future price is $30, which is the current price.

Part Three

Imperfect Markets

Chapter 14

MONOPOLIES AND IMPERFECT COMPETITION

Chapter Review

With the detailed study of perfect competition completed in Part Two, this chapter begins the study of imperfect competition. The real world differs from the basic competitive model in many important ways, and these differences shape the remainder of the text.

The first difference involves setting prices. While the competitive firm must accept the market price as a given fact, most firms in the real world have some control over their prices. How prices are set in monopolies, where there is only one seller, is the first topic taken up in the textbook chapter. The chapter then turns to a discussion of barriers to entry, which keep new firms from competing in an established industry, and competition among many firms producing similar but not identical products. Chapters 15, 16, 17, 18, and parts of Chapter 20 consider related problems and build on this chapter's techniques for analyzing imperfect competition.

ESSENTIAL CONCEPTS

1   There are four important types of **market structure: perfect competition, monopoly, monopolistic competition,** and **oligopoly.** A monopoly has a single seller.

Under monopolistic competition there are many firms, each selling a distinct product. Few firms dominate the industry in oligopolies. The essential differences are summarized in Table 14.1.

Table 14.1

Market structure	Firm's demand curve	Entry	Product differentiation	Examples
Perfect competition	Horizontal	Free entry	Homogenous products	Wheat, corn
Monopoly	Downward sloping	Barriers to entry	Only one firm	Major league baseball, holders of patents
Monopolistic competition	Downward sloping	Free entry	Differentiated products	Restaurants, designer clothing
Oligopoly	Downward sloping	Barriers to entry	Either homogenous or differentiated products	Aluminum manufacturers, automobiles

2   Like all firms, monopolies maximize profit by setting marginal cost equal to marginal revenue. Unlike for

competitive firms, for monopolies marginal revenue is less than price. This fact is shown by the following formula: Marginal revenue = Price (1 − 1/elasticity of demand). Barriers to entry allow monopolists to earn above-normal profits (also called monopoly rents). Finally, as price makers, monopolists can sometimes profitably charge different prices to different customers, a practice known as **price discrimination.**

3   Monopolistic competition and oligopoly are two special types of imperfect competition. In these industries firms have market power, which means that they can raise price without losing all of their sales. **Market power** is greater when the number of firms is lower and when there is more product differentiation. When products are more differentiated, they are more distant substitutes and firms' demands are less elastic. The characteristics of products, locations of the sellers, and the information and perceptions of buyers cause products to differ.

4   Factors that prevent entry into markets are called **barriers to entry.** Government policies such as licence requirements and patents create barriers to entry. The cost structure of the industry can also be a barrier, specifically the fraction of market demand accounted for by the output at the minimum of the firm's average cost curve. If one firm can produce the entire market demand for less than it could if it shared the market, the structure is called a **natural monopoly.** A monopoly can be sustained if a firm has control over an essential resource or if the firm has information advantages. Finally, strategies of existing firms can create barriers, if they can credibly convince potential competitors that entry would be met with fierce competition.

5   Monopolistic competition describes the market structure made up of many firms, each ignoring the reactions of the others. The demand curves facing the firms slope down (thus, price is above marginal cost), but new firms enter when there are profit opportunities (thus, in equilibrium, price equals average cost). New entrants produce close substitutes to the products of existing firms. Each entry shifts the demand curves facing existing firms to the left, reducing their profits.

BEHIND THE ESSENTIAL CONCEPTS

1   One important idea in the theory of imperfect competition is the relationship between marginal revenue and price. Marginal revenue is the extra revenue that the firm takes in when it sells another unit. In perfect competition, this amount is the price. But in imperfect competition, the price falls as more output is sold. Thus, there are two effects on revenue, shown in Figure 14.1. The firm is initially selling 10 units for $10 each. If it chooses to produce and sell 11 units, the price falls to $9.50. The first effect on revenue is that the firm sells more units at $9.50. This is shown as the area with pluses. If the demand curve facing the firm were horizontal, as under perfect competition, this would be the end of

Figure 14.1

the story: the extra revenue would be price times the extra quantity sold. However, the downward-sloping demand curve makes the price drop in order to sell one extra unit. This is the second effect. It means that the firm loses revenue on all its existing sales (because the price is lower for all units). This effect is shown as the area with minuses, and it makes marginal revenue less than the simple price times quantity calculation.

2   All imperfectly competitive firms face a downward-sloping demand curve. Thus, their profit-maximizing price is greater than marginal cost. In monopoly, there are barriers to entry, which allow monopolies to earn pure profits without attracting new competition. Monopoly prices are greater than average costs. In monopolistic competition, however, new entry drives economic profits to zero. When profits are zero, price equals average cost. To sum up,

a   downward-sloping demand implies that price is greater than marginal cost.
b   barriers to entry imply that price is greater than average cost.

3   Monopoly and monopolistic competition are similar in that each firm faces a downward-sloping demand curve and sets marginal revenue equal to marginal cost, which is less than price. The similarities stop here, however, because in a monopoly no new firm may enter even though a firm may earn pure profits. In monopolistically competitive industries, new firms enter, produce close substitutes, and capture customers. This entry shifts demand to the left until price equals average cost. The basic difference in the equilibria is that monopolies earn pure profits.

4   Monopolies are inefficient because price (which equals the marginal benefit of the good to consumers) is greater than marginal cost. Producing another unit would benefit customers more than it would cost. In monopolistic competition, things are not so simple. If all firms produce more goods, there are gains to both consumers and firms because price is greater than marginal cost and also because average cost falls. (Remember that the monopolistically competitive firm produces along the downward-sloping part of average cost.) On the other hand, the overall industry demand is only so

large, and if the firms become bigger, there will be room for fewer firms. Fewer firms mean fewer types of goods, so there is a trade-off between costs and variety.

SELF-TEST

True or False

1 The demand curve facing the firm is downward sloping in perfect competition.

2 The demand curve facing the firm is downward sloping in monopolistic competition.

3 When the demand curve facing the firm is downward sloping, marginal revenue is less than price.

4 Marginal revenue is less than price because price must fall for output to increase.

5 An industry with a single seller is a monopoly.

6 The demand curve facing a monopolist is the same as the industry demand curve.

7 Price is greater than marginal cost in monopoly.

8 Price is greater than marginal cost in monopolistic competition.

9 Compared to perfect competition, monopolies produce more but charge higher prices.

10 If there is a barrier to entry, firms may continue to earn pure profits.

11 Product differentiation is caused by barriers to entry.

12 In a natural monopoly, one firm can produce at a lower average cost than it could if it shared the market with other firms.

13 In equilibrium in monopolistic competition, price is greater than average cost.

14 The extent of a firm's market power is measured by how steeply the industry demand curve slopes downward.

15 The more elastic the demand, the more price exceeds marginal cost in monopolies.

Multiple Choice

1 In the competitive model,

  a marginal revenue for the firm equals the market price;
  b if the firm raises its price above that charged by its competitors, it will lose all its customers;
  c the demand curve facing the firm is horizontal;
  d the firm is a price taker;
  e all of the above.

2 If a single firm supplies the entire market, the market structure is

  a perfect competition;
  b oligopoly;
  c monopoly;
  d monopolistic competition;
  e none of the above.

3 If the market is dominated by several firms, its market structure is

  a perfect competition;
  b oligopoly;
  c monopoly;
  d monopolistic competition;
  e none of the above.

4 Monopolistic competition is distinguished from oligopoly by the fact that

  a in monopolistic competition, firms do not worry about the reactions of their rivals;
  b there is no competition in oligopoly;
  c oligopoly is a form of imperfect competition;
  d the demand curve facing the firm is downward sloping in monopolistic competition;
  e price is above marginal cost in an oligopoly.

5 When there is imperfect competition,

  a the demand curve facing the firm equals the market demand curve;
  b the demand curve facing the firm is horizontal;
  c the demand curve facing the firm is downward sloping;
  d the demand curve facing the firm is upward sloping;
  e the demand curve facing the firm is vertical.

6 When the demand curve facing the firm is downward sloping, marginal revenue is less than price

  a because of the principle of diminishing returns;
  b in the short run, but not in the long run;
  c because as output increases, the price must fall on all units;
  d because taxes must be paid;
  e none of the above.

7 "Marginal cost equals price" is the rule for maximizing profits for firms in which of the following market structures?

  a perfect competition;
  b monopolistic competition;
  c monopoly;
  d oligopoly;
  e all of the above.

8 Compared with competition, a monopoly

  a charges a higher price;
  b sells more output;
  c charges a lower price;
  d sells less output;
  e a and d.

9 The market demand curve is the same as the demand curve facing the firm when the market structure is

  a perfect competition;
  b monopoly;

c   oligopoly;
d   monopolistic competition;
e   all of the above.

10   A monopoly increases price above marginal cost by a greater amount when the demand is

a   more elastic;
b   more inelastic;
c   unitary elastic;
d   perfectly elastic;
e   none of the above.

11   Because they are single sellers, monopolies can earn

a   pure economic profits;
b   pure accounting profits;
c   zero profits;
d   the normal rate of return on invested capital;
e   c and d.

12   The measure of a firm's market power is

a   the number of employees it has;
b   the size of its capital stock;
c   the market price of its stock shares;
d   the extent to which the demand curve it faces is downward sloping;
e   all of the above.

13   How much the demand curve facing the firm slopes downwards is determined by

a   the number of firms in the industry;
b   the extent to which its product is differentiated from those of its competitors;
c   the size of its capital stock;
d   the minimum of its average cost curve.
e   a and b.

14   The four-firm concentration ratio measures

a   the number of firms in the industry;
b   the elasticity of industry demand;
c   the extent to which production is concentrated among a few firms;
d   the extent to which foreign firms dominate the industry;
e   the average elasticity among the four largest firms.

15   Product differentiation is caused by

a   differences in characteristics of products produced by different firms;
b   differences in the location of firms;
c   perceived differences, often induced by advertising;
d   imperfect information about price and availability;
e   all of the above.

16   When the products sold in one industry are differentiated, if one firm raises its price,

a   it will lose all of its customers;
b   it will lose none of its customers;
c   it will lose some but not all of its customers;
d   it will go out of business;
e   its profits will rise.

17   Barriers to entry

a   are factors that prevent new firms from entering the market;
b   are illegal;
c   allow firms in the industry to continue to earn economic profits;
d   imply that marginal revenue is greater than marginal cost.
e   a and c.

18   In the equilibrium of monopolistic competition,

a   firms make zero economic profits;
b   price equals average cost;
c   marginal revenue equals marginal cost;
d   price is greater than marginal cost;
e   all of the above.

19   The practice of charging different prices to different customers is called

a   product differentiation;
b   price discrimination;
c   predatory pricing;
d   limit pricing;
e   natural monopoly.

20   Economies of scale refer to

a   lower average cost as output is increased;
b   charging different prices to different customers;
c   any factor that erects barriers to the entry of new competitors;
d   lower average cost as different goods are produced with the same plant and equipment;
e   charging low prices for a limited time in order to drive competitors from the market.

Completion

1   The way in which an industry is organized is called its _____.

2   A few firms dominate an industry in _____.

3   An industry with a single seller is called _____.

4   In monopolistic competition, there are enough firms that each firm _____ the reactions of rivals.

5   In industries where the characteristics of products are different, there is said to be _____.

6   In imperfect competition, marginal revenue is _____ than price.

7   Any factor that prevents new firms from coming into an industry is called a _____.

8   If the market demand curve intersects the average cost curve for the firm at a point where it is decreasing, the industry is a _____.

9   In monopolistic competition, there is a trade-off between lower prices and more _____.

10   In equilibrium in monopolistic competition, price _____ average cost.

Answers to Self-Test

True or False

1	f	6	t	11	f
2	t	7	t	12	t
3	t	8	t	13	f
4	t	9	f	14	f
5	t	10	t	15	f

Multiple Choice

1	e	6	c	11	a	16	c
2	c	7	a	12	d	17	e
3	b	8	e	13	e	18	e
4	a	9	b	14	c	19	b
5	c	10	b	15	e	20	a

Completion

1 market structure
2 oligopoly
3 monopoly
4 ignores
5 product differentiation
6 less
7 barrier to entry
8 natural monopoly
9 variety
10 equals

Doing Economics: Tools and Practice Problems

In this section, we start with two basic topics and several applications. First, we calculate marginal revenue and find the profit-maximizing price and quantity for the monopolist. The second topic is price discrimination, which is the practice of firms in imperfectly competitive markets charging different prices to different consumers in order to raise profits. The applications that follow include the effects of taxes and price controls in monopoly markets and a couple of puzzles. Artists, entertainers, and authors are often paid a percentage of revenues. Also, they generally prefer lower prices than their producers and publishers. Two problems toward the end of this problem set show why this is true. Other problems explore the effects of taxes and price ceilings in monopoly markets and show that the monopolist always produces along the elastic portion of the demand curve.

MARGINAL REVENUE

The key idea that distinguishes perfect from imperfect competition is that for the latter, marginal revenue is less than price. This is because price must be lowered on all units in order to sell more. Tool Kit 14.1 shows how to calculate marginal revenue from the demand schedule.

Tool Kit 14.1: Calculating Marginal Revenue

The first step in solving the monopolist's problem is to calculate marginal revenue.

Step one: Make a table with four column headings: Price, Quantity, Revenues, and Marginal revenue. Enter the demand curve in the first two columns.

Price   Quantity   Revenues   Marginal revenue

Step two: Calculate revenues for each point on the demand curve, and enter the result in the table. Revenues are price multiplied by quantity:

$$\text{revenues} = \text{price} \times \text{quantity}.$$

Step three: Calculate marginal revenue for each interval along the demand curve, and enter the result in the table. Marginal revenue is the change in total revenue divided by the change in quantity:

marginal revenue =
    change in revenues/change in quantity.

After calculating marginal revenue, choose the price and quantity for which marginal revenue equals marginal cost.

---

1 (Worked problem: marginal revenue) As the only cement producer within 200 miles, Sam's Cement faces a downward-sloping demand curve, which is given in Table 14.2.

Table 14.2

Price	Quantity (tons)
$4.00	400
$3.50	800
$3.00	1,400
$2.50	2,800
$2.00	4,000

Sam's marginal cost is $2.00 per ton, and he has fixed costs of $1,000.

a   Calculate revenues and marginal revenue, and add these two columns to the table.
b   Find the profit-maximizing price and quantity.
c   Compute Sam's costs and profits at this price.
d   Suppose that Sam's fixed costs fall to $500. What is his profit-maximizing price and quantity, and how much does he earn in profits?
e   Illustrate your answer with a diagram.

Step-by-step solution

Step one (a): Make a table.

Price   Quantity   Revenues   Marginal revenue

Step two: Calculate revenues for each point on the demand

curve. When the price is $4, revenues are $4 × 400 = $1,600. Continuing, we derive Table 14.3.

Table 14.3

Price	Quantity	Revenues	Marginal revenue
$4.00	400	$1,600	
$3.50	800	$2,800	
$3.00	1,400	$4,200	
$2.50	2,800	$7,000	
$2.00	4,000	$8,000	

Step three: Calculate marginal revenue for each interval along the demand curve. For the first 400 units, revenue rises from $0 to $1,600. Thus, marginal revenue is $1,600/400 = $4. As output is increased to 800, total revenue grows from $1,600 to $2,800. Marginal revenue is ($2,800 − $1,600)/(800 − 400) = $3. Complete the marginal revenue column as shown in Table 14.4.

Table 14.4

Price	Quantity	Revenues	Marginal revenue
$4.00	400	$1,600	$4.00
$3.50	800	$2,800	$3.00
$3.00	1,400	$4,200	$2.33
$2.50	2,800	$7,000	$2.00
$2.00	4,000	$8,000	$0.83

Step four (b): To find the monopoly output and price, set marginal revenue equal to marginal cost. This occurs when the price is $2.50 and output is 2,800.

Step five (c): To find total costs, add fixed costs, which are $1,000, plus total variable costs. Each unit costs $2, and 2,800 units are produced. Total costs equal $1,000 + ($2 × 2,800) = $6,600. Profits equal revenues minus costs. Revenues are $7,000, so profits equal $7,000 − $6,600 = $400.

Step six (d): If fixed costs fall, marginal cost does not change. The profit-maximizing price is still $2.50, but total profits now equal $7,000 − ($500 + $5,600) = $900. Unless the firm decides to shut down, fixed costs do not affect the output and pricing decisions.

Step seven (e): The solution is illustrated in the diagram.

2   (Practice problem: marginal revenue) The Mudville Nine is the only professional baseball team within several hundred miles. The marginal cost of admitting another fan is $1. Fixed costs, which include player salaries, are $100,000. The demand curve is given in Table 14.5. The quantity column gives the season's attendance.

Table 14.5

Price	Quantity	Revenues	Marginal revenue
$8	100,000		
$7	150,000		
$6	200,000		
$5	250,000		
$4	300,000		
$3	350,000		
$2	400,000		

a   Compute marginal revenue, and complete the column.
b   Find the profit-maximizing price and quantity.
c   Compute Mudville's costs and profits at this price.
d   Suppose that the players win the right to negotiate with any team, and the increase in salaries raises fixed costs to $150,000. What is Mudville's profit-maximizing price and quantity, and how much profit does the team earn?
e   Illustrate your answer with a diagram.

3   (Practice problem: marginal revenue) For each of the following firms, find the profit-maximizing price and quantity and total profits earned.

a   Fixed costs = $0; marginal cost = $8.

Price	Quantity	Revenues	Marginal revenue
$10	1		
$ 9	2		
$ 8	3		
$ 7	4		
$ 6	5		
$ 5	6		
$ 4	7		

b   Fixed costs = $50,000; marginal cost = $.10.

Price	Quantity	Revenues	Marginal revenue
$0.50	500,000		
$0.45	600,000		
$0.40	700,000		
$0.35	800,000		
$0.30	900,000		

c   Compute marginal cost from the table.

Price	Quantity	Revenues	Marginal revenue	Total costs	Marginal costs
$20	400			$ 5,000	
$18	800			$ 7,000	
$16	1,200			$ 9,400	
$14	1,600			$12,600	
$12	2,000			$16,200	
$10	2,400			$21,000	

d   Compute marginal cost from the table.

Price	Quantity	Revenues	Marginal revenue	Total costs	Marginal costs
$1.00	1,000			$ 200	
$0.90	2,000			$ 300	
$0.80	3,500			$ 450	
$0.70	5,500			$ 650	
$0.60	8,000			$ 900	
$0.50	11,000			$1,230	
$0.40	15,000			$1,730	
$0.30	20,000			$2,355	

PRICE DISCRIMINATION

When it is possible to do so, an imperfectly competitive firm can improve profits by charging different prices to different consumers. This is called price discrimination. The idea is to segment the markets and set marginal revenue equal to marginal cost in each market and charge the corresponding price.

4   (Worked problem: price discrimination) Although the sale of the product is illegal, a drug enterprise operates according to sound business practices. It sells addictive designer drugs to two types of customers: nonaddicted experimenters and addicts (former experimenters). The demands for each type of customer are given in Table 14.6. The drug has no fixed costs and has marginal cost equal to $10 per dose.

Table 14.6

	Nonaddicts				Addicts		
Price	Quantity	Revenues	Marginal revenue	Price	Quantity	Revenues	Marginal revenue
$50	100			$50	500		
$40	300			$40	700		
$30	500			$30	1,050		
$20	1,000			$20	1,650		

a   Calculate marginal revenue for each demand curve.
b   Find the profit-maximizing price and quantity for each type of consumer.
c   Calculate total profits.

Step-by-step solution

Step one (a): Follow the procedure outlined above to calculate marginal revenue. The result should look like Table 14.7.

Table 14.7

	Nonaddicts				Addicts		
Price	Quantity	Revenues	Marginal revenue	Price	Quantity	Revenues	Marginal revenue
$50	100	$ 5,000	$50	$50	500	$25,000	$50.00
$40	300	$12,000	$35	$40	700	$28,000	$15.00
$30	500	$15,000	$15	$30	1,050	$31,500	$10.00
$20	1,000	$20,000	$10	$20	1,650	$33,000	$ 2.50

Step two (b): Find the profit-maximizing price in each market. Marginal cost, which is $10, equals marginal revenue for nonaddicts at a price of $20 and a quantity of 1,000. For addicts, marginal revenue equals marginal cost at a price of $30 and a quantity of 1,050.

Step three (c): Calculate total profits. Revenues are $20,000 from the nonaddicts and $31,500 from the addicts. Costs are $10 × (1,000 + 1,050) = $20,500; so profits equal $51,500 − $20,500 = $31,000.

5   (Practice problem: price discrimination) A common instance of price discrimination is dumping, which occurs when a firm faces less competition in its home market than abroad. In these cases, it will pay the company to charge different prices in the two markets. Opus Company sells carpet fibres in the foreign and domestic markets. Its marginal cost is $1 per spool, and it has fixed costs of $5,000. The domestic and foreign demands are given in Table 14.8.

Table 14.8

	Home market				Foreign market		
Price	Quantity	Revenues	Marginal revenue	Price	Quantity	Revenues	Marginal revenue
$10	2,000			$10	2,000		
$ 9	2,500			$ 9	3,000		
$ 8	3,000			$ 8	4,000		
$ 7	3,500			$ 7	5,000		
$ 6	4,000			$ 6	6,000		
$ 5	4,500			$ 5	7,000		
$ 4	5,000			$ 4	8,000		

a   Calculate marginal revenue for each demand curve.
b   Find the profit-maximizing price and quantity for each type of consumer.
c   Calculate total profits.

6   (Practice problem: price discrimination) Mark's Markets is one of the few chains that has not closed its inner-city stores. Mark's has expanded to the suburbs, but he faces more competition there. An example of a product he sells in both markets is hamburger, which has a marginal cost equal to $1. The space required to sell hamburger costs Mark's Markets about $100, and the demand curves in the suburbs and inner city are given in Table 14.9.

Table 14.9

	Suburbs				Inner city		
Price	Quantity	Revenues	Marginal revenue	Price	Quantity	Revenues	Marginal revenue
$4.00	200			$4.00	100		
$3.50	400			$3.50	120		
$3.00	600			$3.00	140		
$2.50	800			$2.50	160		
$2.00	1,000			$2.00	180		
$1.50	1,200			$1.50	200		

a   Calculate marginal revenue for each demand curve.

b   Find the profit-maximizing price and quantity for each type of consumer.

c   Calculate total profits.

APPLICATIONS

The following problems apply the idea of marginal revenue and monopoly decision-making to percentage of gross revenue contracts, tax incidence, price controls, and elasticity. Simply follow the procedure outlined in Tool Kit 14.1.

8   (Worked problem: marginal revenue) After the surprising success of her first novel, Imelda has negotiated a deal in which she receives 20 percent of the revenues from the sale of her second novel. The demand curve is given in Table 14.10. The publisher has fixed costs of $20,000, and the marginal cost of printing and distributing each book printed is $20.

Table 14.10

Price	Quantity	Revenues	Marginal revenue	Imelda's revenue
$40	10,000			
$35	20,000			
$30	30,000			
$25	40,000			
$20	50,000			

a   Calculate marginal revenue, and enter in the table.

b   Find the profit-maximizing price and quantity.

c   Compute Imelda's revenue for each price, and enter in the table.

d   What price maximizes Imelda's revenues?

e   Draw a diagram illustrating your answer.

Step-by-step solution

Step one (a): Calculate marginal revenue. Follow the usual procedure. The answer is in Table 14.11.

Table 14.11

Price	Quantity	Revenues	Marginal revenue	Imelda's revenue
$40	10,000	$ 400,000	$40	
$35	20,000	$ 700,000	$30	
$30	30,000	$ 900,000	$20	
$25	40,000	$1,000,000	$10	
$20	50,000	$1,000,000	$ 0	

Step two (b): Find the profit-maximizing price and quantity. Marginal cost equals marginal revenue for the publisher at a price of $30, where the quantity sold is 30,000.

Step three (c): Calculate Imelda's revenue. She receives 20 percent of the total. At a price of $40, she receives .20 × $400,000 = $80,000. Continue to calculate, and enter the results. They are given in Table 14.12.

Table 14.12

Price	Quantity	Revenues	Marginal revenue	Imelda's revenue
$40	10,000	$ 400,000	$40	$ 80,000
$35	20,000	$ 700,000	$30	$140,000
$30	30,000	$ 900,000	$20	$180,000
$25	40,000	$1,000,000	$10	$200,000
$20	50,000	$1,000,000	$ 0	$200,000

Step four (d): Imelda prefers a price of $25 or $20, which earns her $200,000, more than the $180,000 that she earns at the publisher's preferred price.

Step five (e): Draw a diagram. Note that the publisher sets marginal revenue equal to marginal cost. Imelda is only concerned with revenues, so she prefers the point where marginal revenue equals zero.

9   (Practice problem: marginal revenue) Magdalena, a budding female recording artist, has just completed her first album. She will receive 25 percent of the revenues. The record company reports that its demand curve is as given in Table 14.13, and its marginal costs are $6 per CD.

Table 14.13

Price	Quantity	Revenues	Marginal revenue	Magdalena's revenue
$20	20,000			
$18	25,000			
$16	30,000			
$14	35,000			
$12	40,000			
$10	48,000			

a   Calculate marginal revenue, and enter in the table.

b   Find the profit-maximizing price and quantity.

c   Compute Magdalena's revenue for each price, and enter in the table.

d   What price maximizes Magdalena's revenues?

e   Draw a diagram illustrating your answer.

10 (Practice problem: marginal revenue) Like most cities, South Potato is a one-newspaper town. The *South Potato Truth* distributes its daily paper for a marginal cost of $0.10. The demand curve is given in Table 14.14.

Table 14.14

Price	Quantity	Revenues	Marginal revenue
$1.00	30,000		
$0.95	40,000		
$0.90	50,000		
$0.85	60,000		
$0.80	70,000		
$0.75	80,000		
$0.70	90,000		
$0.65	100,000		
$0.60	110,000		
$0.55	120,000		

a   Calculate marginal revenue, and enter in the table.

b   Find the profit-maximizing price and quantity.

c   Suppose that a tax of $0.10 per paper is instituted. The tax will be paid by the newspaper company. Find the new profit-maximizing price and quantity.

d   How much of the tax is paid by consumers?

e   Draw a diagram illustrating your answer.

11 (Practice problem: marginal revenue) In competitive markets, price ceilings lower price and reduce the quantity sold. This is not true in monopoly markets. The demand for cable subscriptions in Motelville is given in Table 14.15. The marginal cost, including payments to cable programming providers, is $15.

Table 14.15

Price	Quantity	Revenues	Marginal revenue
$45	60,000		
$40	80,000		
$35	100,000		
$30	120,000		
$25	140,000		

a   Calculate marginal revenue, and enter in the table.

b   Find the profit-maximizing price and quantity of subscriptions.

c   Now suppose that the town sets a price ceiling equal to $25. How much will the company charge, and how many subscriptions will be sold?

d   Draw a diagram illustrating your answer.

12 (Practice problem: marginal revenue) Because a monopoly is a single seller of a good, it has no competition. Since price elasticity is generally lower when consumers have little opportunity to find substitutes, you might think that the demand for the monopolist's product is always inelastic. Nevertheless, it is true that the monopolist always produces on the elastic portion of its demand curve. To see this, compute elasticity along the demand curve given in question 3a. Show that at the chosen price and quantity, the price elasticity of demand is greater than 1.

Answers to Problems

2   a   Marginal revenue appears in Table 14.15.

Table 14.16

Price	Quantity	Revenues	Marginal revenue
$8	100,000	$ 800,000	—
$7	150,000	$1,050,000	$5
$6	200,000	$1,200,000	$3
$5	250,000	$1,250,000	$1
$4	300,000	$1,200,000	–$1
$3	350,000	$1,050,000	–$3
$2	400,000	$ 800,000	–$5

b   Profits are maximized when the price is $5 and the number of fans is 250,000.

c   Costs = $100,000 + (250,000 × $1) = $350,000; profits = $1,250,000 – $350,000 = $900,000.

d   The price and quantity remain as in part a, but profits fall to $1,250,000 – $400,000 = $850,000.

e   The solution is illustrated in the diagram.

3   a   Marginal revenue appears in Table 14.17.

Table 14.17

Price	Quantity	Revenues	Marginal revenue
$10	1	$10	—
$ 9	2	$18	$8
$ 8	3	$24	$6
$ 7	4	$28	$4
$ 6	5	$30	$2
$ 5	6	$30	$0
$ 4	7	$28	–$2

Price = $9; quantity = 2; profits = $18 – ($8 × 2) = $2.

  b   Marginal revenue appears in Table 14.18.

Table 14.18

Price	Quantity	Revenues	Marginal revenue
$0.50	500,000	$250,000	—
$0.45	600,000	$270,000	$0.20
$0.40	700,000	$280,000	$0.10
$0.35	800,000	$280,000	$0
$0.30	900,000	$270,000	–$0.10

Price = $0.40; quantity = 700,000; profits = $280,000 – [$50,000 + (700,000 × $0.10)] = $160,000.

  c   The complete table appears in Table 14.19.

Table 14.19

Price	Quantity	Revenues	Marginal revenue	Total costs	Marginal cost
$20	400	$ 8,000	—	$ 5,000	—
$18	800	$14,400	$16	$ 7,000	$ 5
$16	1,200	$19,200	$12	$ 9,400	$ 6
$14	1,600	$22,400	$ 8	$12,600	$ 8
$12	2,000	$24,000	$ 4	$16,200	$ 9
$10	2,400	$24,000	$ 0	$21,000	$12

Price = $14; quantity = 1,600; profits = $22,400 – $12,600 = $9,800.

  d   The completed table appears in Table 14.20.

Table 14.20

Price	Quantity	Revenues	Marginal revenue	Total costs	Marginal cost
$1.00	1,000	$1,000	—	$ 200	—
$0.90	2,000	$1,800	$0.80	$ 300	$0.10
$0.80	3,500	$2,800	$0.67	$ 450	$0.10
$0.70	5,500	$3,850	$0.52	$ 650	$0.10
$0.60	8,000	$4,800	$0.38	$ 900	$0.10
$0.50	11,000	$5,500	$0.23	$1,230	$0.11
$0.40	15,000	$6,000	$0.12	$1,730	$0.12
$0.30	20,000	$6,000	$0	$2,355	$0.14

Price = $0.40; quantity = 15,000; profits = $4,270.

  5   a   The marginal revenue figures appear in Table 14.21.

Table 14.21

	Home market				Foreign market		
Price	Quantity	Revenues	Marginal revenue	Price	Quantity	Revenues	Marginal revenue
$10	2,000	$20,000	—	$10	2,000	$20,000	—
$ 9	2,500	$22,500	$5	$ 9	3,000	$27,000	$7
$ 8	3,000	$24,000	$3	$ 8	4,000	$32,000	$5
$ 7	3,500	$24,500	$1	$ 7	5,000	$35,000	$3
$ 6	4,000	$24,000	–$1	$ 6	6,000	$36,000	$1
$ 5	4,500	$22,500	–$3	$ 5	7,000	$35,000	–$1
$ 4	5,000	$20,000	–$5	$ 4	8,000	$32,000	–$3

  b   Home market price = $7; quantity = 3,500. Foreign market price = $6; quantity = 6,000.

  c   Profits = $24,500 + $36,000 – [(3,500 + 6,000) × $1] – $5,000 = $46,000.

  6   a   The completed table appears in Table 14.22.

Table 14.22

	Home market				Foreign market		
Price	Quantity	Revenues	Marginal revenue	Price	Quantity	Revenues	Marginal revenue
$4.00	200	$ 800	—	$4.00	100	$400	—
$3.50	400	$1,400	$3	$3.50	120	$420	$1
$3.00	600	$1,800	$2	$3.00	140	$420	$0
$2.50	800	$2,000	$1	$2.50	160	$400	–$1
$2.00	1,000	$2,000	$0	$2.00	180	$360	–$2
$1.50	1,200	$1,800	–$1	$1.50	200	$300	–$3

  b   Suburbs price = $2.50; quantity = 800. Inner city price = $3.50; quantity = 120.

  c   Profits = $2,000 + $420 – [(800 + 120) × $1] – $100 = $1,400.

  9 a,c   The marginal revenues and Magdalena's revenues are given in Table 14.23.

Table 14.23

Price	Quantity	Revenues	Marginal revenue	Magdalena's revenue
$20	20,000	$400,000	—	$100,000
$18	25,000	$450,000	$10	$112,500
$16	30,000	$480,000	$ 6	$120,000
$14	35,000	$490,000	$ 2	$122,500
$12	40,000	$480,000	–$ 2	$120,000
$10	48,000	$480,000	$ 0	$120,000

  b,d   The profix-maximizing price is $16 and the quantity is 30,000, but Magdalena's revenues are maximized at a price of $14, where 35,000 CDs are sold.

e   The solution is illustrated in the diagram.

10   *a*   Marginal revenue is given in Table 14.24.

Table 14.24

Price	Quantity	Revenues	Marginal revenue
$1.00	30,000	$30,000	—
$0.95	40,000	$38,000	$0.80
$0.90	50,000	$45,000	$0.70
$0.85	60,000	$51,000	$0.60
$0.80	70,000	$56,000	$0.50
$0.75	80,000	$60,000	$0.40
$0.70	90,000	$63,000	$0.30
$0.65	100,000	$65,000	$0.20
$0.60	110,000	$66,000	$0.10
$0.55	120,000	$66,000	$0

b   Price = $0.60; quantity = 110,000.
c   The tax increases marginal cost to $0.20. The price becomes $0.65 and the quantity, 100,000.
d   Consumers pay $.05 of the tax.
e   The solution is illustrated in the diagram.

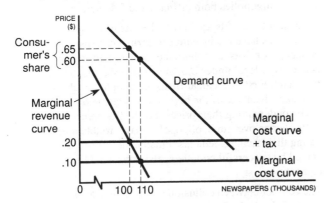

11   *a*   Marginal revenue is given in Table 14.25.

Table 14.25

Price	Quantity	Revenues	Marginal revenue
$45	60,000	$2,700,000	—
$40	80,000	$3,200,000	$25
$35	100,000	$3,500,000	$15
$30	120,000	$3,600,000	$ 5
$25	140,000	$3,500,000	−$ 5

b   Price = $35; quantity = 100,000.
c   Price = $25; quantity = 140,000.
d   The solution is illustrated in the diagram.

12   The elasticity for each point on the demand curve is given in Table 14.26.

Table 14.26

Price	Quantity	Revenues	Marginal revenue	Elasticity
$10	1	$10	—	—
$ 9	2	$18	$8	19/3
$ 8	3	$24	$6	17/5
$ 7	4	$28	$4	15/7
$ 6	5	$30	$2	13/9
$ 5	6	$30	$0	11/11
$ 4	7	$28	−$2	9/11

Along the elastic portion of the demand curve, which is where price exceeds $5, marginal revenue is positive. Marginal revenue equals marginal cost at a price of $9, which is on the elastic portion.

Chapter 15

OLIGOPOLIES

Chapter Review

Chapters 14 and 15 present the three imperfect competitive market structures: monopoly, monopolistic competition, and oligopoly. Chapter 14 dealt with the first two; this chapter rounds out the study with a look at oligopoly.

Oligopolies are industries in which only a few firms dominate. Each firm watches its competitors closely, because each firm's best price, output level, or strategy depends on what its rivals choose. The American automobile industry is a perfect example of an oligopolistic market. Even today, with foreign firms competing in the U.S. market, it is still easy to see how the "big three" (General Motors, Ford, and Chrysler) respond to one another with competing rebate programs, lower prices, or cheap financing. The chapter introduces the Prisoner's Dilemma models to examine the possibilities and motives for collusion. Chapter 16 builds upon the insights of this chapter and Chapter 14 to explore government policy toward imperfect competition.

ESSENTIAL CONCEPTS

1   In **oligopolies**, a few firms dominate the industry. If any one firm changes its price, produces more, or adopts a new strategy, then the other firms in the oligopoly will notice the change and react to it. It is essential, then, that oligopolists pay careful attention and try to anticipate the reactions of rivals. This strategic interaction is the essential feature of oligopolies, and it makes the study of oligopolies both difficult and fascinating.

2   Because total profits are lower when firms compete, oligopolists have the incentive to form a cartel and to collude, fix prices, and share the market. This behavior is not only illegal under U.S. antitrust laws, it is difficult to sustain. First, individual firms are tempted to cheat and take advantage of the higher prices charged by others by undercutting their prices. Further, as demand and costs change over time, oligopolies have trouble renegotiating their tacit agreements. Finally, the pure profits earned by successful colluders attract entry and new competition.

3   The conflict between collusion and competition is at the heart of oligopoly. The combined profits of firms are highest if they collude. Collectively, their incentives are to fix prices and share the market. But each individual firm is tempted by its own self-interest. If the rivals keep their prices high, a firm can undercut and capture the market. The **Prisoner's Dilemma** summarizes this conflict and shows how collusion might work. If the

game is played only once and self-interest quickly takes over, all firms cheat and the equilibrium is competition. If the game is played repeatedly for an indefinite period of time, firms may be able to threaten cheaters with competitive price wars and motivate one another to continue colluding.

4   Certain **restrictive practices** help sustain collusion. These include assigning exclusive territories to individual firms, requiring exclusive dealing at retail outlets, and insisting upon tie-in arrangements that force a customer who buys one product to buy an additional product. These practices can reduce competition by increasing the costs of capturing the customers of rival firms. Firms also facilitate cooperation through such practices as matching low-price offers of rivals.

5   There are three important models of competition in oligopolies.

   a   If firms are committed to producing a given amount of output, as is the case in industries where fixed costs are high and changing capacity is very expensive, there is quantity or **Cournot competition.** One such example is the steel industry. Setting up a factory to commence or expand production is very expensive, so the firm gets locked in at certain capacities. It tries to select capacities corresponding to a price where profits will be maximized.

   b   If the costs of increasing capacity are low, then price or **Bertrand competition** reigns. An example of this is the catalog marketing industry. Setting up a mail-order firm is inexpensive, and the firm can vary the size of its orders from suppliers. It selects a price corresponding to a quantity where profits will be maximized.

   c   The **kinked demand curve** model shows that if firms expect rivals to match a price cut but not price increases, then they are unlikely to change price or quantity.

BEHIND THE ESSENTIAL CONCEPTS

1   The world of perfect competition is simple and precise. The firm cannot affect the market of any competitor; it simply chooses its quantity to maximize profits. The world of oligopoly is rich and varied. Firms try to limit competition and promote collusion. They have a wealth of strategies to choose from: price and quantity, of course, but also such practices as matching offers of rivals and threatening price wars with new entrants or existing firms who cheat on tacit agreements to limit price competition. Oligopoly is an area in which economics has made much progress in the last ten or fifteen years.

2   As a group, firms in an oligopoly want to cooperate, charge high prices, and share monopoly profits, but they always run up against the problem of self-interest. Each individual firm would like to cheat while the others abide by the cooperative strategy. It is this noncooperative behavior by individual firms that promotes economic efficiency, because it keeps the oligopolists from cooperating to gouge customers with high prices. It is ironic that if firms were more cooperative, the economy would not work so well.

SELF-TEST

True or False

1   An oligopolist considering lowering its price must anticipate the reactions of its rivals.

2   A cartel is a group of firms engaging in price competition.

3   Antitrust laws allow cartels to negotiate openly to fix prices.

4   Tacit collusion is an implicit understanding among oligopolists that their profits will be higher if they do not compete too vigorously.

5   Offers to match prices charged by rivals result in more price competition.

6   A price leader can help a cartel adjust to changing conditions.

7   One difficulty that cartels have is that when they succeed in raising price, their members are tempted to undercut the cartel price.

8   If the possibility of entry keeps prices competitive, the market is said to be contestible.

9   The Prisoner's Dilemma is a simple game that shows how parties can overcome their self-interest to achieve the benefits of cooperation.

10   Certain restrictive practices such as resale price maintenance and exclusive territories help oligopolies reduce competition and increase profits.

11   Although restrictive practices such as exclusive territories help oligopolists collude, they also promote economic efficiency.

12   In an oligopoly, firms must worry about the reactions of rivals.

13   In Cournot competition, oligopolists choose their quantity expecting that their rivals will produce the same quantity as they.

14   In Bertrand competition, firms choose their price expecting their rivals to keep price constant.

15   If the firm perceives a kinked demand curve, there is a jump in marginal revenue at the current output.

Multiple Choice

1   Unlike firms operating in monopolistically competitive markets, oligopolists

   a   face downward-sloping demand curves;

   b   are price takers;

   c   must worry about how rivals will react to their decisions;

d   set price above marginal cost;

e   a and d.

2   A group of companies that act jointly to divide the industry and maximize profits is called

   a   a monopoly;

   b   a monopsony;

   c   a cartel;

   d   an antitrust;

   e   none of the above.

3   One difficulty cartels have is that individual firms may cheat and

   a   charge less than the agreed-upon price;

   b   sell more than the agreed-upon quantity;

   c   charge more than the agreed-upon price;

   d   a and b;

   e   b and c.

4   In the Prisoner's Dilemma,

   a   both prisoners act in their own self-interest; this leads to the best alternative from their combined standpoint;

   b   both prisoners cooperate to bring about the best alternative;

   c   acting in their own self-interest, the prisoners bring about the worst alternative;

   d   it is impossible to say what happens because each prisoner must worry about the reactions of the other;

   e   none of the above.

5   Collusion is difficult in practice because

   a   antitrust laws make explicit price-fixing agreements illegal;

   b   individual firms are tempted to cheat and undercut their rivals;

   c   as demand and cost conditions change, it is difficult to renegotiate tacit agreements;

   d   all of the above;

   e   none of the above.

6   When oligopolists publicly offer to match any price charged by any other firm, there will be

   a   more price competition;

   b   the same amount of price competition;

   c   less price competition;

   d   trouble because matching offers are illegal;

   e   none of the above.

7   In contestable markets,

   a   firms can successfully collude to share monopoly profits;

   b   firms are unable to collude because cartel members cheat on tacit agreements;

   c   potential competition ensures competitive pricing;

   d   price returns to the competitive level, but only after entry;

   e   firms deter the entry of new competition by carrying excess capacity.

8   A tie-in is

   a   a requirement that firms offer the same price as their rivals;

   b   an agreement among cartel members to match price cuts but not price increases;

   c   a requirement that any customer who buys one product must buy another;

   d   a practice whereby the prices of the followers are tied to the leader's price;

   e   a threat to meet new entry with resistance.

9   Antitrust laws

   a   prohibit collusive behavior;

   b   require that firms in an oligopoly charge the same price;

   c   punish firms for cheating on collusive agreements;

   d   promote collusion by raising rival's costs;

   e   bar entry into oligopolies.

10   In an oligopoly the price leader

   a   sets the industry's highest price;

   b   sets the industry's price and the other firms follow;

   c   deters entry by threatening to lower price;

   d   ensures cooperation among all firms by threatening to lower price;

   e   offers to match the industry's lowest price.

11   In oligopolies firms often share inventories or combine research and development efforts. These practices

   a   are illegal under antitrust laws;

   b   can facilitate cooperation because firms that cheated on the collusive price agreement may be excluded;

   c   are examples of predatory pricing;

   d   only exist in contestable markets;

   e   are examples of tie-ins.

12   The Prisoner's Dilemma shows

   a   the power of antitrust laws;

   b   the effectiveness of facilitating practices;

   c   the impact of potential competition;

   d   the difficulty of sustaining collusive arrangements;

   e   the importance of the kinked demand curve.

13   In Cournot competition, the firms

   a   compete by choosing quantity, given some conjecture about the quantity that the rival will produce;

   b   compete by choosing price, given some conjecture about the price that the rival will charge;

   c   match price cuts by rivals but not price increases;

   d   collude to fix prices and earn monopoly profits;

   e   divide the market in an orderly way.

14   In Bertrand competition, the firms

   a   compete by choosing quantity, given some conjecture about the quantity that the rival will produce;

   b   compete by choosing price, given some conjecture about the price that the rival will charge;

   c   match price cuts by rivals but not price increases;

   d   collude to fix prices and earn monopoly profits;

   e   divide the market in an orderly way.

15 In laboratory experiments economists have found that

a participants evolve simple strategies to bring about collusion if the game is repeated a number of times;

b collusion is nearly impossible;

c collusion requires the ability to write firm contracts to enforce it;

d complicated strategies are used by most participants;

e none of the above.

16 Restrictive practices restrict competition. These include

a resale price maintenance;

b exclusive territories;

c vertical restrictions;

d horizontal restrictions;

e all of the above.

17 Marginal revenue for the firm with a kinked demand curve

a is greater than in monopoly;

b is less than in monopoly;

c is the same as in monopoly;

d has a jump at the level of current output;

e none of the above.

18 Resale price maintenance is a practice whereby retailers are required to

a compete vigorously with other retailers;

b sell only within their exclusive territory;

c also sell a specific tie-in product;

d carry no competing products;

e sell at the list price.

19 Restrictive practices, such as exclusive dealing and exclusive territories, may

a reduce economic efficiency;

b restrict competition;

c raise costs for rivals;

d lead to duplication of distribution systems;

e all of the above.

20 If rivals match price cuts but do not match price increases, the demand curve facing the firm

a is kinked at the current output level;

b has a jump at the current output level;

c is horizontal at the current price;

d is vertical at the current output level;

e either c or d.

Completion

1 In an oligopoly, there are so few firms that each must consider how its rival will _____ to any change in strategy.

2 A group of companies operating jointly as if they were a monopoly is called a _____.

3 Collusive behavior is prohibited by _____ laws.

4 The _____ is a game that illustrates the problem cartels have in enforcing collusive behavior.

5 Markets in which the threat of competition impels firms to charge the competitive price are called _____.

6 A firm that insists that any other firm selling its products refrain from selling those of its rivals is engaging in _____.

7 _____ is an arrangement whereby retailers agree to sell at the list price.

8 Restrictive practices aimed at wholesalers and retailers selling a producer's goods are called _____.

9 If a firm believes that its rivals will match its price cuts but not its price increases, then it will perceive its demand curve to be _____ at the current price.

10 Firms that conjecture that rival's quantity is fixed are engaging in_____.

Answers to Self-Test

True or False

1	t	6	t	11	f
2	f	7	t	12	t
3	f	8	t	13	f
4	t	9	f	14	t
5	f	10	t	15	t

Multiple Choice

1	c	6	c	11	b	16	e
2	c	7	c	12	d	17	d
3	a	8	c	13	a	18	e
4	c	9	a	14	b	19	e
5	d	10	b	15	a	20	a

Completion

1 react

2 cartel

3 antitrust laws

4 Prisoner's Dilemma

5 contestable

6 exclusive dealing

7 Resale price maintenance

8 vertical restrictions

9 kinked

10 Cournot competition

Doing Economics: Tools and Practice Problems

This section looks at three issues pertaining to oligopoly. First, we consider collusion and the difficulty that cartels have in enforcing their tacit agreements. We see not only how two firms can divide a market and share monopoly profits, but also how difficult it is to maintain a cartel. The cartel's success in restricting output and raising prices tempts each of the cartel members to cheat by producing more than their assigned amounts and undercutting the cartel's price. One way to lessen the incentives to cheat is to assign exclusive territories. We look at collusion and cheating in several problems before turning to some simple game theory problems, using the Prisoner's Dilemma framework to investigate collusion.

CARTELS, COLLUSION, AND CHEATING

Many firms can secretly organize and agree to cooperate to share monopoly profits. Tool Kit 15.1 shows how they might do this. The following problems use this insight to show how individual firms have incentives to cheat and produce more than they agreed. Tool Kit 15.2 shows that when there is quantity competition (Cournot), the same incentive problem arises. This is developed and extended to price competition in the problems.

Tool Kit 15.1: Organizing a Cartel of
Many Price-Taking Firms

To organize a cartel of many firms, one must find the monopoly output and price. Then each firm must be assigned its quota. The following steps show how to proceed.

Step one: Identify and add up the supply curves of the individual firms. The result is the cartel's marginal cost curve.

Step two: Identify the market demand curve, and find its marginal revenue.

Step three: Find the profit-maximizing price and quantity for the cartel by setting marginal revenue equal to marginal cost.

Step four: Determine each firm's output by evenly dividing the cartel's output among its members.

---

1   (Worked problem: collusion and cheating) The Quebec Maple Syrup Board is a cartel of 1,000 maple syrup producers. The demand for maple syrup and the supply curve of one typical producer are given in Table 15.1. The quantity represents gallons.

Table 15.1

Market demand		Firm's supply	
Price	Quantity	Price	Quantity
$10	10,000	$10	60
$ 9	15,000	$ 9	55
$ 8	20,000	$ 8	50
$ 7	25,000	$ 7	45
$ 6	30,000	$ 6	40
$ 5	35,000	$ 5	35
		$ 4	30
		$ 3	25
		$ 2	20

a   Find the profit-maximizing price for the cartel as a whole. How many litres will be sold at this price: How many must each firm produce to sustain this price?

b   If the cartel charges the price computed in part a, how many units would the individual firm like to produce?

c   Now suppose that all firms cheat and the market becomes competitive. Find the equilibrium price and quantity.

Step-by-step solution

Step one (a): Add up the individual supplies. Since there are 1,000 firms, the market supply is simply the quantity supplied by the firm multiplied by 1,000. The market supply is given in Table 15.2.

Table 15.2

Firm's supply		Market supply	
Price	Quantity	Price	Quantity
$10	60	$10	60,000
$ 9	55	$ 9	55,000
$ 8	50	$ 8	50,000
$ 7	45	$ 7	45,000
$ 6	40	$ 6	40,000
$ 5	35	$ 5	35,000
$ 4	30	$ 4	30,000
$ 3	25	$ 3	25,000
$ 2	20	$ 2	20,000

Step two: Derive the marginal revenue curve. First find total revenue, and enter it in the appropriate column. Marginal revenue is the change in total revenue divided by the change in quantity. The answer is given in Table 15.3.

Table 15.3

Market demand		Total	Marginal
Price	Quantity	revenue	revenue
$10	10,000	$100,000	
$ 9	15,000	$135,000	$7
$ 8	20,000	$160,000	$5
$ 7	25,000	$175,000	$3
$ 6	30,000	$180,000	$1
$ 5	35,000	$175,000	–$1

Step three: Find the profit-maximizing price for the cartel. The market supply curve is the cartel's marginal cost. Marginal cost equals marginal revenue when the quantity is 25,000. The corresponding price is $7. Each firm produces 25 gallons.

Step four (b): Find how much the firm would like to supply at the cartel price. At a price of $7, the firm would like to produce 45 units (this number is read off the firm's supply curve), which is 20 more than it is assigned.

Step five (c): If all firms cheat, then the market will become a competitive market and will clear at a price of $5, where each firm produces 35 gallons.

2   (Practice problem: collusion and cheating) The 500 mail-order computer equipment suppliers are (discreetly) forming a cartel. The market demand curve and the supply curve of a typical equipment supplier are given in Table 15.4. The quantity represents the number of computers.

Table 15.4

Market demand		Total revenue	Marginal revenue
Price	Quantity		
$1,000	300,000		
$ 900	400,000		
$ 800	500,000		
$ 700	600,000		
$ 600	700,000		
$ 500	800,000		
$ 400	900,000		
$ 300	1,000,000		

Firm's supply		Market supply	
Price	Quantity	Price	Quantity
$1,000	4,000		
$ 900	3,500		
$ 800	3,000		
$ 700	2,400		
$ 600	2,000		
$ 500	1,600		
$ 400	1,000		
$ 300	500		
$ 200	100		

a   Derive the marginal revenue for the computer equipment supplier market.
b   Add up the 500 individual firm supplies to derive the market supply.
c   Find the profit-maximizing price for the cartel as a whole. How many computers will be sold at this price? How many must each firm sell to sustain this price?
d   If the cartel charges the price computed in part c, how many units would the individual firm like to sell?
e   Now suppose that all firms cheat, and the market becomes competitive. Find the equilibrium price and quantity.

3   (Worked problem: quantity competition) The New Chairs for Old Company shares the furniture-refinishing market in Southpoint with the Like New Company. Each uses enormous vats of chemicals, which are expensive to set up but cheap to operate. One vat will permit the refinishing of 10 pieces of furniture per day. The marginal cost for each firm is constant and equal to $4. Table 15.5 gives the market demand.

Table 15.5

Price	Quantity
$7.50	0
$7.00	10
$6.50	20
$6.00	30
$5.50	40
$5.00	50
$4.50	60
$4.00	70

a   Suppose that the two firms try to operate as a cartel and share the market equally. Find the profit-maximizing quantity for each.
b   Now look at the problem from the point of view of the owner of New Chairs for Old. She conjectures that her rival commit to the quantity solved for in part a. Find the profit-maximizing quantity.

Step-by-step solution

Step one (a): We follow the usual procedure for the monopolist: find the marginal revenue and set marginal revenue equal to marginal cost. Table 15.6 gives the marginal revenue.

Table 15.6

Price	Quantity	Total revenue	Marginal revenue
$7.50	0	$ 0	—
$7.00	10	$ 70	$7
$6.50	20	$130	$6
$6.00	30	$180	$5
$5.50	40	$220	$4
$5.00	50	$250	$3
$4.50	60	$270	$2
$4.00	70	$280	$1

Marginal revenue equals marginal cost when the total quantity is 40. Each firm then buys two vats and refinishes 20 pieces of furniture.

Step two (b): Identify the market demand, marginal cost, and output of the opponent firm. The market demand is given in Table 15.5, the marginal cost is $4, and Like New is expected to produce 20.

Step three: Subtract the output of the opponent firm from the market demand, as shown in Table 15.7.

Table 15.7

Price	Quantity
$7.00	0
$6.50	20 – 20 = 0
$6.00	30 – 20 = 10
$5.50	40 – 20 = 20
$5.00	50 – 20 = 30
$4.50	60 – 20 = 40
$4.00	70 – 20 = 50

Step four: Find the marginal revenue for the residual demand curve, as given in Table 15.8.

Step five: Choose the output for which marginal revenue equals marginal cost. When output is 30, marginal revenue and marginal cost both equal $4.

Table 15.8

Price	Quantity	Total revenue	Marginal revenue
$7.00	0	0	—
$6.50	0	0	—
$6.00	10	$ 60	$6
$5.50	20	$110	$5
$5.00	30	$150	$4
$4.50	40	$180	$3
$4.00	50	$200	$2

4   (Practice problem: quantity competition) The Davis Lead Company competes with its rival Anderson Lead. Because the plant and equipment are so expensive and because marginal production costs are so low (only $5 per ton) until capacity is reached, the two firms compete by choosing quantity. The market demand is given in Table 15.9.

Table 15.9

Price	Quantity (tons)
$22.50	0
$20.00	100
$17.50	200
$15.00	300
$12.50	400
$10.00	500
$ 7.50	600

a   Suppose that the two firms try to operate as a cartel and share the market equally. Find the profit-maximizing quantity for each.

b   Now look at the problem from the point of view of the owner of Davis. The owner conjectures that the rival firm will commit to the quantity solved for in part a. Find the profit-maximizing quantity.

5   (Worked problem: price competition) There are two dry-cleaning establishments in Mudville: Jay's Cleaners and Fay's Cleaners. Although they hate each other personally, the two owners have decided to form a cartel. This is illegal, of course, but they meet discreetly. Each faces a marginal cost of $1 per item. Consumers always patronize the lower-price establishment; therefore, either Jay or Fay can capture the entire market by pricing below the other. One additional fact is that in Mudville people only carry half dollars, so the price must be a multiple of $0.50. Table 15.10 gives the market demand.

Table 15.10

Price	Quantity
$3.00	1,500
$2.50	3,000
$2.00	4,500
$1.50	6,000
$1.00	7,500

a   Derive marginal revenue curve, and enter in the table.

b   Find the profit-maximizing price. If they divide the market equally, how many items will each clean?

c   Compute the profits for each firm.

d   Suppose that Fay decides to undercut Jay and capture the market. What price will Fay charge? How many will Fay sell? Compute Fay's profits.

Step-by-step solution

Step one (a): Derive marginal revenue. Follow the usual procedure, as in Table 15.11.

Table 15.11

Price	Quantity	Total revenue	Marginal revenue
$3.00	1,500	$4,500	$3
$2.50	3,000	$7,500	$2
$2.00	4,500	$9,000	$1
$1.50	6,000	$9,000	$0
$1.00	7,500	$7,500	−$1

Step two (b): Find the profit-maximizing price. Marginal cost equals marginal revenue at a price of $2.

Step three (c): At a price of $2, there are 4,500 items cleaned. If each does one-half, then each cleans 2,250. The profits for each are $2 − $1 = $1 per unit, so each earns $2,250.

Step four (d): Fay can capture the market by charging the next-lower price, which is $1.50. Fay will sell 6,000 units. Fay's profit will be $1.50 − $1.00 = $0.50 per unit for a total of $3,000. Fay gains $750 by cheating on their agreement.

6   (Practice problem: price competition) Yuppie Company and its rival Buppie Company sell dark green and gray rag wool sweaters through catalogs. They buy the sweaters from supplier firms for $10 each. The market demand is given in Table 15.12.

Table 15.12

Quantity (sweaters)	Price
0	$27.50
100	$25.00
200	$22.50
300	$20.00
400	$17.50
500	$15.00
600	$12.50

a   Derive marginal revenue, and enter in the table.
b   Find the profit-maximizing price. If the companies divide the market equally, how many items will each clean?
c   Compute the profits for each firm.
d   Suppose that Yuppie decides to undercut Buppie and capture the market. What price will it charge? How many will it sell? Compute its profits.

PRISONER'S DILEMMA

The Prisoner's Dilemma is one of the most important models in social science. It shows why groups may have difficulty inducing their members to cooperate and act in the group interest. In this section our interest is in the ability of oligopolists to collude. Tool Kit 15.3 shows how to use this model.

Tool Kit 15.3: Using the Prisoner's Dilemma

The Prisoner's Dilemma highlights the conflict between what is good for the cartel as a whole and what is best for the individual firm. Follow these steps to represent this conflict as a game.

Step one: Draw a box with four cells, and label it as shown.

Step two: Identify the payoffs for each party if both cooperate, and enter in the appropriate cell.

Step three: Identify the payoffs for each party if both compete, and enter in the appropriate cell.

Step four: Identify the payoffs for each party if one competes while the other cooperates, and enter in the corresponding cells.

Step five: In the classic Prisoner's Dilemma, competing is always the best strategy, whatever the opponent chooses. Show that competition is the equilibrium.

7   (Worked problem: Prisoner's Dilemma) Chiaravelli and Fiegenshau are the only two dentists in Plainville. They have been colluding, sharing the market and earning monopoly profits of $100,000 each for several years. Fiegenshau is considering reducing his price. He estimates that if Chiaravelli keeps his price at current levels, Fiegenshau would earn $150,000, although Chiaravelli's earnings would fall to $25,000. There is also the possibility that Chiaravelli would compete against Fiegenshau. The resulting price war would reduce the earnings of each to $40,000.

   a   Represent this market as a Prisoner's Dilemma game.
   b   Explain why the equilibrium might be achieved when both dentists compete.

Step-by-step solution

Step one (a): Draw a box with four cells, and label it as shown.

| | CHIARAVELLI | |
	cooperate	compete
FIEGENSHAU cooperate		
compete		

Step two: Identify the payoffs for each party if both cooperate, and enter in the appropriate cell. If both cooperate, they each earn $100,000.

| | CHIARAVELLI | |
	cooperate	compete
FIEGENSHAU cooperate	C = $100,000 F = $100,000	
compete		

Step three: Identify the payoffs for each party if both compete, and enter in the appropriate cell. If both compete, they each earn $40,000.

| | CHIARAVELLI | |
	cooperate	compete
FIEGENSHAU cooperate	C = $100,000 F = $100,000	
compete		C = $40,000 F = $40,000

Step four: Identify the payoffs for each party if one competes while the other cooperates, and enter in the corresponding cell. In this case, the dentist who competes earns $150,000, and the other is left with $25,000.

| | CHIARAVELLI | |
	cooperate	compete
FIEGENSHAU cooperate	C = $100,000 F = $100,000	C = $150,000 F = $ 25,000
compete	C = $ 25,000 F = $150,000	C = $40,000 F = $40,000

Step five (b): Show that competition is the equilibrium. For each party, competition is always the best alternative. If Chiavarelli cooperates, then Fiegenshau can earn more by competing ($150,000 > $100,000). If Chiavarelli competes, again Fiegenshau earns more by competing ($40,000 > $25,000). The same is true for Chiavarelli, and both choose to be competitive.

8   (Practice problem: Prisoner's Dilemma) Upper Peninsula Airlines and Northern Airways share the market from Chicago to the winter resorts in the North. If they cooperate, they can extract enough monopoly profits to earn $400,000 each, but unbridled competition would reduce profits to $50,000 each. If one is foolish enough to cooperate in its pricing policy while the other undercuts it, the cooperating firm would earn $0, and the competing firm would earn $800,000.

   a   Represent this market as a Prisoner's Dilemma game.
   b   Explain why the equilibrium might be that both firms choose a competitive strategy.

9   (Practice problem: Prisoner's Dilemma) Rosewood College and Elmwood College are the best private schools in the state. Each also prides itself on its lacrosse team. If neither offers scholarships for promising players, then obviously the cost of scholarships will be zero. For $20,000 in scholarships, either could attract the best players (if the other did not offer scholarships), win the conference championship, and attract at least $50,000 in new donations. In this case, however, donations at the losing school would fall by $30,000. On the other hand, if both offered scholarships, there would be no advantage, no extra donations, and each would have spent the $20,000 for nothing.

   a   Represent this market as a Prisoner's Dilemma game.
   b   Explain why the equilibrium might be achieved when both schools compete.

FACILITATING AND RESTRICTIVE PRACTICES

Oligopolists can use certain practices to facilitate collusion and restrict competition. These practices may enable them to get around the incentive to cheat on collusive arrangements. These problems illustrate how dividing the market into exclusive territories and promising to match competitors' low prices can promote collusion.

10 (Worked problem: facilitating and restrictive practices) This problem builds upon problem 3. Having accumulated several years of experience with the unpleasant

results of competition, the owners of Southpoint's two furniture-refinishing firms decide to try a new method of collusion. Henceforth, the New Chairs for Old Company will specialize in refinishing chairs, and the Like New Company will take care of the table share of the market. It so happens in Southpoint that exactly half of the business involves tables and half involves chairs. Their marginal costs remain at $4.

a Compute the profit-maximizing quantity of chairs and tables and the corresponding prices for both companies.
b Compare the answer to the answer to part a of problem 3.

Step-by-step solution

Step one (a): Divide the market into chair and table markets. The result is given in Table 15.13.

Table 15.13

Price	Quantity of chairs	Quantity of tables
$7.50	0	0
$7.00	5	5
$6.50	10	10
$6.00	15	15
$5.50	20	20
$5.00	25	25
$4.50	30	30
$4.00	35	35

Step two: Compute the marginal revenue for each firm. These are shown in Table 15.14. Note that since the demands are exactly the same, so are the marginal revenue curves. Only one is shown.

Table 15.14

Price	Quantity of chairs	Quantity of tables	Total revenue	Marginal revenue
$7.50	0	0	$ 0	—
$7.00	5	5	$ 35	$7
$6.50	10	10	$ 65	$6
$6.00	15	15	$ 90	$5
$5.50	20	20	$110	$4
$5.00	25	25	$125	$3
$4.50	30	30	$135	$2
$4.00	35	35	$140	$1

Step three (b): Marginal revenue equals marginal cost at a quantity of 20 for each. The market price will be $5.50, which is exactly the outcome that was solved for in part a of problem 3. Dividing the market promotes collusion.

11 (Practice problem: facilitating and restrictive practices) This problem builds upon problem 4. The Davis and Anderson companies have come up with a scheme to promote collusion. From now on, Davis will advertise and take orders from customers in the West, leaving the eastern half of the market to Anderson. They divide the territories so that exactly half of the customers will go to each firm. The marginal cost remains at $5 per ton, and the market demand is as given in Table 15.9.

a Compute the profit-maximizing quantity and price for each firm.
b Compare with the collusive price and quantity solved for in part a of problem 4.

12 (Worked problem: facilitating and restrictive practices) Let's return to Mudville and problem 5, where Fay is considering undercutting Jay.

a Compute profits if she reduces her price by $50 below the collusive price and Jay matches the price cut. Assume that customers divide themselves equally between the firms charging the same price.
b Derive Fay's demand curve under the assumption that Jay will match any price cuts but not price increases. Draw a diagram illustrating your answer.

Step-by-step solution

Step one (a): The collusive price is $2.00, and Fay's profits are $2,250. If she cuts price to $1.50 and Jay matches the cut, then the quantity demanded is 6,000, and Fay will serve 3,000 of them.

Step two: Fay earns ($1.50 − $1.00) × 3,000 = $1,500. Because this number is less than collusive profits, the offer to match price cuts by Jay will deter Fay from undercutting him.

Step three (b): To find the demand if Jay matches price cuts (below $2) but not price increases, simply divide the market evenly at prices of $2 or below, and give all the customers to Jay for higher prices. Table 15.15 gives the result. Notice the kink at a price of $2.

Table 15.15

Price	Quantity
$3.00	0
$2.50	0
$2.00	2,250
$1.50	3,000
$1.00	3,750

13 (Practice problem: facilitating and restrictive practices) Return to problem 6 and the competition between Yuppie and Buppie. Suppose that each agree to match price offers of the other.

a Compute Yuppie's profits if it cuts price by $2.50 below the collusive price and its cut is matched by Buppie. Assume that customers divide themselves equally between firms charging the same price.
b Derive Yuppie's demand curve assuming that Buppie will match price cuts (below the collusive price) but not price increases.

Answers to Problems

2   *a,b* The marginal revenue and the market supply appear in Table 15.16.

Table 15.16

Market demand		Total revenue	Marginal revenue
Price	Quantity		
$1,000	300,000	$300,000,000	—
$ 900	400,000	$360,000,000	$600
$ 800	500,000	$400,000,000	$400
$ 700	600,000	$420,000,000	$200
$ 600	700,000	$420,000,000	$ 0
$ 500	800,000	$400,000,000	–$200
$ 400	900,000	$360,000,000	–$400
$ 300	1,000,000	$300,000,000	–$600

Firm's supply		Market supply	
Price	Quantity	Price	Quantity
$1,000	4,000	$1,000	2,000,000
$ 900	3,500	$ 900	1,750,000
$ 800	3,000	$ 800	1,500,000
$ 700	2,400	$ 700	1,200,000
$ 600	2,000	$ 600	1,000,000
$ 500	1,600	$ 500	800,000
$ 400	1,000	$ 400	500,000
$ 300	500	$ 300	250,000
$ 200	100	$ 200	50,000

  c   Cartel price = $800; market quantity = 500,000; each firm's quantity = 1,000.
  d   3,000.
  e   Price = $500; quantity = 800,000.

4   *a*   Marginal revenue for the market demand is given in Table 15.17.

Table 15.17

Price	Quantity (tons)	Revenues	Marginal revenue
$22.50	0	$ 0	
$20.00	100	$2,000	$20
$17.50	200	$3,500	$15
$15.00	300	$4,500	$10
$12.50	400	$5,000	$ 5
$10.00	500	$5,000	$ 0
$ 7.50	600	$4,500	–$ 5

       Price = $12.50; market quantity = 400; each firm sells 200 tons.
  b   The residual demand is found by subtracting 200 from the market demand. This and marginal revenue appear in Table 15.18.

Table 15.18

Price	Quantity (tons)	Revenues	Marginal revenue
$22.50	0	$ 0	
$20.00	0	$ 0	
$17.50	0	$ 0	
$15.00	100	$1,500	$15
$12.50	200	$2,500	$10
$10.00	300	$3,000	$ 5
$ 7.50	400	$3,000	$ 0

       Davis will produce 300. The market quantity will be 200 + 300 = 500, and the price will be $10 per ton.

6   *a*   Marginal revenue for the market demand is given in Table 15.19.

Table 15.19

Price	Quantity (sweaters)	Revenues	Marginal revenue
$27.50	0	$ 0	—
$25.00	100	$2,500	$25
$22.50	200	$4,500	$20
$20.00	300	$6,000	$15
$17.50	400	$7,000	$10
$15.00	500	$7,500	$ 5
$12.50	600	$7,500	$ 0

  b   Cartel price = $17.50; market quantity = 400; each firm sells 200.
  c   Profits = (200 × $17.50) – (200 × $10) = $1,500.
  d   Yuppie's price = $15; quantity = 500; profits = ($15 × 500) – ($10 × 500) = $2,500.

8   *a*

Upper Peninsula (UP)

Northern		cooperate	compete
	cooperate	UP = $400,000 N = $400,000	UP = $800,000 N = $50
	compete	UP = $0 N = $800,000	UP = $50,000 N = $50,000

  b   If Northern competes, UP prefers to compete ($800,000 > $400,000). If Northern cooperates, UP still prefers to compete ($50,000 > $0). If UP competes, Northern prefers to compete ($800,000 > $400,000). If UP cooperates, Northern still prefers to compete ($50,000 > $0) Since both always prefer competition, the equilibrium is that both compete and profits are $50,000 each.

9   *a*

Elmwood

Rosewood		cooperate	compete
	cooperate	E = $0 R = $0	E = $30,000 R = –$30,000
	compete	E = –$30,000 R = $30,000	E = –$20,000 R = –$20,000

b If Rosewood cooperates and does not offer scholarships, Elmwood prefers to compete and offer them ($30,000 > $0). If Rosewood competes and offers scholarships, Elmwood still prefers to offer them (–$20,000 > –$30,000). If Elmwood cooperates and does not offer scholarships, Rosewood prefers to offer them ($30,000 > $0). If Elmwood competes and offers scholarships, Rosewood still prefers to offer them (–$20,000 > –$30,000). Since both always prefer competition, the equilibrium is that both compete, offer scholarships, and lose $20,000 each.

11 The demand for each firm's share of the market and the corresponding marginal revenue appear in Table 15.20.

Table 15.20

Price	Quantity (tons)	Revenues	Marginal revenue
$22.50	0	$ 0	—
$20.00	50	$1,000	$20
$17.50	100	$1,750	$15
$15.00	150	$2,250	$10
$12.50	200	$2,500	$ 5
$10.00	250	$2,500	$ 0
$ 7.50	300	$2,250	–$ 5

a Each firm charges $12.50 and sells 200.

b The price and quantity are the same as under monopoly.

13 a If both reduce price by $2.50 to $15.00, the market quantity will equal 500, which implies that each will sell 250. Profits will equal ($15 × 250) – ($10 × 250) = $1,250, which is less than the $1,500 they earn by charging $17.50.

b Yuppie's demand curve if price cuts below $17.50 are matched but price increases are not is given in Table 15.21.

Table 15.21

Price	Quantity (sweaters)
$27.50	0
$25.00	0
$22.50	0
$20.00	0
$17.50	200
$15.00	250
$12.50	300

Chapter 16

GOVERNMENT POLICIES TOWARD COMPETITION

Chapter Review

Monopolies and oligopolies, explored in Chapters 14 and 15, produce too little output and charge inefficiently high prices. This chapter of the text returns to the role government plays in the economy, this time examining government policies to promote competition. Another important topic is government responses to natural monopolies. Natural monopolies occur in markets like home electric service, where a single firm can produce the good more cheaply than multiple firms can. In Chapter 17, the focus shifts to how firms compete to introduce new products and discover better ways of producing.

ESSENTIAL CONCEPTS

1   Competitive industries allocate resources efficiently. Monopolies and other imperfectly competitive industries, however, often operate inefficiently. Economists study four types of inefficiency.

  a   Monopolies restrict output below what it would be if the industry were competitive. The lower output results in higher prices and a transfer of wealth from consumers to the monopoly. There is an additional loss in consumer surplus, because output is below the level at which all gains from trade are realized. This loss is called the deadweight loss of monopoly.

  b   Although monopoly profits are higher when their costs are lower, monopolies are not forced to produce at the lowest cost. There is some room for **managerial slack**, which allows monopolies to be inefficient.

  c   Although there are examples of monopolies that engage in effective **research and development**, the incentives are less under monopoly.

  d   Because monopolies earn rents (profits above the level necessary to compensate investors), resources are expended to acquire and retain these existing . rents. This type of activity is called **rent seeking** and is socially wasteful.

2   In some industries, where there are high fixed and low marginal costs, the lowest cost of production occurs when there is only one firm. Such an industry is called a **natural monopoly**. Figure 16.1 shows that the average cost curve for a natural monopoly is falling and that marginal cost always lies below average cost. Governments sometimes nationalize and operate natural mo-

Figure 16.1

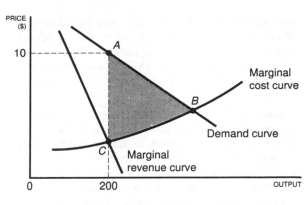

Figure 16.2

nopolies, but more often governments regulate them. A regulatory agency sets prices designed to limit the firm to a normal rate of return. This policy in turn motivates firms to overinvest. Also, because in both the nationalized and regulated cases the pricing decisions are made politically, products may be sold below cost in some markets and above cost in others. This practice is called **cross subsidization.**

3   A final way of dealing with natural monopolies is to increase competition. Examples in the United States include the deregulation of long-distance telephone service and of the trucking and airline industries. Competition provides firms with incentives to innovate and reduce costs, and it eliminates cross subsidization. On the other hand, with more firms in the industry, each firm produces less, that is, chooses a point higher up on the average cost curve.

4   The various ways in which the government attempts to promote competition are called **antitrust policy.** Important pieces of legislation such as the Sherman Act, the Clayton Act, and the establishment of the Federal Trade Commission have outlawed monopolizing, authorized opposition to mergers, and forbidden such types of anti-competitive practices as tying, price discrimination, and exclusive dealing.

BEHIND THE ESSENTIAL CONCEPTS

1   The problem of deadweight loss lies at the heart of economic arguments about making exchange efficient. As an example, look at Figure 16.2, which shows a monopoly output equal to 200. The firm sets the price at $10 and maximizes its profits. Notice, however, that at this point the marginal benefit to consumers of one or more unit (measured, as usual, by the price they're willing to pay) is greater than the marginal cost. This means that producing and selling additional units would create value—there would be gains from trade. The total possible additional gains equal the area of the triangle *ABC*. But these gains are not realized, and therefore they are called the deadweight loss of monopoly.

The idea that exchange creates value and that any reduction in the amount of exchange below the competitive level leads to a deadweight loss (as seen in Figure 16.2) is very important in economics.

2   Firms desiring greater profits seek them in two different ways. First, they offer better products or devise better ways of producing and doing business. These activities do make profits, and they create value and enhance efficiency as well. Firms can also try to convince government to protect them against competition or devise strategies to deter entry. Practices of this type do not create anything, they only redistribute money and reduce economic efficiency. The latter behavior is called rent seeking.

3   In competitive industries, firms are forced to produce at the lowest possible cost. If they do not, new firms will enter the market, undercut the price, and drive existing firms out. In a monopoly, however, whether it is private, nationalized, or regulated, the firm can get away with some slack. It can pay its workers a little more than the going wage, it can postpone adopting the most efficient production techniques, or it can overlook the low-cost suppliers. You can probably see how this could happen in an unregulated monopoly, where there are extra profits, or in a nationalized industry, where the government makes up any losses, but it is also possible in a regulated monopoly because regulators do not always know the lowest cost. The firm has an incentive and the ability to make the regulators believe that it is more costly to do business than it really is. Regulators can prevent fraud, but it is very difficult to find and eliminate waste.

4   In order to determine whether a merger will inhibit competition, the number of firms in an industry and their size relative to the market need to be determined. The geographical size of the market should be considered, as some industries are local, while many have become international. For example, the gold market is a world market. The cement industry, on the other hand, is local. The product is very expensive to transport, and only nearby firms could merge. The similarity of the products also needs to be considered. Is plastic wrap in the same industry as aluminum foil? If so,

does a single producer of plastic wrap have a monopoly, or is it simply another firm in the food-wrapping industry? Economists look at the cross-price effect to determine the extent to which firms are competing. How much does a price decrease by one firm reduce another's demand?

5   Antritrust policy is concerned with prohibiting market domination. This brings up the question of what it means to dominate a market. First, there is the issue of the bounds of the market. What products belong in the market? Economists look at the effect of one good's increase in price on the demand for another. If demand rises significantly, then the goods are part of the same market. The second issue is how different are the products. Here, we look at how much business is lost when price rises. In each case, how prices affect demands is the central idea.

SELF-TEST

True or False

1   Monopolies produce less output than would be produced if the industry were competitive.

2   Monopolies must produce at the lowest cost.

3   Rent seeking refers to anything done in pursuit of monopoly profits.

4   Monopolies have stronger incentives to undertake research and development than do competitive firms.

5   In a natural monopoly, the cost of production is higher because of the lack of competition.

6   Cross subsidization refers to the practice of selling below cost in one market and above cost in another.

7   Regulated natural monopolies are usually forced to charge a price equal to marginal cost.

8   Subjecting a natural monopolist to competition can be an effective strategy if the average cost curve is not too steep.

9   In a horizontal merger, a firm acquires an upstream supplier.

10   Vertical mergers are illegal *per se* in the United States.

11   Enforcement of antitrust laws is the exclusive domain of the U.S. government.

12   One important goal of antitrust policy is to limit the absolute size of firms.

13   Under the rule of reason, a business practice is not illegal if it can be shown to enhance economic efficiency.

14   The Clayton Act outlawed some specific monopoly practices, such as price discrimination.

15   Most current antitrust efforts involve attempting to break up excessively large firms.

Multiple Choice

1   Monopolists set the price

a   equal to marginal cost;
b   equal to average cost;
c   above marginal cost;
d   below marginal cost;
e   below average cost.

2   Monopoly output is

a   the same as the competitive output;
b   less than the competitive output;
c   more than the competitive output;
d   sometimes more and sometimes less than the competitive output;
e   determined by setting marginal revenue equal to price.

3   The deadweight loss caused by monopoly is

a   the difference between consumer surplus under the monopoly and what consumer surplus would have been if the industry were competitive;
b   the amount of monopoly profits;
c   the increase in cost brought about by managerial slack;
d   the total of rent-seeking expenditures;
e   the difference between consumer surplus under the monopoly and what consumer surplus would have been if the industry were competitive minus the transfer from consumers to the monopolist.

4   Managerial slack refers to

a   the lack of efficiency in some monopolies;
b   activities designed to protect a monopoly position;
c   the loss in consumer surplus as a result of restricted output;
d   the lessened incentives for research and development under monopoly;
e   the failure of antitrust policies.

5   Among the problems of monopolies are

a   restricted output;
b   managerial slack;
c   reduced incentives for research and development;
d   rent seeking to protect the monopoly position;
e   all of the above.

6   Which of the following is not a type of rent seeking?

a   research aimed at reducing the cost of production;
b   lobbying the legislature for protection against foreign competition;
c   contributions to political campaigns for candidates who support regulations favored by the monopoly;
d   entry-deterring activities;
e   designing the product to be incompatible with competitors' products.

7   If the cost of production is lowest when there is only one firm, then the industry is a

a   trust;
b   natural oligopoly;
c   natural monopoly;

d horizontal merger;
e vertical merger.

8 In a natural monopoly, marginal cost

a equals price;
b equals average cost;
c is less than average cost;
d is greater than average cost;
e is greater than price.

9 Cross subsidization involves

a selling at below cost in some markets and above cost in others;
b selling at cost in all markets;
c selling above cost in each market;
d selling below cost in each market;
e a and b.

10 Cross subsidization

a occurs in nationalized monopolies but not in regulated monopolies;
b occurs in regulated monopolies but not in nationalized monopolies;
c occurs in neither regulated nor nationalized monopolies;
d occurs in both regulated and nationalized monopolies;
e never occurs.

11 Natural monopoly regulation usually sets price equal to

a marginal revenue;
b marginal cost;
c average revenue;
d average cost;
e average variable cost.

12 Regulated natural monopolies often

a invest too much;
b invest too little;
c hire too much labor;
d hire too few workers;
e sell too much output.

13 Government policies to promote competition are called

a antitrust;
b rent seeking;
c managerial slack;
d natural monopoly;
e horizontal mergers.

14 Which of the following is an example of a horizontal merger?

a One steel producer buys another steel producer.
b A meat-packing firm buys a large cattle ranch.
c A maker of chalk buys a pizza delivery firm.
d A foreign company buys an American company.
e A U.S. company buys a foreign company.

15 Which of the following is an example of a vertical merger?

a One steel producer buys another steel producer.
b A meat-packing firm buys a large cattle ranch.

c A maker of chalk buys a pizza delivery firm.
d A foreign company buys an American company.
e A U.S. company buys a foreign company.

16 Which of the following is not a goal of antitrust policy?

a limit anticompetitive practices;
b prevent market domination;
c limit the absolute size of firms;
d make use of private incentive to sue under antitrust law.
e All of the above are goals of antitrust policy.

17 The Federal Trade Commission

a issues the regulation that made monopolies illegal;
b investigates unfairly competitive practices;
c issues orders to cease and desist from unfair practices;
d determines whether foreign firms engage in unfair trade practices, such as dumping;
e b and c.

18 The act that made monopolizing an industry illegal was the

a Sherman Act;
b Federal Trade Commission Act;
c Robinson-Patman Act;
d Celler-Kefauver Act;
e Taft-Hartley Act.

19 The hypothesis that regulators eventually serve the interests of the industry that they regulate and not the customers is called the

a antitrust hypothesis;
b rent-seeking hypothesis;
c regulatory capture hypothesis;
d natural monopoly hypothesis;
e none of the above.

20 A business practice is anticompetitive under the rule of reason if

a it is illegal *per se*;
b it is in violation of the Clayton Act;
c it cannot be shown to be a sensible business practice that promotes efficiency;
d it leads to vertical mergers;
e it leads to horizontal mergers.

Completion

1 Monopolies restrict output and cause a loss in consumer surplus, part of which is a transfer to the monopolist, and the remainder is called the _____.

2 The fact that, shielded from competition, monopolists may not produce for the lowest costs is called _____.

3 Political contributions and lobbying expenses for the purpose of winning regulations to restrict competition are examples of _____.

4 Regulated or nationalized firms may sell below cost in some markets and above cost in others, a practice known as _____.

5   In a _____, the cost of production is lowest if there is only one firm in the industry.

6   Government efforts to promote competition by restricting anticompetitive tactics or opposing mergers are called _____.

7   When a firm buys a competitor that was producing a competing product, it is called a _____.

8   The purchase by one firm of an upstream supplier or downstream distributor is called a _____.

9   The monopolization of an industry was made illegal by the _____.

10 The _____ investigates and proscribes unfair trade practices.

Answers to Self-Test

True or False

1	t	6	t	11	f
2	f	7	f	12	f
3	f	8	t	13	t
4	f	9	f	14	t
5	f	10	f	15	f

Multiple Choice

1	c	6	a	11	d	16	c
2	b	7	c	12	a	17	e
3	e	8	c	13	a	18	a
4	a	9	a	14	a	19	c
5	e	10	d	15	b	20	c

Completion

1   deadweight loss
2   managerial slack
3   rent seeking
4   cross subsidization
5   natural monopoly
6   antitrust
7   horizontal merger
8   vertical merger
9   Sherman Act
10 Federal Trade Commission

Doing Economics: Tools and Practice Problems

One of the important costs that monopolies impose on the economy is the deadweight loss, which reflects the losses resulting from the fact that monopolies restrict output. Here, we study how to compute the deadweight loss and then move on to consider the regulation of natural monopolies.

DEADWEIGHT LOSS

When a monopoly controls an industry, it can increase its profits by restricting output below the level where price equals marginal cost. By doing so, the monopoly reduces the number of mutually beneficial trades. Because these trades do not occur, there is a loss in consumer surplus, and this loss is called the deadweight burden. (Consumer sur-

plus falls still further because of the higher price that the monopoly charges, but this loss in consumer surplus is only a transfer from consumers to the monopolist and is not part of the deadweight loss.) Tool Kit 16.1 shows how to compute deadweigt loss.

Tool Kit 16.1: Finding the Deadweight Loss of Monopoly

When price is set above marginal cost, the market contracts and there is a deadweight loss. Follow these five steps to compute it.

Step one: Identify the demand and marginal cost curves.

Step two: Calculate marginal revenue.

Step three: Find the monopoly output (Q_m) and price (p_m) by choosing the quantity for which marginal revenue equals marginal cost (MC_m).

Step four: Find the "competitive" quantity (Q_c) by choosing the quantity for which demand equals marginal cost.

Step five: Compute the deadweight loss as the area between the demand and marginal cost curves:

$$\text{deadweight loss} = \tfrac{1}{2}\,(Q_c - Q_m) \times (p_m - MC_m).$$

(This formula exactly measures the area only when demand is a straight line.)

1 (Worked problem: deadweight loss) The West India Tea Company has been granted the sole franchise to sell green tea in Greenville. Its marginal cost is $5 per box. Demand is given in Table 16.1. Solve for its output and price and the deadweight loss.

Table 16.1

Price	Quantity
$10	10,000
$ 9	15,000
$ 8	20,000
$ 7	25,000
$ 6	30,000
$ 5	35,000

Step-by-step solution

Step one: Identify the demand and marginal cost curves. The demand curve is given in Table 16.1; marginal cost is constant and equal to $5.

Step two: Calculate marginal revenue. Follow the usual procedure outlined in Tool Kit 14.1. The marginal revenue for the West India Tea Company is given in Table 16.2.

Table 16.2

Price	Quantity	Total revenue	Marginal revenue
$10	10,000	$100,000	—
$ 9	15,000	$135,000	$7
$ 8	20,000	$160,000	$5
$ 7	25,000	$175,000	$3
$ 6	30,000	$180,000	$1
$ 5	35,000	$175,000	–$1

Step three: Find the monopoly output by choosing the quantity for which marginal revenue equals marginal cost. Mar-

ginal revenue equals marginal cost when price is $8 and 20,000 boxes are sold.

Step four: Find the competitive quantity by choosing the quantity for which demand equals marginal cost. The competitive price is $5, and the quantity is 35,000.

Step five: Compute the deadweight loss as the area between the demand and marginal cost curves.

$$
\begin{aligned}
\text{Deadweight loss} &= \tfrac{1}{2}\,(Q_c - Q_m) \times (p_m - MC_m)\\
&= \tfrac{1}{2}\,(35{,}000 - 20{,}000) \times (\$8 - \$5)\\
&= \$22{,}500.
\end{aligned}
$$

2 (Practice problem: deadweight loss) Although its marginal cost is only $4 for each ride, the Calloway Cab Company has bribed the city council in Venal City to grant it monopoly status at the local airport. The demand for rides is given in Table 16.3.

Table 16.3

Price	Quantity
$7.50	0
$7.00	10
$6.50	20
$6.00	30
$5.50	40
$5.00	50
$4.50	60
$4.00	70

Solve for the company's output and price and the deadweight loss.

3 (Practice problem: deadweight loss) As all baseball fans know, there is only one team in Mudville. The marginal cost of another fan in the park is $1, and the demand is given in Table 16.4.

Table 16.4

Price	Quantity
$3.00	1,500
$2.50	3,000
$2.00	4,500
$1.50	6,000
$1.00	7,500

Solve for the team's output and price and the deadweight loss.

NATURAL MONOPOLY

Natural monopolies are industries with high fixed and low marginal costs. Costs in these industries are lowest when there is only one firm. Many so-called natural monopolies, such as public utilities, cable television companies, and phone companies, are regulated by a public commission that prevents the entry of competitors and sets prices just high enough to allow the firms to earn a normal rate of return. This practice mandates that price equal average cost. Tool Kit 16.2 shows how to set price in a regulated monopoly.

Tool Kit 16.2: Finding the Price for a Regulated Natural Monopoly

Public utility commissions often regulate natural monopolies so that they make a normal rate of return. To this end price must equal average cost. Follow these steps.

Step one: Identify the demand curve, marginal cost, and fixed costs.

Step two: Compute the average cost by dividing total cost by quantity:

average cost = total cost/quantity.

Step three: Find the price for which average cost crosses the demand curve. This is the price for a regulated natural monopoly.

---

4   (Worked problem: natural monopoly) Cutthroat Cable Company is the only provider of cable television services in Kings. Most of its costs are access fees and maintenance expenses, and these fixed costs, which do not vary with the number of customers, total $760,000 monthly. The marginal cost of another subscriber is only $1 per month. The company's demand curve is given in Table 16.5.

Table 16.5

Price (per month)	Number of subscribers
$50	10,000
$40	20,000
$30	30,000
$20	40,000
$10	50,000
$ 1	100,000

The Kings Borough Utility Commission regulates the price of cable service and wants to set the price so that

Cutthroat makes a normal rate of return. What price should it mandate?

Step-by-step solution

Step one: Identify the demand curve, marginal cost, and fixed costs. Demand is given in Table 16.5; marginal cost is $1, and fixed costs are $760,000.

Step two: Compute average cost. When price is $50, there are 10,000 subscribers, and total costs are $760,000 + (10,000 × $1) = $770,000. Average cost is $770,000/10,000 = $77. Continuing this procedure, we derive Table 16.6.

Table 16.6

Price	Number of subscribers	Total cost	Average cost
$50	10,000	$770,000	$77.00
$40	20,000	$780,000	$39.00
$30	30,000	$790,000	$26.33
$20	40,000	$800,000	$20.00
$10	50,000	$810,000	$16.20
$ 1	100,000	$860,000	$ 8.60

Step three: Find the price for which average cost crosses the demand curve. This price is $20, and it is the price that the public utility commission will choose.

5   (Practice problem: natural monopoly) The new big-cat exhibit at the Potter Park Zoo is bringing in the public. Demand is given in Table 16.7. The zoo costs the park service only $1 per visitor, but its fixed costs equal $12,000. Governor Scissorhands has declared that no public funds will be used to support zoos, so Potter Park must charge a price just high enough to cover its costs. What price will solve this problem?

Table 16.7

Price	Number of visitors
$8	1,000
$7	2,000
$6	3,000
$5	4,000
$4	5,000
$3	6,000
$2	7,000
$1	8,000

6   (Practice problem: natural monopoly) Country Line Commuter Service runs from rural areas into the city. It has fixed costs of $20,400 and a marginal cost of $10 per commuter. Demand is given in Table 16.8. The Metropolitan Transportation Commission sets the monthly price for a pass on Country Line, and it wants to allow the firm to earn a normal rate of return. Find the price that allows the service to cover its costs.

Table 16.8

Price (per month)	Number of commuters
$200	100
$180	120
$160	140
$140	160
$120	180
$100	200

Answers to Problems

2   The marginal revenue is given in Table 16.9.

Table 16.9

Price	Quantity	Revenues	Marginal revenue
$7.50	0	$ 0	—
$7.00	10	$ 70	$7
$6.50	20	$130	$6
$6.00	30	$180	$5
$5.50	40	$220	$4
$5.00	50	$250	$3
$4.50	60	$270	$2
$4.00	70	$280	$1

The monopoly output and price are 40 and $5.50, respectively. The competitive output and price would be 70 and $4, respectively. The deadweight loss is

$$\tfrac{1}{2}\,(70 - 40) \times (\$5.50 - \$4.00) = \$22.50.$$

3   The marginal revenue is given in Table 16.10.

Table 16.10

Price	Quantity	Revenues	Marginal revenue
$3.00	1,500	$4,500	$3
$2.50	3,000	$7,500	$2
$2.00	4,500	$9,000	$1
$1.50	6,000	$9,000	$0
$1.00	7,500	$7,500	−$1

The monopoly price and output are $2 and 4,500, respectively. The competitive price and output would be $1 and 7,500, respectively. The deadweight loss is

$$\tfrac{1}{2} \times (7,500 - 4,500) \times (\$2 - \$1) = \$1,500.$$

5   Average cost is given in Table 16.11.

Table 16.11

Price	Number of visitors	Total cost	Average cost
$8	1,000	$13,000	$13.00
$7	2,000	$14,000	$ 7.00
$6	3,000	$15,000	$ 5.00
$5	4,000	$16,000	$ 4.00
$4	5,000	$17,000	$ 3.40
$3	6,000	$18,000	$ 3.00
$2	7,000	$19,000	$ 2.70
$1	8,000	$20,000	$ 2.50

The price that allows Potter Park to cover its costs is $3.

6   Average cost is given in Table 16.12.

Table 16.12

Price	Number of commuters	Total cost	Average cost
$200	100	$21,400	$214.00
$180	120	$21,600	$180.00
$160	140	$21,800	$156.00
$140	160	$22,000	$138.00
$120	180	$22,200	$123.00
$100	200	$22,400	$112.00

Average cost equals price when price is $180. The commission should choose this price.

Chapter 17

TECHNOLOGICAL CHANGE

Chapter Review

Think back once again to the history of the automobile in Chapter 1. At the beginning of this century, the automobile had not been invented, much less produced in any quantity or in the form we know it today. The enormous technological change in the automobile industry during this century is astounding. Yet the basic model of perfect competition assumes that the goods produced and the technology used to produce them do not change. In this chapter, the emphasis shifts to firms as they actively compete to discover new products and new ways of producing. Although many firms may be involved, the race for new ideas brings with it many of the aspects of imperfect competition covered in Chapters 14–16.

The most important point made in this chapter is that imperfect competition is not all bad. It brings with it the positive benefits of technological advance. Government policy to promote technological change includes granting patents, subsidizing research and development (R & D), and occasionally protecting infant industries.

ESSENTIAL CONCEPTS

1   In the basic competitive model, there is one lowest-cost way of producing, and all firms adopt this technology.

The entry of new firms into the market soon drives away any profits, and all firms settle down to produce at the minimum of the average cost curve. The world of **technological change**, however, is vastly different. Firms compete aggressively to develop new products or production processes so that they can earn monopoly profits, at least for a while. For various reasons, the study of technological change must focus on imperfect competition.

2   A **patent** is a property right to an idea, and it gives the owner monopoly status and the opportunity to earn monopoly profits for the duration of the patent. Firms compete in **patent races**, a winner-take-all system in which the first firm with a discovery is awarded that patent, and its competitors get nothing. Because not all ideas are patentable and because to obtain a patent the firm must disclose details of the idea, firms sometimes forgo applying for one and keep the idea a **trade secret.** In this case, the firm earns monopoly profits until its competitors discover the idea or a better one.

3   Patent policy involves two types of trade-offs:

   a   The first issue is the **life** of the patent. Longer patents offer greater rewards for winning the race, and at the same time they promote research and development. On the other hand, for the duration of the patent, the firm sells at the monopoly price, which is above marginal cost, and so causes short-run inefficiencies; i.e., deadweight losses.

b   The second issue is the **breadth** of the patent. Should patents be given for the narrowly defined idea or something more general? More broadly defined patents increase the rewards for R & D; however, access to the idea is restricted, and this restriction inhibits any subsequent innovative activity that might build on the patented idea.

4   Several features of research and development encourage large-sized firms.

a   First, R & D is a *fixed cost*, in the sense that once discovered, an idea can be used many times without additional cost. Fixed costs increase the efficient scale of the firm.

b   Second, the **learning curve** shows that costs fall with experience. The more the firm learns, the more it produces, and thus learning by doing encourages firms to increase their size.

c   Third, firms have difficulty borrowing to finance R & D. Larger firms with more retained earnings can finance more of their own research.

5   **Basic research** on the nature of fundamental ideas generates such widespread external benefits that it has the two characteristics of **public goods:** Basic research produces knowledge, and it is difficult (not to mention undesirable) to exclude others from learning and taking advantage of new knowledge. Also, the marginal cost of giving another user access to new knowledge is certainly zero. Because basic research has the characteristic features of public goods, the government has an important role to play in providing funding for such work.

6   Because R & D creates external benefits not captured through patents, most economists advocate additional government policies to encourage it. Tax credits for increased R & D spending are one form of subsidy used in the United States. Also, the **infant industry argument for protection** says that new industries require protection against foreign competition until they move down the learning curve and acquire sufficient expertise to compete effectively. Further, antitrust laws can be relaxed to allow for joint ventures.

BEHIND THE ESSENTIAL CONCEPTS

1   Most of microeconomics sings the praises of perfect competition, especially to the extent that it allocates resources efficiently given the existing production technology. But does a perfectly competitive economy always find the best way to generate more advanced technologies of production, better products, and new ways of doing things? This chapter suggests that the answer is no. In order to encourage R & D, the government set up the patent system to motivate firms toward innovation by rewarding the winner with a period of freedom from competition. Perhaps paradoxically, government creates monopoly to encourage competition.

2   Technological advance is a vital engine of economic growth. Because it is so important, government promotes it with a wide range of complementary policies. Longer-lived and more broadly defined patents increase the rewards for R & D, while tax subsidies reduce the cost. Government also provides direct funding for basic research.

3   Economists consider the infant industry argument for protection to be valid but dangerous. Sometimes the protected industry gains expertise through experience and becomes a world-class competitor; other times the industry becomes inefficient and requires constant government support to survive. The difficulty is determining which industries will thrive and which will not.

4   You learned the basic logic of externalities in Chapter 7: whenever costs or benefits of some decision are not borne entirely by the decision maker, there is inefficiency. Most important to note in this chapter are the external benefits not captured by the firm that invests in R & D. These positive externalities include the fruits of subsequent R & D following an initial discovery, the gains after the expiration of the patent, and the consumer surplus arising from the application of the new idea. The firm ignores these externalities and thus undervalues the true social benefit of the R & D. Government policy can improve matters by promoting additional research efforts.

SELF-TEST

True or False

1   Firms engage in R & D expenditures so that they can participate in competitive markets.

2   A patent confers the exclusive right to produce and market an innovation for a limited period of time.

3   Patents and copyrights are forms of intellectual property.

4   The firm that finishes second in a patent race wins nothing.

5   Holders of patents set the price of their goods equal to marginal cost.

6   Patents promote dynamic efficiency at the expense of short-run inefficiency.

7   The length of patents is set to balance the costs of monopoly pricing by patent holders against the incentives to innovate.

8   Defining a patent more broadly might reduce the rate of innovation by denying access to previous innovations.

9   Any firm eligible for a patent will surely apply for one.

10   R & D is a variable cost of production.

11   The learning curve shows how fixed costs decline with experience.

12   One advantage that smaller firms have in R & D is their better access to capital markets.

13   Venture capital firms specialize in assessing the prospects of R & D ventures and providing capital to innovating firms.

14   The market is unlikely to provide enough basic research because basic research is a public good.

15   The antitrust laws inhibit firms from engaging in joint ventures.

Multiple Choice

1   Capitalism is a process of

   a   steady and smooth growth in the living standards of every individual;
   b   stagnation, in which the same goods are produced in the same way and distributed to the same people;
   c   creative destruction, in which new products and technologies continually destroy existing jobs, firms, and even entire industries;
   d   efficient allocation of resources in the short run, without any incentives for technological advance;
   e   b and d.

2   Firms engage in research and development expenditures in order to

   a   destroy their rivals;
   b   provide beneficial externalities to society;
   c   advance knowledge, which is a public good;
   d   gain market power and charge prices above costs;
   e   promote perfect competition.

3   Research and development refers to expenditures intended to

   a   discover new ideas and products;
   b   discover new technologies;
   c   develop products and bring them to market;
   d   all of the above;
   e   a and b.

4   A patent is

   a   a property right to an idea;
   b   the right to produce and sell an invention or innovation for all time;
   c   the right to produce and sell an invention or innovation for a limited time;
   d   a and b;
   e   a and c.

5   Patents

   a   promote short-run efficiency by encouraging firms to set price equal to marginal cost;
   b   stimulate research and innovation and promote dynamic efficiency;
   c   are awarded to the firm that has devoted the most resources to researching and developing the idea;
   d   are given for advances in basic knowledge;
   e   all of the above.

6   In the United States, the typical patent life is 17 years. The length involves a trade-off between

   a   short-run inefficiency and incentives to innovate;
   b   greater incentives to innovate and stimulation of subsequent innovation through greater access to past innovations;
   c   promoting research and fostering new product development;
   d   the profits of innovators and those of rivals;
   e   all of the above.

7   The breadth of patent coverage involves a trade-off between

   a   short-run inefficiency and incentives to innovate;
   b   greater incentives to innovate and stimulation of subsequent innovation through greater access to past innovations;
   c   promoting research and fostering new product development;
   d   the profits of innovators and those of rivals;
   e   all of the above.

8   Direct rewards from R & D are given

   a   in proportion to R & D expenditures;
   b   in proportion to market share;
   c   based on how many positive externalities are generated;
   d   on a winner-take-all basis;
   e   equally to all who entered the race.

9   A patent might not be awarded for an innovation if

   a   the innovator chose not to apply for the patent, preferring to hide the advance as a trade secret;
   b   the idea was too broad to be patentable;
   c   other firms had tried harder to find this particular innovation;
   d   too many jobs would be destroyed if the patent were awarded;
   e   a and b.

10   When patent holders raise price above marginal cost, there is a sacrifice of

   a   trade secrets;
   b   dynamic efficiency;
   c   infant industries;
   d   public goods;
   e   short-run efficiency.

11   R & D expenditures are

   a   variable costs;
   b   fixed costs;
   c   marginal costs;
   d   U-shaped average costs;
   e   none of the above.

12   Which of the following is true?

   a   Large firms have advantages in R & D because they may have better access to capital markets.
   b   Large firms have advantages in R & D because they can reap the cost savings on sales of more units.

c   Small firms have advantages in R & D because of the bureaucratic environment in large corporations.

d   All of the above.

e   a and b.

13   Learning by doing refers to

a   the fact that education only signals higher productivity; it does not increase productivity;

b   the idea that as firms gain experience from production, their costs fall;

c   the fact that R & D is wasteful because firms must produce products before they can innovate;

d   the fact that R & D is the only way to lower costs;

e   none of the above.

14   The learning curve

a   shows the trade-off between short-run and dynamic efficiency;

b   shows the trade-off between providing incentives to innovate and allowing access to previous innovations;

c   shows that patents lead to monopoly profits;

d   shows how marginal cost declines as cumulative experience increases;

e   disproves the infant industry argument.

15   According to the infant industry argument,

a   firms that have higher costs than their foreign rivals should be protected in order to save jobs;

b   firms should be protected if foreign labor costs are so low that the domestic firm cannot compete;

c   firms that have higher costs than their foreign rivals should be protected until they move down the learning curve;

d   free trade is efficient;

e   a, b, and c.

16   Which of the following is not true?

a   Competition drives firms that do not innovate from the market.

b   Competition inhibits innovation by eliminating profits that could be used to finance R & D.

c   Competition leads firms to imitate innovations, eroding returns.

d   Competition spurs R & D by making it clear that the principal way to earn profits is to innovate and capture market power.

e   All of the above.

17   The market will not supply enough R & D because

a   firms that win patent races do not have to pay for the patents;

b   the benefits of R & D spill over to others not directly involved;

c   firms that lose patent races cannot market the innovation;

d   firms that win patent races set price higher than marginal cost;

e   all of the above.

18   Which of the following is not a property of public goods?

a   It is difficult to exclude anyone from the benefits.

b   The marginal cost of an additional user is close to zero.

c   The market is likely to supply too few public goods.

d   All of the above are properties of public goods.

e   a and b.

19   Which of the following types of R & D is most likely to be a public good?

a   basic research;

b   product development;

c   applied research;

d   the costs of marketing new goods and services;

e   all of the above.

20   When firms share research and development efforts,

a   they are in violation of antitrust law;

b   they forgo the right to patent their innovations;

c   they may restrict access to their discoveries, thereby creating an entry barrier;

d   they forgo the right to ask for government subsidies;

e   they undermine dynamic efficiency.

Completion

1   As new products and technologies drive older jobs, technologies, and industries from the market, capitalism, in the words of Joseph Schumpeter, is a process of _____.

2   Expenditures designed to discover new ideas, products, and technologies and bring them to market are called _____.

3   The exclusive right to produce and sell an invention or innovation is a _____.

4   The fact that the rewards of research and development are given on a winner-take-all basis makes R & D a _____.

5   Rather than seek a patent, an innovator may try to hide the new knowledge as a _____.

6   _____ refers to the idea that as firms gain experience, their costs fall.

7   The curve showing how marginal costs of production decline as total experience increases is called the _____.

8   The benefits of research and development spill over to others not directly involved and generate positive _____.

9   Basic research produces knowledge from which it is difficult to exclude potential users and which can be used by others at no cost to the producers; therefore, it is an example of a _____.

10   The hope that an industry not currently able to com-

pete with foreign firms may in time acquire the experience to move down the learning curve is called the _____ argument for protection.

Answers to Self-Test

True or False

1	f	6	t	11	f
2	t	7	t	12	f
3	t	8	t	13	t
4	t	9	f	14	t
5	f	10	f	15	t

Multiple Choice

1	c	6	a	11	b	16	e
2	d	7	b	12	d	17	b
3	d	8	d	13	b	18	d
4	e	9	e	14	d	19	a
5	b	10	e	15	c	20	c

Completion

1 creative destruction
2 research and development
3 patent
4 patent race
5 trade secret
6 Learning by doing
7 learning curve
8 externalities
9 public good
10 infant industry

Doing Economics: Tools and Practice Problems

Firms undertake research and development in order to market new products or to find new and less costly ways of producing. They compete to win patents or secure trade secrets that will allow them to enjoy some protection against competition and to earn above-normal profits. In this section we study the rewards that motivate R & D. First, several problems explore the value of new product patents and trade secrets. Next, we study innovations that result in lower production costs and consider whether incumbent monopolies have as much incentive to innovate as do potential entrants.

PATENTS

The incentive to undertake research and development is the expectation of future profits. Patents allow firms to earn these profits by conferring monopoly status for the duration of the patent. Tool Kit 17.1 shows how to compute the value of a patent and thus the reward for successful innovation.

Tool Kit 17.1: Calculating the Value of a Patent

The developer of a new product may be able to win a patent, which grants the exclusive right to market the product for 17 years. The value of the patent is then the present discounted value of monopoly profits for the duration of the patent. Follow these steps to compute the value of a patent.

Step one: Compute monopoly profits resulting from the patent.

Step two: Find the present discounted value of 17 years of profits. This number is the value of the patent:

$$\text{value of the patent} = \text{profits} + [(\text{profits})] \times 1(1 + r)^1]$$
$$+ [(\text{profits}) \times 1/(1 + r)^2] + \ldots$$
$$+ [(\text{profits}) \times 1/(1 + r)^{16}].$$

(The variable r stands for the real rate of interest. In the problems below, we will set r equal to 3 percent. A shortcut for step two is to multiply profits by 13.47.)

---

1 (Worked problem: patents) Nu Products, Inc., has come up with another winning idea—a rubberized surface for premium, no-injury waterslide parks. The company wins the patent. Demand for resurfacings is given in Table 17.1, and costs are $20,000 per park. Calculate the value of the patent.

Table 17.1

Price	Parks resurfaced
$60,000	10
$50,000	20
$40,000	30
$30,000	40
$20,000	50

Step-by-step solution

Step one: Compute the monopoly profits resulting from the patent. Table 17.2 gives the marginal revenue for resurfacings.

Table 17.2

Price	Park resurfaced	Revenues	Marginal revenue
$60,000	10	$ 600,000	$60,000
$50,000	20	$1,000,000	$40,000
$40,000	30	$1,200,000	$20,000
$30,000	40	$1,200,000	$ 0
$20,000	50	$1,000,000	–$20,000

Marginal cost equals marginal revenue when price is $40,000 and 30 parks are resurfaced. Profits then equal ($40,000 × 30) – ($20,000 × 30) = $600,000.

Step two: Find the present discounted value of 17 years of profits. This number is the value of the patent.

Value of the patent $= \$600,000 + [(\$600,000) \times 1/(1 + r)^1]$
$+ [(\$600,000) \times 1/(1 + r)^2] +$
$+ \dots [(\$600,000) \times 1/(1 + r)^{16}]$
$= \$600,000 \times 13.47 = \$8,082,000.$

2 (Practice problem: patents) Bugout Pesticide has discovered a new product that kills potato bugs. It wins the patent. The firm's economics department computes that it can expect to earn $100,000 for the length of the patent. Compute the value of the patent.

3 (Practice problem: patents) Nip and Tuck Bodyshapers have developed a new procedure for smoothing those wrinkles that trouble the after-40 generation. They have decided not to apply for a patent, but rather to keep the technique secret. They expect that others will be able to duplicate the procedure in 4 years and that the resulting competition will allow only a normal rate of return thereafter. Their costs are $5,000 per face, and they estimate that the demand curve is as given in Table 17.3.

Table 17.3

Price	Quantity
$30,000	20
$25,000	30
$20,000	40
$15,000	50
$10,000	60
$ 5,000	70

The real interest rate is expected to remain at 5 percent over the period. Find the value of the trade secret.

THE ENTRANT VS. THE INCUMBENT

A firm that discovers and patents a new, lower-cost production technique will be able to earn above-normal profits for the duration of the patent. If the firm is already a monopoly, then it merely takes advantage of the lower costs. If the firm is a potential entrant, it can undercut the existing firm, drive it from the market, and take its place as the incumbent monopolist. Here, we compare the incentives that incumbent and entrant firms have to innovate, and demonstrate that monopolists do have lower incentives to innovate, as we learned in Chapter 16. Tool Kit 17.2 shows how to predict the outcome of competition between a new entrant and the incumbent monopolist. The following problems use this idea to compare incentives to innovate.

Tool Kit 17.2: Finding Equilibrium with an Incumbent Monopolist and a Potential Entrant

When a firm discovers how to produce for less, it is in position to take over an industry. It can set price just below the average cost of its rival and capture all sales. Follow these steps.

Step one: Identify the incumbent's costs, the potential entrant's costs, and the demand curve.

Step two: Find the equilibrium. The incumbent sets price equal to the entrant's average cost and captures the entire market. (Actually, the price must be 1 cent less than the average cost of the entrant, but we will round up in the problems below.)

---

4 (Worked problem: monopolist and potential entrant) Dentalcomp has had the monopoly in the market for computerizing dental offices in Roseville. While other firms could set up a computer system for $20,000, Dentalcomp's costs are only $15,000. Demand is given in Table 17.4.

Table 17.4

Price	Offices computerized
$30,000	20
$25,000	30
$20,000	40
$15,000	50
$10,000	60

a Find the equilibrium.
b Suppose that a new innovation in programming would lower costs to $10,000. Assume that the incumbent, Dentalcomp, discovers and patents the innovation first. Find the new equilibrium and the incumbent's profits. How much is the innovation worth to Dentalcomp?
c Now assume that a potential entrant discovers and patents the innovation first. Find the new equilibrium and the entrant's profits.
d Who has stronger incentives to innovate?

Step-by-step solution

Step one (a): Identify the incumbent's costs, the potential entrant's costs, and the demand curve. The incumbent, Dentalcomp, has an average cost of $15,000; the entrant has an average cost of $20,000. The demand appears in Table 17.4.

Step two: Find the equilibrium. The incumbent sets price equal to the entrant's average cost, which is $20,000, and captures the entire market of 40 offices. Its profits are ($20,000 × 40) – ($15,000 × 40) = $200,000.

Step three (b): If it discovers the innovation and wins the patent, Dentalcomp is still the low-cost firm. It captures the entire market with the same price of $20,000 and earns profits of ($20,000 × 40) – ($10,000 × 40) = $400,000.

Step four (c): If a potential entrant discovers the patent first, it becomes the low-price firm. It sets price equal to Dentalcomp's average cost, which is $15,000, and captures the entire market of 50 offices. Its profits are ($15,000 × 50) – ($10,000 × 50) = $250,000.

Step five (d): The gain to innovation for Dentalcomp is the difference between its profits before and after the innovation, which equals $400,000 – $200,000 = $200,000. The entrant gains $250,000 by innovating and thus has stronger incentives.

5   (Practice problem: monopolist and potential entrant) Blackdare has patented its unique process for extinguishing oil fires. It can put out a typical well fire for $150,000, but its competitors, without access to the patented process, have average costs equal to $200,000. The demand for extinguishing oil fires is given in Table 17.5.

Table 17.5

Price	Fires
$400,000	10
$350,000	12
$300,000	14
$250,000	16
$200,000	18
$150,000	20
$100,000	22

a   Find the equilibrium price and quantity and profits.
b   Suppose that a new innovation in firefighting would lower costs to $100,000. Assume that the incumbent, Blackdare, discovers and patents the innovation first. Find the new equilibrium and the incumbent's profits. How much is the innovation worth to Blackdare?
c   Now assume that a potential entrant discovers and patents the innovation first. Find the new equilibrium and the entrant's profits.
d   Who has the stronger incentives to innovate?

6   (Practice problem: monopolist and potential entrant) PhXXX Pharmaceuticals has a monopoly on the treatment of Rubinksi's Trauma, an obscure ailment of the saliva glands. The average cost of curing a patient is $2,000 for PhXXX. The only other treatment available costs $5,000. Demand for the treatment of Rubinski's Trauma is given in Table 17.6.

Table 17.6

Price	Treatments
$8,000	100
$7,000	200
$6,000	300
$5,000	400
$4,000	500
$3,000	600
$2,000	700
$1,000	800

a   Find the equilibrium price and quantity.
b   Suppose that a new genetically engineered drug would lower treatment costs to $1,000. Assume that the incumbent, PhXXX, discovers and patents the new drug first. Find the new equilibrium and the incumbent's profits. How much is the innovation worth to PhXXX?
c   Now assume that a potential entrant discovers and patents the innovation first. Find the new equilibrium and the entrant's profits.
d   Who has the stronger incentives to innovate?

Answers to Problems

2   Value of patent = $100,000 × 13.47 = $1,347,000.
3   Marginal revenue is given in Table 17.7.

Table 17.7

Price	Quantity	Revenues	Marginal revenue
$30,000	20	$600,000	—
$25,000	30	$750,000	$15,000
$20,000	40	$800,000	$ 5,000
$15,000	50	$750,000	–$ 5,000
$10,000	60	$600,000	–$15,000
$ 5,000	70	$350,000	–$25,000

Marginal revenue equals marginal cost at a price of $20,000, where 40 faces are smoothed. Profits = ($20,000 × 40) – ($5,000 × 40) = $600,000. The value of the trade secret is $600,000 + [($600,000) × 1/(1.05)] + [($600,000) × 1/(1.05)²] + [($600,000) × 1/(1.05)³] = $2,209,380.

5   a   Price = $200,000; quantity = 18; profits = $900,000.
    b   Price = $200,000; quantity = 18; profits = $1,800,000.
    c   Price = $150,000; quantity = 20; profits = $1,000,000.
    d   The entrant would gain $1,000,000, while Blackdare would only gain $1,800,000 – $900,000 = $900,000. The entrant has stronger incentives.

6   a   Price = $5,000; quantity = 400; profits = $1,200,000;
    b   Price = $5,000; quantity = 400; profits = $1,600,000;
    c   Price = $2,000; quantity = 700; profits = $700,000.
    d   The entrant would gain $700,000, while PhXXX would only gain $1,600,000 – $1,200,000 = $400,000. The entrant has stronger incentives.

IMPERFECT INFORMATION IN THE PRODUCT MARKET

Chapter Review

Chapter 18 begins the exploration of the economics of information with a look at information problems in the product market. Why can't customers always be sure of the quality of a good? Why do customers sometimes pay a higher price for a good than the good is worth? This chapter explains the various ways in which the economy attempts to solve these problems. In doing so, the chapter deviates from the basic competitive model to introduce a fascinating world of signaling, reputation, search, and advertising. Imperfect information causes markets to look a lot like the imperfect competition models discussed in Chapters 14–16 (on monopoly and oligopoly). Chapters 19 and 20 will take up imperfect information as well, in the labor and capital markets.

ESSENTIAL CONCEPTS

1   The basic competitive model assumes that information is perfect, that households are well-informed about the prices, quality, and availability of goods and services, and that firms know all input and output prices and the best available technology. Economists now believe that there are important aspects of the economy's performance that are the result of **imperfect information.** For instance, mutually beneficial trades may not occur if customers cannot judge accurately a product's quality.

   If there were such a thing as a market for information, it would not solve the problem. There would be no way for a customer to evaluate information before buying it, and if she already had the information, she would have no need to buy it.

2   **Asymmetric information** exists when one side of the market knows something that the other does not. For example, the seller of a used car may know more about its reliability than the buyer. Asymmetric information can cause the demand curve to be upward sloping, because buyers reason that only low-quality cars would be sold at low prices and that quality increases with price. This odd situation can lead to more than one possible equilibrium, and can cause markets to be thin or nonexistent in spite of potential gains from trade.

3   One way to send buyers a message in a market with asymmetric information is called **signaling.** For example, a seller of quality used cars can distinguish his product by offering warranties or by building expensive showrooms. Buyers will reason that a seller of lemons

could not afford the expenses of honoring the warranty and will conclude that this seller's used cars are reliable. The seller can also charge higher prices, another potentially informative signal. Buyers understand that only lemons would be sold at low prices, and thus they judge the quality according to the price.

4   If buyers can observe the quality of what is sold, then they can provide sellers with good incentives by basing pay on quality. For example, an employer can pay a typist according to the number of errors made. When buyers do not know the quality of goods before purchasing them, markets do not provide built-in incentives for firms to produce high-quality merchandise. Two possible solutions to this incentive problem are **contracts** and **reputations.**

   a   Contracts typically include **contingency clauses**, which make payment depend on the quality of the service. For example, a contract might specify that the service must be performed by a certain date unless there is a strike or bad weather. Spelling out contingencies provides incentives and shares the risk, but it makes contracts complicated. When the terms of a contract are violated, one party is said to be in breach, but if the reasons for the breach are ambiguous, contract enforcement becomes an issue. Certainly, contracts help, but they provide only an imperfect solution to the incentive problems accompanying trade in the presence of asymmetric information.

   b   By repeatedly providing quality goods and service, a firm establishes a reputation, which enables it to earn extra profits. To preserve its valuable reputation, the firm must continue to provide quality. Reputations thus provide firms with incentives to perform well.

5   Because quality is uncertain and also because the same good may be sold at different prices in different locations (**price dispersion**), customers spend time and money in **search**. Rational search balances the benefits (finding better goods at lower prices) against the costs. Customers usually stop searching even though there is more to learn. **Information intermediaries** are firms that gather information to make customer search easier and more effective. Department stores and travel agents are examples of information intermediaries.

6   Firms try to influence customers' purchasing decisions through **informative** and **persuasive advertising.** The goal of advertising is to shift the demand curve to the right, enabling the firm to raise prices and sell more goods. Advertising may also serve as a signal. Customers may reason that only a high-quality product with good sales would justify a large expenditure on advertising.

7   Concern for poorly informed consumers and deceptive advertising has led to **consumer protection legislation**, which attempts to stop false advertising. Such legislation includes truth-in-lending regulations, which require lenders to disclose the true interest rate. Even so, distinguishing between illegal, false advertising and its legal counterparts (confusing and persuasive advertising) is difficult.

BEHIND THE ESSENTIAL CONCEPTS

1   Markets do not necessarily fail when information is imperfect. The market for assets is an example of a very efficient market. Uncertainty in these markets exists, but the uncertainty is symmetric. Neither side knows the ultimate value of the assets they are trading. Efficiency problems arise, however, when information is asymmetric, that is, when one side of the market knows something that the other does not. Many mutually beneficial exchanges do not take place because buyers cannot be sure about quality, and they fear that sellers may exploit their informational advantage and sell lemons.

2   In the basic competitive model, customers ask simple questions such as, "Is the good worth its price?" In the presence of asymmetric information, and, especially signaling, customers must be more sophisticated. The seller of a quality item wants to signal that his goods have value. He could just say, "My goods are great!" but few customers would believe him. If he provides a guarantee and builds an expensive shop, customers may be more confident that he would be there to honor his word should the product fail. The customer infers from the warranty and the shop that the seller's goods are quality goods.

3   The information problems discussed in this chapter lead the market structure away from perfect competition, creating two possible situations: **barriers to entry** and firms with **downward-sloping demand curves.**

   a   Customers who cannot know the quality of goods buy from businesses with good reputations. Because a reputation is built up over time, firms that would otherwise enter an industry will not be able to justify the investment necessary to establish a good reputation. In this scenario, reputation becomes a barrier to entry and results in less competition.

   b   Because customers must search to learn about price and quality, it becomes cheaper for them to shop at familiar stores. Although the goods themselves may be identical, the stores are different in the eyes of the customer because he knows about some stores and is ignorant of others. Thus, a firm faces a downward-sloping demand curve, where high demanders are those who have information about the firm and lower demanders do not as yet.

4   Information problems in the product market run parallel to the problems in the insurance market discussed in Chapter 6. Again, there are two types of information problems.

   a   In the insurance market, when the price of insurance

is high, only the risky customers buy insurance. The mix of customers is adversely selected when the price rises. Adverse selection also appears in the market for lemons. Customers reason that as the price rises, more quality cars are offered for sale, and the fraction of lemons declines. In other words, there is *adverse selection* in the average quality of used cars when the price falls.

b   *Moral hazard* troubles the insurance market because people who have insurance tend to be less cautious. They lose their incentives to be careful when they are protected against loss. Similarly, in this chapter, we see that suppliers must be given incentives to live up to the terms of their contracts. There is a moral hazard that the other party may not fulfill his promise and instead give some excuse that cannot be verified.

5   Although this chapter is about information problems, you should also keep in mind that markets do economize on the need for gathering information. In deciding what to produce and in what quantities and the method of production, firms do not need to know the preferences or incomes of households, the production techniques of other firms, or the overall quantities of inputs available. They only need to know the price. Similarly, households do not need to know others' tastes or anything about firms. Price conveys all relevant information, a great advantage of markets.

SELF-TEST

True or False

1   In the basic competitive model, individuals know their opportunity sets.

2   In the basic competitive model, firms know the opportunity sets of individuals.

3   Markets for information do not work well because once the consumer has enough information to evaluate the worth of the information, she no longer has the incentive to pay for it.

4   In the lemons model, demand may slope upward if average quality increases as price increases.

5   Supply and demand may cross more than once if customers do not know the quality of the goods they are asked to buy.

6   Lemons markets have adverse selection in that as the price falls, the mix of goods offered for sale contains more low-quality goods.

7   Customers may believe that a product that carries a warranty is reliable because if the product were not reliable, the firm would incur costs honoring the warranty.

8   Even if customers judge the quality of goods by their price, the market always clears in equilibrium.

9   In the rental car market, there is an incentive problem because customers have less reason to drive carefully.

10   Contracts attempt to provide incentives through contingency clauses that specify what each party agrees to do in different situations.

11   Problems of specifying and enforcing quality make it difficult to overcome the incentive problems with contracts.

12   The reputation of a firm may persuade customers that its goods are of high quality because if the firm were to lose its reputation, its profits would fall.

13   The reputations of existing firms attract new competitors to the market because these firms earn higher profits.

14   Markets where customers must search to learn price are characterized by perfect competition.

15   Information intermediaries reduce the search costs of firms and customers.

Multiple Choice

1   In the basic competitive model, households are assumed to know

a   their opportunity set;
b   the prices of all goods and services offered for sale;
c   the characteristics of all goods and services;
d   their preferences;
e   all of the above.

2   In the basic competitive model, firms are assumed to know

a   the best available technology;
b   the productivity of each job applicant;
c   all input prices from every possible supplier;
d   the present and future prices for their outputs;
e   all of the above.

3   In the basic competitive model, firms are assumed to know

a   the preferences of individual consumers;
b   the costs of production for their suppliers;
c   the overall quantities of available inputs;
d   all of the above;
e   none of the above.

4   Markets for information do not work well because

a   no firm would be willing to sell information;
b   consumers are not willing to pay for information;
c   consumers cannot know what they are buying before they actually buy the information;
d   markets only work to allocate material goods;
e   all of the above.

5   In the lemons model,

a   customers know the quality of the goods, but sellers do not;
b   sellers know the quality of the goods, but customers do not;

c   neither customers nor sellers know the quality of the goods;

d   both customers and sellers know that the quality of the goods is low;

e   none of the above.

6   In the lemons model,

a   average quality rises as price falls;

b   average quality falls as price falls because sellers know the quality, and owners of lower-quality goods are willing to sell at lower prices;

c   average quality does not change as price falls because consumers know quality and will not buy lower-quality goods;

d   average quality may rise or fall as price falls;

e   none of the above.

7   In the lemons model,

a   demand is downward sloping;

b   supply is upward sloping;

c   demand may slope up or down;

d   supply may slope up or down;

e   b and c.

8   Which of the following involve(s) adverse selection?

a   Consumers sometimes make mistakes and select inferior products.

b   Consumers may not be able to find the lowest-price supplier.

c   As the price falls, the fraction of used cars that are lemons increases.

d   As the automobile insurance premium is increased, those least likely to have an accident drop out of the market.

e   c and d.

9   In markets with imperfect information,

a   firms are price takers;

b   firms set prices, taking into account the effect that price has as a signal of quality;

c   price plays no role because consumers are uncertain about quality;

d   markets clear for the usual reasons;

e   there is a uniform market price per unit of quality, but the goods of different firms sell for different prices.

10   Which of the following are examples of informative signals?

a   The seller claims that her goods are high quality.

b   The seller offers a warranty.

c   The seller constructs an expensive showroom.

d   All of the above.

e   b and c.

11   In markets with imperfect information, the incentive problem arises because

a   firms have no incentive to pay lower prices because they do not know the quality;

b   firms have limited incentive to produce good-

quality items if they cannot convince consumers;

c   firms can raise price above the consumer's willingness to pay;

d   firms have no incentive to produce quality items unless they can be patented;

e   firms have no incentive to build reputations.

12   Contracts with provisions that specify what each of the parties must do in certain situations are called

a   signals;

b   adverse selection;

c   contingency clauses;

d   reputations;

e   none of the above.

13   When a party to contract violates its terms, he

a   is in adverse selection;

b   writes a contingency clause;

c   creates price dispersion;

d   is an information intermediary;

e   is in breach.

14   In some markets, the reputations of firms help persuade customers that their products are high quality. In these markets,

a   price remains above the cost of production;

b   firms earn reputation rents;

c   the reputations of existing firms act as a barrier to the entry of new competitors;

d   all of the above;

e   a and b.

15   A firm with a reputation for high-quality goods might not cut its price because

a   cutting price would attract more customers;

b   customers might infer that at the low price, the firm will not have enough incentive to maintain its reputation;

c   lower prices would attract new competitors;

d   the firm cannot set its price—it must be a price taker;

e   a and b.

16   When customers do not have perfect information about price, there may be price dispersion, which means

a   the same good is sold at different prices;

b   the expenses of searching eliminate the gains from trade;

c   customers will search for the best value;

d   all of the above;

e   a and c.

17   When search is costly for customers,

a   the demand curves for a firm's products will be downward sloping;

b   firms will be price takers;

c   the firm will lose all its customers if it raises its price above the prices of its competitor;

d the firm will gain all its competitors' business if it charges lower prices;

e c and d.

18 Markets in which customers must search to learn prices and qualities are best described by the

   a competitive model;

   b pure monopoly model;

   c monopolistic competition model;

   d a or b;

   e none of the above.

19 An information intermediary

   a helps bring together buyers and sellers;

   b cannot make money because markets for information do not work well;

   c writes contracts for buyers and sellers;

   d eliminates the need for advertising;

   e c and d.

20 Advertising

   a provides price information to potential customers;

   b informs customers about which products are available;

   c attempts to persuade customers to buy certain products;

   d all of the above;

   e a and b.

Completion

1 In the market for _____, customers do not know the quality of the goods being sold.

2 Actions taken by sellers to convince buyers of the high quality of their goods are called _____.

3 The _____ arises when the individual is not rewarded for what she does or when she does not have to pay the full costs of what she does.

4 Clauses in contracts that make the payment depend on precisely how the service is performed are called _____.

5 Someone who brings buyers and sellers together is called an _____.

6 The reputations of existing firms act as a _____ against new competition.

7 When the same good is sold at different prices, there is _____.

8 When customers must search for price and quality information, competition is _____.

9 Advertising that conveys information about price, product availability, and quality is called _____ advertising.

10 Advertising may _____ to customers that the product is of high quality because if the quality were poor, the firm would soon lose its new customers and would have wasted its advertising expenses.

Answers to Self-Test

True or False

1	t	6	t	11	t
2	f	7	t	12	t
3	t	8	f	13	f
4	t	9	t	14	f
5	t	10	t	15	t

Multiple Choice

1	e	6	b	11	b	16	e
2	e	7	e	12	c	17	a
3	e	8	e	13	e	18	c
4	c	9	b	14	d	19	a
5	b	10	e	15	b	20	d

Completion

1 lemons
2 signals
3 incentive problem
4 contingency clauses
5 information intermediary
6 barrier to entry
7 price dispersion
8 imperfect
9 informative
10 signal

Doing Economics: Tools and Practice Problems

Three topics are discussed in this section. First, we look at the important **lemons model**, where average quality is higher as price increases. In this situation, we may see upward-sloping demand curves, which may cause markets to fail to exist or may create the possibility of more than one equilibrium. Also, when firms are able to set prices in this model, there is the possibility of excess supply. Second, we turn to price dispersion and search. We explore the benefits and costs of searching and see why the consumer will likely stop searching before the lowest price is found. Finally, we study how advertising increases profits.

LEMONS

When consumers do not know the quality of a good until after they make the purchase, there is asymmetric information in the product market. Firms that produce low-quality goods (lemons) can sell their goods in the high-quality market. If information were perfect, there would be two markets; now there is one. In figuring out their own demand, consumers must estimate how average quality changes as the market expands. Tool Kit 18.1 shows how to derive the demand curve under these circumstances and that it may slope upwards, and some problems explore the consequences.

Tool Kit 18.1: Deriving the Demand Curve When Consumers Do Not Know the Quality of the Good

If they cannot observe the quality of a good at the time of purchase, customers must estimate and base their demand on the average quality available on the market. Follow this four-step procedure.

Step one: Add the supplies of low- and high-quality goods to find the market supply curve.

Price	Quantity supplied
p_1	$Q_{low} + Q_{high}$
p_2	$Q_{low} + Q_{high}$
etc.	

Step two: Find the fractions of high- and low-quality goods at each point on the supply curve.

Fraction of high-quality goods = $Q_{high}/(Q_{low} + Q_{high})$.

Fraction of low-quality goods = $Q_{low}/(Q_{low} + Q_{high})$.

Step three: Find the average value at each point. This number is what consumers are willing to pay; therefore, it is the demand price.

Average value = demand price
= (fraction of high quality ×
value of high quality)
+ (fraction of low quality ×
value of low quality).

Step four: Construct the demand curve.

Price = average value	Quantity demanded
p_1	$Q_{low} + Q_{high}$
p_2	$Q_{low} + Q_{high}$
etc.	

---

1 (Worked problem: lemons) Many firms sell 50-pound packages of meat at the local farmers' market. Customers place a value of $20 on fatty, low-quality beef, and they place a value of $50 on lean, good-quality beef. The beef is wrapped and frozen, so at the time of purchase, customers cannot distinguish the quality of beef they are buying. The supply curves for low- and high-quality beef appear in Table 18.1.

Table 18.1

Low quality		High quality	
Price	Quantity	Price	Quantity
$15	1,000	$15	0
$20	2,000	$20	0
$25	3,000	$25	1,000
$30	4,000	$30	4,000
$35	5,000	$35	10,000
$40	6,000	$40	12,000
$45	7,000	$45	14,000
$50	8,000	$50	16,000

a Derive the demand curve for beef.
b Find the market-clearing price (or prices) and quantity (or quantities).
c For purposes of comparison, suppose that consumers could tell the difference and that there were separate markets for the two types of beef. Find the equilibrium price and quantity for each type of beef. How does the asymmetric information about quality affect the market for high-quality beef?

Step-by-step solution

Step one (a): Add the supplies to find the market supply. For example, if the price is $325, there will be 5,000 low-quality packages of beef and 10,000 high-quality packages for a total of 15,000. Proceeding in this way gives the market supply as shown in Table 18.2.

Table 18.2

Market supply	
Price	Quantity both high (and low quality)
$15	1,000
$20	2,000
$25	4,000
$30	8,000
$35	15,000
$40	18,000
$45	21,000
$50	24,000

Step two: Find the fractions of the total that are high and low quality at each point. For example, if the price is $35, there are 10,000 high-quality packages. The total number of packages is 15,000. The fraction is $(10,000/15,000) \times 100 = 2/3$. Enter the number and continue. The corresponding fraction of low-quality goods is then 1/3. The complete information appears in Table 18.3.

Table 18.3

Price	Low-quality quantity	High-quality quantity	Fraction high	Fraction low
$15	1,000	0	0	1
$20	2,000	0	0	1
$25	3,000	1,000	1/4	3/4
$30	4,000	4,000	1/2	1/2
$35	5,000	10,000	2/3	1/3
$40	6,000	12,000	2/3	1/3
$45	7,000	14,000	2/3	1/3
$50	8,000	16,000	2/3	1/3

Step three: Compute the average value for each price. For example, when the price is $35, there are 5,000 packages valued at $20 and 10,000 valued at $50. The average value is $[(\$20 \times 5,000) + (\$50 \times 10,000)]/15,000 = \$40$. Continue and complete the table as shown in Table 18.4. Note that average value increases with price. This is because at a higher price, the percentage of packages that are high quality is greater.

Table 18.4

Price	Low-quality quantity	High-quality quantity	Fraction high	Average value
$15	1,000	0	0	$20.00
$20	2,000	0	0	$20.00
$25	3,000	1,000	1/4	$27.50
$30	4,000	4,000	1/2	$35.00
$35	5,000	10,000	2/3	$40.00
$40	6,000	12,000	2/3	$40.00
$45	7,000	14,000	2/3	$40.00
$50	8,000	16,000	2/3	$40.00

Step four: Construct the demand curve. It is given in Table 18.5 and drawn in the diagram. The price column is the average value, and the quantity column is the sum of the low- and high-quality quantities.

Table 18.5

Market demand	
Price	Quantity
$20.00	1,000
$20.00	2,000
$27.50	4,000
$35.00	8,000
$40.00	15,000
$40.00	18,000
$40.00	21,000
$40.00	24,000

Step five (b): Find the market-clearing prices and quantities. The market clears at a price of $20, where the quantity demanded equals the quantity supplied at 2,000. At this equilibrium, there are no high-quality packages sold. Also, the market clears at a price of $40, where the quantity demanded and the quantity supplied equal 18,000. At this equilibrium, there are 6,000 low-quality and 12,000 high-quality packages. The two equilibria are shown in the diagram.

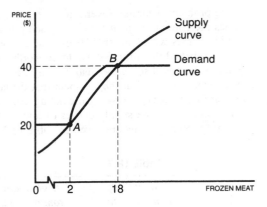

Step six (c): If consumers had perfect information about quality, then there would be a separate low-quality market with 2,000 sold at a price of $20 and a high-quality market with a price of $50 and 16,000 units sold. The asymmetric information destroys the high-quality market in equilibrium A. In equilibrium B, the high-quality market survives, but the quantity is smaller than it would be with perfect information.

2   (Practice problem: lemons) Trying to appear better educated, many Americans are buying abbreviated guides to culture—lists of novels, operas, and works of art an educated person should know. The guides also include a paragraph or two of witty things to say. The consumers of these books, obviously, cannot judge the quality until they say the wrong thing at the next important social function. The supply curves of low- and high-quality guides are given in Table 18.6. The value of a high-quality guide (complete with video tapes and workbooks) is $300. Low-quality guides are worthless.

Table 18.6

Price	Low-quality guides	High-quality guides
$ 50	1,000	0
$100	2,000	1,000
$150	4,000	6,000
$200	8,000	16,000
$250	12,000	36,000
$300	16,000	48,000

a   Derive the demand curve for guides.
b   Find the market-clearing price (or prices) and quantity (or quantities).
c   For the purposes of comparison, suppose that consumers could tell the difference and that there were separate markets for the two types of guides. Find the equilibrium price and quantity for each type of guide. How does the asymmetric information about quality affect the market for high-quality guides?

3   (Practice problem: lemons) Several new varieties of tomatoes are coming on to the market. Each promises tasty tomatoes with long shelf lives, and a tomato plant that fulfilled this promise would be worth $4. Consumers cannot observe the quality until the end of the growing season, but they suspect that the new hybrids are no better or worse than existing ones valued at $1 per plant. The supply curves of low- and high-quality tomato plants are given in Table 18.7.

Table 18.7

Price	Low-quality tomato plants	High-quality tomato plants
$1.00	10,000	0
$1.50	20,000	5,000
$2.00	30,000	20,000
$2.50	40,000	60,000
$3.00	50,000	100,000
$3.50	60,000	300,000
$4.00	70,000	500,000

a   Derive the demand curve for tomato plants.
b   Find the market-clearing price (or prices) and quantity (or quantities).
c   For the purposes of comparison, suppose that consumers could tell the difference and that there were separate markets for each of the two types of plants. Find the equilibrium price and quantity for each type of plant. How does the asymmetric information about quality affect the market for high-quality plants?

Judging Quality by Price

Because it is more expensive to produce high-quality goods than low, consumers may reason that at low prices only the poor-quality items are offered for sale, and that as price increases, so does average quality. If firms understand this sort of reasoning, they will set price so that quality per dollar is as high as possible, even though this price may not be the market-clearing price. It is possible that shortages will occur, and yet no firm will reduce its price because it knows that it will not gain customers, who believe that lower prices imply lower quality. This is a profound result. In normal competitive markets, the role of prices is only to clear the market. In markets where customers do not know quality, however, price acts as a signal of quality. The price that does the best job of signaling quality may not clear the market. Tool Kit 18.2 shows how price is set in this case.

Tool Kit 18.2: Finding the Price That Maximizes Quality per Dollar

If customers judge quality by price, firms will set price to maximize quality per dollar. Follow these steps to find the right price.

Step one: Identify and plot the relationship between quality and price.

Step two: For each price, find the quality-price ratio: quality-price ratio = quality/price.

Step three: Choose the highest quality-price ratio. Label this point *A*.

Step four: Draw a line from the origin to point *A*. It should be tangent to the quality-price curve, and its slope equals the maximum quality-price ratio.

---

4   (Worked problem: quality and price) Consumers of 12-gallon fire extinguishers care deeply about the quality of the item, but they cannot distinguish effective and ineffective goods at the time of purchase. The quality of the fire extinguisher only matters if and when it is used. Consumers may reason that at low prices, firms could not afford the quality-control procedures necessary to ensure effective operation. Suppose consumers believe that the relationship between quality and price is as given in Table 18.8.

Table 18.8

Price	Quality (gallons of fire retardant released)
$ 5	0
$10	1.0
$15	4.5
$20	7.0
$25	10.0
$30	11.0
$35	12.0
$40	12.0

a   Find the price that maximizes quality per dollar.

b   Suppose that demand and supply are as given in Table 18.9. Find the equilibrium price. Does it clear the market? Why or why not?

Table 18.9

Price	Demand	Supply
$40	10,000	28,000
$35	12,000	25,000
$30	14,000	21,000
$25	16,000	20,000
$20	17,000	19,000
$15	19,000	17,000
$10	21,000	11,000

Step-by-step solution

Step one (a): Identify and plot the relationship between quality and price. It is given in Table 18.8 and drawn in the diagram.

Step two: For each price, find the quality-price ratio. When the price is $40, the quality-price ratio is 12/$40 = 0.30. Continuing, we derive Table 18.10.

Table 18.10

Price	Quality	Quality-price ratio
$ 5	0	—
$10	1.0	0.10
$15	4.5	0.30
$20	7.0	0.35
$25	10.0	0.40
$30	11.0	0.37
$35	12.0	0.34
$40	12.0	0.30

Step three: Choose the highest quality-price ratio. It is 0.40, which occurs at a price of $25.

Step four: Draw a line from the origin to point A. It should be tangent to the quality-price curve, and its slope should equal the maximum quality-price ratio, as shown in the diagram.

Step five (b): At a price of $25, the quantity demanded is 16,000, and the quantity supplied is 20,000. Even though there is a surplus of 4,000, firms do not reduce the price. They know that customers would interpret the lower price as a signal of lower quality.

5   (Practice problem: quality and price) Tourists come to San Gordo for the shrimp. Dozens of small establishments offer shrimp, but tourists have little ability to judge the quality before eating. They reason, however, that at low prices the firms cannot afford to ensure that the shrimp are tasty. Suppose consumers believe that the relationship between quality and price is as given in Table 18.11.

Table 18.11

Price (dozen shrimp)	Quality (percentage of tasty shrimp)
$1	10
$2	30
$3	60
$4	70
$5	80
$6	85

a   Find the price that maximizes quality per dollar.

b   Suppose that demand and supply are as given in Table 18.12. Find the equilibrium price. Does it clear the market? Why or why not?

Table 18.12

Price	Demand	Supply
$6	2,000	6,000
$5	2,500	5,500
$4	3,000	5,000
$3	3,500	4,500
$2	4,000	4,000
$1	6,000	3,000

6   (Practice problem: quality and price) The boom in home exercise equipment continues, but there are many purchasers who have given up the quest for the perfect body. These purchasers offer their used equipment for sale. The market also includes those who are selling used lemons, worthless devices that do not perform as advertised. Consumers of used exercise equipment judge that the relationship between price and quality is as given in Table 18.13.

Table 18.13

Price	Quality (calories burned per hour)
$100	100
$200	500
$300	1,100
$400	1,600
$500	1,750

Find the price that maximizes quality per dollar.

SEARCH

In imperfectly competitive markets, different firms may offer the same good for sale at different prices. This situation, called price dispersion, means that consumers must not only decide which goods to purchase, they also must expend time and effort to locate lower price offers and decide which offer to accept. The optimal amount to search is the subject of these problems. As usual, the solution involves carefully balancing benefits and costs. Tool Kit 18.3 shows how.

Tool Kit 18.3: Searching for
Lower Prices

When there is price dispersion, customers must search. These steps show how to balance the benefits and costs of searching for lower prices.

Step one: Identify the marginal cost of search and the relationship between search effort and price.

Step two: Calculate the marginal benefits of search: marginal benefit = (change in lowest price)/change in search effort.

Step three: Find the amount of search for which the marginal benefits equal the marginal cost.

Step four: Draw a diagram illustrating the solution.

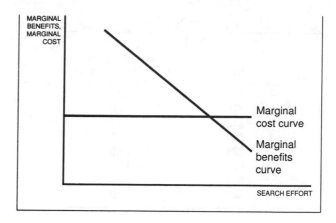

7   (Worked problem: search) Jennifer would like to build a deck behind her new condominium. She has in mind the type she would like and is considering sending away for catalogs offering deck kits. Each catalogue costs $5. The relationship between the lowest appropriate deck kit price and the number of catalogs is given in Table 18.14.

Table 18.14

Number of catalogs ordered	Lowest price found	Marginal benefit
1	$250	
2	$225	
3	$210	
4	$205	
5	$202	
6	$200	

a   What is the optimal number of catalogs for Jennifer to order?
b   What price does she expect to pay for a deck kit?
c   Draw a diagram illustrating your solution.

Step-by-step solution

Step one (a): Identify the marginal cost of search and the relationship between search effort and price. The marginal cost is $5, and the relationship appears in Table 18.14.

Step two: Calculate the marginal benefit of search. The expected price is $250 from the first catalog and $225 from the second. The marginal benefit is thus $25. Continuing, we derive the marginal benefits as shown in Table 18.15.

Table 18.15

Number of catalogs ordered	Lowest price found	Marginal benefit
1	$250	—
2	$225	$25
3	$210	$15
4	$205	$ 5
5	$202	$ 3
6	$200	$ 2

Step three: Find the amount of search for which the marginal benefit equals the marginal cost. This is 4 catalogs, which is the answer to part a.

Step four (b): The expected lowest price is $205, when she buys 4 catalogs.

Step five (c): The solution appears in the diagram.

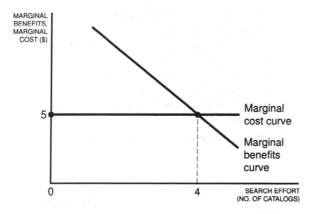

8 (Practice problem: search) Raul wants to refinish his floors. This type of home improvement project is very popular in his neighborhood, and appointments for estimates must be made and paid for weeks in advance. Estimates cost $25, and Raul guesses that the relationship between the number of estimates and the lowest price is as given in Table 18.16.

Table 18.16

Number of estimates	Expected lowest price
1	$800
2	$650
3	$550
4	$500
5	$475
6	$465
7	$460

a   What is the optimal number of estimates for Raul to schedule?

b   What price does he expect to pay for refinishing his floors?

c   Draw a diagram illustrating your solution.

9 (Practice problem: search) The Melling Forging Company needs a new robotic lathe. Several companies offer the lathes, but Melling's management feels there is enough variety that an on-site inspection is needed for each. Time is short, so the company plans to send engineers simultaneously to the plants of some of the firms that sell robotic lathes. The company would like to visit all robotic lathe producers, but a plant visit costs the company $1,000. The relationship between the number of visits and the profits that the new system will earn is given in Table 18.17.

Table 18.17

Number of visits	Expected maximum profitability
1	$18,000
2	$23,000
3	$26,000
4	$27,000
5	$27,500

How many engineers should Melling send?

10 (Practice problem: advertising) Advertising is designed to shift the demand curve to the right. This allows a firm to charge higher prices on the goods that it sells and to adjust the quantity to the profit-maximizing level along the new demand curve. To see how profits change with a successful advertising program, simply follow the procedure outlined in Chapter 14 for deriving marginal revenue and finding the monopoly price and quantity.

Fay's Cleaners has been advertising its new service, which offers customers the opportunity to leave and pick up their dry cleaning at the commuter train station. The demand curves before and after the advertising campaign are given in Table 18.18. Quantity measures suits cleaned and pressed. The marginal cost of each item is $1. Fixed costs equal $1,000.

Table 18.18

Before		After	
Price	Quantity	Price	Quantity
$5.00	100	$5.00	500
$4.50	200	$4.50	1,000
$4.00	300	$4.00	1,500
$3.50	400	$3.50	2,000
$3.00	500	$3.00	2,500
$2.50	600	$2.50	3,000
$2.00	700	$2.00	3,500

a   Find the profit-maximizing price and quantity and level of profits before the advertising campaign.

b   Find the profit-maximizing price and quantity and level of profits after the advertising campaign.

c   How much is the advertising campaign worth to Fay's Cleaners?

11 (Practice problem: advertising) The Gainesville Gekkos, a minor league franchise in the A league, is evaluating its advertising program. The demand curves before and after the advertising campaign are given in Table 18.19. Quantity measures the attendance. The marginal cost of another customer in the park is $0.50. Fixed costs are $50,000.

Table 18.19

Low quality		High quality	
Price	Quantity	Price	Quantity
$10.00	15,000	$10.00	20,000
$ 9.50	17,500	$ 9.50	30,000
$ 9.00	20,000	$ 9.00	40,000
$ 8.50	22,500	$ 8.50	50,000
$ 8.00	25,000	$ 8.00	60,000
$ 7.50	27,500	$ 7.50	70,000
$ 7.00	30,000	$ 7.00	80,000
$ 6.50	32,500	$ 6.50	90,000
$ 6.00	35,000	$ 6.00	100,000
$ 5.50	37,500	$ 5.50	110,000

a   Find the profit-maximizing price and quantity and level of profits before the advertising campaign.

b   Find the profit-maximizing price and quantity and level of profits after the advertising campaign.

c   How much is the advertising campaign worth to the Gainesville Gekkos?

Answers to Problems

2   a   The market demand and supply curves appear in Table 18.20.

Table 18.20

Price	Low-quality guides	High-quality guides	Total market quantity	Demand price
$ 50	1,000	0	1,000	$ 0
$100	2,000	1,000	3,000	$100
$150	4,000	6,000	10,000	$180
$200	8,000	16,000	24,000	$200
$250	12,000	36,000	48,000	$225
$300	16,000	48,000	64,000	$225

b   The market clears at a price of $100, with 1,000 high- and 2,000 low-quality guides. Another market-clearing price is $200, where high-quality guides number 16,000 and low-quality, 8,000.

c   If there were perfect information, there would be no low-quality guides, 48,000 high-quality guides, and an equilibrium price equal to $300.

3   a   The market demand and supply curves appear in Table 18.21.

Table 18.21

Price	Low-quality tomato plants	High-quality tomato plants	Total market quantity	Demand price
$1.00	10,000	0	10,000	$1.00
$1.50	20,000	5,000	25,000	$1.60
$2.00	30,000	20,000	50,000	$2.20
$2.50	40,000	60,000	100,000	$2.80
$3.00	50,000	100,000	150,000	$3.00
$3.50	60,000	300,000	360,000	$3.50
$4.00	70,000	500,000	570,000	$3.63

a   The market clears at a price of $1.00 where 10,000 low-quality plants are sold and also at a price of $3.00 where 50,000 low-quality and 100,000 high-quality plants are sold.

c   The equilibrium price of low-quality plants would be $1.00 with 10,000 sold. In the high-quality market, the price would equal $4.00, and 500,000 would be sold.

5   a   The quality-price ratio appears in Table 18.22.

Table 18.22

Price	Quality	Quality-price ratio
$1	10	10.0
$2	30	15.0
$3	60	20.0
$4	70	17.5
$5	80	16.0
$6	85	14.2

Firms choose a price of $3.

b   This results in a surplus of $4,500 - 3,500 = 1,000$.

6   The quality-price ratio appears in Table 18.23.

Table 18.23

Price	Quality	Quality-price ratio
$100	100	1.00
$200	500	2.50
$300	1,100	3.67
$400	1,600	4.00
$500	1,750	3.50

8   The marginal benefits of searching appear in Table 18.24.

Table 18.24

Number of estimates	Expected lowest price	Marginal benefits
1	$800	—
2	$650	$150
3	$550	$100
4	$500	$ 50
5	$475	$ 25
6	$465	$ 10
7	$460	$ 5

a   Raul should get 5 estimates.
b   He expects to pay $475.
c

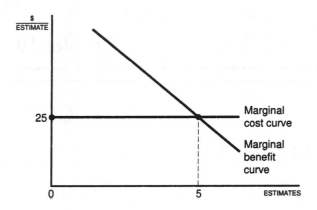

9   The marginal benefits of search appear in Table 18.25.

Table 18.25

Number of visits	Expected maximum profitability	Marginal benefits
1	$18,000	—
2	$23,000	$5,000
3	$26,000	$3,000
4	$27,000	$1,000
5	$27,500	$ 500

The company should send 4 engineers and expect to earn $27,000.

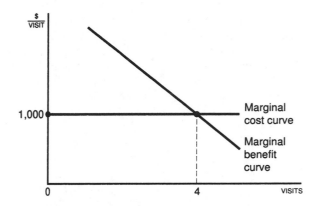

10   a   Price = $3; quantity = 500; profits = ($3 × 500) − ($1 × 500) − $1,000 − $0.
     b   Price = $3; quantity = 2,500; profits = ($3 × 2,500) − ($1 × 2,500) − $1,000 = $4,000.
     c   The advertising campaign increases profits by $4,000 −$0 = $4,000.

11   a   Price = $6; quantity = 32,500; profits = ($7 × 30,000) − ($0.50 × 30,000) − $50,000 = $145,000.
     b   Price = $5.50; quantity = 110,000; profits = ($5.50 × 110,000) − ($0.50 × 110,000) − $50,000 = $500,000.
     c   The advertising campaign increases profits by $500,000 − $145,000 = $355,000.

Chapter 19

IMPERFECTIONS IN THE LABOR MARKET

Chapter Review

This chapter of the text returns to the labor market and applies the lessons of imperfect competition from Chapter 14 and imperfect information from Chapter 18. The chapter first explores labor unions and compares them to monopolies in the context of the labor they supply to the firm. Next the chapter examines reasons for wage differences. Finally, it takes up the problems of motivating and selecting employees. Particular attention is paid to how different compensation schemes affect incentives. Chapter 20 moves on to explore the capital market from the perspective of imperfect information and the management of the firm.

ESSENTIAL CONCEPTS

1   Employees band together in **unions** to negotiate better working conditions and higher wages. After increasing for decades, the unionized share of the work force has declined since the mid-1950s. Reasons for the decline include an overall improvement in working conditions, relative declines in the sectors of the economy with more unionization, more competitive product markets,

and unfavorable government policy, expecially the Taft-Hartley Act.

2   Unions can be thought of as *monopolies* in the supply of labor to the firm. As such, they raise the wage and allow employment to fall. When the employer firm makes monopoly profits in its own product market, however, it is possible for unions to secure higher wages without reduced employment, at least for a while. Overall, higher union wages probably result in somewhat lower wages for nonunion workers and lower union employment in the long run. Unions also promote job security and have advocated job safety regulations, minimum wages, and immigration restrictions through the political process.

3   Because of imperfect information and other factors, labor is somewhat immobile, and wage differentials exist. Wage differentials may be caused by factors:

   a   **Compensating differentials** are wage differences that reflect characteristics of the job. For example, a police officer may earn more than a firefighter, reflecting the greater danger of police work.

   b   **Information-based differentials** reflect a worker's imperfect information. Workers must search for job offers. A worker currently receiving a low wage may not be able to convince another employer to offer a higher wage because the prospective employer will not know the quality of the worker. This is the lemons model from Chapter 18 applied to the labor market. The difficulty that workers have in moving from job to job gives firms some market power and leads to lower wages.

  c **Productivity wage differentials** simply account for differences in abilities to produce output.

4 **Discrimination** reduces the wages of certain groups. This may involve outright prejudice or just **statistical discrimination**, which results from the use of screening devices (such as degrees from well-established schools) that unintentionally sort out certain classes of workers from the hiring pool. **Affirmative action** requires that firms must actively seek out minorities and women and include them in the applicant pool.

5 Employers must **motivate** workers to perform the task for which they were hired. When the marginal product of a worker is observable, a firm can base pay on output. Thus, **piece-rate systems** provide strong incentives to workers but can subject them to substantial risk. Again, there is a risk-incentive trade-off. When there is concern for the quality, piece-rate systems may fail to give good incentives.

6 Especially when a worker's output is difficult for the employer to observe, the employer may want to **monitor** workers. Also, paying relatively high **efficiency wages** gives workers incentives to work hard and be more productive. Employers can reduce turnover (and training costs) by letting pay and fringe benefits increase with seniority.

7 Sometimes the employer may not know whether output is high because the employees are working hard and well or because the demand for the product is high. In this case, one option is to set up **contests** where workers are paid according to how well they do relative to their peers. Also, basing pay on team performance can encourage workers to monitor and help each other.

just as workers need incentives to be productive. There is always the risk-incentive trade-off. Contracts and reputations create incentives in product markets. Monitoring, efficiency wages, seniority benefits, contests, and team rewards create incentives in labor markets.

2 Not only is information imperfect, but exactly what the employer does not know is important. Based upon what she does not know, the employer must choose a means of selecting and motivating her workers. For example:

  a If the employer does not know the productivity of a job applicant, she may rely on signals. A low wage in the current job may indicate low productivity. A college degree may indicate innate abilities.

  b If the employer can observe the marginal productivity of his workers, then he may offer a piece-rate schedule of wages, but this scheme may expose the employee to substantial risk.

  c If the employer cannot observe the effort of her workers, she can monitor them and pay above-market efficiency wages. High wages make the job valuable and make losing the job something to motivate the worker.

  d If the employer thinks that the worker might have other employment opportunities, the employer may offer higher wages and better working conditions to discourage more senior workers from quitting. This becomes especially important if the employer must pay to train new workers.

  e If the employer does not know whether the output of her workers is due to their productivity or due to market conditions, she may set up contests, paying more to workers who do relatively better.

  f If the employer cannot observe the productivity of his employees but if he thinks that the employees are aware of one another's productivity, he can reward good performance by a team, which serves to induces employees to motivate one another.

BEHIND THE ESSENTIAL CONCEPTS

1 The most important idea to keep in mind when thinking about the labor market is that it is a market. Many of the same models that explained aspects of imperfect product markets appear here in the labor market. Consider the following.

  a Just as the firm may be a monopoly in the product market, a union has monopoly power over the labor supply to the firm. In each case, the price (wage) is set above marginal cost (supply curve of labor), and the quantity (employment) is less.

  b Consumers must search for price and quality information, while workers must search for job offers. In the product market, there is price dispersion; in the labor market, there are information-based wage differentials.

  c Firms need incentives to produce quality products

SELF-TEST

True or False

1 The Wagner Act set up the National Labor Relations Board, which provided procedures for the certification of unions and the prevention of unfair labor practices.

2 The Taft-Hartley Act allowed states to pass right-to-work laws and authorized the president to temporarily suspend strikes.

3 One reason for the decline in the percent of the work force in the private sector that belongs to unions is that consumers have shifted their demand toward more manufacturing and fewer services.

4 Unions act like monopolies in the supply of labor to the firm.

5 Unions power is limited by threats of replacing striking workers and also by unemployment.

6 Wage differentials resulting from differences in job characteristics are called compensating differentials.

7 Imperfect information will not lead to wage differentials if workers search for job opportunities.

8 Employers may be reluctant to offer jobs to workers who currently earn low wages, if they believe that current wages signal low productivity.

9 Statistical discrimination results from overt prejudice.

10 Affirmative action is designed to eliminate union shops.

11 Under a piece-rate system, workers are insured against any risk related to the overall success of the business.

12 Piece-rate systems do not work well if the firm cannot easily and accurately measure the marginal product of workers.

13 Paying higher efficiency wages may motivate workers to be more productive because they perceive that the high-wage job is worth keeping.

14 Firms that are unsure about a task's difficulty can motivate workers by using contests.

15 When pay depends on team performance, workers have incentives to cooperate, work together, and monitor each other's effort.

Multiple Choice

1 In 1935, Congress passed the Wagner Act, which

  a gave legal status to unions;
  b outlawed right-to-work laws;
  c set up the National Labor Relations Board, which provided procedures for the certification of labor unions and for the prevention of unfair labor practices;
  d all of the above;
  e a and c.

2 The Taft-Hartley Act of 1947

  a allowed individual states to pass right-to-work laws;
  b gave the president the power to declare an 80-day cooling off period during which striking workers must return to work;
  c eliminated the National Labor Relations Board;
  d all of the above;
  e a and b.

3 Reasons for the decline in the percentage of the work force that belongs to unions include the following.

  a An overall improvement in working conditions has reduced the demand of workers for unions.
  b Consumer demand has shifted toward the relatively less unionized sectors, such as services.
  c Increasingly competitive markets have limited the power of unions to negotiate increased wages.
  d All of the above.
  e None of the above.

4 In negotiating wages with firms, unions are most like

  a monopolies;
  b monopsonies;
  c competitive firms;
  d individual consumers;
  e none of the above.

5 Unless the firm is making monopoly profits in its product market, the higher wages negotiated by a union must

  a increase the level of employment at the firm;
  b have no effect on the level of employment at the firm;
  c reduce the level of employment at the firm;
  d lead the firm to substitute labor for capital;
  e a and d.

6 Higher wages for union labor

  a increase the supply of nonunion labor;
  b decrease the supply of nonunion labor;
  c reduce wages received by nonunion labor;
  d a and c;
  e b and c.

7 In a labor-management negotiation, the bargaining surplus refers to

  a the fact that although the firm can hire other workers and workers can find other jobs, both sides can gain by reaching agreement;
  b the costs of negotiation in lawyers' and arbitrators' salaries;
  c the strike funds built up by the firms and unions in anticipation of possible work stoppages;
  d the extra workers that union force management to hire;
  e b and d.

8 Compensating differentials are wage differences resulting from

  a the fact that workers must search to find job offers and learn of alternative wages;
  b the fact that employers are unlikely to make offers to workers who currently earn low wages, inferring that these workers may be less productive;
  c differences in job characteristics;
  d wage differences that compensate for differences in productivity;
  e a and b.

9 Jobs that are similar in all respects

  a must pay the same wage, because no worker would take the lower-paying job when higher-paying ones are available;
  b can have different wages according to the theory of compensating differentials;
  c may pay different wages if it takes time and effort for workers to learn about the alternative job possibilities;
  d may pay different wages because employers can pay whatever they want and workers must accept;
  e none of the above.

10 Wage differences that are due to differences in ability to produce output are called

 a   compensating differentials;
 b   information-based differentials;
 c   statistical discrimination;
 d   productivity differentials;
 e   affirmative action.

11 When workers are not aware of alternative job possibilities,

 a   firms may take advantage of their information-based market power and raise wages;
 b   information-based wage differentials may occur;
 c   workers can earn compensating differentials;
 d   all similar workers must earn the same wage for jobs with the same characteristics;
 e   none of the above.

12 Statistical discrimination refers to

 a   wage differences based on statistical measures of productivity differentials;
 b   requirements that firms keep statistics on the numbers of employees in each ethnic group;
 c   requirements that firms actively seek out women and minorities for hiring and promotion;
 d   the use of screening devices that unintentionally sort out members of certain groups;
 e   paying lower wages to workers who have little statistical information about the labor market and alternative job possibilities.

13 Affirmative action refers to

 a   wage differences based on statistical measures of productivity differentials;
 b   requirements that firms keep statistics on the numbers of employees in each ethnic group;
 c   requirements that firms actively seek out women and minorities for hiring and promotion;
 d   the use of screening devices that unintentionally sort out members of certain groups;
 e   paying lower wages to workers who have little statistical information about the labor market and alternative job possibilities.

14 The system of payment in which a worker is paid for each item produced is called

 a   a compensating differential system;
 b   an adverse selection system;
 c   a signaling system;
 d   monopsony;
 e   a piece-rate system.

15 One difficulty with basing workers' pay on their output is that

 a   although workers are given appropriate incentives to work hard, they bear considerable risk;
 b   although they bear the appropriate amount of risk, workers are given little incentive to work hard;
 c   piece-rate schemes are illegal under the Wagner Act;
 d   a and c;
 e   none of the above.

16 Most workers are not paid on a piece-rate basis, because

 a   piece-rate pay is illegal under the Wagner Act;
 b   workers are risk lovers;
 c   it is often difficult to measure the quantity and quality of an individual worker's output;
 d   all of the above;
 e   none of the above.

17 If the employer cannot observe the contribution to output of each worker, she can

 a   monitor a worker's effort;
 b   pay higher wages to increase the cost to the worker of being fired;
 c   set up a piece-work system;
 d   all of the above;
 e   a and b.

18 Efficiency wages

 a   reduce job turnover;
 b   attract more productive job applicants;
 c   motivate workers to put forth more effort;
 d   increase payments to workers;
 e   all of the above.

19 When workers are paid on the basis of relative performance, as in contests,

 a   they are given incentives to be productive, even though management does not know their job's difficulty;
 b   workers are better off because they bear less risk;
 c   workers receive efficiency wages and thus work hard;
 d   turnover is reduced;
 e   all of the above.

20 When pay is based on team performance,

 a   workers are motivated to monitor each other's efforts;
 b   worker are motivated to help each other;
 c   promotions go the those workers who have been more productive;
 d   a and b;
 e   all of the above.

Completion

1 Under _____ legislation, all laborers at unionized establishments must join the union.

2 Unions can raise wages because they have a _____ on the supply of labor to the firm.

3 _____ outlaw union shops.

4 _____ are differences in wages that reflect different job characteristics, such as working conditions or advancement possibilities.

5 _____ results from firms using screening devices that unintentionally sort out members of certain groups from the applicant pool.

6   The system of payment in which a worker is paid for each item produced or each task performed is called a _____ system.

7   The theory that paying higher wages leads to a more productive work force is called _____ theory.

8   Some compensation schemes, such as bonuses for the top sales representatives, base pay on _____ performance.

9   The safety of working conditions is regulated by the _____.

10 The "glass ceiling" that prevents the promotion of women to higher management is an example of _____ discrimination.

Answers to Self-Test

True or False

1	t	6	t	11	f
2	t	7	f	12	t
3	f	8	t	13	t
4	t	9	f	14	t
5	t	10	f	15	t

Multiple Choice

1	e	6	d	11	b	16	c
2	e	7	a	12	d	17	e
3	d	8	c	13	c	18	e
4	a	9	c	14	e	19	a
5	c	10	d	15	a	20	d

Completion

1   union shops
2   monopoly
3   Right to work laws
4   Compensating differentials
5   Statistical discrimination
6   piece-work
7   efficiency wage
8   relative
9   Occupational Safety and Health Administration
10 job

Doing Economics: Tools and Practice Problems

A successful union forms a monopoly in the supply of labor to a firm or industry. We apply the tools of monopoly to study the behavior of unions in several problems in this section. Then we move to compensating differentials, an important source of wage differences among workers. In accepting a job offer, a worker also buys a list of job characteristics, such as safety, advancement potential, training, and the aesthetics of the workplace. We use the budget constraint to show how the labor market offers a choice among job characteristics and establishes an implicit market price for them.

THE WAGE-EMPLOYMENT TRADE-OFF

If a union is able to force the signing of a contract, guaranteeing that only union members will be hired, it is in the position of a monopolist in the supply of labor. Unions may control the supply of labor to an industry, a craft, or an individual firm. The problems here focus on the latter case. Usually unions set wages and let management choose the quantity of labor to hire. In this case, the firm's demand for labor, which is the marginal revenue product, includes all the combinations of wages and employment that the union can achieve. These combinations, in turn, show the trade-off faced by the union. Tool Kit 19.1 shows how to construct the demand for labor and some possible choices that a union might make.

Tool Kit 19.1: Constructing the Union's Trade-off between Wages and Employment

Higher wages usually bring about reduced employment. Follow this procedure to construct the trade-off.

Step one: Identify the production function and the price of the product, and set up a table as follows.

Workers	Output	Revenues	Marginal revenue product

Step two: Find the revenue corresponding to each level of labor use by multiplying the output level by price, and enter the results in the table:

revenues = output × price.

Step three: Compute the marginal revenue product, which is the change in revenue divided by the change in labor, and enter the results in the table:

marginal revenue product
= change in revenues/change in output.

Step four: Plot the marginal revenue product. This curve is the schedule of possible wage and employment levels.

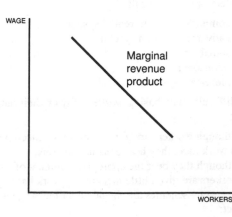

---

1 (Worked problem: unions) The miners of Davis Lead are represented by the Lead Workers Union, which is considering its stance for the upcoming contract negotiations. The union's economist has estimated a production function for lead, as given in Table 19.1. Its current price is $10 per ton.

Table 19.1

Workers	Output (tons per month)
10	20,000
20	40,000
30	60,000
40	75,000
50	85,000
60	90,000
70	90,000

a Calculate the marginal revenue product, plot it, and interpret it as a schedule of wage and employment possibilities.
b What is the maximum wage? How much employment would result at this wage?
c Workers can earn $5,000 elsewhere. What is the maximum level of employment?

Step-by-step solution

Step one (a): Identify the production function and the price of the product. The production function is given in Table 19.1, and the price of lead is $10 per ton.

Step two: Find the revenue corresponding to each level of labor use. We multiply output by $10, which is the price of lead. When there are 10 workers, output is 20,000, and revenue is 20,000 × $10 = $200,000. Continuing, we derive Table 19.2.

Table 19.2

Workers	Output	Revenues
10	20,000	$200,000
20	40,000	$400,000
30	60,000	$600,000
40	75,000	$750,000
50	85,000	$850,000
60	90,000	$900,000
70	90,000	$900,000

Step three: Compute the marginal revenue product, which is the change in revenue divided by the change in labor. The marginal revenue product for the first 10 workers is $200,000/10 = $20,000. Continuing, we derive Table 19.3.

Table 19.3

Workers	Output	Revenues	Marginal revenue product
10	20,000	$200,000	$20,000
20	40,000	$400,000	$20,000
30	60,000	$600,000	$20,000
40	75,000	$750,000	$15,000
50	85,000	$850,000	$10,000
60	90,000	$900,000	$ 5,000
70	90,000	$900,000	$ 0

Step four: Plot the marginal revenue product.

Step five (b): The maximum possible wage is $20,000 per month, and 30 workers will have jobs at this wage.

Step six (c): If the company pays $5,000, which is the alternative wage, there will be 60 workers hired.

2 (Practice problem: unions) Rosewood College's faculty has voted to join the United Professorial Workers Union to win high wages from the administration. Its economics department has estimated the production function, which is given in Table 19.4. Tuition nets Rosewood a profit of $1,000 per student after all expenses (except salaries for professors) are deducted.

Table 19.4

Faculty	Students
20	100
30	600
40	1,000
50	1,300
60	1,500
70	1,600
80	1,600

a Calculate and plot the marginal revenue product schedule. Interpret it as a schedule of salary and employment possibilities.

b   What is the maximum salary that the union could negotiate? Keep in mind that with its enormous endowment, Rosewood would not shut down even if it lost money.

c   The alternative salary for a typical Rosewood professor is $20,000. What is the maximum level of employment?

3   (Practice problem: unions) The cherry pickers at Bingo's Cherry Orchard have won an agreement that the owner will only hire union workers. The production function is given in Table 19.5, and cherries sell for $2 per bushel.

Table 19.5

Pickers	Cherries (bushels per day)
1	24
2	64
3	96
4	120
5	136
6	144
7	148
8	150

a   Calculate and plot the marginal revenue product. Interpret it as a schedule of wage and employment possibilities.

b   What is the maximum wage? Will the orchard shut down if labor is its only nonsunk cost?

c   The workers have an alternative wage of $16 per day. What is the maximum level of employment?

COMPENSATING DIFFERENTIALS

A job offer brings with it a promised wage and a bundle of job characteristics. Workers may not accept the highest-paying job, preferring a lower wage alternative if it offers more attractive nonwage benefits. The additional wage that accompanies a job with some undesirable nonwage aspect is called the compensating differential. The budget constraint allows us to identify and study the trade-off between wages and job characteristics. Tool Kit 19.2 shows the technique.

Tool Kit 19.2: Using Budget Constraints to Analyze Compensating Differentials

When an individual has several job offers, she faces a trade-off between higher wages and other desirable job characteristics. These steps show how to illustrate the trade-off with a budget constraint.

Step one: Draw a set of axes with the wage measured on the vertical axis and the nonwage characteristic on the horizontal.

Step two: Plot a point corresponding to each job offer.

Job offers

Step three: Cancel the "dominated" offers. The dominated offers represent jobs with both lower wages and less-attractive job characteristics.

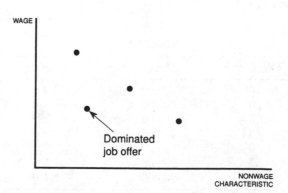

Dominated job offer

Step four: Draw a smooth curve through the undominated job offers. These are the ones that include higher wages and/or more attractive job characteristics. This curve is the budget constraint, reflecting the alternative combinations of wages and job characteristics available to the worker.

Step five: Identify the trade-off between several points on the budget constraint. The slope is the compensating differential.

4 (Worked problem: compensating differentials) Many parents in two-earner families worry about day care for infants. Recognizing this concern, some progressive companies offer on-site day care, although the facilities vary greatly in quality. Table 19.6 lists some local firms, the entry-level salaries for management trainees, and the expenditure per child for the day care facility.

Table 19.6

Firm	Salary	Expenditure per child
ALX Corp.	$30,000	$5,000
ABX Corp.	$35,000	$3,000
PBX Corp.	$37,000	$4,000
APX Corp.	$46,000	$ 0
AXX Corp.	$40,000	$1,000

a Represent the salaries and day care expenditures as an opportunity set.
b Are there any dominated offers?
c What is the compensating differential for reducing day care expenditures from $5,000 to $4,000? from $1,000 to $0?

Step-by-step solution

Step one (a): Draw a set of axes.

Step two: Plot a point corresponding to each job offer.

Step three (b): Cancel the dominated offers. The ABX offer, which entails less money and child care expenditure, is dominated by the PBX offer.

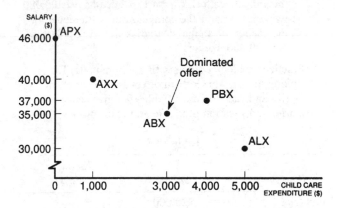

Step four: Draw a smooth curve through the undominated job offers.

Step five (c): Identify the trade-offs between several points on the budget constraint. As the day care expenditure falls from $5,000 to $4,000, salary rises by $37,000 − $30,000 = $7,000. The compensating differential for a decrease from $1,000 to $0 is $46,000 − $40,000 = $6,000.

5 (Practice problem: compensating differentials) Sylvester Stallion is looking for a job. The alternatives, the corresponding annual salaries, and some data on accidental deaths are given in Table 19.7. Sylvester has offers for

each type of job, he is qualified for each, and he considers them equally satisfying except for the risk of death.

Table 19.7

Job	Salary	Deaths per 100,000
Night watchman	$16,000	2
Shoe salesman	$15,000	1 (irate customer)
Clerk in convenience store	$24,000	5
Cab driver	$19,000	6
Armed guard	$22,000	3

a   Represent the job offers as an opportunity set.
b   Without knowing anything about Stallion's willingness to risk death, can you say if there is a job offer he will definitely refuse? Explain.
c   What is the compensating differential for increasing the annual death risk from 1 to 2 deaths per 100,000 workers? What is the compensating differential for increasing the annual death risk from 3 to 5 deaths per 100,000 workers?

6   (Practice problem: compensating differentials) The banking industry in Gotham offers a wide variety of salaries and vacation days. Table 19.8 gives entry salaries and vacation time offered to new hires.

Table 19.8

Bank	Salary	Vacation days
First One	$20,000	5
Bank One	$25,000	8
First Bank	$32,000	5
Premier Bank	$30,000	6
Second Bank	$28,000	7

a   Represent the salaries and vacation days as an opportunity set.
b   Are there any dominated offers?
c   What is the compensating differential for reducing vacation days from 8 to 7? From 6 to 5?

Answers to Problems

2   a   The marginal revenue product schedule is given in Table 19.9.

Table 19.9

Faculty	Students	Revenues	Marginal revenue product
20	100	$ 100,000	—
30	600	$ 600,000	$50,000
40	1,000	$1,000,000	$40,000
50	1,300	$1,300,000	$30,000
60	1,500	$1,500,000	$20,000
70	1,600	$1,600,000	$10,000
80	1,600	$1,600,000	$ 0

b   The maximum wage is $50,000, at which 30 faculty will be hired.
c   The maximum employment occurs at a wage of $20,000, with 60 faculty.

3   a   The marginal revenue product schedule is given in Table 19.10.

Table 19.10

Pickers	Cherries	Revenues	Marginal revenue product
1	24	$ 48	$48
2	64	$128	$80
3	96	$192	$64
4	120	$240	$48
5	136	$272	$32
6	144	$288	$16
7	148	$296	$ 8
8	150	$300	$ 4

b   The maximum wage is $80, at which there will be 2 pickers.
c   The maximum employment is 6, where the wage equals $16.

5 *a*

6 *a*

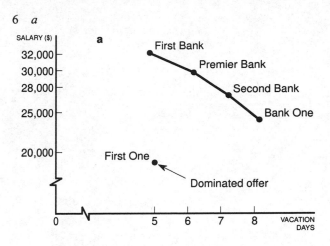

b   Stallion will refuse the cab driver offer, which is dominated by the job of clerk in a convenience store.

c $1,000, $2,000.

b   First One.

c $3,000, $2,000.

Chapter 20

FINANCING, CONTROLLING, AND MANAGING THE FIRM

Chapter Review

Information problems pervade the entire economy. This chapter continues the discussion of information problems in markets by turning to the market for financial capital. The same problems caused by asymmetric information in product markets (Chapter 18) and labor markets (Chapter 19) reappear in this chapter, when we consider how the firm is financed, how it is managed, and who owns it.

ESSENTIAL CONCEPTS

1 There are three legal forms for businesses in the United States. A single-owner firm is called a **proprietorship.** A firm with two or more owners is a **partnership.** Ownership of **corporations** is divided into shares, and each owner of a share has voting rights in management elections. The most important feature of the corporate form, however, is **limited liability.** Each owner can lose no more than his or her original investment. In contrast, if a partnership incurs large losses, each partner is fully liable for all the debts.

2 Corporations can finance their investments by borrowing, either from banks or by selling bonds, by issuing new shares of stock (equity finance), or from retained earnings, which are accounting profits not paid out as dividends to owners. If corporate managers act in the interest of the owners, they will maximize the market value of the firm. Surprisingly, the mix of debt and equity finance makes no difference to the market value of the firm.

3 The result that debt does not affect a corporation's market value is the starting point for the analysis of the financial structure of corporations. Nevertheless, there are certain features of real-world corporations that make the level of debt important.

a A heavy debt load raises the probability of a costly **bankruptcy.** Banks are reluctant to let a firm's indebtedness grow too large without charging higher interest rates as a risk premium in case of default.

b The **tax code** encourages debt because interest is deductible. The fact that capital gains are also treated favorably, however, offsets some of the tilt toward debt finance.

c Higher debt loads force managers to keep costs

low and profits high to stave off bankruptcy. Equity finance, on the other hand, may allow managers some freedom to pursue goals other than maximizing the market value.

d   Markets may perceive a firm's issuing debt as a *signal* that managers have confidence in the prospects for the profitability of the firm. This perception will drive up the market value of the firm.

e   Firms that borrow may have to cede substantial *control* to banks or bondholders. This can provide management with different incentives, because shareholders lack information about what management is doing and why.

4   If lenders had perfect information about the default risk of borrowers, then the interest rate would adjust to clear the market for loans. In the real world, however, lenders do not know how risky each borrower is; thus, they give each borrower incentives to pay the loans back. Furthermore, charging higher interest rates attracts especially risky borrowers and motivates borrowers to take on extra risks to earn enough to repay the interest. Rather than raise the interest rate, lenders may ration loans. This phenomenon is known as **credit rationing.**

5   Issuing new shares is one way firms can raise new capital, but this practice may also pose problems. Prospective buyers of shares may reason that managers believe that the firm is overvalued or that it has been turned down on previous loan applications. Such expectations will cause the stock price to fall when new shares are issued. When the price of a stock falls significantly in response to the issuing of new shares, economists say that the firm is **equity rationed.** Few firms raise capital through equity finance in modern economies.

6   Inefficient management lowers the market value of a firm, but shareholders often do not have good enough information to monitor the managers. Other investors may buy up a majority voting share, replace the inefficient managers, and make profits. In this way, the **market for takeovers** can promote efficient management. Some economists have reservations about the effects of hostile takeovers, noting that takeovers are usually financed with additional debt and that the increased indebtedness injures other bondholders. Another important criticism is that the takeover firm may be managed inefficiently itself and may be pursuing the takeover for reasons other than the well-being of its shareholders. These criticisms have led to proposals to limit takeovers, but most economists favor leaving the control of firms to markets.

7   **The principal-agent problem** summarizes the difficulty of providing good incentives to employees. One important example is the case in which the owners of a firm are the principal and the managers are their agents. The owners (the stockholders) want managers to act in the best interest of the firm. The managers, however, may have other interests, and it is difficult for the owners to judge whether a manager takes appropriate actions. The problem for the principal is to design incentives to motivate the managers to work hard and to take the appropriate risks in order to further its own interests.

8   One approach to solving the principal-agent problem is for the manager to buy her share of the enterprise. As an *owner*, she has the appropriate incentives. Another approach to solving the principal-agent problem involves **incentive pay,** such as sales commissions or stock options, which give the manager the right to buy a number of shares at a given price. If she can increase the market value of the firm, she can profit. Finally, the principal can monitor the agent's performance.

9   A fundamental issue in the structure of a large organization is the degree of **centralization.** A centralized, top-down structure has many layers of decision making and review. Its advantages include the approval of fewer bad projects, coordination to account for interdependencies and externalitites within the organization, and a lack of duplication. Decentralized structures grant more autonomy to subunits; they usually approve more good projects and act more quickly with more diversity and experimentation; and they allow management to compare the performance of subunits and decide how to allocate resources within the firm.

10   The issue of how large the firm should be involves how many activites it will do in-house, how many it will contract out, and whether it should **vertically** integrate with its suppliers or its customer firms. If **transactions costs,** which are the extra costs over and above the price of purchasing an item on the market, are high, it may be less costly to do the activities within the firm. One problem with outside contracting may occur if the outside firm must make specialized investments and thereby risk becoming dependent. This is known as a "hold-up problem." Usually the threat of dependency results in higher costs. Generally, it is more efficient to produce some services in-house and purchase others outside.

BEHIND THE ESSENTIAL CONCEPTS

1   Over and over again, economists approach a problem by first understanding a simple situation and then moving on to more realistic complications. When studying corporate finance, the simple starting point is the idea that the method of corporate finance makes no difference to the market value of the firm. It is important for you to understand both the logic of this and why the real world of corporate finance is different.

a   How does the market adjust when the firm uses borrowing rather than new shares to finance new investment? First, what the firm does with the money is unaffected by the means of raising it. Second, a higher debt load makes the stock riskier and lowers its price. The lower price is just enough to keep the market value of the firm the same under debt and equity finance.

b   What is missing from this story? In the real world of corporate finance, firms must worry about the high costs of bankruptcy, and they must consider the tax consequences of debt and equity. Managerial incentives, market perceptions of value based on these incentives, and the ultimate control of the firm's decisions may all be affected by the financial structure of the firm.

2   If a firm raises money by borrowing, the lenders receive interest payments. If it raises money through new equity, then the investors receive dividends and capital gains as the stock price rises. The U.S. tax system affects the firm's decision in the following way: the system encourages borrowing because interest is tax deductible, while it discourages equity finance because dividends are not tax deductible. Offsetting this to some extent is the more favorable treatment capital gains receive in the tax code. The net effect is that the U.S. tax system encourages borrowing to some extent.

3   Whenever one side of the market knows something that the other side does not, there is asymmetric information. In the corporate world, an important example of this is that the owners of the firms (shareholders) will not know everything that management is doing and will not be able to judge whether management's decisions are the right ones. Management may be able to get away with activities that lower profits without the owners knowing. Here is where the market for corporate control comes in with the threat of takeovers. Inefficient management risks being discovered not so much by owners as by other investors, who can purchase the outstanding stock, acquire majority voting status, and replace the laggards.

4   Asymmetric information is also important when the firm goes to the market for loanable funds in search of capital to finance investments. Suppose you are thinking of providing some of this capital by purchasing a corporate bond. You do not know as much about the default risk as the firm issuing the bond, and you should therefore be suspicious about bonds that pay very high interest rates. After all, why would a firm pay high interest rates unless it is selling a risky bond? Other investors reason as you do, and therefore the interest rate does not rise to clear the market for bonds. Firms are credit rationed because of asymmetric information in credit markets.

5   Chapter 10 focused on the efficiency of capital markets. Because each investor seeks the highest rate of return, it will be impossible to beat the market consistently. The credit market problems discussed in this chapter (credit and equity rationing) pertain to the inability of borrowers to obtain loans or raise capital even though they are willing to pay the going rate of return. The conclusion is that capital markets are efficient in valuing different assets, but not efficient in that the market for loanable funds does not clear.

6   This chapter goes a long way beyond the firm in the basic competitive model. The competitive firm has two simple problems to solve: how much should it produce and by what means. Competitive firms hardly need managers. The firms in this chapter are much more realistic and, naturally, more complicated. In addition to the problem of competitive firms, these firms must select employees for tasks, motivate them, monitor their efforts, and account for their outputs. Further, they must deal with uncertainty, determine the degree of centralization, and decide on the number of activities to produce in-house and contract out. It is in solving these problems that real-world managers earn their salaries.

7   As an organization grows, the level of direct control owners exercise diminishes and the problem of providing incentives crops out. When incentives are the issue, the usual suspects appear: asymmetric information in that the principal (the owner) cannot observe and evaluate the activities of her employees (the agents), and moral hazard in that the agents may pursue their own interests and not those of the principal. Solutions to the problem involve the risk-incentive trade-off. For example, basing pay on performance or tying pay to profitability provides stronger incentives but also subjects the agents to more risk. These are fundamental problems within any organization. An understanding of their source and nature, however, may enable you to manage better in any organization that you work for or join.

8   Centralization versus decentralization is a question raised in organizations such as business firms, nonprofit organizations, and government. It is also a fundamental question about the economic system itself. Socialism can be seen as a more centralized system, in which the state makes more economic decisions. Market economies are more decentralized, leaving more decisions to individuals and firms. The debate between socialists and advocates of markets has taken place over the same issues that are discussed in this chapter. Adherents of socialism claim that fewer bad projects are adopted, activities are coordinated better, and there is less duplication. Advocates of market economies point to the abundance of good projects and the diversity, experimentation, and incentives that market economies provide.

9   Transaction costs do not include the purchase price, but rather all those costs in addition to the price. Transactions costs are the costs of using the market: the time, effort, and expense involved in searching the market to find high quality at a good price. Contracts must then be drawn up (at least implicitly) to specify the terms. If it were always easy, reliable, and cheap to use the market, then firms could be quite small and simply buy and sell what they needed among themselves. Often transactions costs are high, and it is cheaper to integrate an activity within the firm even though the added size brings about the problems discussed above.

SELF-TEST

True or False

1   A proprietorship is a firm owned by two or more proprietors.

2   Partnerships offer each partner limited liability in case of bankruptcy.

3   One risk of owning shares of a corporation is that should the firm go out of business, each shareholder is liable for all the debts.

4   If a firm has a heavy debt load, it is said to be highly leveraged.

5   Dividends are tax deductible for firms, because individuals must pay income tax on their dividend earnings.

6   If a firm cannot afford the interest rate charged by banks for loans, then it is credit rationed.

7   Credit rationing occurs because banks and other lenders do not have as much information about default risks as borrowers.

8   Because of credit rationing, the supply of loans exceeds the demand.

9   Investors may infer that the managers of a firm issuing new shares feel that the firm is overvalued by the market.

10   When issuing new shares causes the price of shares to fall substantially, there is credit rationing.

11   The market for takeovers may motivate managers to work hard to increase profits.

12   The principal-agent problem refers to the difficulty in providing incentives within organizations.

13   Centralized decision making provides strong incentives because the directives come from the top.

14   Decentralized decision making leads to the acceptance of more good projects and more bad projects.

15   When transaction costs are high, firms usually will decide to contract out for the service.

Multiple Choice

1   A business with two or more owners, each fully responsible for the liabilities, is called a

a   proprietorship;
b   partnership;
c   limited partnership;
d   corporation;
e   none of the above.

2   Under the partnership form of business,

a   each partner is liable for no more than the amount invested;
b   each partner is liable for her share of the debts;
c   each partner is fully responsible for all the liabilities of the business;
d   neither partner has any liability;
e   none of the above.

3   If there is a single owner, the business is called a

a   monopsony;
b   monopoly;
c   partnership;
d   proprietorship;
e   corporation.

4   Because of limited liability, the owners of corporations

a   are exempt from taxes on capital gains that are due to inflation;
b   are not taxed on their share of the retained earnings of the firm;
c   have only a limited say in the operation of the corporation;
d   can lose no more than the amount they invest;
e   a and b.

5   Retained earnings equal

a   revenues minus expenses minus debt payments minus dividend distributions;
b   revenues minus expenses;
c   revenues minus debt and dividend distributions;
d   revenues minus expenses and interest;
e   revenues.

6   A firm is highly leveraged if

a   the company union has a representative on the board;
b   its outstanding debt is large relative to the value of the firm;
c   its equity is large relative to the value of the firm;
d   its retained earnings are large relative to the value of the firm;
e   c or d.

7   The result that debt does not affect the market value of a firm

a   is an accurate description of corporate finance;
b   would be true if corporate managers understood economics;
c   does not accurately describe the world of corporate finance;
d   is true only in monopolistic product markets;
e   would be true in the absence of government involvement in capital markets.

8   Because increased debt imposes a greater risk of bankruptcy on the corporation,

a   lenders limit the amount they are willing to lend and monitor closely their borrowers;
b   banks that are willing to lend require higher interest rates to compensate them for the risk of bankruptcy;
c   there is no effect on borrowing and lending incentives because the value of the firm does not depend upon the debt-to-equity ratio;
d   there is no effect on borrowing and lending because the financial capital market always clears, and any firm seeking a loan at the going rate can secure one;
e   a and b.

9   Overall, the tax code

    a   treats debt and equity finance equally;

    b   favors debt finance because interest is deductible but dividends are not;

    c   favors debt finance because stockholders must pay taxes on dividend income, and this affects their willingness to supply capital;

    d   favors debt because capital gains receive some tax advantages;

    e   b and c.

10 Markets may perceive that a heavy debt position

    a   indicates that managers have confidence in the prospects of the firm;

    b   has no effect on managerial incentives;

    c   indicates that managers have little confidence in the prospects of the firm;

    d   indicates nothing because of the Modigliani-Miller theorem;

    e   b and d.

11 Credit rationing refers to

    a   the means by which prospective borrowers are allocated to banks;

    b   the fact that there is a limited number of seats on the stock exchanges;

    c   the policy that firms must first go to domestic banks before seeking foreign funds;

    d   any situation where individuals or firms cannot obtain funds at the going rate for borrowers of similar risk;

    e   the fact that issuing new shares of stock may cause the stock price to fall.

12 Information in the market for loanable funds is imperfect because

    a   borrowers cannot know the going interest rate;

    b   lenders and borrowers cannot find each other;

    c   good banks are hard to find;

    d   lenders cannot monitor a borrower to ensure that enough care is being taken to prevent default;

    e   a and b.

13 The idea of credit rationing says that if the lender is unsure of the likelihood of default by a certain class of borrowers, he will likely

    a   raise the interest rate to compensate for added risk;

    b   not be willing to raise the interest rate because higher rates may attract a relatively riskier mix of borrowers;

    c   charge an interest rate that leads to excess for funds;

    d   b and c;

    e   none of the above.

14 If a firm issues more shares, the stock price

    a   should not change because the stock market is an example of a competitive market;

    b   should increase because investors will interpret the sale as a signal of confidence in the future;

    c   should decrease because investors will infer that a confident firm would have sought funds from banks;

    d   should not change because of the Modigliani-Miller theorem;

    e   a and d.

15 Takeovers of corporations by others

    a   are never justified because stockholders can oversee the operation of the firm and motivate managers to be efficient;

    b   are never justified because banks and stockholders can oversee the operation of the firm and motivate managers to be efficient;

    c   can be important because other methods of controlling managers are relatively ineffective;

    d   reduce the wealth of shareholders;

    e   a and b.

16 Suppose the owner of the firm wants to motivate the manager to make the decision that he would make in the same situation, but does not have the information necessary to evaluate the decisions made by the manager. This is an example of

    a   comparative advantage;

    b   diminishing returns;

    c   the principal-agent problem;

    d   adverse selection;

    e   none of the above.

17 In the principal-agent problem,

    a   the interests of the principal and agent differ;

    b   the principal cannot judge whether the agent takes the appropriate action by looking at the results;

    c   the agent cannot judge whether the principal takes the appropriate action by looking at the results;

    d   a and c;

    e   a and b.

18 Which of the following is not an advantage of centralized decision making?

    a   Fewer bad projects are accepted.

    b   There is better coordination.

    c   There is less duplication.

    d   There is more experimentation.

    e   Externalities within the organization are accounted for.

19 Which of the following is not an advantage of decentralized decision making?

    a   More good projects are accepted.

    b   There is less duplication.

    c   Decisions are made and implemented more quickly.

    d   There is greater diversity and experimentation.

    e   Incentives are stronger.

20 Which of the following is not a component of transactions costs?

    a   the purchase price;

    b   the time and effort involved in searching the market;

    c   the expense of drawing up contracts;

d the risk that the supplier will place a low priority on the firm's business.

e All of the above are transactions costs.

Completion

1 A business with a single owner is called a _____.

2 Two or more individuals owning a business together form a _____.

3 The key distinguishing characteristic of corporations is that their owners have _____.

4 Cash left over after expenses, debt payment, and dividend distributions is called _____.

5 Although it offers some special advantages to equity and debt finance, overall the tax code favors _____.

6 When individuals or firms cannot borrow all they desire at the going interest rate, they are subject to _____.

7 If firms are reluctant to issue new shares of stock because the market may perceive this action as a signal that management does not have enough confidence in the business to borrow, then firms are said to be _____.

8 The difficulty that owners have in motivating managers to act in the interest of ownership is an example of the _____.

9 A firm using _____ decision making usually has a hierarchial structure with a well-defined set of approval layers.

10 Considerable autonomy is granted to subunits of a firm using _____ decision making.

Answers to Self-Test

True or False

1	f	6	f	11	t
2	f	7	t	12	t
3	f	8	f	13	f
4	t	9	t	14	t
5	f	10	f	15	f

Multiple Choice

1	b	6	b	11	d	16	c
2	c	7	c	12	d	17	e
3	d	8	e	13	d	18	d
4	d	9	e	14	c	19	b
5	a	10	a	15	c	20	a

Completion

1 proprietorship
2 partnership
3 limited liability
4 retained earnings
5 debt

6 credit rationing
7 equity rationed
8 principal agent problem
9 centralized
10 decentralized

Doing Economics: Tools and Practice Problems

CREDIT RATIONING

In the basic competitive model, markets clear (supply equals demand) and firms minimize costs. One reason that these outcomes might not occur in the real world is imperfect information. In this section we see how, if banks cannot observe the credit-worthiness of potential borrowers, they may choose to ration credit. Also, we look at incentives issues with some problems concerning the principal-agent relationship. Credit rationing is a reason why firms may not be able to obtain loans even when they are willing to pay the going interest rate. As in the lemon and efficiency wage models, the price (the interest rate in the loanable funds market) has two jobs: it balances supply and demand and influences the riskiness of loan applicants. The latter job refers to the fact that at higher rates of interest, firms may seek funds for riskier projects with greater default rates. Because the interest rate that maximizes the expected rate of return on loans encourages a high percentage of safe loan applicants, it may be too low to clear the market. In this case, supply is less than demand, and there is credit rationing. Tool Kit 20.1 illustrates credit rationing.

Tool Kit 20.1: Credit Rationing

If the mix of applicants grows riskier as the interest rate rises, lenders may choose to ration credit. These steps show how credit rationing brings about a surplus of loanable funds.

Step one: Identify and plot the relationship between the interest rate and the expected rate of return on loans. Also, identify the supply and demand for loans. Note that the demand depends on the interest rate actually charged by banks, but the supply depends on the expected rate of return.

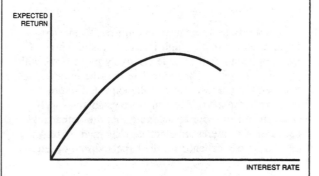

Step two: Find the interest rate that maximizes the expected rate of return. This will be the equilibrium interest rate.

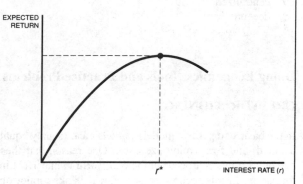

Step three: Find the quantity supplied by substituting the maximum expected rate of return into the supply curve.

Step four: Find the quantity demanded by substituting the equilibrium interest rate (found in step two) into the demand curve.

Step five: Find the amount of credit rationing by subtracting the loans supplied from the loans demanded:

credit rationing = loans demanded – loans supplied.

1   (Worked problem: credit rationing) Banks in West Dakota realize that at high interest rates, the pool of loan applicants will include relatively more firms with high default rates. They calculate that the relationship between the interest rate and the expected returns is as given in Table 20.1. The table also gives the supply and demand for new loans. Note that the demand depends on the interest rate actually charged by banks, but the supply depends on the expected rate of return.

Find the equilibrium interest rate and the level of credit rationing.

Table 20.1

Interest rate	Expected rate of return
4.0%	4.0%
4.5%	4.4%
5.0%	4.8%
5.5%	5.2%
6.0%	5.0%
6.5%	4.8%
7.0%	4.0%

Demand for loans		Supply of loans	
Interest rate	Quantity (thousands)	Expected rate of return	Quantity (thousands)
4.0%	$2,500	4.0%	$ 300
4.5%	$1,900	4.4%	$ 400
5.0%	$1,500	4.8%	$ 600
5.5%	$1,200	5.0%	$ 800
6.0%	$1,000	5.2%	$1,000
6.5%	$ 700		
7.0%	$ 400		

Step-by-step solution

Step one: Identify the relationship between the interest rate and the expected rate of return on loans, and the supply and demand for loans. They are given in Table 20.1.

Step two: Find the interest rate that maximizes the expected rate of return. The expected rate of return reaches its maximum of 5.2 percent when the interest rate is 5.5 percent.

Step three: Find the quantity supplied by substituting the maximum expected rate of return into the supply curve; $1,000,000 is supplied when the expected rate of return is 5.2 percent.

Step four: Find the quantity demanded by substituting the equilibrium interest rate into the demand curve; $1,200,000 is supplied when the interest rate is 5.5 percent.

Step five: Find the amount of credit rationing. It is $1,200,000 – $1,000,000 = $200,000. Although there is a shortage, banks will not raise the interest rate because higher interest rates bring about more defaults and a lower expected rate of return.

2   (Practice problem: credit rationing) The relationship between the interest rate and the expected rate of return is given in Table 20.2, which also gives the supply and demand curves for university loans in Gotham. Find the equilibrium interest rate and the amount of credit rationing.

Table 20.2

Interest rate	Expected rate of return
6.0%	5.8%
6.5%	6.0%
7.0%	6.2%
7.5%	6.3%
8.0%	6.2%
8.5%	6.0%
9.0%	5.0%

Demand for loans		Supply of loans	
Interest rate	Quantity (thousands)	Expected rate of return	Quantity (thousands)
6.0%	$8,000	5.0%	$1,000
6.5%	$7,000	5.8%	$1,500
7.0%	$6,000	6.0%	$2,000
7.5%	$5,000	6.2%	$2,500
8.0%	$4,000	6.3%	$3,000
8.5%	$3,000		
9.0%	$2,000		

3   (Practice problem: credit rationing) The relationship between the interest rate and the expected rate of return is given in Table 20.3, which also gives the supply and demand curves for small-business loans in Eastpointe. Find the equilibrium interest rate and the amount of credit rationing.

Table 20.3

Interest rate	Expected rate of return
6.0%	5.0%
6.5%	6.0%
7.0%	6.1%
7.5%	6.0%
8.0%	5.5%
8.5%	5.0%
9.0%	5.0%

Demand for loans		Supply of loans	
Interest rate	Quantity (thousands)	Expected rate of return	Quantity (thousands)
6.0%	$17,000	5.0%	$6,000
6.5%	$15,000	5.5%	$7,000
7.0%	$13,000	6.0%	$8,000
7.5%	$11,000	6.1%	$9,000
8.0%	$ 9,000		
8.5%	$ 7,000		
9.0%	$ 5,000		

INCENTIVES AND THE PRINCIPAL AGENT PROBLEM

Once individuals have been assigned to tasks within an organization, they must be given incentives to perform the tasks in the manner that furthers the goals of the organization. We will look at two aspects of the incentive problem. First, how does the absence of prices within organizations lead to inefficiency? Second, what are the incentive problems associated with sharing the profits?

4   (Worked problem: incentives) The Add advertising agency has several creative teams in its employ, and for years each team has been given a budget of $10,000 for any services that their work requires. The teams hire outside contractors to do layouts and printing. The price of each service is $200 per day.

   a   Plot the budget constraint for the typical creative team.

   b   The typical team has spent half its budget on each service. Plot the point that corresponds to this choice.

   c   Following the recommendation of a consultant, the agency decides to do all its printing in-house. Now the creative teams purchase only layout services from outside the agency. Since they can have their printing services performed at the agency and do not need to purchase printing, their budgets are cut to $5,000. Plot the budget constraint.

   d   The agency finds that the print shop is always overcrowded. Why?

Step-by-step solution

Step one (a): Draw coordinate axes, and label the horizontal one "Printing services" and the vertical one "Layout services."

Step two: If the team spends all its budget on printing, it can purchase $10,000/$200 = 50 days. Plot this point along the horizontal axis.

Step three: If the team spends all its budget on layouts, it can purchase $10,000/$200 = 50 days. Plot this point along the vertical axis.

Step four (b): The team spends $5,000 on each service and buys $5,000/$200 = 25 days of each. Plot the point (25, 25) and label it *A*.

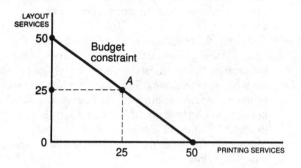

Step five (c): The team has a budget of $5,000. The price of layout service is still $200 per day, but printing is free. The team can still purchase 25 days of layout services, and it can have all of the printing that it wants. The budget constraint is a horizontal line intersecting the vertical axis at 25.

Step six (d): The new way of doing things at the agency allows teams to use printing services without paying for them. In terms of the budget constraint, the teams now can choose all the combinations to the right of point *A*. As long as printing has any value to the team, they will buy more and the shop will be overcrowded.

5   (Practice problem: incentives) Betty and Wilma are copy editors. They pore over manuscripts looking for typographical, grammatical, and other errors. Betty is self-employed and receives $2 per page. Wilma works for Meglith Publishers and receives a straight salary of $800 each week. Each can edit 10 pages an hour, and each has 60 hours available every week. They both like to goof off, and they both like money.

   a   Plot Betty's budget constraint. Put income on the vertical axis and time spent goofing off on the

horizontal. What is the slope of her budget constraint?

   b   Plot Wilma's budget constraint. What is its slope?

   c   Which editor has the greater incentive to goof off? Why?

6   (Worked problem: incentives) Michael and Eliot have part-time jobs as Mexway distributors; they sell soap. The amount that each can sell depends on the time that he puts in knocking on doors. The relationship is given in Table 20.4.

Table 20.4

Time	Revenues
1 hour	$ 40
2 hours	$ 70
3 hours	$ 90
4 hours	$100
5 hours	$105
6 hours	$106

Both Michael and Eliot place a value of $10 on 1 hour of their time.

   a   Complete the marginal benefit column.

   b   How many hours will each work? How much revenue will each earn?

   c   Now suppose that Michael and Eliot form a business to sell soap. They agree to share the revenues. If Michael works 1 hour, he brings in $40, but he gives $20 to Eliot. Michael's personal reward is only $20. Revise the table above to reflect the agreement that revenues are shared.

   d   Complete a marginal benefit column for the revised revenue numbers.

   e   How many hours will each work now?

Step-by-step solution

Step one (a): Complete the marginal benefit column. If Michael works 1 hour, he earns $40, which is the marginal benefit. If he works 2 hours, his revenues rise from $40 to $70, which is a marginal benefit of $30. The results are given in Table 20.5.

Table 20.5

Time	Revenues	Marginal benefit
1 hour	$ 40	$40
2 hours	$ 70	$30
3 hours	$ 90	$20
4 hours	$100	$10
5 hours	$105	$ 5
6 hours	$106	$ 1

Step two (b): The marginal cost of an hour is $10. Setting marginal cost equal to marginal benefit implies 4 hours of work, which brings in $100.

Step three (c): Accounting for the sharing of revenues means that the relationship between time spent selling and the revenues that each gets to keep for himself are in Table 20.6.

Table 20.6

Time	Revenues
1 hour	$20.00
2 hours	$35.00
3 hours	$45.00
4 hours	$50.00
5 hours	$52.50
6 hours	$53.00

Step four (d): Now the marginal benefit is half what it was before, as shown in Table 20.7.

Table 20.7

Time	Revenues	Marginal benefit
1 hour	$20.00	$20.00
2 hours	$35.00	$15.00
3 hours	$45.00	$10.00
4 hours	$50.00	$ 5.00
5 hours	$52.50	$ 2.50
6 hours	$53.00	$ 0.50

Step five (e): Now marginal benefit equals marginal cost at 3 hours worked, which brings in only $45. Sharing the profits means that neither person receives the full benefits of his time and effort. This is the classic incentive problem. Because of bad incentives, each is led to work less.

7   (Practice problem: incentives) Mr. Davis is a sharecropper on a farm owned by Miss Tilly. He gives her one-third of his revenues from farming her 20 acres in rural Mississippi. Table 20.8 gives the relationship between his effort and the revenues from the farm.

Table 20.8

Time	Total revenues	Mr. Davis' revenues	Marginal benefit
1 hour	$18		
2 hours	$33		
3 hours	$45		
4 hours	$54		
5 hours	$60		
6 hours	$63		

Mr. Davis, when not sharecropping, can work in town and make $6 per hour.

a   Complete the table.
b   How much does Mr. Davis choose to work on the farm?
c   If he owned the farm himself and did not share revenues with Miss Tilly, how much would he work on the farm?

Answers to Problems

2   Equilibrium interest rate = 7.5%; expected return = 6.3%; credit rationing = $5,000,000 – $3,000,000 = $2,000,000.

3   Equilibrium interest rate = 7%; expected return = 6.1%; credit rationing = $13,000,000 – $9,000,000 = $4,000,000.

5   a,b

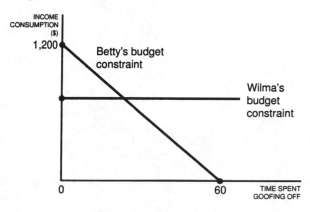

c   Wilma has more opportunities that involve less work; thus, she has more incentive to goof off.

7   a   The completed information is given in Table 20.9.

Table 20.9

Time	Total revenues	Mr. Davis' revenues	Marginal benefit
1 hour	$18	$12	$12
2 hours	$33	$22	$10
3 hours	$45	$30	$ 8
4 hours	$54	$36	$ 6
5 hours	$60	$40	$ 4
6 hours	$63	$42	$ 2

b   He works 4 hours, where the marginal benefit equals marginal cost, which is $6 per hour.
c   If he owned the farm, the marginal benefit would be as given in Table 20.10.

Table 20.10

Time	Revenues	Marginal benefit
1 hour	$18	$18
2 hours	$33	$15
3 hours	$45	$12
4 hours	$54	$ 9
5 hours	$60	$ 6
6 hours	$63	$ 3

Mr. Davis would work 5 hours.

Part Four

Policy Issues

Chapter 21

EXTERNALITIES AND THE ENVIRONMENT

Chapter Review

Of the three major economic players—individuals, firms, and government—the first two have been center stage so far in the text, while the third has mainly stood silently at the side. Government has been the central focus only of Chapters 7 and 16. This is appropriate, because the critical points for you to understand are where markets succeed at answering the main economic questions, where they fail, and how.

Where markets fail, government may have an economic role to play. This chapter wraps up some loose ends with respect to government's role. You have already seen problems of competition, information, and technological change that interfere when private markets are used to answer economic questions. Another major category of market failure is externalities, a concept first introduced in Chapter 7. As you may remember, externalities can be positive or negative. The distinguishing characteristic of externalities is that, positive or negative, they represent benefits or costs that are not captured in the market price. The first example studied in Chapter 21 is pollution. The chapter moves on to natural resources, where the key idea is whether correct incentives exist to conserve.

ESSENTIAL CONCEPTS

1   A market transaction is a voluntary exchange between two parties. Any costs or benefits not captured by market transactions are called **externalities. Positive externalities** are benefits received by others. Markets produce too little activities that generate positive externalities, such as research and development or on-the-job training. Other activities, such as pollution, noise, or congestion, confer costs on others that often do not figure into the market price. Markets create too many of these **negative externalities.**

2   Markets require clearly defined *property rights* in order to allocate resources efficiently. The **Coase's theorem** says that any externality problem could be solved if the government would assign property rights for the externalities. For example, direct pollution of a privately owned lake would not occur unless the owner judged that the benefits exceeded the costs. General environmental pollution is a serious problem because the environment is commonly, not privately, owned.

3   Externalities lead to **market failure** because resources are not allocated efficiently. Individuals consider only their private costs and benefits and ignore the larger so-

cial costs and benefits. Potential governmental solutions to the problems fall into two categories: **command and control regulations** and marketlike devices such as taxes, subsidies, and **marketable permits.** For example, in the case of pollution, governments can issue regulations requiring pollution-control equipment or banning the use of hazardous materials. Alternatively, they can employ more market-oriented policies, such as taxes on pollution emissions, subsidies for pollution abatement, or even creating a market for pollution permits.

4   Private property and the price system enhance the conservation of natural resources. If all is well, current prices reflect the value of natural resources used today and expected future prices equal their expected value in the future. Seeking the highest value for his property, the natural resource owner sells today if the current price exceeds the present discounted value of the future price. If not, he conserves. Thus, private owners make socially efficient decisions.

5   Two problems with private incentive for natural resource conservation exist. First, property rights may not be secure, especially in resource-rich, less-developed countries. If an owner sees a risk of confiscation, she will likely use her resource at a faster than efficient rate. In the same vein, governments often make poor guardians of commonly owned public lands. Second, if capital markets impose borrowing constraints on resource owners, they may substitute faster extraction for borrowing and thereby foil conservation.

BEHIND THE ESSENTIAL CONCEPTS

1   Individuals and firms make efficient decisions when they bear the full costs and benefits of their choice. When externalities are present, some benefit or cost is ignored, and the decision becomes inefficient. The missing ingredient is property rights. Coase's theorem says that if property rights are clearly assigned, decisions will be efficient. The logic can best be understood with an example.

   Suppose that your neighbor likes to play the stereo very loudly each evening while you are reading this book. Clearly, there is an externality. You complain to the building manager, and there are two possible reactions. The manager might say that playing the stereo is a right of all tenants, in effect giving the property right (to make noise) to your neighbor. Or the manager may insist on quiet and give the property right (to silence) to you. According to Coase's theorem, either way of assigning property rights will do. If your neighbor has the right, then you can buy the right to silence by paying your neighbor to be quiet. If you have the right, she must buy your permission to play the music. Of course, you would prefer the latter; nevertheless, in either case, the externality is eliminated and replaced by a market transaction. (Any reader who lives in a college dorm can judge how realistic it is to apply Coase's theorem to externalities.)

2   Pollution is an example of a negative externality. It is a cost ignored by the polluter and borne by others. The inefficiency can be corrected by raising the polluter's private marginal opportunity cost of pollution to the level of the social marginal cost. There are three marketlike ways to do this: taxes on pollution, subsidies for pollution abatement, and marketable pollution permits. Here is how they work.

   a   Suppose that the firm must pay a *tax* of $10 per unit of pollution. Clearly, any pollution now has a private marginal cost of $10, because the tax must be paid.

   b   Suppose that the government pays a *subsidy* of $10 per unit of pollution abatement. Again, the marginal opportunity cost of the pollution is $10, because if the pollution is emitted, it is not abated, and the subsidy is not received.

   c   Under the marketable permits scheme, pollution requires a permit, which must be purchased. The purchase price of the permit is the marginal cost of the pollution. All three marketlike policies put a price on pollution and encourage polluters to find economical ways to reduce emissions.

3   Whether we are using our limited natural resources efficiently and whether we are likely to run out of these resources are important economic questions. The key aspects in the answer to these questions are property rights and markets.

   a   For those resources, such as oil, minerals, and arable farmland, that are *privately owned*, markets provide good incentives for conservation. Future shortages mean high prices in the future. The profit opportunities from future sales motivate owners to conserve resources for the future.

   b   For those resources, such as the ozone layer and endangered species, that are not privately owned, there is no reason for optimism. Since there are *no markets* for these resources, there is no financial incentive to conserve.

SELF-TEST

True or False

1   When there is no government interference, markets will always produce efficient outcomes.

2   The market failures approach assigns to government the task of improving matters when markets allocate resources inefficiently.

3   Markets fail because too many people are motivated by greed.

4   The market will supply too many goods for which there are positive externalities.

5   The social marginal cost is greater than the private marginal cost for a good that generates negative externalities.

6   Coase's theorem contends that externality problems require government intervention.

7 Reassigning property rights can sometimes correct a market failure.

8 Because pollution is an example of a negative externality, economists recommend taxing pollution abatement.

9 Goods for which there are negative externalities should be taxed so that the price captures more of the social costs.

10 The regulation requiring catalytic converters on automobiles is an example of the command and control approach.

11 Marketable permits give no incentive to reduce pollution, because firms that want to pollute can simply buy the permits.

12 Because pollution is a negative externality, it should be eliminated on efficiency grounds.

13 We are using up our limited supply of natural resources because they are sold without concern for the needs of potential future users.

14 Both current and future property rights are essential to provide private owners with incentives to conserve natural resources.

15 If natural resource owners face borrowing constraints, they may conserve more natural resources than is socially efficient.

Multiple Choice

1 The market failures approach to the role of government in the economy says that

a because markets fail, governments must do as much as they can afford;
b governments have a role to play when markets fail to produce efficient outcomes;
c government is less likely to fail than markets;
d the Coase theorem is correct about the role of property rights in producing efficient market outcomes;
e marketable prices will fail to give incentives for natural resource conservation.

2 Examples of market failures include

a externalities;
b a lack of sufficient competition;
c information problems;
d insufficient technological innovation;
e all of the above.

3 The costs of environmental pollution are examples of

a positive externalities;
b public goods;
c negative externalities;
d private costs;
e diminishing returns.

4 Social marginal cost includes

a all marginal costs borne by all individuals in the economy;

b only those marginal costs not included in private marginal cost;
c only those marginal costs included in private marginal cost;
d total revenues minus total private costs;
e marginal revenue minus marginal cost.

5 Coase's theorem claims that

a market outcomes are always efficient;
b when markets fail to produce efficient outcomes, the government should allocate resources;
c negative externalities should be subsidized;
d reassigning property rights can solve externality problems;
e the decisions made by a majority of voters may be inconsistent.

6 Which of the following is not an example of a negative externality?

a Freon gas destroys some of the ozone layer.
b Carbon dioxide emissions bring about global warming.
c Industrial smoke emissions increase lung cancer rates.
d Customers must pay more when the prices of natural resources are increased.
e Runoff of pesticides pollutes streams and rivers.

7 Which of the following is an example of command and control regulations?

a subsidies for the production of goods with positive externalities;
b taxation of goods with negative externalities;
c regulations limiting the allowable level of pollution emissions;
d assigning property rights to victims of environmental pollution;
e nonrivalrous consumption.

8 To reduce emissions of pollution, the government can

a tax pollution abatement;
b subsidize pollution abatement;
c subsidize the sale of polluting goods, such as steel and chemicals;
d reassign to polluters the property rights to pollute;
e take over the production facilities of firms.

9 Under the marketable permits approach to curbing pollution,

a firms purchase permits from the government;
b permits allow firms to emit a certain amount of pollution;
c a market for pollution permits exists for firms to buy and sell the permits;
d firms have strong incentives to reduce pollution;
e all of the above.

10 The market system encourages conservation because

a the price of a natural resource, such as an oil well, equals the present discounted value of potential future uses;

  b wasteful exploitation is punished by fines or imprisonment;

  c markets always allocate resources efficiently;

  d permits from the government are required before natural resources may be sold;

  e there is such an abundance of natural resources.

11 Private owners may undervalue future demand for natural resources if

  a there are negative externalities associated with the current use of the resource;

  b there are positive externalities associated with the current use of the resource;

  c property rights are not secure;

  d owners may face limited borrowing opportunities;

  e b, c, and d.

12 The view that there is a role for government when markets do not produce efficient outcomes is called

  a Coase's theorem;

  b the market failures approach;

  c marketable permits;

  d the command and control approach;

  e none of the above.

13 How does Coase's theorem recommend that government solve the problem of overgrazing public lands?

  a The government should put a tax on beef.

  b The government should sell the grazing land to private owners.

  c The government should subsidize beef feedlots.

  d The government should issue regulations mandating how many cattle can graze per acre in each season.

  e Coase's theorem allows no role for government.

14 Which of the following is not an example of a problem with command and control regulations of environmental pollution?

  a Firms cannot afford to clean up their pollution.

  b Regulations do not allow for variations in circumstances among firms.

  c The least cost cleanup technology may not be the mandated one.

  d There are limited incentives for technological advance in pollution abatement.

  e All of the above are problems with command and control regulations.

15 Which of the following methods can reduce environmental pollution?

  a taxes on pollution emissions;

  b subsidies for pollution abatement;

  c marketable permits;

  d command and control regulations;

  e all of the above.

16 When the social marginal cost of an activity exceeds its private marginal cost,

  a it should be subsidized;

  b it should be taxed;

  c it should be outlawed;

  d a or b;

  e a, b, or c.

17 If the government uses the marketable permits policy,

  a firms must purchase permits from the government;

  b firms may sell their permits to the government but not to other firms;

  c firms may buy their permits from the government but not from other firms;

  d firms may sell their unused permits, but they may not buy additional permits;

  e firms may buy or sell permits as they choose.

18 The marketable permits system specifies that

  a firms purchase permits in order to pollute;

  b firms may buy permits from other firms;

  c firms may sell unused permits to other firms;

  d all of the above;

  e none of the above.

19 The production of too many goods with negative externalities is an example of

  a paternalism;

  b consumer sovereignty;

  c public failure;

  d market failure;

  e the voting paradox.

20 In deciding when to extract and sell a mineral deposit, the private owner compares

  a the present and expected future prices;

  b the present net return and the discounted present value of the future net return;

  c the discounted present value of future costs and prices;

  d the expected value of future costs and prices;

  e present costs and price.

Completion

1 The _____ approach to the role of government calls upon the government when markets fail to produce efficient outcomes.

2 The extra costs and benefits not captured by market transactions are called _____.

3 The _____ cost of pollution is borne entirely by the polluter, while the _____ cost includes all costs borne by individuals in the economy.

4 _____ claims that externality problems can be solved by reassigning property rights.

5 Regulatory measures that set limits on pollution emissions and mandate the use of specific types of pollution-control technologies are examples of the _____ approach.

6 The _____ approach issues to firms permits, which allow them to emit a certain amount of pollution and which can be traded.

7 Government can bring about a reduction in pollution emmissions by subsidizing _____.

8 When social marginal costs exceed private marginal costs there is a _____ externality.

9 High expected future prices motivate private owners to _____ natural resources.

10 When there are negative externalities associated with a good the market will produce too _____.

Answers to Self-Test

True or False

1	f	6	f	11	f
2	t	7	t	12	f
3	f	8	f	13	f
4	f	9	t	14	t
5	t	10	t	15	f

Multiple Choice

1	b	6	d	11	e	16	b
2	e	7	c	12	b	17	e
3	c	8	b	13	b	18	a
4	a	9	e	14	a	19	d
5	d	10	a	15	e	20	b

Completion

1 market failure
2 externalities
3 private, social
4 Coase's theorem
5 command and control
6 marketable permits
7 pollution abatement
8 negative
9 conserve
10 much

Doing Economics: Tools and Practice Problems

The first topic of this section is how taxes and subsidies can be used to encourage an activity for which there are positive externalities. We see how firms can be induced to emit less pollution by engaging in pollution abatement. Next, we turn to markets for goods that generate negative externalities such as noise, congestion, and pollution. A few problems show situations in which market equilibrium levels are too high and investigate how taxes can be used to make the market more efficient. The last topic focuses directly on the market for pollution and the way in which the marketable permits system brings about efficient use of the environment.

POLLUTION ABATEMENT

Like other decisions made by firms, the question of the level of pollution abatement involves marginal benefit and cost reasoning. If the government taxes pollution emissions, then abating pollution saves the tax. If the government subsidizes

pollution abatement, then abating pollution earns the subsidy. In each case, the marginal benefit of pollution abatement is determined by the government's policy. Tool Kit 21.1 demonstrates this.

Tool Kit 21.1: Determining the Level of Pollution Abatement

Pollution abatement is encouraged by taxing pollution or subsidizing abatements. Each raises the marginal cost of polluting. Follow these steps to find the resulting level of abatement.

Step one: Identify the cost of pollution emission and abatement.

Step two: Calculate the marginal abatement costs:

marginal abatement cost = change in cost/change in level of pollution abatement.

Step three: Determine the marginal benefit of abatement.

Step four: Set the marginal benefit of pollution abatement equal to its marginal cost.

---

1 (Worked problem: pollution abatement) Runoff from the Lower Indiana Quarta Lead Mine has raised lead levels in the Maumee River. The current level of lead effluent is 10 pounds per month. A filtering technology would enable the company to reduce its effluent. The abatement costs are given in Table 21.1.

Table 21.1

Pollution emitted (pounds/month)	Pollution abated (pounds/month)	Total cost	Marginal cost
10	0	$ 0	—
9	1	$ 10	
8	2	$ 25	
7	3	$ 45	
6	4	$ 70	
5	5	$100	
4	6	$135	
3	7	$175	
2	8	$225	
1	9	$290	
0	10	$400	

a Suppose that a pollution tax (or fine) of $40 is assessed per kilogram of lead emitted. How much will the company emit? What quantity of pollution will be abated?

b Suppose that rather than a tax, a subsidy of $40 is given per unit of pollution abated. How much will the company emit? What quantity of pollution will be abated?

c The firm's profits from the production and sale of lead total $10,000. Compare its profits under the tax and the subsidy plan.

Step-by-step solution

Step one (a): The cost of pollution emission and abatement is given in Table 21.1.

Step two: Calculate the marginal abatement cost. The marginal abatement cost is the extra cost incurred in reducing pollution emissions by 1 more unit. For example, reducing pollution from 10 to 9 units raises costs from $0 to $10; therefore, the marginal abatement cost is $10 for the first unit. The remainder of the schedule is given in Table 21.2.

Table 21.2

Pollution emitted	Pollution abated	Total cost	Marginal cost
10	0	$ 0	—
9	1	$ 10	$ 10
8	2	$ 25	$ 15
7	3	$ 45	$ 20
6	4	$ 70	$ 25
5	5	$100	$ 30
4	6	$135	$ 35
3	7	$175	$ 40
2	8	$225	$ 50
1	9	$290	$ 65
0	10	$400	$110

Step three: Determine the marginal benefit of abatement. Each unit of pollution emitted incurs a tax of $40; thus, the marginal benefit of abatement is $40.

Step four: Set the marginal benefit of pollution abatement equal to its marginal cost. This results in 3 pounds of lead emitted and 7 pounds abated.

Step five (b): When the policy is to subsidize abatement, the marginal benefit is the subsidy, which is $40. Setting $40 equal to the marginal abatement cost again gives 3 pounds of lead emitted and 7 pounds abated. The answer is the same as for part a. Notice that under the subsidy scheme, each unit emitted still costs the firm $40, in the sense that any unit emitted is a unit not abated and a subsidy not received.

Step six (c): Profits under the tax equal $10,000 less the abatement cost and the tax, or

$$\text{profits} = \$10,000 - \$175 - \$40\ (3) = \$9,705.$$

Under the subsidy, however,

$$\text{profits} = \$10,000 - \$175 + \$40\ (7) = \$10,105.$$

Notice that the difference in profits is $10,105 − $9,705 = $400, which is the magnitude of the tax/subsidy multiplied by the number of units that the firm emits with no regulation. It is the total value of the property right to pollute.

2   (Practice problem: pollution abatement) Avenger of the Sea Tuna kills 20 dolphins during an average harvest. It has various options for reducing the dolphin kill, and the costs are given in Table 21.3.

Table 21.3

Dolphins killed	Dolphins saved	Total cost	Marginal cost
20	0	$ 0	—
18	2	$ 100	
16	4	$ 240	
14	6	$ 400	
12	8	$ 600	
10	10	$ 1,000	
8	12	$ 1,500	
6	14	$ 2,200	
4	16	$ 3,000	
2	18	$ 5,000	
0	20	$10,000	

a   Suppose that a tax (or fine) of $100 is assessed per dolphin killed. How many dolphins will be killed? What number of dolphins will be saved?

b   Suppose that rather than a tax, a subsidy of $100 per dolphin is granted for reductions in the dolphin kill. How many will the company kill? How many will be saved?

c   With no tax or subsidy, the company's profits are $10,000. Compute its profits with the tax and with the subsidy.

3   (Practice problem: pollution abatement) Flying Turkey Air Transport has its hub in Franklin. Dozens of planes land and take off each night causing considerable noise. By muffling engines or other more advanced techniques, the company can reduce its noise. The costs are given in Table 21.4.

Table 21.4

Average level of noise (decibels)	Total cost	Marginal cost
1,000	$ 0	—
900	$ 50	
800	$ 150	
700	$ 300	
600	$ 500	
500	$ 750	
400	$1,100	

a   Suppose that a pollution tax (or fine) of $2.50 is assessed per decibel of noise created. How much will the company create? What quantity of noise will be abated?

b   Suppose that rather than a tax, a subsidy of $2.50 is granted per unit of noise abated. How much will the company create? What quantity of noise will be abated?

c   With no tax or subsidy, the company's profits are $5,000. Compute its profits with the tax and with the subsidy.

MARKETS AND EXTERNALITIES

When there are negative externalities, such as pollution, noise, and congestion, market outcomes will be inefficient. Specifically, there will be more than the socially efficient level. The socially efficient level just balances the social marginal costs with the marginal benefits. But markets ignore the externality and focus only on the private marginal benefits. Tool Kit 21.2 shows how to distinguish private and social benefits and how to compare the market and socially efficient levels.

Tool Kit 21.2: Finding the Efficient Quantity in Markets with Negative Externalities

The production and consumption of many goods causes negative externalities. In these cases, markets bring about too much production and consumption. Follow these steps to compare market and efficient levels.

Step one: Determine the market equilibrium at the intersection of the supply and demand curves.

Step two: Add the marginal external cost to the supply curve, which is the private marginal cost, to determine the social marginal cost curve.

Step three: Find the efficient quantity at the intersection of the demand curve and the social marginal cost curve.

Step four: Compare the market equilibrium and efficient quantities.

---

4 (Worked problem: negative externalities) Runoff from local feedlots is polluting the Red Cedar River. The negative externality per steer is $100. The demand and supply curves for steer are given in Table 21.5.

Table 21.5

Demand		Supply	
Price	Quantity	Price	Quantity
$200	350	$200	1,100
$180	500	$180	1,000
$160	650	$160	900
$140	800	$140	800
$120	950	$120	700
$100	1,100	$100	600
$ 80	1,300	$ 80	500

a   Find the market equilibrium quantity and price.
b   Calculate the social marginal cost, and determine the efficient quantity of steers.

Step-by-step solution

Step one (a): Find the market equilibrium quantity and price. At a price of $140, the market clears with 800 sold.

Step two (b): Find the social marginal cost curve. We add the marginal external cost, which is $100, to the supply curve, which is the private marginal cost. Table 21.6 gives the solution.

Table 21.6

Quantity	Social marginal cost
500	$180
600	$200
700	$220
800	$240
900	$260
1,000	$280
1,100	$300

Step three: Find the efficient quantity at the intersection of the demand curve and the social marginal cost curve. This occurs at a quantity of 500 and a price of $180.

Step four: Compare the market equilibrium and efficient quantities. Notice that the efficient quantity is only 500, while the market produces 800. Incorporating the external cost into the supply curve would raise the price and reduce the quantity to the efficient level.

5 (Practice problem: negative externalities) The private flying lessons at Daredevil Airport cause noise that disturbs local residents. The residents are also uneasy about the periodic crashes. One estimate of the magnitude of the negative externalities is $15 per flight. The market supply and demand curves for flight lessons are given in Table 21.7.

Table 21.7

Demand		Supply	
Price	Quantity	Price	Quantity
$75	10	$75	100
$70	20	$70	80
$65	30	$65	60
$60	40	$60	40
$55	50	$55	20
$50	60	$50	0

a   Find the market equilibrium price and quantity.
b   Calculate the social marginal cost, and find the efficient quantity.

6 (Practice problem: negative externalities) New developments of townhouses are springing up in the ex-urban community of Outland. The supply and demand curves for new townhouses are given in Table 21.8.

Table 21.8

Demand		Supply	
Price	Quantity	Price	Quantity
$140,000	100	$140,000	900
$130,000	200	$130,000	800
$120,000	300	$120,000	700
$110,000	400	$110,000	600
$100,000	500	$100,000	500
$ 90,000	600	$ 90,000	400
$ 80,000	700	$ 80,000	300

a Find the market equilibrium quantity of townhouses and the corresponding price.

b The new developments impose costs on other current residents for sewage, transportation, and congestion. An estimate of the magnitude of these negative externalities is $20,000 per townhouse. Find the efficient level of townhouse production and the corresponding price.

MARKETABLE PERMITS

The problem of pollution (and other negative externalities) can be attacked more directly by considering the "market" for pollution itself. The polluters are the demanders for pollution, and their demand curve is just the marginal abatement cost curve. If it costs a firm $40 to clean up a ton of sludge from its emissions, then that firm is willing to pay $40 to be given the right to emit the sludge. The efficient level of pollution occurs where the demand curve intersects the social marginal cost curve, which is the marginal damage done by the pollution. These problems explore the issue of the efficient level of pollution and how a marketable permit scheme can bring about this outcome. Use Tool Kit 21.3.

Tool Kit 21.3: Using Marketable Permits to Bring About the Efficient Level of Pollution

The marketable permit policy sells permits to pollute. The market price for these permits gives firms incentives to reduce pollution. The following procedure shows how to find the number of permits to sell and the market price.

Step one: Identify the demand for pollution (the sum of all the marginal abatement cost curves) and the social marginal cost curve.

Step two: Find the efficient level of pollution, which is at the intersection of the demand for pollution and the marginal abatement cost curve.

Step three: Determine how many permits to sell. This quantity is the efficient level of pollution found in step two.

Step four: Find the market price for the permits. Read this price off the demand curve.

---

7 (Worked problem: marketable permits) Discharges from factories, runoff from farmlands, and many other activities pollute the Metatarsal Lakes. The pollution could be reduced, but any reduction would involve expensive abatement procedures. The marginal abatement cost schedule is given in Table 21.9 along with the social marginal cost of the pollution. (BOD means biochemical oxygen demand.)

Table 21.9

Pollution (millions of pounds/BOD)	Marginal abatement cost	Social marginal cost
100	$1,200	$ 0
200	$1,000	$ 0
300	$ 900	$ 150
400	$ 800	$ 300
500	$ 700	$ 450
600	$ 600	$ 600
700	$ 500	$ 800
800	$ 300	$1,000

Find the efficient level of pollution, and explain how a marketable permits scheme can achieve an efficient outcome.

Step-by-step solution

Step one: Identify the demand for pollution and the social marginal cost curve. The demand is the marginal abatement cost curve given in Table 21.9, which also includes the social marginal cost curve.

Step two: Find the efficient level of pollution. The intersection of the demand for pollution and the marginal abatement cost curve occurs at 600 parts/million.

Step three: Determine how many permits to sell. This number is 600, and each permit entitles the holder to emit 1 part/million of pollution.

Step four: Find the market price for the permits. If 600 permits are offered for sale, their market price will be $600. This price is read off the marginal abatement cost curve at 600 units.

8 (Practice problem: marketable permits) The marginal abatement cost and social marginal cost of pollution in the Northwest Air Shed are given in Table 21.10. Find the efficient level of pollution, and explain how a marketable permits scheme can achieve an efficient outcome. Pollution is measured as metric tons of sulphur oxide.

Table 21.10

Pollution	Marginal abatement cost	Social marginal cost
10	$100	$ 0
20	$ 80	$ 0
30	$ 60	$ 5
40	$ 50	$10
50	$ 40	$20
60	$ 30	$30
70	$ 15	$50

9 (Practice problem: marketable permits) Pesticides, engine oil, chemicals, and other pollutants are finding their way into the groundwater. Abatement is possible but expensive. The marginal abatement cost and social marginal cost of this type of pollution for the Alago Aquifer are given in Table 21.11. Find the efficient level of pollution, and explain how a marketable permits scheme can achieve it.

Table 21.11

Pollution	Marginal abatement cost	Social marginal cost
100	$10,000	$ 10
150	$ 8,000	$ 100
200	$ 6,000	$ 1,000
250	$ 5,000	$ 5,000
300	$ 4,000	$10,000
350	$ 3,000	$20,000

Answers to Problems

2 The marginal abatement cost for reducing the dolphin kill is given in Table 21.12.

Table 21.12

Dolphins killed	Dolphins saved	Total cost	Marginal cost
20	0	$ 0	—
18	2	$ 100	$ 50
16	4	$ 240	$ 70
14	6	$ 400	$ 80
12	8	$ 600	$ 100
10	10	$ 1,000	$ 200
8	12	$ 1,500	$ 250
6	14	$ 2,200	$ 350
4	16	$ 3,000	$ 400
2	18	$ 5,000	$1,000
0	20	$10,000	$2,500

a The firm reduces its dolphin kill by 8 for a total of 12 killed.
b Again, the firm reduces its dolphin kill by 8 for a total of 12 killed.
c Profits under the tax = $10,000 – (12 × $100) = $8,800; profits under the subsidy = $10,000 + (8 × $100) = $10,800.

3 The marginal abatement cost for noise is given in Table 21.13.

Table 21.13

Average level of noise	Total cost	Marginal cost
1,000	$ 0	—
900	$ 50	$0.50
800	$ 150	$1.00
700	$ 300	$1.50
600	$ 500	$2.00
500	$ 750	$2.50
400	$1,100	$3.50

a The firm will emit 500 decibels (abating 500).
b The firm will abate 500 decibels (emitting 500).
c Profits under tax = $5,000 – (500 × $2.50) = $3,750; profits under subsidy = $5,000 + (500 × $2.50) = $6,250.

5 a Market equilibrium quantity = 40; price = $60;
b The social marginal cost is given in Table 21.14.

Table 21.14

Quantity	Social marginal cost
0	$65
20	$70
40	$75
60	$80
80	$85
100	$90

Efficient quantity = 20; price = $70.

6 a Market equilibrium quantity = 500; price = $100,000.
b The social marginal cost is given in Table 21.15.

Table 21.15

Quantity	Social marginal cost
300	$100,000
400	$110,000
500	$120,000
600	$130,000
700	$140,000
800	$150,000
900	$160,000

Efficient quantity = 400; price = $110,000.

8 Efficient level = 60. If 60 permits are sold, the market price will be $30 each, 60 permits will be purchased, and the level of pollution will be 60.

9 Efficient level = 250. If 250 permits are sold, the market price will be $5,000 each, 250 permits will be purchased, and the level of pollution will be 250.

TAXES, TRANSFERS, AND REDISTRIBUTION

Chapter Review

Chapter 22 is about why governments redistribute income and how they do so. It begins with the basic argument of why markets may not provide a satisfactory answer to the question of for whom goods are produced. It looks separately at the tax and transfer system and at social insurance and asks how each promotes a more equitable distribution of the economy's output. The chapter examines the fundamental trade-off between efficiency and equality and discusses various current public-policy controversies.

ESSENTIAL CONCEPTS

1   While the idea of market failure justifies many government policies aimed at improving the efficiency of the economy, the case for **redistribution** of the economy's output depends on overriding social values relating to equality. Markets allocate too small a share of output to those at the lower end of the economic spectrum and too much to those at the upper end, and the distribution has grown more unequal in the last 20 years. Redistribution programs often interfere with economic efficiency, so it is important to pay attention to their design.

2   A good tax system has five important characteristics, the first of which is **fairness**. Economists have emphasized two principles of fairness. **Horizontal equity** says that individuals in the same circumstances should pay the same tax, and **vertical equity** says that taxes should be based on ability to pay. By the standard of vertical equity, the tax system should be **progressive**, which means that the fraction of income paid in taxes should be larger for those with more income.

3   The second characteristic of a good tax system is **efficiency**. The system should change the economy's resource allocation decisions as little as possible and also impose few extra costs on taxpayers. The U.S. tax system often encourages more consumption and production of some goods with special tax provisions called **tax subsidies**. These reduce taxes for those who engage in the favoured activity and result in lower tax revenues for the government. The lost tax revenue is called a **tax expenditure.** Other characteristics of a good tax system include **administrative simplicity, flexibility,** and **transparency**, which means that it should be clear who is paying how much of each tax.

4 Government transfer programs fall into two categories: income tested, need based programs and social insurance. The former includes AFDC (Aid to Families with Dependent Children), EITC (Earned Income Tax Credit), and public housing. AFDC provides cash assistance to poor families, and the EITC encourages low wage workers to work by making them eligible for a subsidy through the income tax system. AFDC reform proposals center around encouraging work, increasing opportunities, and fostering responsibility.

5 Many social insurance programs, such as Social Security, unemployment insurance, disability insurance, and Medicare, benefit the middle class. They are financed by payroll taxes, but the ultimate burden is in the form of lower wages. Although they are called insurance programs, the provisions of each cause some income to be redistributed.

6 Any program or tax provision that promotes quality inevitably reduces efficiency. This basic **equity-efficiency trade-off** must be faced in making choices about social programs and tax reforms. Overall, income equality in United States, as shown by the **Lorenz curve**, is reduced somewhat by taxation and government programs, but it remains significantly more unequal than in other developed countries.

BEHIND THE ESSENTIAL CONCEPTS

1 You can judge the U.S. tax system on how well it meets the five criteria outlined in the text. The following are some arguments.

  a Fairness: The marginal tax rate, which is the tax paid out of the extra dollar of income, is higher for higher incomes. This aspect and refundable tax credits combine to make the income tax system mildly progressive, although the progressivity is offset somewhat by a variety of special provisions that help higher-income households, such as mortgage interest deductions and capital gains exclusions. Payroll taxes and federal and provincial sales taxes are regressive, however, and in sum, the total tax system is probably fairly flat, slightly progressive at best.

  b Efficiency: Although the 1981 reduction in marginal tax rates and the 1986 tax reform improved the efficiency of the income tax system, many special provisions remain. Further, in 1993 marginal rates rose again.

  c Administrative simplicity: By removing many lower-income individuals from the tax rolls and making tax avoidance less profitable (because marginal tax rates are lower), recent tax reforms have made the U.S. income tax system simpler for some. Overall, the goal remains unmet.

  d Flexibility: In practice, the U.S. income tax system is not flexible because any proposed tax change seems to open up debate on all aspects of the tax code.

  e Transparency: For some taxes, such as the corporation income tax and sales taxes, it is difficult to determine the actual tax burden.

2 The equity-efficiency trade-off is similar to the risk-incentive trade-off you studied in earlier chapters. You learned that an employer who pays commissions, for example, will provide stronger incentives to her sales force than another who pays a straight salary. The result of the strong incentives, however, is risk for the employees. The risk is not only that incomes may be high in some months and low in others, but also that some employees may earn more than others. Just as an employer can have strong incentives at a cost of risk for the employees, an economy can have efficiency at a cost of inequality. Social programs that alleviate poverty also reduce the incentives to earn income. Similarly, progressive income taxation pays for social programs, but discourages effort.

SELF-TEST

True or False

1 Redistribution is necessary to promote a more efficient allocation of resources than the market provides.

2 Horizontal equity says that upper-income individuals should pay a larger fraction of income in taxes.

3 Vertical equity says that people in similar situations should pay the same tax.

4 A tax system is progressive if upper-income individuals pay a larger fraction of income in taxes.

5 The payroll tax is an example of a progressive tax.

6 The U.S. income tax system is quite flexible and able to respond quickly to changes in economic circumstances.

7 The 1986 tax reform reduced administrative complexity somewhat by removing some low-income individuals from the tax rolls and reducing marginal tax rates.

8 The corporate income tax is an example of a transparent tax in that it is easy to see how much each person effectively pays.

9 The earned-income tax credit increases the after-tax income of the working poor.

10 Tax expenditures refer to the lost revenue from tax subsidies, such as the mortgage interest deduction.

11 The Gini coefficient equals twice the area between the Lorenz curve and the 45 degree line.

12 The burden of payroll taxes is the same whether they are paid by workers or their employers.

13 Social Security is an example of a middle-class entitlement program.

14 The Lorenz curve illustrates the efficiency of the economy.

15   The United States has a more equal distribution of economic goods than most other developed economies.

Multiple Choice

1   Which of the following is not an excise tax?

   a   cigarette tax;
   b   tax on alcohol;
   c   gasoline tax;
   d   tax on air travel;
   e   corporate income tax.

2   Horizontal equity means that

   a   people in the same economic situation should pay the same amount in tax;
   b   richer individuals should pay a larger fraction of their income in taxes;
   c   richer individuals should pay a larger monetary amount in taxes;
   d   the marginal tax rate should be higher for higher-income individuals;
   e   the tax schedule should be flat.

3   Vertical equity means that

   a   people in the same economic situation should pay the same amount in taxes;
   b   richer individuals should pay a larger fraction of their income in taxes;
   c   richer individuals should pay a larger monetary amount in taxes;
   d   the marginal tax rate should be higher for higher-income individuals;
   e   the tax schedule should be flat.

4   If lower-income individuals pay a larger fraction of their income in tax, the system is

   a   progressive;
   b   regressive;
   c   transparent;
   d   efficient;
   e   flexible.

5   If the income tax allows a tax credit for any money spent on some item, then there is said to be a

   a   tax subsidy;
   b   tax incidence;
   c   excise tax;
   d   tax burden;
   e   earned-income tax credit.

6   The marginal tax rate is the

   a   extra tax owed on an additional dollar of income;
   b   amount of tax expenditure on an additional dollar of income;
   c   amount of tax subsidy on an additional dollar of income;
   d   ratio of taxes to taxable income;
   e   tax rate at which the earned-income credit no longer applies.

7   The burden of a tax refers to

   a   how many people must pay it;
   b   how difficult it is to determine how much is paid;
   c   who really bears the burden of the tax, taking into account its economic repercussions;
   d   who actually sends the money to the tax authority;
   e   how much the tax distorts economic decisions.

8   An efficient tax system

   a   distorts economic decisions as little as possible;
   b   collects its revenue with as little additional cost to taxpayers as possible;
   c   is flexible;
   d   all of the above;
   e   a and b.

9   Which of the following is not an attribute of a good tax system?

   a   efficiency;
   b   vertical equity;
   c   horizontal equity;
   d   transparency.
   e   All of the above are attributes of good tax systems.

10   Which of the following is not an important issue in welfare reform?

   a   time limited welfare;
   b   job training;
   c   job search training;
   d   fostering responsibility by making parents provide financial support to their children.
   e   All of the above are important issues.

11   Which of the following is not a problem associated with public housing?

   a   reduced labor mobility;
   b   lower quality than that available in the private sector at similar cost;
   c   segregation of the poor;
   d   unequal treatment of families of similar size and income.
   e   all of the above are problems.

12   Assuming that labor supply is inelastic, the effect of the payroll tax is to

   a   reduce wages by the amount that the worker pays;
   b   reduce wages by the amount that the employer pays;
   c   reduce wages by the total amount of the tax regardless of who pays;
   d   leave wage unchanged;
   e   increase wages somewhat.

13   A subsidy that the tax system currently provides to low-wage workers is

   a   unemployment insurance;
   b   the earned-income tax credit;
   c   minimum wage laws;
   d   AFDC;
   e   b and d.

14 The AFDC program

   a is the same as the earned income tax credit;

   b only offers support to those laid off from their last job;

   c is a tax subsidy for low-wage workers;

   d provides support to single parent and other low-income families;

   e all of the above.

15 Social insurance programs in the United States

   a have no redistribution effect;

   b are purely redistributive;

   c provide insurance and also redistribute from higher- to lower-income households;

   d are financed by taxes that have disincentive effects;

   e c and d.

16 Government programs that redistribute income to the poor with money raised by taxes are examples of

   a the equity-efficiency trade-off;

   b middle class entitlements;

   c market failures;

   d consumer sovereignty;

   e none of the above.

17 Economists represent inequality using the

   a Lorenz curve;

   b Stigliz curve;

   c redistribution curve;

   d equity-efficiency trade-off;

   e market failure approach.

18 The Gini coefficient measures inequality by

   a the slope of the Lorenz curve;

   b twice the area between the Lorenz curve and the 45 degree line;

   c the area between the Lorenz curve and the 45 degree line;

   d one half the area between the Lorenz curve and the 45 degree line;

   e the curvature of the Lorenz curve.

19 The incidence of the payroll tax for Social Security almost surely falls

   a evenly between the employer and the employee;

   b entirely on the employee;

   c entirely on the employer;

   d on upper-income salaried workers;

   e on the self-employed.

20 The government's role in redistribution is primarily motivated by

   a market failure;

   b social values concerning those unable to sustain a minimum standard of living;

   c imperfect information;

   d distrust of consumer sovereignty;

   e noncompetitive markets.

Completion

1 The idea that individuals who are in identical situations should pay the same tax is called _____.

2 The idea that people who have more income or wealth should pay more tax is called _____.

3 A tax system in which individuals pay a larger fraction of income as income increases is called _____.

4 The term _____ refers to the revenue lost as a result of tax credits and deductions.

5 A good tax system has the characteristics of _____, which means that it is clear what each person is paying in taxes.

6 The tax owed on an additional dollar of income is the _____.

7 The _____ of a tax refers to who actually bears its economic burden.

8 Under the _____, low wage workers receive tax credits.

9 The _____ measures economic inequality as twice the area between the 45 degree line and the Lorenz curve.

10 The _____ shows the fraction of income earned by the poorest 10 percent, 20 percent, etc.

Answers to Self-Test

True or False

1	f	6	f	11	t
2	f	7	t	12	t
3	f	8	f	13	t
4	t	9	t	14	f
5	f	10	t	15	f

Multiple Choice

1	e	6	a	11	e	16	a
2	a	7	c	12	c	17	a
3	b	8	e	13	b	18	b
4	b	9	e	14	d	19	b
5	a	10	e	15	e	20	b

Completion

1 horizontal equity
2 vertical equity
3 progressive
4 tax expenditure
5 transparency
6 marginal tax rate
7 burden
8 earned-income tax credit
9 Gini coefficient
10 Lorenz curve

Doing Economics: Tools and Practice Problems

One nice way to measure inequality is with the Lorenz curve. It shows how the cumulative percentage of income (or wealth) varies with the population as we move up the income scale. Complete equality implies that the Lorenz curve is a 45 degree line. Tool Kit 22.1 shows how to plot it.

Tool Kit 22.1: Plotting the Lorenz Curve

The Lorenz curve is a convenient way to represent graphically the inequality in income (or any other economic variable). It shows what percentage of income is earned by the lowest 10 percent of the population, the lowest 20 percent, etc. Here is how to plot it.

Step one: Order the groups from lowest income to highest.

Step two: Make a table with headings as follows.

Group	% population	Cumulative % population	% income	Cumulative % income

Step three: Compute the percentage of income for each group, and enter in the table.

Step four: Compute the percentage of the population for each group, and enter in the table.

Step five: Compute the cumulative percentage of income for each group by adding its percentage to all percentages of the lower-income groups, and enter in the table.

Step six: Compute the cumulative percentage of the population for each group by adding its percentage to all percentages of the lower-income groups, and enter in the table.

Step seven: Draw coordinate axes. Label the horizontal one "Cumulative percentage of population" and the vertical one "Cumulative percentage of income."

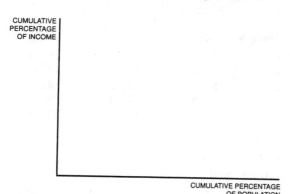

Step eight: Plot points corresponding to each group.

Step nine: Draw a curve connecting the points. This curve is the Lorenz curve.

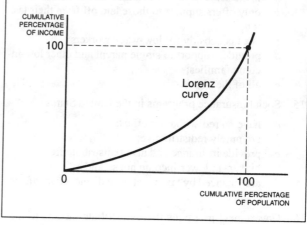

1   (Worked problem: Lorenz curve) In Costa Guano, there are four types of households: peasant farmers, ranchers, shopkeepers, and business owners. The population of each group (in millions) and the income (in U.S. dollar equivalent) of each are given in Table 22.1.

Table 22.1

Income		Population (millions)
Peasant farmers	$ 5,000	40
Ranchers	$50,000	20
Shopkeepers	$10,000	30
Business owners	$80,000	10

Plot the Lorenz curve.

Step-by-step solution

Step one: Order the groups from lowest income to highest.

Peasant farmers	$ 5,000	40
Shopkeepers	$10,000	30
Ranchers	$50,000	20
Business owners	$80,000	10

Step two: Make a table.

Group	% population	Cumulative % population	% income	Cumulative % income
Peasant farmers				
Shopkeepers				
Ranchers				
Business owners				

Step three: Compute the percentage of income for each group, and enter in the table. For peasant farmers, it is {40 × $5,000/[(40 × $5,000) + (30 × $10,000) + (20 × $50,000) + (10 × $80,000)]} = 14 percent. The completed column is given in Table 22.2.

Step four: Compute the percentage of the population for each group, and enter in the table. For peasant farmers, it is 40/(40 + 30 + 20 + 10) = 40 percent. Continue, and complete the column, which is given in Table 22.2.

Table 22.2

Group	% population	Cumulative % population	% income	Cumulative % income
Peasant farmers	40		14	
Shopkeepers	30		21	
Ranchers	20		7	
Business owners	10		57	

Step five: Compute the cumulative percentage of income for each group by adding its percentages to all percentages of the lower-income groups, and enter in the table. For peasant farmers, it is simply 9 percent. For shopkeepers, it is 14 + 21 = 35 percent. Continue.

Step six: Compute the cumulative percentage of the population for each group by adding its percentage to all percentages of the lower income groups, and enter in the table. For peasant farmers, it is simply 40 percent. For shopkeepers, it is 40 + 30 = 70 percent. Continue. The complete information appears in Table 22.3.

Table 22.3

Group	% population	Cumulative % population	% income	Cumulative % income
Peasant farmers	40	40	14	14
Shopkeepers	30	70	21	35
Ranchers	20	90	7	42
Business owners	10	100	57	100

Step seven: Draw coordinate axes. Label the horizontal one "Cumulative percentage of population" and the vertical one "Cumulative percentage of the income."

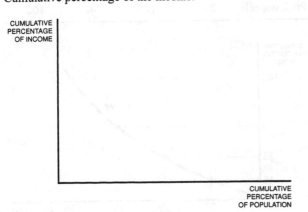

Step eight: Plot points corresponding to each group.

Step nine: Draw a curve connecting the points. This curve is the Lorenz curve.

2 (Practice problem: Lorenz curve) Enormous State University is reconsidering the equity of its pay structure. The number of professors in each department and their salaries are given in Table 22.4.

Table 22.4

Department	Number of professors	Salary
Sociology	8	$50,000
Economics	10	$60,000
Marketing	2	$80,000
Literature	16	$30,000
Philosophy	4	$40,000

a   Plot the Lorenz curve.
b   An organization of faculty members proposes paying each professor $50,000. Plot the Lorenz curve for the faculty if this proposal were adopted.
c   What would the Lorenz curve look like if each professor were paid $80,000?

3   (Practice problem: Lorenz curve) Exurbia, a pleasant town outside Gotham City, is populated by factory workers, bureaucrats, professionals, and retirees. The number of each, their income, and wealth of each individual in the group are given in Table 22.5.

Table 22.5

Career	Number	Income	Wealth
Factory workers	100	$30,000	$ 30,000
Bureaucrats	100	$40,000	$ 40,000
Professionals	100	$80,000	$ 80,000
Retirees	100	$50,000	$350,000

a   Plot the Lorenz curve for income.
b   Plot the Lorenz curve for wealth.
c   Compare the two. Is there more inequality in income or in wealth?

Answers to Problems

2   a   The Lorenz curve appears in Table 22.6 and the diagram.

Table 22.6

Department	% population	Cumulative % population	% income	Cumulative % income
Literature	40	40	40	40
Philosophy	10	50	10	50
Sociology	20	70	20	70
Economics	25	95	25	95
Marketing	5	100	5	100

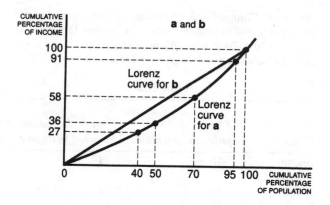

b   The complete information is given in Table 22.7. The Lorenz curve is the 45-degree line if there is equality.

Table 22.7

Department	% population	Cumulative % population	% income	Cumulative % income
Literature	40	40	40	40
Philosophy	10	50	10	50
Sociology	20	70	20	70
Economics	25	95	25	95
Marketing	5	100	5	100

c   The answer does not depend on the magnitude of income, only on its distribution. The answer is the same as for part b.

3   a   The Lorenz curve for income is given in Table 22.8 and the diagram.

Table 22.8

Career	% population	Cumulative % population	% income	Cumulative % income
Factory workers	25	25	15	15
Bureaucrats	25	50	20	35
Retirees	25	75	25	60
Professionals	25	100	40	100

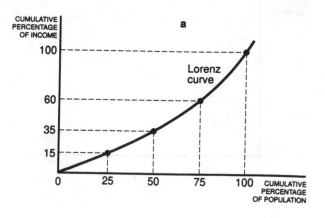

b   The Lorenz curve for wealth is given in Table 22.9 and the diagram.

Table 22.9

Career	% population	Cumulative % population	% income	Cumulative % income
Factory workers	25	25	6	6
Bureaucrats	25	50	8	14
Retirees	25	75	16	30
Professionals	25	100	70	100

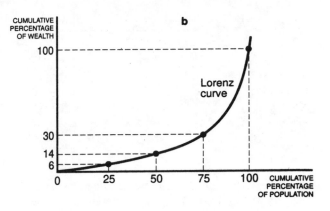

c   Wealth is distributed more unequally than income. The Lorenz curve for wealth is farther from the diagonal (45-degree line) than is the Lorenz curve for income.

Chapter 23

PUBLIC DECISION MAKING

Chapter Review

The economic theory of government, which is called public choice, fills this chapter. In previous chapters we have asked when and how government can improve the economy's resource allocation. Here, the subject concerns how actual governments allocate resources. The focus is on voting, lobbying, and the functioning of bureaucracies. Reasons why governments may fail to work efficiently are explored and decentralization within the federal system is discussed.

ESSENTIAL CONCEPTS

1 According to the economic approach, government is not a coordinated, benign decision-maker, but rather a collection of rational individuals playing a variety of roles. There are voters, candidates, interest groups, and bureaucrats. Economists focus on their choices and on the outcome of the political process.

2 An important way of making public decisions is majority voting. The **voting paradox** illustrates one problem: a majority of the electorate may not hold consistent views as to desirable policies. When it comes to such

matters as deciding how much to spend on fire protection, on the other hand, the median voter model demonstrates that government responds to the preferences of the voter who stands between equal numbers of voters desiring more spending or less spending.

3 The incentives concerning interest groups and bureaucrats may stand in the way of efficient public decisions. The **rent-seeking** activities of interest groups may lead to inefficient policies that benefit their members at the expense of the relatively poorly organized general electorate. Further, once a policy is set, there is the principal agent problem, which inhibits the ability to motivate bureaucrats to act in the public interest.

4 Although there are many examples of efficient government enterprises and helpful programs, government often allocates resources wastefully. Reasons for **public failures** include improper incentives attributable to the constraints of due process, inability to make long-term commitments, and political pressures. Also budgetary and spending problems such as soft budget constraints, the annual appropriations process, and inflexible cost containment restrictions like competitive bidding requirements undermine efficiency. Finally, there is the general problem of unintended consequences and unforeseen incentives and behavior brought about by the

interaction of government policy and the very complex economy.

5   The United States operates a **federal system** of government with functions and responsibilities divided among the various levels of government. The appropriate assignment of task balances the costs and benefits of decentralization. Arguing for a stronger federal government role are the externalities involved in local government decision making, national public goods, and the problem of the national income distribution. On the other side are some factors that argue for allocating functions to state and local government. These include local public goods, the diversity of preferences, and the possibility of experimenting with different solutions to common problems.

BEHIND THE ESSENTIAL CONCEPTS

1   It is important to understand what the voting paradox is and what is is not. It tells us that in certain circumstances majority voting may not be able to make consistent choices or even rank alternatives. This implies that even if all citizens are rational, when they act collectively, they may not be. The voting paradox does not say that every public decision is irrational or inconsistent.

2   One example of a situation where majority voting is consistent is when the decision concerns a single variable for which each individual voter has a preferred level and also favors alternatives closer to this level than others farther away. Examples include funding levels for local public goods such as parks and education. In these cases, the **median voter theory** says that public decisions will reflect the preferences of the median voter. Assuming that the median voter is consistent, public decisions will be consistent. (Nothing in the median voter theory implies that public decisions will be efficient, only that they will be consistent.)

3   The **free rider problem** helps us to understand why special interests may succeed in pushing inefficient programs. People have incentives to free ride when they can draw the benefits of some activity without paying. In smaller groups it is more difficult to avoid paying one's share. Therefore, relatively small groups may be able to lobby more forcefully than larger groups, where people can easily avoid contributing. As an example, consider the sugar quotas that limit the import of foreign sugar. This is surely an inefficient program. Why then do taxpayers not insist that it cease? The reason is that removing sugar quotas would give only a small benefit to any individual.

4   You can understand certain constraints placed on government decision making as imperfect solutions to larger problems. For example, due process constraints prohibit the arbitrary exercise of government power to seize assets. While this is undoubtedly a good thing, due process unfortunately limits the discretion of bureaucrats to tailor decisions to individual circumstances. Similarly, competitive bidding requirements help to minimize corruption in government procurement, but they mandate cumbersome and costly procedures. The government's ability to make long-term commitments does lead to inefficiencies, but it also limits the ability of current legislature from imposing undue burdens on future generations.

5   When you think about the federalism question—which tasks should be assigned to each level of government—you may relate it to the broad issue of decentralized decision making within organizations. As we have seen in other chapters, centralized decision making has the advantage of better coordination. Here, this relates to the ability of the federal government to account for externalities among local governments. On the other hand, decentralization leads to greater experimentation and innovation. Thus we can expect new ways of dealing with policy problems to originate in the U.S. states, which are sometimes called laboratories of democracy.

SELF-TEST

True or False

1   Economists focus on the voting behavior of rational individuals and on the public choices that are the outcome of the political process.

2   The voting paradox shows that majority vote cannot result in a determinate political outcome, and thus it argues for dictatorship.

3   The voting paradox states that political parties will advocate the alternative most preferred by the average voter.

4   Median voter theory shows that when there is a vote over a single issue, individuals have a most-preferred alternative and they vote for alternatives closer to it; the outcome of majority vote reflects the preferences of the median voter.

5   The median voter in a community is the person who earns the average income.

6   Rent seeking refers to activities and expenditures designed to secure special favors from government.

7   Due to the realities of the principal agent problem, public managers may not act in the interest of the electorate.

8   Public enterprises are always less efficient than their private counterparts.

9   Due process is designed to protect against arbitrary use of government's coercive powers.

10   The inability to make long-term commitments can undermine the efficiency of public agencies.

11   Soft budget constraints, the annual appropriations process, and rigid procurement rules constrain government budgetary and spending decisions.

12   Decentralization refers to the provision of government goods and services at the state or local level.

F 13   When there are externalities in the provision of state and local services, more decentralized decision-making is appropriate.

F 14   The distribution of income is an example of a local public good.

T 15   Decentralization allows for experimentation with different solutions to common problems.

Multiple Choice

1   In their study of public decision-making, economists focus on

   a   coalition formation;
   b   the media;
   c   voting behavior and the outcomes of the political process;
   d   biographies of great political leaders;
   e   all of the above.

2   The voting paradox refers to

   a   the tendency of democratic governments to make inconsistent choices;
   b   the reasons for market failure;
   c   the reasons for public failure;
   d   the principle that political parties gravitate toward the political center;
   e   the principal agent problem as applied to motivating bureaucrats.

3   Which of the following voting systems did Kenneth Arrow show to be troubled by potential inconsistencies?

   a   simple majority voting;
   b   weighted majority voting;
   c   two-thirds majority voting;
   d   three-fourths majority voting;
   e   all of the above.

4   Which of the following is not a characteristic of a public choice described by the median voter theory?

   a   The vote concerns a single variable.
   b   Individual voters have a most-preferred outcome.
   c   Voters vote for an alternative based on how close it is to their most-preferred outcome.
   d   Only two alternatives are considered.
   e   All of the above are characteristics of public choices described by the median voter theory.

5   On issues such as school finance, where people have different views about the desirable level of public support, the median voter theory predicts that the majority vote will result in

   a   inconsistent decisions;
   b   no money allocated to schools because everyone cannot agree;
   c   the preferences of the median voter determining the level of funding;
   d   property rights being reassigned;
   e   inefficient public decisions as a result of imperfect information.

6   Consider a majority vote to decide how much land to set aside for a local park. The median voter

   a   earns the average level of income;
   b   desires less park land than half of the voters, but also desires more park land than half of the voters;
   c   lives an average distance from the park;
   d   neither likes nor dislikes parks;
   e   is governed by the voting paradox.

7   Which of the following best describes the relationship between the voting paradox and the median voter theory?

   a   Political scientists believe in the voting paradox, but economists argue that median voter theory more closely describes public decision-making in a democracy.
   b   The median voter theory resolves the voting paradox.
   c   Inconsistencies in democratic decision-making are inevitable; therefore the median voter is an interesting, but incorrect description.
   d   Inconsistencies in democratic decision-making are not inevitable. The median voter theory explains one type of situation where choices are consistent.
   e   While economists once believed in the voting paradox, now they only use the median voter model to study public choices in a democracy.

8   Rents are

   a   moneys paid to landlords;
   b   returns enjoyed by a factor of production that go beyond those required to elicit its supply;
   c   political contributions;
   d   inefficient public decisions resulting from lobbying for special favors from government;
   e   activities, such as lobbying and political contributions, designed to promote the agenda of special interests.

9   Rent seeking refers to

   a   advertising by landlords;
   b   returns enjoyed by a factor of production that go beyond those required to elicit its supply;
   c   special favors from government, such as subsidies and protection from foreign competition;
   d   inefficient public decisions resulting from lobbying for special favors from government;
   e   activities, such as lobbying and political contributions, designed to promote the agenda of special interests.

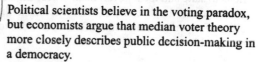

10   Public managers may not actively pursue the agenda of the electorate because of the

   a   voting paradox;
   b   principal agent problem;
   c   free rider problem;
   d   race to the bottom;
   e   public choice theory.

11   Which of the following is not an example of the principal agent problem as it applies to the administration of government programs?

a Bureaucrats may act in a risk-averse manner.
b Public managers may seek to advance their careers by expanding their spheres of influence.
c Special interests lobby politicians for favors, such as subsidies and protection from competition.
d Performance of public administrators may be judged by how they conform to procedures.
e All of the above are examples of the principal agent problem.

12 U.S. government farm policy

a raises, but does not stabilize, prices of agricultural commodities;
b stabilizes, but does not raise, prices of agricultural commodities;
c both raises and stabilizes prices of agricultural commodities;
d eliminates income risk for farmers;
e leaves farming decisions to the market.

13 Which of the following contributes to the explanation of United States farm policy?

a effective rent seeking by farm groups;
b the ability of relatively small special interests to advance their agenda at the expense of the taxpayer and food consumer;
c ineffective lobbying by groups representing consumers and taxpayers, due to the free rider problem;
d all of the above;
e none of the above.

14 Procedures developed to protect the public against arbitrary use of government power are called

a due process;
b soft budget constraints;
c the law of unintended consequences;
d rent seeking;
e federalism.

15 The idea that public enterprises can make losses that are funded by taxpayer moneys is called

a due process;
b soft budget constraints;
c the law of unintended consequences;
d rent seeking;
e the principal agent problem.

16 The concept of public failures refers to

a inefficient decisions by government;
b inefficient allocations of resources by market;
c a socially unacceptable distribution of income;
d the voting paradox;
e the free rider problem.

17 When government subsidies increase demand and raise costs, it is an example of

a soft budget constraints;
b unintended consequences;
c due process;
d externalities;
e market failure.

18 Which of the following are sources of government failure?

a Due process regulations limit flexibility.
b Governments have limited ability to make long-term commitments.
c Expenditures are appropriated on an annual basis.
d Rigid procurement rules impose excessive costs.
e All of the above are sources of government failure.

19 Which of the following concerns argues for provision of government goods and services at the state or local level?

a Some government activities are national public goods.
b Some government activities generate externalities on neighboring jurisdictions.
c States and localities can experiment with alternative solutions to common problems.
d Left to itself, the market may not yield a socially acceptable distribution of income.
e All of the above argue against provision at the local level.

20 Which of the following concerns argues against provision of government goods and services at the state or local level?

a Some government activities are local public goods.
b Left to itself, the market may not yield a socially acceptable distribution of income.
c States and localities can experiment with alternative solutions to common problems.
d Preferences and needs of communities may vary.
e All of the above argue against provision at the local level.

Completion

1 The _____ illustrates the tendency for public decisions to be inconsistent.

2 _____ predicts that in certain cases public decisions will reflect the preferences of the voters whose most-preferred alternative lies in the middle of the distribution of voters, with an equal number of voters desiring more or less of the public good.

3 Activities, such as lobbying and political contributions, designed to secure tax breaks or subsidies are called _____

4 The notion that the self-interest of public managers may not coincide with the will of the electorate is an example of the _____

5 Procedures designed to limit the arbitrary use of government power are called _____

6 Due to _____, government enterprises can suffer financial losses with the deficit funded out of government revenues.

7 Government education loan programs that gave strong incentives to declare bankruptcy are examples of

8 ~~Public Failures~~ _____ refers to inefficient decisions by governments.

9 When local government programs create benefits and costs that extend to nonresidents, there are ~~unintended conse~~ externalities

10 The ~~race to bottom~~ refers to the incentives that states and localities have to lower benefits to the poor and reduce their population of low-income people.

Answers to Self-Test

True or False

1	t	6	t	11	t
2	f	7	t	12	t
3	f	8	t	13	f
4	t	9	t	14	f
5	f	10	t	15	t

Multiple Choice

1	c	6	b	11	c	16	a
2	a	7	d	12	c	17	b
3	e	8	b	13	d	18	e
4	d	9	e	14	a	19	c
5	c	10	b	15	b	20	b

Completion

1 voting paradox
2 Median voter theory
3 rent seeking
4 principal agent problem
5 due process
6 soft budget constraints
7 unintended consequences
8 Public failures
9 externalities
10 race to the bottom

Doing Economics: Tools and Practice Problems

Public choice theory analyzes the voting behavior of rational individuals and the collective choices that result from the political process. Two important models are the voting paradox and the median voter theory. Together they show that majority voting sometimes, but not always, leads to a determinate outcome. Some problems explore these ideas.

VOTING PARADOX

The voting paradox can arise when people vote to choose among at least three alternatives. If the outcome of majority voting cannot provide a ranking or even pick out unambiguously the best alternative, it reveals a voting paradox. Of course, this may not always occur. Tool Kit 23.1 shows how to use the majority voting model to discover inconsistencies arising from the voting paradox.

Tool Kit 23.1: Finding the Voting Paradox

When at least three individuals must choose among at least three alternatives, the outcome of their majority vote may lead to inconsistencies. Follow this procedure to discover voting paradoxes.

Step one: Identify the alternatives, the voters, and their preferences.

Step two: Choose two alternatives and hold a majority election. Conclude that the winner is chosen over the loser.

Step three: Conduct similar majority votes for each pair of alternatives. (For three alternatives there will be three elections; four alternatives require six.)

Step four: Rank the alternatives on the basis of the outcome of the elections. If the alternative cannot be ranked unambiguously, there is a voting paradox.

---

1 (Worked problem: voting paradox) Alice, Bob, and Colleen are considering lunch at one of three local restaurants: Xerxes, Yellowfoot, and Zeke's. Their preferences are given in Table 23.1.

Table 23.1

		Alternatives	
Voter	Most preferred	Second best	Worst
Alice	Xerxes	Yellowfoot	Zeke's
Bob	Yellowfoot	Zeke's	Xerxes
Colleen	Zeke's	Xerxes	Yellowfoot

a Suppose that they decide by majority vote. Can they rank the three alternatives?

b Is there a most preferred alternative?

Step-by-step solution

Step one: Identify the alternatives (Xerxes, Yellowfoot, and Zeke's), the voters (Alice, Bob, and Colleen), and their preferences (given in the table).

Step two: Choose two alternatives and hold a majority vote election. Let's vote on Xerxes versus Yellowfoot. Alice votes for Xerxes. Bob votes for Yellowfoot. Colleen votes for Xerxes. Xerxes wins two to one; therefore Xerxes is preferred to Yellowfoot.

Step three: Conduct similar majority votes for every pair. Continuing as in step two, Yellowfoot is preferred to Zeke's (Alice and Bob vote for Yellowfoot, defeating Colleen, who votes for Zeke's). Finally, Zeke's wins a majority vote over Xerxes.

Step four: Rank the alternatives. The outcome of the vote is as follows. Xerxes is preferred to Yellowfoot. Yellowfoot is preferred to Zeke's. But Zeke's is preferred to Xerxes. There is an inconsistency, and there is no single most-preferred alternative. This is an example of the voting paradox.

2 (Practice problem: voting paradox) Representatives of the three dormitories at Enormous State University are meeting to vote on how to allocate the Trustee's Grant. There are three alternatives: library expansion, football scholarships, and campus beautification. The preferences are given in Table 23.2.

Table 23.2

Dormatory	Most preferred	Second best	Worst
North Towers	football	library	beautification
Shady Acres	library	football	beautification
Cement Block	library	beautification	football

a Does majority voting give an unambiguous ranking of the three alternatives?

b Does majority voting select a single best alternative?

3 (Practice problem: voting paradox) The city council consists of three voting members, who must decide among four alternative sources of funds to make up the budget shortfall. The alternatives are property tax increase, sales tax increase, a cut in recreation funding, and reduced payments into the retirement fund for retired city council members. Their preferences are given in Table 23.3.

Table 23.3

Member	First choice	Second	Third	Fourth
Hammermesh	property	sales	recreation	retirement
Menchik	sales	recreation	property	retirement
Davidson	recreation	property	sales	retirement

a Does majority voting give an unambiguous ranking of the four alternatives?

b Does majority voting select a single best alternative?

MEDIAN VOTER THEORY

Many elections, such as school bond issues, sales tax referenda, and funding for parks and recreation, involve the choice of a single variable: how much to spend or tax. Usually, voters will have a most-preferred alternative and will vote for the proposal closest to their liking. In this case median voter theory predicts that the outcome will reflect the preferences of the median voter, who is the one preferring the level in the middle of the distribution of voters. Half of the voters prefer more and half prefer less. This theory has been used extensively to analyze funding for local public goods and many other issues decided by local elections. Tool Kit 23.2 shows how to find the median voter and predict the outcome of majority voting.

Tool Kit 23.2: Using Median Voter Theory

When the vote concerns the magnitude of a single variable about which people have a most preferred level and always vote for alternatives closer to that level, the preferences of the median voter will determine the outcome. That is the majority vote will choose the level most preferred by the median voter.

Step one: Identify the variable subject to vote, the voters, and their most-preferred level.

Step two: Order the voters from highest to lowest according to their most-preferred level of the variable.

Step three: Find the median voter. This is the voter in the middle of the list constructed in step two. If there is an odd number of voters, there will be an equal number of voters preferring more than the median voter and an equal number preferring less.

Step four: Predict the outcome of the vote. According to median voter theory, it is the level preferred by the median voter found in step three. (If there is an even number of voters, then take an average of the two in the middle.)

4 (Worked problem: median voter theory) Grove City's school board is planning to ask the voters for a new bond issue. The voters and their preferred (per student) level of school funding are given in Table 23.4.

Table 23.4

Voter	Preferred funding
Kowalski	$5,000
Stokowski	$4,000
Litovsk	$3,500
Stanislav	$6,200
Jones	$8,000

a Who is the median voter?

b Find the outcome of the election according to the median voter theory.

Step-by-step solution

Step one: Identify the variable subject to vote, the voters, and their most preferred level. The variable is per student school funding. The voters and their preferred level are given above in Table 23.4.

Step two: Order the voters. From high to low, the ordering appears in Table 23.5.

Table 23.5

Voter	Preferred funding
Jones	$8,000
Stanislav	$6,200
Kowalski	$5,000
Stokowski	$4,000
Litovsk	$3,500

Step three: Find the median voter. He is Kowalski. Jones and Stanislav want more; an equal number of voters, Stokowski and Litovsk, want less.

Step four: Predict the outcome. Kowalski, the median voter, desires $5,000 per student. According to median voter theory the outcome will be $5,000 per student.

5   Suppose that four new voters move into Grove City. Their names and preferences are given in Table 23.6.

Table 23.6

Voter	Preferred funding
Cheong	$7,500
Davis	$8,000
Samuels	$7,000
Biddle	$8,000

a   Who is the median voter?
b   Find the outcome of the election according to the median voter theory.

6   Frightened of the recent surge in crime, voters in Pleasantville vow to increase the size of the police department. There are five voters, and their preferences and names are given in Table 23.7.

Table 23.7

Voter	Preferred number of police officers
Davis	1
Lee	1
Gaudin	2
Stevens	1
Mathews	4

a   Who is the median voter?
b   Find the outcome of the election according to the median voter theory.

Answers to Problems

2   a   Yes. Football is preferred to beautification. The library is preferred to football. The library is preferred to beautification. There is a ranking: library, football scholarships, campus beautification. In this case there is no voter's paradox.
     b   Yes. Library expansion is the most preferred alternative.

3   a   No. Property tax increase defeats sales tax increase; sales defeats recreation cut; recreation cut defeats property tax.
     b   No, there is no single best alternative.

5   a   Samuels is the median voter.
     b   The preferred funding is $7,000.

6   a   Davis, Lee, or Stevens is the median voter.
     b   The preferred number of officers is 1.